ISBN 978-1-331-64549-8
PIBN 10217280

1 MONTH OF
FREE
READING

at

www.ForgottenBooks.com

By purchasing this book you are eligible for one month membership to ForgottenBooks.com, giving you unlimited access to our entire collection of over 700,000 titles via our web site and mobile apps.

To claim your free month visit: www.forgottenbooks.com/free217280

English
Français
Deutsche
Italiano
Español
Português

www.forgottenbooks.com

Mythology Photography **Fiction**
Fishing Christianity **Art** Cooking
Essays Buddhism Freemasonry
Medicine **Biology** Music **Ancient
Egypt** Evolution Carpentry Physics
Dance Geology **Mathematics** Fitness
Shakespeare **Folklore** Yoga Marketing
Confidence Immortality Biographies
Poetry **Psychology** Witchcraft
Electronics Chemistry History **Law**
Accounting **Philosophy** Anthropology
Alchemy Drama Quantum Mechanics
Atheism Sexual Health **Ancient History**
Entrepreneurship Languages Sport
Paleontology Needlework Islam
Metaphysics Investment Archaeology
Parenting Statistics Criminology
Motivational

Puritan Discipline Tracts.

AN

ADMONITION

TO THE

PEOPLE OF ENGLAND:

AGAINST

Martin Mar-Prelate.

BY

THOMAS COOPER, D.D.

BISHOP OF WINCHESTER.

LONDON:

JOHN PETHERAM, 94, HIGH HOLBORN.

1847.

LONDON:

HUGH WILLIAMS, PRINTER, ASHBY-STREET,
NORTHAMPTON-SQUARE.

INTRODUCTION.

Of the Admonition there are two editions, both bearing the date of 1589, the title-pages of which are so much alike that the most minute examination fails to discover any difference in them. This similarity extends only to the early part of the work, for a difference in the width of the page, in pagination, and other circumstances soon lead to the conclusion of two distinct impressions. By a careful collation of the two editions, a few slight verbal differences occur, though they are unimportant, and the following passage in the corrected edition, "I will nowe come to answere briefly some particular slanders vttered against some Bishops and other by name," does not occur in the original. The second, or corrected edition is that chosen as the text of the reprint. The Author of the Admonition has not affixed his name to it, but the initials T. C. will be found at the end of the short preface; and the work is well known to have been written by Thomas Cooper, at that time Bishop of Winchester, respecting whom some particulars may be found in Sir John Harington's *State of the Church*, and in Wood's *Athenæ Oxonienses*, by Dr. Bliss. Soon after the publication of the Admonition it was answered by Martin Mar-Prelate in *Hay any worke for Cooper*, wherein that author pointed out two passages in the Admonition, that, for some reason or other, it had been found necessary to cancel. At page 40 of the original edition, Bishop Cooper says, "The Libeller doth but dreame, let him and his doe what they *dare*,"—over this last word is pasted the word *can.* At page 135 of the same edition, its author seems to have admitted too much, where he says, "I will not deny it;" over this is pasted, "That is not yet proued." It is perhaps not unimportant to add that in the second impression these passages are printed as corrected. Were we acquainted with the secret history of the Admonition we should not have to conjecture that Martin's calling attention to these variations led to the suppression of the original edition in which they occur, and to the substitution of another whose title page should mislead the reader; or else, why not call it, what in reality it is, a second, or new edition? The truth seems to be that the Admonition unquestionably was, as Strype states it to have been, a book of authority, written by command of Archbishop Whitgift, and in which the bishops answered for themselves; not in writing certainly, but by communicating to its author the facts necessary for their vindication; because he tells us, "For as much as I haue *not* bene curious in all my life to examine the doings of other, hauing ynough to do with mine owne, I haue in these matters vsed the instructiō of them, whom no honest man may in Christian dutie suspect of vntrueth:" evidently indicating that he had been specially selected and instructed for the purpose. And in the case of Bishop Aylmer, he adds, "This have I laid downe word by worde, as I receiued the same from my Lorde of London." I know nothing that can be plainer than this, for if, to use the words of a learned modern writer, "There are many statements in Bishop Cooper's work which we must utterly dissent from," or, "when matters of doctrine are involved we should always give suspected parties the benefit of a doubt;" whomsoever it may affect by admitting the statement above, we are not justified in attempting to throw discredit on such direct and credible testimony.

                                                        J. P.

London, Nov. 18, 1846.

AN

ADMONITION
TO THE PEOPLE OF
ENGLAND:

WHEREIN ARE AN-
SVVERED, NOT ONELY THE
slaunderous vntruethes, reprochfully vt-
tered by Martin *the Libeller, but also many other*
Crimes by some of his broode, obiected gene-
rally against all Bishops, and the chiefe of the
Cleargie, purposely to deface and
discredite the present state of
the Church.

Detractor & libens auditor, vterque
Diabolum portat in lingua.

Seene and allowed by authoritie.

Imprinted at London by the Deputies
of Christopher Barker, Printer to the
Queenes most excellent Maiestie.

1 5 8 9.

TO THE READER.

I AM not ignorant (Gentle Reader) what daunger I drawe vpon my selfe, by this attempt to answere the quarrels and slaunders of late time published in certaine Libelles, against the Bishops and other chiefe of the Clergie of the Church of *England.* We see the eagernesse and boldnesse of their spirit that be the authors of them: we taste alreadie the bitternes of their tongues and pennes. The raging furie of their reuenge vpon all which they mislike, themselues dissemble not, but lay it downe in words of great threatnings. I must needs therfore looke for any hurt, that venemous, scoffing, and vnbridled tongues can worke toward me. And how shoulde I hope to escape that, when the Saints of God in Heauen doe feele it? In the course of their whole Libell, when they speake of *Peter, Paul,* or the *Blessed Virgin Marie,* &c: whome other iustlie call Saintes, their phrase in derision is, *Sir Peter, Sir Paule, Sir Marie.* Surely it had becommed right well the same vnmodest Spirite, to haue said also *Sir Christ,* and so throughly to haue bewrayed himself. Seeing they haue sharpned their tongues and hearts against heauen, wee poore creatures on earth must be content in our weaknesse to beare them. The dartes, I confesse, of deceitfull and slaunderous tongues, are verye sharpe, and the burning of the woundes made by them, will as hardly in the hearts of many bee quenched, as the coales of Iuniper. But I thanke God I feare them not, though they bring mee greater harme, eyther in credite, liuing or life, then I trust that God that seeth, knoweth, and defendeth the trueth, will suffer them. *Ambrose* beeing in case somewhat like, sayeth thus, " Non tanti est vnius vita, quanti est dignitas omnium Sacerdotum." If I therefore shoulde bazarde the one for the defence of the other : I trust the godlye woulde iudge that I did that duetie which I owe to the Church of God, and to my brethren of the same function and calling.

What is the cause why wee bee with such spight and malice discredited ? Surely, because as the duty of fayth-full Subiectes dooth binde vs, liuing in the state of a Church refourmed, we doo indeuour to preserue those Lawes, which her Maiesties authoritie and the whole state of the Realme hath allowed and established, and doe not admitte a newe platforme of gouernment, deuised, I knowe not by whome.

The reasons that mooue vs so to doe, are these two. First, wee see no proofe brought out of the word of God, that of necessitie such forme of Gouernement ought to be : Secondly, that by the placing of the same, it woulde bring so many alterations and inconueniences, as in our opinion woulde bee dangerous to the Prince and to the Realme. Some of those inconueniences I haue in this treatise laid downe, and leaue them to the consideration of them, whom God hath set in place of gouernment.

It may be some will iudge that I am worldly affected, because I shewe my selfe so much grieued with losse of our credite, and hinderance of good name among the people. In trueth, although a godly Minister shoulde haue no worldly thing so deere vnto him, as his credite : yet if the hurt went no further then to our selues, wee should make lesse account of it. But, seeing by our reproche and infamie, the doctrine which wee teache is greatly hindered, we ought by all lawfull meanes to defend it. Christ himselfe, in this respect, answered such reproches, as the enemies obiected against him. As, " that hee was a friende vnto Publicanes, and Matth. 9. sinners : That hee wrought his miracles by the power Matth. 12. of Beelsebub : That hee broke the Sabbaoth day : John 8. That hee was a Samaritane : That hee had a deuill &c." *Saint Paul* also to the *Corinthians* against his Aduersaries sheweth, that hee was not a " vaine Promiser :" That hee was not " light" and " vnconstant," and " a wauering Teacher :" That he did not teache " craftily," or " corruptly dispensing the worde of God :" That hee did not " teach ambitiously, as seeking his owne glorie" &c. The like did a nomber of learned Fathers of the Primitiue Church, at large Tertul. Justin. answering those vile and reprochefull Slaunders Melito, &c. raysed against the Christians in those dayes. *Augustine* in a whole woorke answered Assertions falsly fathered vpon him : and so did many other. Wee seeke not therein our owne prayse and commendation. If I doe insert particular prayses and commendations, I must say vnto the *Libellers,* as *S. Paul* sayde to the *Corinthians,* " Si insipiens fui in laudando, vos me coegistis." If I haue bene foolish in ouermuch praising, your immodest reproches, vntrueths, and slaunders do driue me to it. In this mine answere, I seeke not to satisfie all kinde of men, but onely the moderate and godly. For the malicious

Back-biter and Rayler will neuer be satisfied : but the more he is answered, the worse he will be. If my defence may take moderate place with the better sort, I shall be glad : if not, I may not be excessiuely grieued with sorowe, but I must say with *Paul*, " Gloria nostra hæc est, testimonium conscientiæ nostræ." And with *Iob*, " Ecce in cælis testis meus." This witnesse in heauen, and the witnesse of our owne heart and conscience, is sufficient to comfort vs. And for our further helpe, we must pray with *Dauid*, who was lamentably beaten and bitten with viperous tongues, " Leade vs, O Lorde, in thy righteousnesse, because of our enemies : make thy way plaine before vs." This God I trust, will deliuer vs from the daunger of euill tongues, and open their eyes and hearts, that they may see and vnderstande what hinderance they bring to the Gospel of Christ, which they will seeme to professe so earnestly. Amen.

(· ·)

T. C.

The

THE CONTENTS OF THIS TREATISE.

¶ AN ADMONITION TO THE CHURCH AND

people of England, to take heede of the contempt of *those Bishops and Preachers, which God hath sent to them as messengers to bring vnto them the doctrine of their Saluation.*

WHEN I call to my remembrance, the loathsome contempt, hatred, and disdaine, that the most part of men in these dayes beare, and in the face of the worlde declare towarde the Ministers of the Church of God, aswell Bishops as other among vs here in Englande : my heart can not but greatly feare and tremble at the consideration thereof. It hath pleased God now a long time most plentifully to powre downe vpon vs his manifold and great benefites of wealth, riches, peace and quietnesse, euen in the middest of the flames of discord, dissention and miserie rounde about vs, yea, and that more is, by the space of these thirtie yeeres, by the continuall preaching of the Gospell hath called vs vnto him (as before time he called his chosen people of the Iewes by his Prophets) and yet do we not onely not shew any sound token, either of our returning to him that called vs, or of our thankefull receiuing his worde which he hath sent vs, or of conforming our liues thereunto, as hee willeth vs: but also euidently to the eyes and eares of all men, shew our hatred and misliking of those reuerend persons, whome it hath pleased God to vse as his messengers to call vs vnto him, and as his instruments to bring vnto vs the ʽglad tidings of the Gospel, which before with sworde and fire was taken from vs. For who seeth not in these dayes, that hee who can most bitterly inueigh against Bishops and Preachers, that can most boldely ·blaze their discredites, that can most vncharitably slaunder

B

their liues and doings, thinketh of himselfe, and is esteemed of
other, as the most zealous and earnest furtherer of the Gospel?
Yea, they thinke it almost the best way, and most ready, to
bring themselues in credite and estimation with many.   A lamentable state of time it is, wherein such vntemperat boldnesse
is permitted without any bridle at all.   What man therefore
that feareth God, that loueth his Church, that hath care of his
Prince and countrey, can remember this thing, and not dread
4 Reg. 17. in his heart, the sequele thereof?   When the *Israel-*
& 18.   *ites* derided and contemned the Prophets which God
had sent among them, his wrath was so kindled, that hee
        brought the *Assyrians* vpon them to their confusion.
4 Reg. 24. When the tribe of *Iuda* did the like to *Ieremie* and
other messengers of God, they were cast into the captiuitie
Matt. 23. of *Babylon.*   When the Iewes reprochefully vsed
Luke 13.   Christ, and with wicked slaunder persecuted his Apostles that brought to them the light of saluation, their Citie and
Temple was burned, their people slaine, and (as Christ threatned) their countrey made desolate, and giuen ouer to the
spoyle.   And shall wee thinke that God will not remaine the
same God toward vs?   Is his minde changed? is his iustice
slaked? is his hand shortned, that either he wil not, or cannot reuenge, as he hath bin wont to doe? No (good Christians)
let vs neuer deceiue our selues with such vaine and godlesse
cogitations.   God remaineth alwayes one, and is not mutable.
His benefits to the Israelites and Iewes were neuer greater,
then they now these many yeeres haue bene toward vs:
they were neuer more earnestly, eyther by Gods blessings
allured, or by preaching called to repentance then we haue
bene.   And yet our vnthankefulnesse, in some respectes is
greater then theirs, and our vncourteous vsing of his messengers not much inferiour: yea, if the willes of many were not
brideled by Gods singular grace, in our Prince and gouernours, it is to bee feared, it woulde shewe it selfe as outragious
as theirs did.   We haue iust cause therefore to feare the like

plague, which they in like case sustained: And surely, it cannot bee, but that it hasteneth fast vpon vs.

Obiection.

But some will say (I knowe) " That I doe great iniurie to the Prophets, the Apostles, and other messengers of God, to compare them with such wicked men, such blinde guides, such couetous hypocrites, such antichristian Prelates, such symonicall Preachers, as our cleargie men now are."

Answere.

I doe not compare them (good Reader) in worthines of grace and vertue, but in likenesse of office and ministerie. These haue brought vnto this realme, the same light of the gospell, the same trueth of doctrine, the same way of saluation, that the Apostles brought to the people of God in their time. They are the mouth of God whereby hee speaketh to vs and calleth vs to his knowledge, as hee did his chosen by other in the Primitiue church. And howsoeuer by the libertie of this time, it pleaseth men in the heate of their spirite to boyle out with reprochfull choler against them: yet I am sure, they are not able to vse more bitter and vncourteous speech, then the like affection vttered against the Prophets, against Christ himselfe, and his Apostles, as after more euidently shall appeare. I knowe, they being but fraile and sinfull men in comparison of those blessed Saints of God beforetime, may giue more iust cause of reproche, and minister more matter to euill tongues, then they did: And yet I doubt not, but the tenth part of that euill that vnthankefull mindes vtter against them, shall neuer be found to be true. They that haue the feare of God, will not rashly iudge of other, and christian charitie will hide the blemishes and faultes of their brethren, and specially of the preachers of the gospell sincerely teaching Gods trueth. Charitie woulde consider, that the times are dangerous, and that wee are lighted into

these corrupt and perillous last dayes, whereof Christ prophe-
cied in the Euangelists, and therfore may thinke our selues
thrise happy, if we haue tollerable Ministers, though they bee
farre from that rule that Christian perfection requireth.

Apolog.   These dayes bee like the times *Nazianzen* writeth
of. "When they heare any thing spoken of a Minis-
ter or Priest, they by and by conceiue that of all, which is
reported of one.   And wee are become a Theater, not to Angels
and men, (as that Champion Saint *Paul* sayth,) But wee are
become a Stage to the most vile and abiect men at all times,
and in all places, in the Streetes, in Shoppes, at Tables, at
Feasts, at Councels, euen to the very playing scaffolds, which
I speake with teares, and are scoffed at, euen of the vile and
contemptible players." &c.

"The time was (sayth *Caluine*) when no man durst open
his mouth against the Ministers or Preachers of the worde:
But nowe there is no speech more plausible.   None of these
base persons would speake a word, if they did not see themselues backed by men of great authoritie, and receiue reward
for so dealing.   Such vntrueths woulde soone vanish and bee
forgotten, vnlesse they were nourished by them for whose
pleasure they were deuised."   It may be hardly thought, that
the true zeale of God, and loue of his Gospell is in that heart,
that can easily breake out to the discrediting of the ministers
and teachers therof.   They woulde rather sigh in their hearts
and groane in their consciences, and pray vnto God in the
spirit of mildenes, to take away such blemishes from the face
of his church, and to amende the faults thereof, if not all at
once, yet by little and little, as to his gratious prouidence
might seem best.   For surely where hatred and contempt of
the ministers is, there all goodnes must needes growe to confusion.   And that maketh mee to feare, that to our great
euil, the ruine of the gospell is at hand among vs.   For
where God is loued and feared, there his word is imbraced,
and his ministers reuerenced.

" This is the cause of all euil (sayth *Chrysostome*) In 2. epist.
that the authoritie of spirituall gouernours is decayed, ad Tim. 2.1.
no reuerēce, no honor, no feare is vsed toward them. Obey
your gouernours (saith *Paul*) and be subiect to them. But
now al things are ouerthrowen and cleane confounded:
Neither speake I this for the gouernours sake, but for your
owne." And a little after, "He that honoureth the Priest
honoureth God, and hee that despiseth the Priest, by little
and little falleth to this also, that he will vse reproch against
God himself. He that receiueth you (sayth Christ)
receiueth me." And in another place, sayth the Matt. 10.
Scripture, "Haue his Priestes in honour." "Hence commeth
it (sayth *Cyprian*) that the bonde of the Lordes De zelo
peace is broken: Hence is it that brotherly loue is & liuore.
violated: Of this cause is it, that trueth is corrupted, vnitie is
broken, that men leane to Schismes: because Priestes are
slaundered, Bishops are enuied, and euery man, either complaineth that hee is not ordeined rather then another, or else
disdaineth to haue another aboue him." &c.

The Iewes were esteemed to despise God, because they made so small account of his seruant Nom. 16.
Moses. And to *Samuel* (saith the Lord) "They haue not
despised thee, but me." "Yea, if it be an euill Minister, (sayth
Chrysostome) yet God marketh, that for his sake thou doest
reuerence and obey him, that is not worthie honour of himselfe, and therefore will he pay thee thy rewarde. If he that
receiueth a Prophet in the name of a Prophet, receiue the
rewarde of a Prophet, it cannot be that he that reuerenceth
and obeyeth his ordinarie Minister, shall want his reward."
Christians should remember that Bishops and Preachers are
the *Angels of God*, the *Ambassadours of Christ*, the Mal. 2.
Ministers of our saluation, and therefore that they 2 Cor. 5.
can not be slaundered or abused, but the reproche Ephes. 2.
must touch God himselfe. *Esay* sheweth, when the vnthanke-
ful and disobedient Iewes did mocke the Prophets, Esay 57.

did put out their lips, and lell out their tongues in disdaine
of them, that God was dishonoured with the reproch thereof. Happily it will be doubted, whether our Bishops and
Preachers bee the Ministers and messengers of God, or
no. Yea, some dare affirme boldly, "that in deede they be
not." But (good christians) beware of such cogitations, as
displeasant and misliking affections may raise in you. If they
be not the ministers and messengers of God, if they bee not
sent of him, then it is not the message of God that they haue
brought vs: it is not his worde that they haue taught vs:
they bee not Gods Sacraments that they deliuered vnto vs,
and so doe a great nomber of vs remain as no Christians.
Though they were such vnworthie persons, as the vnthankfull mindes of many doe imagine them, or as the vncharitable
tongues and pennes of some of late time haue blazed them:
yet bringing nothing vnto you, but Gods will out of his holy
Scriptures, (for in deede they haue not done otherwise, howsoeuer their doctrine be defaced) you should assuredly be
perswaded, that they are the instruments of Gods blessing
vnto you. "Although they that bee superiours," saith
Chrysostome, "and Gouernours, were euill, and spotted with manye faultes: yet shoulde not the Disciples
withdrawe them from their instruction. For if Christ speaking of the Doctours of the Iewes, that because they sate in
Moyses Chayre, they were worthie to bee heard of their Disciples, although their workes were not commendable: what
fauour are they woorthie of, which contemne and trample
vnder foote (as it were) the Prelates of the Church, which by
Gods goodnesse liue moderately? If it bee a foule matter for
one to iudge an other, howe much more is it vnlawfull to
iudge their Maisters and instructers?" *Baalam* was a couetous prophet, and yet by him GOD blessed his people. Nowe
surely, if you haue receiued at their bandes the blessing of
Gods trueth, and the light of his holie word, as in deede you
haue: the cogitation of this benefite shoulde moue your mindes

Chrysost.
in 2. ad
Corin.

more fauourably to thinke of them, and more charitably to iudge of their doinges. Or if you doe not, looke that you leaue not great occasion to men to think of you, that you make light accompt of that doctrine of the Gospell, which aswell their predecessours as they, haue, and doe daily preach vnto you: and so that you bee not those men that you would pretende to be. For men will thinke this: If these persons did fauour the Gospell, they woulde rather seeke meanes to hide the blemishes and imperfections of their Prelates and Preachers, then thus odiously to amplifie and paint foorth their discredite to their vtter shame and reproche in the worlde. For, as much as in them lyeth, through their sides (in the heartes and mindes of manie) they giue a mortal wound to the doctrine, which by them hath now these manie yeeres beene taught in this Realme. For will men iudge (trowe you) that after so great darkenesse and ignoraunce of Gods woorde, as the Churche of Christ is reported by vs to haue beene wrapped in, that God woulde restore and sende vnto the same the light of his trueth, by so wicked and naughtie instruments, as these men be imagined to be? (For they condemne not onelie those Bishops and ministers that be now in place, but their predecessors also, whose place these men occupie, and whose doctrine they confirme.) Men will thinke surely, either that that doctrine which we call darknesse and errour, was the true light, or that these Preachers can not be so euill persons, as malice doth make them. Christ would not suffer that the deuill shoulde vtter any thing to the glorie of God, and will he suffer " deuillish and Antichristian persons" to bee the chiefe Preachers and restorers of his Gospell? GOD alwaies hath appointed godlie men to be the teachers and reuiuers of his trueth, as *Abraham* with the other Patriarches, *Moses, Aaron, Dauid,* the *Prophets,* the *Apostles.* And in our dayes *Luther, Zuinglius, Oecolampadius, Cranmer, Ridley, Iewell, &c.* For God is neuer destitute of his godly captaines to gouerne his Church, and to set foorth his word.

Obiection.

" Oh, but our Bishops and preachers be couetous : they
giue not to the poore : they imbesill the goodes of the Church :
they bee woorkers and clokers of Simonie : they hinder reformation of the Church," &c.

Answere.

But how know you that? It were safe for your consciences
first to trie and knowe the trueth, before you rashly, to con-
Chrys. in 2. demnation, iudge your brother. Common speeches,
ad Timoth. and coniecturall collections doe oftentimes prooue
false. Doe you think that al is true which is spoken of your
selues ? I appeale to your owne consciences. Surely hee must
bee a very bappie man in these dayes, of whome some euill is
not spoken, which, in his owne conscience, hee knoweth not to
bee true. Nowe if this may, and doeth happen to most priuate
persons, howe is it not likely that it happeneth also to Bishops
and ecclesiasticall Ministers? Yea, of all other it is most
like, that they shoulde feele the bitternesse of false and backbiting speeches : The Ministers of God haue beene alwayes
subiect to that crosse. And in these dayes, they haue to doe
with so manie and diuers kindes of enemies, as it is not possible for them to escape the daunger thereof. On the one side
is the *Papist*, whose errours they confute, whose obstinacie
they punish : On the other side are the *phantasticall spirites
of Anabaptists, Of the families of the loue,* and sundry others o
the like sort, whose wickednesse and corrupting of the church, is
by our ecclesiasticall gouernors drawen into the light, reproued,
and repressed. Yea, and beside these, there are an infinit
number of *Epicures,* and *Atheistes,* which hate the Bishops
and speake euil of them, and wish them to be taken away :
partly because they are as bridles to their loose and wicked life :
partlie because they staye from them, that spoyle and praye,
which nowe for a fewe yeeres with great hope they haue gaped
after, and with much adoe is holden out of their iawes.

Moreouer, who knoweth not that they which haue the office of iudging, correcting, and reprooing other, bee their doinges neuer so sincere, shall often light into the displeasure and misliking of manie, and thereby gette misreport? Therefore seeing Bishoppes, and other chiefe of the Clergie, are besette with so manie difficulties, and lie in danger of so manie aduersaries : no maruaile though their blemishes bee amplified, and (as the prouerbe is) of euerie moul-hill made a great mountayne. Yea, no maruaile, though their best doinges and sincerest meaninges, by mislikers are depraued, and with harde and vncharitable interpretations wrested to their reproofe. Wherfore al Christians that haue the feare of God, and loue his trueth, but principally the chiefe gouernours, that haue authoritie to deale with the Clergie, ought to take great heed, that by such deprauing reports they bee not carried to mislike or discredite them, which neuer iustly deserued so great reproofe. Let them diligently consider what may fall vnto themselues also, beeyng in place subiect to like obloquie. What meant Saint *Paul*, when he saide, "Against an elder, receiue no accusation vnder two or three witnesses?" Surely hee did see that 1. Tim. 5.
the office of teachers and reproouers, iudges and gouernors, lieth in great daunger of euill speech and false accusations, and therefore would not haue them rashly condemned, either in priuate or publike iudgement, much lesse to bee defaced and contemned, to be disobeyed and resisted, yea, though they were more grieuous offenders, then standeth with the worthinesse of their offices. *Aaron* had grieuously offended, and greatly distained his calling, when hee was Nom. 16.
the Minister to make the golden Calfe, and to further the peoples horrible and shamefull idolatrie. I trust all the enemies that the Bishops and Cleargie men of *England* haue, shall neuer bee able to prooue, that in this time of the Gospell, any one of them did euer commit an offence either so horrible, and displeasant in the sight of God, or so hurtfull and offensiue to the Church. And yet after that, when *Corah, Dathan*

and other did call him proude Prelate, and sayde that hee, and
his brother vsed tyrannie ouer the people of God, howe grieuously God did take it, and howe dreadfull punishment came
vpon them for misusing the Ministers of GOD, the historie
doeth sufficiently declare: yea, though many of the offenders
were of the highest state, birth and linage, among the people.

Obiection.

But it is a common Obiection, and many thinke they sufficiently excuse their contempt, when they say, " That our
Bishops and Preachers speake well, and teach other to doe
well, but they followe not the same themselues, and therefore
men doe not beleeue them, nor be any thing mooued with
their preaching"

Answere.

But I say vnto you, if you followe any doctrine in respect
of the person that speaketh it, you doe not like good Christians: yea, if Paul speake any thing of himselfe, you doe not
well, if in that respect you beleeue him: but you shoulde
1 Thes. 1.   embrace his doctrine and followe his teaching, because he is the Apostle and messenger of God sent
to deliuer his holy will out of the scriptures, and as it were
from the mouth of God himselfe.

Obiection.

Matth. 5.   It wil be sayd that Bishops should be "The light
1. Pet. 2.   of the world, the salt of the earth, patternes and
examples to the flocke of Christ."

Answere.

I graunt they should be so, and if they be not, the daunger is
theirs: but Christ is the iudge, whose office thou mayest not
presume without danger, to take vpon thee, in iudg-
Rom. 14.   ing his Minister. If they be not such as they
shoulde be, wilt thou headlong therefore runne to thine owne

perdition, and cast they selfe into the danger of Gods wrath and displeasure, aswell by reiecting the trueth of his doctrine, as also by rashly iudging and condemning his Minister? Doest thou not remember that Christ sayeth, " That men shall make an accompt of euery idle worde that _{Matth. 12.} they speake?" And shall they not make a streight account, thinke you, for their vncurteous and vnsauorie speeches, for their vncharitable and bitter raylings against them, by whose meanes they haue receiued the doctrine of saluation? Who can be worse then a Publicane? And yet the Pharisey is greatly reproued, for that he spake so contemptuously of the Publicane, and so arrogantly preferred himselfe before him. " The Pharisey (saith *Chrisostome*) by his euill _{Chrys. in} speech did hurt the Publican nothing, but rather _{epist. ad.} did him good, yea, though the thinges were true that _{Rom.} hee spake of him. Wee also drawe vnto our selues extreame euill, by our euill speeches, euen as the Pharisey (as it were) did thrust a sworde into himselfe, and receiuing a sore wounde, departed. Let vs therefore rule our vntamed tongues, least wee also haue a like rewarde: for if hee that spake euill of a Publican, escaped not punishment, what defence shall we haue, that are wont to raile against our fathers? If *Marie* which once blasphemed her brother, was so sore punished, what hope of health shal we haue, which dayly ouerwhelme our superiors with railing speeches and taunts?"

They that haue the right feare of God, looke first into their owne bosomes: they be inquisitiue of their owne liues: they sitte as iudges and examiners of their owne consciences: but nowe a dayes (the more it is to bee lamented) men forget them-selues: they looke not into their owne doings: they cast that end of the wallet behinde them, wherein their owne faultes are wrapped, and be alwayes curiously prying into the liues and doings of other, and specially of Gouernours, Bishops, and Ecclesiasticall Ministers. In them, if they see neuer so light a blemish, if in their face they can finde neuer so small a

warte, or espie in their eye neuer so little a moate, they are
esteemed by and by " misshapen Bishops, blinde guides,
Monsters of Antichrist, not meete for any roome in Christes
Church, not to bee suffered in any Christian common weale."
Yea, they loath their doctrine, Counsell and instruction, be it
neuer so true and good : they will not take any aduise at their
handes : yea, they say their teaching can doe no man good.
Thus doe they make those men stumbling stockes for themselues to perdition, whome GOD of his singular grace and
prouidence hath sent with his worde among them, as Ministers of their saluation.

Thinke of Bishops and Preachers, how basely and unchari-
tably soeuer it shall please you, they are not onely the Sur-
geons of your soules, but your spirituall fathers also. A
naturall childe, though he suffer griefe and iniuries at his
fathers hande, will not be in a rage against him, but wil take
the hurts patiently and mildely, so long as any way they may
be borne. Although hee see faultes in his father, (as that he
is euill of sight, or doateth for age, or that he be weake and
staggereth as hee goeth, yea, and sometime falleth to the
grounde) he will not therefore vndutifully chide his father, but
by such meanes as hee can wil helpe, and with his best indeuour, wipe away the filth, that he gathereth by his oft falling :
hee will bee mindeful of that good lesson, " Noli gloriari in ig-
nominia Patris tui, neque enim tibi tam gloria quàm
probrum est." So surely, those good and kindly
children that loue God their great father, wil vse themselues
toward their spiritual fathers in his Church. If *Noah* happen
in his sleepe to lye somewhat vncomely, and leaue open his
nakednesse, they will not follow the example of cursed
Cham, and with derision fetch not their brethren onely, but
their fathers enemies also to beholde it, that hee may bee for
euer shamed, and the aduersaries mouthes opened against
him : They will rather with blessed and obedient *Sem* and
Iaphet, take the garment of christian charitie, and going back-

Eccle. 3.

warde hide their fathers nakednesse, yea, and happily with
the rusling of their feet, or by casting on of the garment,
purposely wake him out of his sleepe, that he may vnderstand howe vncomely hee doth lie, in the derision, not onely
of their vnkind brother, but of other also that seeke his
reproche, and by that meanes be taught to take heed that he
doe not fal on sleepe againe in such vncomely maner.

Chrysostome complaineth at this vnkindnesse:
" What coulde be more happie then they? what more
miserable then wee? for they gaue their blood, and
their life for their Maisters, but wee will not vouchsafe to
vtter so much as a few wordes for our common fathers, when
wee heare them reproched, backebited, slaundered, both of
their owne and of others: for wee neither reproue or represse
such cursed speakers: yea, I woulde to God we our selues
were not the first accusers. Surely wee heare not such opprobrious rebukes at the mouthes of Infidels, as wee see powred
out against our superiours, by them that are of the same religion." Thus much haue I spoken, and the longer stoode
vppon this matter (the Lord knoweth) not so much to helpe the
credite of them that bee blamed, as, if it may be possible, to
turne away from vs Englishmen the great daunger of our vn-
kindenesse in abusing them, by whome God hath deliuered
vnto vs so great and inestimable benefites.

Chrys. in Epist. ad Rom.

Obiection.

" Some perchance will aske me, whether I entend by this
meanes to cloake and hide the corrupt and naughtie life of the
chiefe ministers of the Church, whereby they slaunder the
Gospel, deface their calling, and be an open offence to a great
number of godly."

Answere.

I answere, God forbid I should haue any such meaning.
Their great offences I greatly reproue, and thinke them

woorthy, vpon triall of trueth, not only of blame, but also of more sharpe punishment, then any other, for that the offence giuen by them is greater. And we haue a Prince and Magistrate, who by Gods lawe, if there be so iust cause, both may, and ought to deale with them, neither can their authoritie bee refused, they claime not exemption.

But as for their smaller faultes, Christian charitie forceth me to winke at them, because I know greater matter in my selfe. And I see they are men, and no Angels, and they liue in a perillous time, and haue many occasions to offend, so that it is harder for them to stande vpright, then for some other that are in priuate state. Hee is an Angell that neuer falleth, hee is no man. Men are fraile, and in daunger to sinne, though they haue otherwise great graces. If any of them haue fallen with Aaron, to anie great and horrible offence, I trust they are with him also risen by repentaunce, and with teares, in the mercie of God, washed away their wickednesse: Or, if they haue not, I must needes say with Christ, "Better it were that a Milstone were hanged about their neckes, and they cast into the sea," then that by their continuance in euil, they shoulde bee occasion that anie shoulde fall from God, or reiect his Gospell. As their vertues are more profitable and beneficial to the Church of God, then the vertues of other priuate persons: so are their vices and faults more hurtfull and daungerous. They stande on an high place where all mens eyes are fastened vppon them: their least faultes cannot be hidde, and the greatest are of all men abhorred. A wart in the face, and a blemish in a Bishoppe, is no small disfiguring of either of them. If other mens faults be seene, the offence is not accounted great: but if a bishops be espied, it is esteemed, not according to the greatnes of the thing, but according to the dignitie of the person. "Hee that knoweth the will of his Master and doth it not, shalbe beaten with many stripes."

In Matt. 8.   "Sacerdos (saith *Chrysostome*) si pariter cum homil. 27. Subditis peccat, non eadem sed acerbiora patietur."

If a Priest shall offend as the inferiour doeth, hee shall suffer not the same punishment, but farre greater.

It behooueth them therefore in the feare of God, to looke more diligently about them then any other, and specially in these miserable dayes, wherein all mens eyes are so curiously set vpon them, that they almost cleane forget to looke any thing vpon themselues, or to finde fault with any other, then with Ecclesiasticall persons and officers.

Obiection.

Heere some perchaunce will take mee in mine owne turne, and conclude against all that hitherto I haue spoken, yea and against the whole purpose of my writing: " That if Bishoppes offences bee so grieuous and hurtfull, more then other mens are, and that our Bishops and Ecclesiastical Ministers, are seene to commit so foule and heynous faultes: that they are worthie of all that euill that is spoken against them, and that I cannot iustly blame these persons, that with great zeale doe reproue these their doings, so hurtful to the Church of Christ, and so dangerous to the people of God."

Answere.

Surely, if all bee true that is written and spoken against them, (as I trust, and in part I knowe, it is not) I must needes confesse, and were wicked if I woulde denie, that they had iustly deserued whatsoeuer euill coulde bee vttered of them. For sure I am, if, as I say, all were true that is spoken, that they should be as detestable as anie heretikes that euer were in the Church, yea, as the Pope and Antichrist himselfe, whose pillars and vpholders, they are called and accounted with many. And yet can I not excuse them, which in such manner doe persecute them with the bitternesse of their tongue and penne, no more then I can excuse *Nabuchodonosor*, or any other tyrant that plagued the people of God, offending against his lawe. For whatsoeuer God in his prouidence respected, they looked onely to the satisfying of their coue-

tous, ambitious, cruell and bloody affection: And so, whatsoeuer God regardeth in chastening his negligent Ministers,
or in waking them out of sleepe with the spurre of infamie
and reproch: yet by their virulent and vnseasoned speeches,
that are vsed, by the scornefull and disdainefull reproches, by
the rash and vncharitable vntruethes, I feare it may bee toc
truely gathered, that they which bee the instruments thereof,
seeke to fulfill their enuious, proude and disdainefull appetites,
or the working of some other purpose, which they looke to
bring to passe, by the discrediting of the Bishops, and other
chiefe of the Clergie, which be as great blockes and stops in
their way. *Qui habet aures ad audiendum, audiat.* But let
such persons in time take heede, when God as a mercifull
father, hath chastised his children sufficiently, and stirred
them to remember their dueties, that he cast not the rod into the
fire, as before time he hath vsed to do, and bring the rewarde
of their vnchristian dealing vpon their owne heads. If right
zeale, with conscience and detestation of euil, were the roote
of these inuectiues, which so boyle in loathsome choller and
bitter gall against the Bishops and other of the Clergie: surely,
the same spirit would mooue them to breake out into like
vehement lamentations against the euils and vices, whic
shew themselues in a great nomber of this Realme: I meane,
the deepe ignorance and contempt of God in the midst of the
light of the Gospell, the heathenish securitie in sinne and wickednesse, the monstrous pride in apparell, the voluptuous riot
and sensualitie, the excessiue buildings and needelesse nestes
of mens treasures, which bee as cankers consuming the riches
of this Realme.

What shall I say of the loosenesse of whoredome and adulterie? the wrongfull wresting by extortion, bribery, and vsury
the crafty cosening for priuate commoditie? the libertie in false
swearing and periurie? with the heape almost of all other
vices wherewith mans life may be distained? so that if some
stay were not by moderat gouernment, and some meane num-

ber restrained in conscience, by the doctrine of the Gospell:
it were greatly to be feared, that our wickednesse woulde growe
in haste to such perfection, as it woulde presently pull out of
heauen Gods wrath against vs. But all these thinges are
wrapt vp in deepe silence among most of these men, vnlesse it
bee to vpbraid Bishops as causes thereof, and the corrupt
gouernment, as it is thought, of this Church, with the rich and
wealthy states of Bishops, pretended to bee the onely cause of
Gods indignation toward vs. But this is the wicked working
of the deuill, to turne mens eyes from their owne sinnes, that
they may not acknowledge them, and by repentance turne
away the displeasure of God and his iustice hanging ouer vs,
and, if it be possible, also to destroy the course of the Gospell, that hath bene so long with so small fruit among vs.

But here I haue to aduertise the godly, and chiefely the
Prince and Magistrates, that they be not abused and ledde by
the cunning that Sathan hath alwayes vsed, to deface the glory of God, and disturbe his Church. When Sathan seeth the
doctrine of Trueth to spring vp amongst men, and somewhat
to prosper: when hee seeth wickednesse and vice by diligent
preaching to bee repressed, and thereby his kingdome of
errour and wickednesse to decay, and the glorie of God to
increase: then hee bestirreth him by all meanes hee can.
And if by Gods good prouidence the Princes and Magistrates
bee such, as by sword and fire he cannot either ouerthrowe
it, or worke some mischiefe against it: then seeketh hee by
lying and slander to discredit and deface the messengers that
GOD sendeth with his worde, and instruments that he vseth to
aduance and sette foorth his trueth, by this meanes to worke
hinderance to the trueth it selfe. When *Ieremie* preached the
will of God earnestly and truely vnto the Iewes, were there
not false Prophets, and other verie neere the Prince, which
perswaded him and other rulers, that hee was a naughtie man,
not worthie to liue? that hee was an enemie to his Countrey?
that hee conspired with the *Babylonians,* and was with money

or otherwise corrupted by them, to perswade the people of
Hest. 3. & 4. *Iuda*, not to refuse their subiection? When God by
the Iewes in captiuitie, and by the fauour of the
Queene *Hester*, began to spread his knowledge among the
Gentiles, so that their heathenish idolatrie was somewhat ble-
mished, the deuil raised vp a fit instrument by such meanes as
before is mentioned, to worke their confusion. For *Haman*
came to king *Assuerus*, and said, "There is a people disper-
sed throughout all the prouinces of thine Empire, not agreeing
among themselues, vsing newe lawes, and contemning thy
ordinances, and thou knowest it is not expedient for thy kingdome, that they should be suffered to waxe so insolent. And
if it shall please thee to appoynt, that they may be all put to
death, I will bring in tenne thousand talents into the kings
treasure." It was a shrewd tale to perswade a Prince. For
he tempered his hatefull and slaunderous lying with the sweete
sawce of gaine and commoditie. The subtile Sathan did see,
that sometime they which otherwise are good Princes, when
hope of great benefite is offered, will be more easily persuaded
to some kinde of hard dealing, which otherwise they themselues would not like. When *Iohn Baptist* was sent to prepare the way for the comming of Christ, though hee were a
man of very austere liuing, did not the Pharisees perswade
the people and chiefe rulers, that hee was but an hypocrite?
Matth. 11. that hee was possessed with a deuill, and therfore
Iohn 8. that his doctrine should not be beleeued? When
Christ himselfe came, a perfect patterne of all temperance and
godly vertue, did they not say, that he was a glutton, and
wine bibber? a Samaritane? a friend of Publicanes and sinners? a worker with deuils? a seducer of the people? &c
and by this means in the hearts of many wrought the discredite both of his doctrine, and of his myracles? In like manner
dealt Sathan with his instruments against the Apostles an
godlie professors of Christian religion in the Primitiue Church,
as it appeareth in the Ecclesiasticall Histories and auncient

Fathers. For malitious tongues and pennes did
spreade abroade of them, that they murdered their
children, and did eate them: that vsually at their
assemblies they committed incest: that they woorship-
ped the sunne: that they worshipped an asse head:
that they were traitours to the Empire: that they were generall enemies of all mankinde: with an infinite number of other
like false and slaunderous crimes, and by this meanes the
wicked enemies of Christ raised those grieuous and terrible
persecutions, wherewith the Church was vexed the space of
three hundred yeeres vnder the Emperours. Yea, and this
craft of the deuill ceased not vnder the Christian Emperours.
For then stirred he vp schismes and factions, errours and
heresies, almost in number infinite, and still by backebiters
and slaunderous instrumentes, defaced and brought out of
credite the godly and learned bishops, which were as the
pillars of Christian trueth, against the enemies of God and his
Church.

Constantine that woorthy and godlie prince, at the beginning fauoured and furthered all those reuerend and learned
Bishops that did mainteine the doctrine of *Nicene* Councell
against the *Arians*: but after that *Eusebius* of *Nicomedia*, the
great patrone of that heresie, had procured friendes in the
court, and therby crept in some credite with the Emperour,
he, and the residue of his sort, deuised shamefull slaunders
against *Athanasius* and other, that, in the ende, with great
displeasure of the Emperour, he was banished into *Fraunce*,
and there continued all the reigne of the saide *Con-*
stantine. His enemies with great impudencie, had
charged him with shamefull vntruths, as that he
cruelly and vniustly had excommunicated diuers
persons: that as a couetous extortioner, he had
oppressed the countrey of *Egypt* with exactions: that hee had
committed adultery with a strumpet, who was brought before
his face to auouch it to be true: that he had murthered

Arsenius, and vsed his arme to worke sorcery : that he sent
Socrat. lib. 1. cap. 35. money to one that went about treason against the
Emperor: that hee had affirmed in threatning wordes,
that he would cause the city of *Alexandria* to send no more
tribute-corne to *Constantinople* for the Emperors prouision, as
before time it had vsed to doe. As they dealt with *Athanasius,*
so did they in like manner with *Eustathius, Macarius,* and al
other godly Fathers which defended the true faith of Christ,
and set themselues against the indeuours of heretikes, and
other seditious and factious spirites. And in like maner were
other vsed after that time, as *Ambrose, Cyrill,* and *Chrysostome.*
It were a matter almost infinite to recite the examples thereof,
and to shewe how like they are to the attempts of some in
these dayes.

And although it pleased GOD by strange meanes at that
time to reprooue sundry of those shamefull vntrueths deuised
against manie : yet by stoute affirmation and colourable proofe,
thorow friendship, many of them tooke suche effect, that sundrie woorthy and good men were put out of their bishoprikes,
driuen into banishment, and put to death, to the great trouble of
the Church, and exceeding hinderaunce of christian faith for the
space of many yeeres. We reade in histories, that *Philip* king
of *Macedony,* a subtile and politique prince, who is thought to
haue conquered more by craft and cunning, then by force of
warre and dint of sworde, minding to bring the *Græcians,* vnder
his subiection, in concluding an agreement with them, conditioned
that they shoulde deliuer vnto him their Orators as the very
firebrands of discord among them, and the onely occasioners
of that displeasure and misliking, that was betweene him and
them. At which time *Demosthenes* one of the Orators, speaking for himselfe, admonished the *Athenians* to call to their remembraunce, the parable betweene the shepheardes and the
wolues. The wolues pretending desire of agreement between them and the shepheards, perswaded them, that all the
cause of their displeasure, was the vnseasonable barking of

the dogges : and promised great amitie, so that they woulde put away their ill-fauoured curres and mastiues. But when the dogs were remooued, the wolues tooke their pleasure in spoyling the flocke more cruelly then euer they did before. So (saieth *Demosthenes*) this King *Philip*, vnder pretence of friendship, seeking his owne benefite, would haue you to deliuer vp your Orators, which from time to time call vppon you, and giue you warning of his subtile and craftie deuises, to the ende, that when you haue so done, ere you bee ware, he may bring you and your citie vnder his tyrannie. And this saying of *Demosthenes* proued after verie true indeede. Euen so (good Christians) the subtile serpent Sathan, prince of darkenesse, seeking to bring the Church of *England* vnder his kingdome againe, from which by the mightie hand of God it hath beene deliuered, indeuoureth cunningly to perswade the shepheardes, that is, the chiefe Gouernours of this realme to put away their barking dogges, that is, to put downe the state of Bishops, and other chiefe of the Cleargie, to take away their lands and liuings, and set them to their pensions, the sooner by that meanes to worke his purpose. And heerein he turneth himselfe into an Angel of light, and pretendeth great holines and the authoritie of Gods worde, and the holy Scriptures. For such a subtile *Protheus* he is, that he can turne himselfe into all maner of shapes, to bring forward his deuise.

The craftie enemie of the Church of GOD, doeth well knowe the frailetie and corruption of mennes nature, that they will not of themselues easily bende to that is good, vnlesse they be allured vnto it, by the hope of benefite. He vnderstandeth that *Honos alit artes*, and if he shall by any cunning bee able to pull away the reward of learning, hee right well seeth that hee shall haue farre fewer dogges to barke at him, and almost none that shall haue teeth to bite those hell houndes, that hee will sende to deuoure and destroy the flocke of Christ. Happily there may be some young Spanielles that will quest lauishly ynough, but hee will not feare them, because hee knoweth they will haue no teeth to bite. If the state of the Cleargie shall bee made contemptible, and the best reward of learning a meane pension: hee foreseeth that neither yong flourishing wittes will easily incline themselues to godly learning, neither wil their parents and friendes suffer them to make that the ende of their trauaile. To bring this to passe, hee worketh his deuises by sundry kindes of men: first, by such as be Papists in heart, and yet can clap their handes, and set forwarde this purpose, because they see it the next way, either to ouerthrowe the course of the Gospell, or by great and needelesse alteration, to hazard and indanger the state of the common weale. The second sort are certaine worldly and godlesse Epicures, which can pretend religion, and yet passe not which end thereof goe forwarde, so they may bee partakers of that spoyle, which in this alteration is hoped for. The thirde sorte, in some respect the best, but of all other most dangerous, because they giue the opportunity and countenance to the residue, and make their indeuours seeme zealous and godly. These bee such which in doctrine agree with the present state, and shewe themselues to haue a desire of a perfection in all things, and in some respect, in deede, haue no euill meaning, but through inordinate zeale are so caried, that they see not howe great dangers by such deuises they drawe into the Church and state of this Realme. Howe great perils, euen small mutations haue brought to Common-weales, the knowledge of Histories, and the obseruation of times, will easily teach vs.

Obiection.

But in this place " mee thinketh I heare some crie out with earnest affection against me, and say that I shewe my selfe to bee a carnall man, and in this matter of the Church vse carnall and fleshly reasons out of humaine policie, and do not stay my conscience vpon Gods word and the holy Scriptures, whereunto only in the gouernment of the Church wee shoulde cleaue, though all reason, and policie seeme contrary."

Answere.

If I doe stay my selfe, and grounde my conscience vpon humane policie, in any matter of faith and religion, I must needes confesse my selfe to be worthie great blame: But if in some things perteining to the externall fourme of gouerne-ment, or the outwarde state of the Church, I haue respect to Christian policie, not contrary to Gods word, I see no iust cause, why I shoulde be misliked, if, in consideration of the corrupt affection of mans nature, I wish the state of a Christian Church and common weale to bee such, that yong and towardly wittes, not yet mortified by Gods spirit, may bee allured with the hope of benefite, to the studie of learning, and principally of the holy Scriptures, leauing the secret direction of their minde to God. I trust no man can with good reason reprooue this my desire, and in the course of my writing, no man shall iustly say, that either I doe stay mine owne conscience, or will other men to grounde theirs, vpon reason and policie onely, without the word of God. For neither will the feare of God suffer mee so to deale, in matter of such weight, neither doe I see, that by such meanes I can further the cause that I write of.

Many Pamphlets haue bene of late yeres partly written, and partly printed, against the whole gouernment of the Church by Bishops, and those in sundrie sortes, according to the nature and disposition of the Authors, but in all, great pro-testation of euident and strong proofe out of the Scriptures, and other writers: But especially there is one which I haue seene, the writer whereof maketh this solemne protestation following.

" That as he looketh to be acceptable to the Lord, at the iudgmēt of the immaculate lambe, in his accusation that he maketh against the Clergie of this Realme, he will not cleaue to

his owne iudgement, nor will followe his owne braine, nor wil
of himselfe inuent ought, nor vntruly blame ought, but will
faythfully and truely, sincerely and incorruptly, rehearse the
holy Scriptures, and the sentences, actes, and deedes of other
learned men, which determine and agree vpon those things,
that hee layeth downe against them."

You may well vnderstand therefore, that such an accusation will not bee answered and shifted away with humane
reason onely. The matter must haue more pith and substance in it. But howsoeuer that accusation will bee answered, I woulde the authour had perfourmed his protestation
as faithfully, as, to carry some credite and fauour, hee layde
it out solemnely. Then shoulde not his writing containe
so many vncharitable, and contemptuous speeches, so many
slaunderous vntruethes, so many wrested Scriptures, so many
false conclusions, so many impertinent allegations, as he
doth vse.

The purpose to perswade so great and daungerous a mutation in a common weale, shoulde haue caried with it, not
onely more trueth, and comelinesse of speech, but also more
weight of matter, and sounde substance of proofe. But such
is the libertie of this time, and such is the maner of them,
that to slaunder and deface other, passe not what they
speake or write.

I will nowe come to answere briefly some particular slanders vttered against some Bishops and other by name.

Against

Against the slaunderous Libels of late published vnder a
fained and fonde name of MARTIN MARPRELATE.

OH my good Brethren and louing Countrey men, what a
lamētable thing is this, that euen nowe, when the viewe of
the mightie Nauie of the *Spaniards* is scant passed out of
our sight: when the terrible sound of their shot ringeth, as
it were, yet in our eares: when the certaine purpose of most
cruel and bloody conquest of this Realme is confessed by
themselues, and blazed before our eyes: whē our sighes and
grones with our fasting and prayers, in shewe of our repentance, are fresh in memorie, and the teares not washed from
the eyes of many good men: when the mightie workes of God,
and his marueilous mercies in deliuering vs, and in scattering
and confounding our enemies, is bruted ouer all the world, and
with humble thanks renowmed by all them that loue the
Gospell: when our Christian duetie requireth for ioy and
thankesgiuing, that we should bee seene yet still lifting vp
our hands and hearts to heauen, and with thankefull mindes
setting foorth the glorie of God, and with *Moses* and the
Israelites singing prayses vnto his Name, and saying, " The
Lorde hath triumphed gloriously, the horse and the Rider, the
Ships and the Saylers, the souldiers and their Captaines hee
hath ouerthrowen in the Sea: the Lorde is our strength, the
Lorde is become our saluation, &c." That euen nowe (I say) at
this present time, wee shoulde see in mens bandes and bosomes,
commonly slaunderous Pamphlets fresh from the Presse,
against the best of the Church of Englande, and that wee
should heare at euery table, and in Sermons and Lectures, at
priuate Conuenticles, the voyces of many not giuing prayse to
God, but scoffing, mocking, rayling, and deprauing the liues
and doings of Bishoppes, and other of the Ministerie, and contemptuously defacing the state of Gouernment of this Church,
begunne in the time of that godly and blessed Prince, King

Edward the sixt, and confirmed and established by our most
gracious Soueraigne. What an vnthankfulnesse is this? what
a forgetting of our duetie towarde God, and towarde our
brethren? what a reproche to our profession of the Gospell?
what an euident testimonie to the **Aduersarie**, of our hypocrisie, and deepe malice layde vp in the bottome of our
breastes, euen in the middest of our troubles, when these
Pamphlets were in penning? The common report goeth, and
intelligence is sundry wayes giuen, that the Enemies of this
lande haue rather their malice increased towarde vs, then sustained a full ouerthrowe: and therefore by confederacie, are
in making prouision for a newe inuasion, more terrible in
threatning, then the other. Which may seeme more easie to
them, because they now know their owne wants, and our imperfections: For which vndoubtedly, they will prepare most
carefully. "For the children of this worlde, are wiser in
their generation, then the children of God." What then
meaneth this vntemperate, vncharitable and vnchristian dealings among our selues, at such an vnseasonable time? but as
it were, to ioyne handes with the Seminaries, Iesuites, and
Massing priests, and other Messengers of Antichrist, in furthering their deuises, by distracting the mindes of the Subiects, and drawing them into parets and factions, in increasing
the nomber of Mal-contents, and mislikers of the state: which
make no account of religion, but to make their commoditie,
though it bee with spoyle of their owne countrey, if oppor-
tunitie serue? In pulling away the good and faithfull hearts
of many subiects from her Maiestie, because she mainteineth
that state of Church-gouernment, which they mislike, and
which is protested to them, to bee prophane and Antichristian
    There are of late time, euen within these fewe weekes, three
or foure odious Libels against the Bishops, and other of the
Clergie, printed and spread abroad almost into all Countreyes
of this Realme, so fraught with vntrueths, slaunders, re-

proches, raylings, reuilings, scoffings, and other vntemperate speeches : as I thinke the like was neuer committed to Presse or paper, no not against the vilest sort of men, that haue liued vpon the earth. Such a preiudice this is to the honour of this State and Gouernment, as neuer was offered in any age.

For these things bee done with such impudencie and desperate boldnesse, as if they thought there were neither Prince, nor Lawe, nor Magistrate, nor Ruler, that durst controll them, or seeke to represse them.

The Author of them calleth himselfe by a fained name, *Martin Marprelate :* a very fit name vndoubtedly. But if this outragious spirit of boldenesse be not stopped speedily, I feare he wil proue himselfe to bee, not onely *Mar-prelate*, but *Mar-prince, Mar-state, Mar-lawe, Mar-magistrate*, and all together, vntil he bring it to an Anabaptisticall equalitie and communitie.

When there is seene in any Common wealth such a loose boldenesse of speech, against a setled lawe or State, it is a certaine proofe of a loose boldenesse of minde. For, *Sermo est index animi*, that is, Such as the speeche is, such is the minde. *Ex abundantia cordis os loquitur.* It hath also in all Histories bene obserued, that loose boldenesse of minde toward the Superiours, is ioyned alwayes with contempt : and contemptuous boldenesse is the very roote and spring of discord, dissention, vprores, ciuill warres, and all desperate attemptes, that may breede trouble and danger in the State. Yea, and if they be hardened with some continuance of time, and hope of impunitie, and some multitude of assistāce gathering vnto them : what may followe, I leaue to the wisedome and discretion of them, that God hath set in place of Gouernment.

These Libellers are not contented to lay downe great crimes generally, as some other haue done, but with very vndecent tearmes, charge some particular Bishops with particular faultes, with what trueth you shall now vnderstand.

They first beginne with *the most Reuerend, the Archbishop*

of *Canterburie :* which crimes and reproches, because they are many, and of no weight or likelihoode of trueth, I take onely the chiefe, and note the pages wherein they are, setting the answere after, answering them very briefly.

But in those that touch my Lord of *London,* because they are by lewd tongues drawen into more common talke, and his person most slanderously inueighed against and discredited : I thought it necessarie the thinges should bee more fully and amplie declared, that the trueth of them might be better conceiued.

For as much as I haue not bene curious in all my life to examine the doings of other, hauing ynough to do with mine owne, I haue in these matters vsed the instructiō of them, whom no honest man may in Christian duetie suspect o vntrueth : and therefore in conscience I thinke the things to be true as I haue layde them downe.

An answere to such thinges as the most Reuerend

the Archbishop of Canterburie is particularly charge withall in the Libell.

Libel pag. 2. " His Grace I warrant you, will carie to his graue the blowes &c."

Answere. God be thanked, he neuer felt blowe giuen b him or any other in that cause, except the blowes of thei despitefull and malitious tongues, which notwithstandin hee contemneth, remembring how true it is that *Hierom* saith, " Istæ machinæ hæreticorm sunt, vt conuicti de per fidia ad maledicta se conferant." When heretikes are con uinced of falsehood and vntrueths, their shift is to flee t railing and slandering. And againe, " Detractio vilium sati hominum est, et suam laudem quærentium." To backebit is the shift of base men, and such as seeke their owne praise.

He did indeede peruse *Doctor Bridges* booke before i went to the Presse, and hee knoweth that the sufficienci thereof causeth these men thus to storme, as not being able otherwise to answere it: which maketh them so bitterly to inueigh against his person, and therefore, " Si insectari personam deploratæ causæ signum est, (as it is in deede) illorum causa est deploratissima."

" It is shame for your Grace *Iohn of Cant.* that Cartwrights bookes are not answered." ^{Libell. Pa. 3.}

Hee neuer thought them so necessarie to bee ^{Answere.} answered, as the factious authors of the Libel pretend. And of that opinion are not a fewe wise and learned men, that beare good will vnto the party, and with all their hearts wishe, that God woulde direct him to vse his good giftes to the peace and quietnesse of the Church. There is sufficient written already to satisfie an indifferent reader. Hee that with indifferent minde shall read the answere of the one, and the replie of the other, shall see great difference in learning betweene them.

The desire of disputation is but a vaine brag: they haue bene disputed and conferred with oftner then either the worthines of their persōs or cause did require. Wherin their inability to defend such a cause hath manifestlie appeared, as it is well knowen to. very many, wel able to iudge. But what brags are here by the Libeller vttered, which doe not agree with the old *Heretikes and Schismatikes ?*

" His Grace threatned to send Mistres *Lawson* to ^{Libel. pag. 10.} Bridewel, because &c."

This is a notorious vntrueth. For neither did hee, ^{Answere.} nor *D. Perne* euer heare (but of this Libeller) that shee spake anie such wordes of him. But in trueth, aswell for the immodestie of her tongue, wherein she excelleth beyond the seemelinesse of an honest woman, as also for her vnwomanlie and skittish gadding vp and downe to Lambehith, and frō thence in cōpanie vnfit for her, without her owne husband, he threatned to send her to Bridewell, if she reformed not the same: which he meaneth to performe, if she

continue her lightnesse.   And yet *Dame Lawson* so notorious,
for the vilenesse of her tongue, and other vnwomanly beha‾
uiour, is one of *Martins* canonized Saints : " Quia quod
volumus sanctum est," as *Augustine* said of their predecessors
the *Donatists.*   It is likewise an vntruth, which is reported in
that page of her words spoken by *M. Shaller.*   For surely if
she had vttered them, hee would haue sent her thither with‾
out faile.   But *Dame Lawson* glorieth in her owne shame, and
so do her teachers.

That which he calleth a " Protection," *Chard* had from the
Lords of her Maiesties priuie Counsell, vpon charitable and
good causes moouing their Lordships.

Libel. pag.   " He seemeth to charge the Archbishop with in-
15.   fidelitie &c."

Answere.   This needeth no answere, it sheweth of what
spirit they are.

Libel. pag.   " Touching the *Premunire &c.*"
21.

Answere.   The Libeller doth but dreame, let him and his doe
what they can.

The same may bee answered to their " threatning of
fists &c."

That which hee speaketh of " buying a Pardon &c." as it is
most vntrue, so is it slaunderous to the *State.*   If there were
any such matter, it may soone appeare by search : but the
impudencie of these men is great, and villanous slaunder will
neuer long be without iust reward.

Libel. pag.   " He saith we fauour Recusants rather then
22.   Puritans &c."

Answere.   Herein he doeth notoriously abuse vs : though the
Recusant for the most part, behaueth himself more ciuilly
before the Magistrate then doth the *Puritane :* who is com_
monly most insolent, and thereby deserueth more sharpe
wordes and reproofes then the other.

That which he speaketh of *Recusants* threats against *Puritane* Preachers, hath no sense.   For how can the ·*Recusant*

so threaten the *Puritane*, when he neuer commeth to heare his Sermons? But these wicked *Martinists* account her Maiesties louing subiectes, liking and allowing the orders of the Church, and procuring the contrary to be reformed by authoritie, as Papists and Recusants. By which sinister practise and iudgement many are discomforted, and obedience greatly impeached.

" Doth your Grace remember, what the Iesuite at Libel. pa, 23. Newgate &c."

No truely, for he neuer heard of any such matter, Answere. but by this lewde Libeller: neyther doeth he thinke that there was euer any such thing spoken. Schismatikes are impudent lyars, the worlde knoweth what he hath euer bene, and what hee is: he doth disdaine to answere such senselesse calumniations.

That which he speaketh of *Thackwell* the Printer, &c. is a matter nothing pertaining to him. M. *Richard Yong*, was the dealer therein without his priuitie, who is able to iustify his doings in that matter, and to conuince the libeller of a malicious slaunder. The man is knowen and liuing: the Libeller may talke with him, and knowe his owne wickednesse. " The mouth that lyeth killeth the soule. The Lord will destroy lying lippes, and the tongue that speaketh proude things."

Waldegraue receiued iustly according to his deserts, hauing founde before that time, greater fauour then he deserued, being a notorious disobedient and godlesse person, an vnthriftie spender, and consumer of the fruits of his owne labours, one that hath violated his faith to his best and dearest friends, and wittingly brought them into danger, to their vndoing. His wife and children haue cause to curse all wicked and vngodly Libellers.

The Calumniation touching the Presse and Letters Pag. 24 in the Charterhouse (which presse *Waldgraue* himselfe soulde to one of the *Earle of Arundels* men, as it is since con-

fessed) must receiue the same answere with the other o
Thackwell : sauing that to M. *Yong* must bee added also, some
other of greater authority, who can tel *Martin,* that his
spirite is not the spirit of God, which is the spirit of trueth,
but the spirite of Sathan, the author of lyes.   Charge them,
O shamelesse man, with this matter, who are able to answere
thee, and not the Archbishop, whome it toucheth not, though
it becommeth not euery common and base person, to demaund
an account of the doings of men in authoritie.

The decree there mentioned, being first perused by the
Queenes learned counsell, and allowed by the Lords of her
Maiesties most honourable priuie Counsell, had his furtherance
in deede, and should haue, if it were to doe againe.   It is
but for the maintenance of good orders amōg the printers,
approued and allowed by the most, the best, and the wisest
of that cōpany, and for the suppression of inordinate persons,
such as *Waldegraue* is.

Pag. 25.   Hee erected no newe Printer, contrary to that
decree : but vsed meanes by way of perswasion for
that party, commended to him by his neighbors, to be a very
honest and poore man, hauing maried also the widowe of a
Printer : and hee did very well like and allowe of his placing
by such as haue interest therein.   Neither did hee euer heare,
(but by this Libeller who hath no conscience in lying) that
hee euer printed any such bookes.   This I knowe of a cer-
taintie, that *Thomas Orwin* himselfe hath vpon his booke oath
denied, that he euer printed, either the *Iesus Psalter,* or *Our
Lady Psalter,* or that he euer was any worker about them, or
about any the like bookes.   " But the poisoned serpent careth
not whome hee stingeth."

Whether *Waldgraue* haue printed any thing against the
state, or no, let the bookes by him printed, be iudges.

I doe not thinke, that eyther hee, or any *Martinist* euer
heard any Papist say, that there was no great iarre betweene
the Papistes and the Archbishop in matters of Religion.   It

is but the Libellers Calumniation. If they did, what is that to him ? I thinke *Martin* him selfe doubteth not of the Archbishops soundnesse in such matters of Religion, as are in controuersie betwixt the Papists and vs. If hee doe, the matter is not great.

The *Vniuersitie* of *Cambridge*, where hee liued aboue thirtie yeeres, and publiquely red the Diuinitie Lecture aboue seuen yeeres, and other places where he hath since remained, will testify for him therein, and condemne the Libeller for a meere *Sycophant*, and me also of follie, for answering so godlesse and lewde a person.

It is no disparagement to receiue testimonie of a mans aduersarie : and therefore if Master *Reinolds* haue giuen that commendation to his booke in comparison of others, it is no impeachment to the trueth therof. I haue not seene *Reinolds* his booke : the Libell is so full of lies, that an honest man can not beleeue any thing conteined in it.

My Lorde of *Canterburie* would be sorie from the bottome of his heart, if his perswasion, and the grounds thereof were not Catholike : hee detesteth and abhorreth schismaticall grounds and perswasions : and thereunto hee professeth him-selfe an open enemie, which he woulde haue all *Martinists* to knowe.

" That of the Spaniards stealing him away, &c:" is foolish and ridiculous. I would the best *Martinist* in *England* durst say it to his face before witnesse.

Hee firmely beleeueth that Christ in soule descended into hell. All the *Martinists* in Christendome are not able to proue the contrary : and they that indeuour it, doe abuse the scriptures, and fall into many absurdities.

Hee is likewise perswaded that there ought to be by the worde of God a superioritie among the Ministers of the Church, which is sufficiently prooued in his booke against *T. C.* and in D. *Bridges* booke likewise, and he is all times ready to iustifie it, by the holy Scriptures, and by the testimony of all antiquitie. *Epiphanius* and *August.* account them heretikes, that holde the contrary. The Arguments to the contrary, are vaine, their answeres absurd, the authorities they vse, shamefully abused, and the Scriptures wrested.

He hath shewed sufficient reason in his booke against *T. C.* why Ministers of the Gospell, may be called Priests. The ancient fathers so cal them. The church of *England* imbraceth that name, and that by the authoritie of the highest court in *England.* And why may not *Presbyter* be called *Priest?*

In these three points (whereof the last is of the least moment) he doth agree with the holy Scriptures, with the vniuersall Church of God, with all antiquitie, and in some sort with the Church of *Rome.* But hee doth disagree from the Church of *Rome* that now is in the dregges, which it hath added: as " that Christ should harrow hell : that the Pope should be head of the vniuersall Church: that hee, or any other Priest, should haue authoritie ouer Kinges and Princes to depose them, to deliuer their subiects from the othe of their obedience." These thinges haue neither the word of God nor the decrees of ancient Councels, nor the authoritie of antiquitie to approoue them, but directly the contrarie. As for the name of Priest, as they take it, hee doeth likewise condemne in our Ministers, neyther doe themselues ascribe it to them. And therefore the Libeller in these poyntes writeth like himselfe.

Libel. pag. 26. 27. " Touching Wigginton, &c."

nswere. That which he speaketh of *Wigginton,* is like the rest, sauing for his saucie and malapert behauiour towarde the Archbishoppe : wherein in trueth, hee did beare with him too much. *Wigginton* is a man well knowen vnto him, and i hee knewe himselfe, hee would confesse that hee had great cause to thanke the Archbishoppe. As hee was a foolish proude, and vaine boy, a laughing stocke for his follie to al the societie with whom hee liued : so doeth hee retaine the same qualities being a man, sauing that his follie, pride, and vanitie is much increased: so that nowe hee is become ridiculous euen to his owne faction.

The honestest, the most, and the best of his parish did exhibite to the high Commissioners, articles of very great moment against him : the like whereof haue seldome bene seene in that Court. The most and woorst of them are prooued by diuers sufficient witnesses, and some of them confessed by himselfe, as it appeareth in record. For which enormities, and for that hee refused to make condigne satisfaction for the same, and to conforme himselfe to the orders of the Church, by lawe established: he was by due order of lawe deposed from his Ministerie, and depriued of his benefice, and so remayneth, being vnfit and vnworthie of either.

The tale of *Atkinson* is a lowde, notorious, and knowen lie. For neither did he euer say so to the Archbishop, neither would hee haue taken it at his hands, neither was that any cause of *Wiggintons* depriuation : but vanitie and hypocrisie causeth this man to haue so small conscience in lying, according to that saying, " Omnis hypocrisis mendacio plena est."

That heathenish vntruth vttered diuers times in this booke, that the Archbishoppe should accompt preaching of the word of God to be heresie, and mortally abhorre and persecute it, is rather to bee pitied then answered. If man punish not such sycophants, God will do it, to whose iust iudgement the reuenge of this iniurie is referred. He doth bridle factious and vnlearned Preachers, such as the more part of that sect are, who notwithstanding crie out for a learned Ministerie, themselues being vnlearned, and so would be accounted of all men, if it were not *propter studium partium.* I say with S. *Hierome,* " Nunc loquentibus et pronunciantibus plenus est orbis : loquuntur quæ nesciunt, docent quæ non didicerunt, magistri sunt eum discipuli antè non fuerint." The world is full of them that can speake and talke : but they speake the thinges they knowe not : they teach the thinges they have not learned : they take vpon them to teach before they were

schollers to learne. Indeede our Church is too full of such
talkers, rather then sober teachers, whome hee profæsseth
himselfe greatly to mislike. Otherwise hee defieth all *Mar-*
tinistes in *Englande*, and doeth appeale vnto the whole State
of the learned and obedient Clergie for his innocencie therein.

Libel. pag. 31 " Touching master *Euans*, &c :"

Answere.   That of *Euans* concerning the Vicarage of *War-*
wike, is maliciously reported. He reiected him for lacke o
conformitie to the orders of the Church. If hee haue done
him any wrong thereby, the lawe is open, hee might haue
had his remedie. That honourable person mentioned by the
Libeller, I am sure, accepted of his answer. And I knowe,
that according to his honourable disposition, hee thinketh himselfe greatly abused by the libeller in this point. But what
careth such a corner-creeper what he saith of any man, be hé
neuer so honourable ? The rest of that tale is vntrue, not
worth answering. And if the relator thereof durst appeare
and shewe himselfe, *Martin* could not be long vnknowen. If
any of his men at any time reported, that hee shoulde say,
hee woulde not be beholding to neuer a noble man in this
land, &c. hee sheweth himselfe to be of the Libellers conditions, that is, a common lyar. For hee neuer spake the
wordes to any man, neither doeth he vse that familiaritie with
his men. But the Libeller careth not what hee speaketh,
either of him, or of his men, so that he may fill vp his libel
with vntrue slaunders.

That which followeth of the Archbishops words to the
knight, " that he was the second person of the land, &c." is
of the same kinde. The knight I am sure is liuing, let him
be examined of that matter. True it is, that there was a good
knight with him, an olde friend of his about such a sute :
but that he euer spake any such wordes vnto him, as the
Libeller woulde make the worlde beleeue, is most false : the
Knight liueth and can testifie the same. But the Libeller
thinketh all men to be as proude and malapert as himselfe and

other of his faction are, whose pride the world seeth, and it is vntolerable.

He was neuer *D. Perns* boy, nor vnder him at ~Pag. 32.~ any time, but as felow of the house where he was master. Neither did he euer cary his, or any other mans cloake bagge: Although if he had so done, it had bin no disgrace to him. Better mens sonnes then the Libeller is, haue caried cloakebags. But the lewde man is not ashamed to lye in those things, that are open to euery mans eyes: such is his malice and impudencie.

How *Dauisons* Catechisme was allowed, or how ~Pag. 34.~ long in perusing, I know not: some paultrie pamphlet belike it is, like to that busie and vnlearned *Scot*, now termed to be the author thereof. *D. Wood* is better able to iudge of such matters, then either *Dauison*, or any *Martinist*, that dare be knowen.

" Touching the Apocrypha, &c."   ~Libel. pag. 37~

He gaue commandement in deede, and meaneth to see it obserued. For who euer separated this *Apocrypha* from the rest of the *Bible*, from the beginning of Christianity to this day? Or what Church in the world, refourmed or other, doth yet at this present? And shal we suffer this singularitie in the church of England, to the aduauntage of the aduersary, offence of the godly, and contrary to al the world besides? I knowe there is great difference betweene the one and the other: yet all learned men haue from the beginning, giuen to the *Apocrypha* authoritie, next to the Canonicall Scriptures. And therfore such giddie heads, as seeke to deface them, are to be bridled. A foule shame it is, and not to be suffered, that such speeches should be vttered against those bookes, as by some hath bene: enough to cause ignorant people to discredite the whole Bible.

" Touching Doctor Sparke, &c."   ~Libel. pag. 44~   ~Answere.~

Their Honors that were thē present, can and wil, I am sure, answere for the bishops to this vntrueth. They

made report to diuers in publike place, and some to the
highest, of that cōference, after an other sort, and to another
end, thē the Libeller doth.   That seely *Obiection* God knoweth, was soone answered in few words, viz. That the trās-
lation read in our Churches, was in that point according to
the *Septuagint*, and correspondent to the Analogie of faith.
For if the word be vnderstood of the Israelites, then is it true
to say, that " they were not obedient to his cōmandement :"
but if of the signes and wonders, that *Moses* and *Aaron* did
before *Pharao*, or of *Moses* and *Aaron* themselues, then is it
on the other side true, that " they were obedient to his commandement."   This might haue satisfied any learned and
peaceable Diuine, and pacified their immoderate contention
against the booke of common praier.   This was then, and is
now, the answere to that friuolous obiection, and this is the
Nonplus that the Libeller vaunteth of.   More modestie might
haue become both *D. Sparke*, and the reporter, euen *con-
scientia suæ imbecillitatis*, in that conference.

Libel. pa. 50.   " Touching Patrike, &c."

Answere.   He neuer made *Patrike* Minister, neither intended
to make him, neither was hee of his acquaintance at all in
Worcester.   It is wel knowen that the Archbishop hath not
ordeined moe, then onelie two Ministers, since his comming
to this Archbishoprike.   And therefore this *Calumniation*
must be placed with the former.

Thus is this godlesse Libeller answered in few words,
touching such matters wherwith he chargeth the most reuerend father the Archbishop of *Cant.* whereby the world may
perceiue, with what spirit he is possessed.   The wisemā
Prouer. 24.   saith, " that destruction shall suddenly come vpō the
backbiter and calumniator."   The *Psalmist* saith, " The Lord
Psalm 55.   wil destroy lying lips, and the tōgue which speaketh
proud things :" and " that death shal suddenly come vpon
them, and hell shall receiue them."   *S. Ambrose* saith, " that
Detractors are scarcely to be accounted Christians."   And

Cyprian saith, " Non qui audit, sed qui facit conuitium, miser est." Not he that is railed at, but he that raileth, is the wretched man. The wicked Iewes, when they could not otherwise answere Christ, called him Samaritan, and saide he had a deuill, and shortly after tooke vp stones, and cast at him. So the Anabaptists, within our memory, after slaunderous and opprobrious calumniations against the godly preachers and magistrates then liuing, fell to blowes and open violence. The Libeller in this booke hath performed the one, and threatned the other.

> This haue I laid downe word by worde, as I receiued the same from my Lorde of London: who desireth to haue the matter heard by indifferent Iudges, and will shew the Suggestions to be very vntrue.

AND as to *Martins* lewd exclamation against the B. of *London* cōcerning the cloth thought to be stollen frō the Dyars, this is the truth of the case : that vpon notice giuē to the said B. that such like cloth was wayued within his Manor of *Fulham*, and left in a ditch there, and no owner knowen, hee presently hoping to take them that brought it thither, or at the least to saue the same from purloyning or miscarying, appoynted the same to be watched diuers nights : and in the end hearing neyther of the owners, nor of thē that so waiued it, willed the same to bee brought to his house in Fulham, and there to be kept for him or them which by law ought to haue it, were it in respect of the first property, or of the altēratiō therof by means of the liberties. Whereupon, a good space after, the Dyars indeed came to the Bishop, and claimed the cloth, and sought by earnest means to haue it again, without making any proofe, that the cloth was theirs, or that the same cloth was it, for which the theeues were executed, or that fresh sute was made after the saide theeues for the same. But vpon cō-ference had with learned Lawyers therein, it was resolued, that the propertie of this cloth was altered and transferred to the lyberties: and so it seemeth the Dyars themselues haue found, els would they by lawe haue sought remedy therefore yer nowe, it beeing well nie towards three yeares since. Yet neuerthelesse, so far hath the said bishop beene from exacting the extremity, that offer hath bene made to the Dyars of a good part of the cloth, where in rigour of the law, they haue lost all: And further to restore all, or to make sufficient recompence therefore, if by law it ought to be so, vpon the examination of the trueth of the case. And as for *Martins* erronious iudgment, that this is theft, beeing taken and claymed by right and lawe, as aforesayd, because the true owners are defeated (as hee saith) surely, hee might knowe if it were matter for his humor, that the Lawe worketh this in other cases, as in strayes proclaymed and kept a yeere and a daye, according to the law, the propertie is altered, and transferred to the Lord from the true owner: so is it for stolen cattell, brought *bona fide* to the ouert market: The first owners propertie is gone, and the buyer hath it: And so is it for waiued goods, as was this cloth. And to shewe that the sayde Bishop had not so great a desire to detaine the cloth as the Libeller hath presumed, hee often times asked an officer of his, howe it happened that the Dyars came not for it: for hee was euer ready, and yet is, to deliuer it to them, or the value thereof, i it prooue to be theirs. And thus much is to be answered to that matter.

The Libeller obiecteth against the Bishop as a great heinous fault, that of his Porter he made a Minister: which, al things considered, he thinketh that doing to be iustifiable and lawfully done, and not to lacke example of many such that haue bene after that sort admitted, both since her Maiesties comming to the Crown, by many good Bishops, and by sound histories Ecclesiasticall, that where the Church by reason o persecutiō or multitude of Hamlets, and free Chappels, which haue commonly very small stipends for the Minister, hones godly men, vppon the discretion of the Gouernours of th

Church, haue and might be brought in to serue in the want of learned men, in prayer, administration of Sacraments, good example of life, and in some sort of exhortation. And this man therefore, when the Bishop founde him by good and long experience to be one that feared God, to be conuersant in the scriptures, and of very honest life and conuersation : he allowed of him, to serue in a small congregation at *Padington*, where cōmonly for the meannesse of the stipend, no Preacher coulde be had, as in many places it commeth to passe where the Parsonage is impropriat, and the prouision for the Vicar or Curat is very smal. And how this poore man behaued him-selfe there, time and tryall prooued him : for he continued in that place with good liking of the people 8. or 9. yeres, till he grew dull of sight for age, and thereby vnable for to serue any longer. It is to be founde among the Greeke Canons, that in *Spaine* and *Africa* when the Goathes and Vandalles had by extreme persecution made hauocke of the Church men, those fewe that were left there aliue, made their moane to the Churches of *Rome* and *Italy*, that their Churches stoode emptie, because they could get none to serue, no not such as were vnlearned. Whereby it appeareth, that in the time of necessitie, and such great want, the Church did allowe of very meane Clarkes, and so did they in the beginning of hir Maiesties raigne. But *Martin* and his complices, hauing a desire to throwe out of the Church, the booke of common prayer, would rather haue the Churches serued by none, then by such as by praier and administration of Sacraments should keepe the people together in godly assemblies. But this Libeller being as a botch in the body, wherunto all bad hu-mors cōmonly resort, and fewe good, was cōtent to take this report of this poore man, and not at all to make mention, as he might haue done, of that precise and straight order which the Bishoppe obserueth in making Ministers. For most true it is that the said B. admitteth none to orders, but such as he him-self doth examine in his owne person in poynts of Diuinitie,

and that in the latin tongue, in the hearing of many : whereby
it cōmeth to passe, that none lightly come at him, but such as
be Graduats, and of the vniuersities.   But *Martin* neither
himselfe nor his cole cariers seeke for any thing that is cō-
mendable, but like the spider that gathereth all that may turne
to poyson.

Further, for lacke of true matter, *M. Maddockes* must be
brought in by the Libeller to furnish his railing comedy.   It
were ynough to say of that thus much, that the most reuerent
Father the Archbishop of *Canterburie* examining that matter
betweene the Bishop and *Maddockes*, with some other Bishops
assisting him, founde the matter to make so sore against the
Bishop, that *Maddockes* himselfe was content before them to
aske him forgiuenes, and to promise that he would euer after
haue a reuerent regard of his duetie towards the saide Bishop,
as his Ordinarie.   For if he should so vntruely haue played
with the name of *Aelmer*, by turning it into the name of Marelme, hee shoulde haue spoken against his conscience, as he
himselfe knoweth, and all the Court, and her Maiestie her
selfe can testifie, that it was a most shamefull vntrueth blased
abroade by one *Lichfield* a Musicion, which is nowe departed.

Here might bee noted, howe *Doctor Perne*, beeing at no
meane mans table, and hearing of such slanderous rayling of
felling of the Elmes at *Fulham*, he asked one of the company
being an ancient Lawyer, howe long the Elmes of *Fulham* had
bene felled.   Said the Lawyer, some halfe yere past.   Nowe
truly saide *D. Perne*, they are marueilouslie growen in that
time, for I assure you I was there within these foure daies, and
they seeme to be two hundred yeeres old.   And maister *Vice-
chamberlaine* at her Maiesties being at *Fulham*, tolde the
Bishop that her Maiestie misliked nothing, but that her Highnesse lodging was kept from all good prospects by the thick-
nesse of the trees.   Lo, you may see hereby, that the Libeller
to set out his *Pasquill*, raketh all things by all reportes from all

the Sycophants in the world, and maketh no choise of man or matter, so that it may serue his turne.

And for any Letter written by the maister of Requests so iestinglie, as the Libeller reporteth, Maddockes hath deceiued him : for there was no such matter, nor the man from whome the Bishop wrote, was none of his seruant, nor is.

Nowe commeth in Dame *Lawson* to frumpe the bishoppe with impudent and vnwomanlie speech, and vnfit for that sexe, whome *Paul* vtterly forbiddeth to speake in the congregation. But considering the circumstaunces of time, place, and persons, it is to bee thought that Dame *Lawson* came at no time to the bishoppe in that brauerie : for if she had, the bishop is not so soft but shee shoulde haue felt of Discipline, and of the Queenes authoritie. Surelie the bishop and such other of the Reuerend fathers that are so bitten by this Libeller, may comfort themselues by the exāple of *Athanasius* and others as I before haue said, which were most shamefully accused by the heretikes, of murder, robbery, enchantment, whoredome, and other most detestable crimes, to deface them to the worlde, to the ende that their heresies might be the better liked of. But *Martin* remember that saying " Væ bomini per quem scandalum venit," and that *Iude* saith, " that *Michael* when he disputed with the Deuill about the body of *Moses*, the Angell gaue no railing sentence against him, but said, the Lord rebuke thee, Satā." And if it pleased you to remēber that booke that is fathered vpon *Ignatius* in *Greeke* which attributeth so much to the bishops, you would be good master to bishops, against whom so vnreuerently you cast out your stomacke.

And for your iesting at the Bishop for bowling vpon the Sabboth, you must vnderstand that the best expositor of the Sabboth, which is Christ, hath saide, that the Sabboth was made for man, and not marr for the Sabboth : and man may haue his meate dressed for his health vpon the Sabboth, and

why may he not then haue some conuenient exercise of the
body, for the health of the body?

You will take small occasion to raile, before you will hold
your tongue. If you can charge the Bishop that euer he
withdrew himself from Sermon or seruice by any such exercise, you might bee the bolder with him: but contrariwise it
is wel knowen, that he and his whole familie doeth euery day
in the weeke twise say the whole seruice, calling upon God
for them selues, the State, and the Queenes Maiestie, pray-
ing for her highnesse by that meanes deuoutly and heartily
many times: I pray God you do the like. But, " oratio
animæ maleuolæ non placet Deo:" The prayer of a malicious
heart neuer pleaseth God.

Martin with his bitter stile of malicious *Momus* dipt in the
gall of vngodlinesse, proceedeth in a shamelesse vntrueth
touching the Bishops answere to the executors of *Allein* the
Grocer, as though he should flatly denie the payment of a
certaine debt, due to the sayde *Allein*: which is as true as
all the rest of *Martins* writings is honest and sober. For
bee it that at the first demaunde, the Bishoppe was somewhat mooued to heare his name to be in the Merchants
bookes, which hee euer so precisely auoyded, that commonly
he sendeth to them whom hee hath to doe with, warning
them to deliuer nothing in his name, without his owne hand
or ready money, vsed peraduenture some sharpe wordes in a
matter that was so suddaine and so strange to him: Yet most
certaine it is, that though not at that time, yet very shortly
after, the debt was discharged, as shall be prooued, long
before *Martins* railing booke was heard of or seene: ten
pound excepted, which the sayde executors for a time
respited. But this fellowe will trauaile farre before he will
lacke matter to furnish a lye.

Another mountaine that he maketh of molehils (for such is
all his blasphemous buildings) is, that one *Benison* a poore
man, was kept in the Clincke I cannot tell howe long, vniustly

without cause, &c. The trueth is this: *Benison* comming
from *Geneua*, full fraught with studie of *Innouations*, and
vtterly emptie of obedience, which *Beza* that learned Father
had or might haue taught him, as by his Epistles appeareth,
both to the Queene and the gouernors of the Church:
set vp in *London* his shop of disobedience, being maried
in a contrary order to the booke and vsage of the Church
of *England*, abusing good M. *Foxe* as hee himselfe in
griefe of heart after confessed. After that, the said *Benison*
gathering conuenticles, and refusing to goe to his owne parish
church, seeking to set al in combustion with schisme in the
Citie, was long before the B. heard any thing of him, called
before Sir *Nicholas Woodrofe* a graue Citizen, and the
Recorder: who found him in such an humour, that they ment
to haue sent him to prison. But because he was of the
Clergie, they thought good to commit him to his Ordinarie,
who trauailing with him most earnestly to bring him to the
Church and become· orderly, when he coulde profite nothing
with him, sent him againe to the Sessions to the Lord Maior
and the Iudges. After they had dealt with him, and could
finde at his hands nothing but railing, they sent him againe to
the Bishop, and he finding him in vnspeakeable disobedience
to her Maiestie and her Lawes, offered him the oath, which
he contemptuously and spitefully refused. Which being cer-
tified according to order, hee was sent to the Queenes bench,
and was condemned, and thereupon sent to prison. And
this is that· wonderful tragedie wherin this fellow so greatly
triumpheth, wishing belike (as his whole Libell seemeth to
desire) that no malicious schismatike should be punished
for moouing sedition in the lande. But to this vnbrideled
tongue, it may be said as the Psalme sayth, "Quid gloriaris
in malitia tua? &c." Where he courseth the Bishop of
London with the lewde lying Epithete of *Dumbe Iohn*, fetched
I cannot tell from what grosse conceite, either as willingly
stumbling upon *Dumbe* for *Don*, or for that he preacheth not

so oft, as hee and other of his crewe babbling in their verball
sermons vse to doe, or from whence else I knowe not, vnlesse
it please his wisedome to play with his owne conceite, and
minister matter to the Prentises and Women of *London*, to
sport himselfe in that pretie deuised and newe founde name.
If the Bishop shoulde answere for himselfe, I knowe he might
say somewhat after this sort : Good charitable *Martin*, how
olde are you ? how long haue you knowen the man ? what
reports in the booke of Martyrs, in Master *Askams* booke
of his Schoolemaster, and in some learned men that haue
written from beyond the Seas, haue you heard of him ?
Master *Foxe* saith of him, that hee was one of the fiue, and
now onely aliue, that stoode in the solemne disputations in
the first of Queene *Mary*, with a hundred hauberdes about
his eares : (the like whereof you threaten now him and others)
in the defence of the Gospell, against all the learned Papists
in *England*.   For the which hee was driuen into banishment,
and there continued for the space of fiue or sixe yeeres,
visiting almost all Vniuersities in *Italie* and *Germanie*, hauing
great conference with the most and best learned men : at the
last being stayed at *Iany*, an vniuersitie erected by the dukes
of *Saxonie*, and should, if he had not come away, had the
Hebrewe lecture, which *Snepphinus* had, intertained by thē
to read in their said vniuersity both Greeke and Latin,
in the company and with the good loue and liking of
those famous men, *Flaccus Illyricus*, *Victorius*, *Strigellus*,
D. Snepphinus, called *alter Luther*, with diuers others, where
belike he was not dumb.   And after cōming home, was
appointed among the famous learned men, to dispute againe
with the enemies of the religion, the papisticall Bishops, and
like, that if the disputations had continued, to shewe him not
ignorant in all the three tongues, as he wil yet, if *Martin
Malapert* prouoke him too far, not to be dumbe.   Is he
dumbe because hee was the onely preacher in *Leicestershire*
for a space, as the noble Earle of *Huntington* can witnesse ?

and by their two meanes, that shire, God be blessed, was conuerted and brought to that state that it is now in? which in
true religion is aboue any other place, because they retaine
the Gospell without contention, which fewe other places doe.
And in *Lincolneshire* did he nothing? did he not first purge
the Cathedral Church, being at that time a neast of vncleane
birdes, and so by preaching and executing the Commission, so
preuailed in the countrey (God blessing his labours) that not
one recusant was left in the countrey, at his comming away to
this sea of *London?* Is this to be dumbe? how many Sermons hath hee preached at *Paules* crosse? sometime three
in a yeere, yea, sometime two or three together, being an
olde man, to supply some yonger mens negligence.

It is omitted, that Episcopomastix had a fling at the
Bishoppe of *London* for swearing by his faith, wherefore he
termeth him a Swag. What hee meaneth by that, I will not
diuine : but as all the rest is lewd, so surely herein he hath a
lewde meaning. It is to be thought, that the Bishop wil take
profite hereby, being a man that hath diligently read *Plutarke,*
" De vtilitate capienda ab inimico." If it bee an othe, as this
gentleman hath censured it, it is not to be doubted, but that he
wil amend it: but if it were lawful, as it may bee for any
thing *Martin* can say, to aske his brotherhood, what *Amen* signifieth, or whether it be an othe : then in his wicked and malicious wishes for the ouerthrow of the Clergie, how oft is he
to be found to say *Amen?* for in the phrase of our speech, *by
my faith* signifieth no more, but, *in very trueth, bona fide, in
trueth, assuredly, id est, Amen.*

It is to be thought, that *Martin* misliketh to say by his faith,
because a railing and slanderous spirit can haue no faith : for
where Charitie is away (the soule of all good workes) there
can be no faith. Read that of *Paul,* " Charitas non inuidet,
non est suspicax, &c." The contraries whereof swell in *Martin*
as venemous humours in an infectious sore.

Among other their reproches, they affirme of the bishop of

Rochester, that hee presented him selfe to a benefice. I doe not thinke it to be true, for that I know it can not be good in Lawe. If he hath procured a benefice in way of *Commendam* (as they call it) it is by lawe allowed, and hath bene done by other.

The bishop of *Lincolne* is knowen to bee learned and zealous in religion. There are few men towarde her Maiestie that haue preached in the court, either oftner times, or with more commendation, or better liking, as well before he was bishop, as since. It is therefore maruaile, that none in all this time could espie his inclination vnto corrupt and Papisticall doctrine, vntill the chickens of the scratching kite yong *Martinists*, got wings to flee abroad, and crie out vntrueths against euerie man that displeaseth them.

If the bishop of *Lincolne* had not euen of late shewed himselfe in the Commission Court, at the examination of some of them, he had nowe escaped this scratch of the lewde lying *Martin Marprelate*. What his wordes were I haue forgotten, and yet I heard them deliuered by a learned man that was present. For I did not then meane to deale in this cause, but they were nothing soũding to that which the Libell layeth downe. And the person considered at whose funerall hee preached, hee could not with comelinesse speake lesse in her commendation then he did, vnlesse they woulde haue had him as rash and furious as themselues, and to enter into Gods secrete iudgement, and openly to condemne her as a reprobate. God may worke great matters in a moment.

THE bishop of *Winchester* is charged with certeine wordes vttered in two sermons the last Lent : the one in the Queenes Chappell, the other at S. *Marie Oueries* in *Southwarke*. The wordes of the challenge are these, " Like a flattering hypocrite, he protested before God and the congregation, that there was not in the worlde at this day, nay, there had not beene since the Apostles time such a flourishing state of a Church, as nowe

wee haue in England." Surely, if hee had vttered these
wordes for the state of the Church appointed by lawe and
order, not respecting the faultes of particular persons, it might
in Christian duetie bee well defended. But it was not vttered
in this manner, nor for the matter, nor for the time. The first
part of those wordes hee doth not acknowledge at all, for they
are purposely inserted to stirre enuie.

Thus in deede it was deliuered: " As for the trueth of doctrine, according to the worde of God, for the right administration
of the Sacramēts, for the true worship of God in our prayer,
layde downe in the booke of seruice : since the Apostles age,
vnto this present age of the restoring of the gospell, there was
neuer Church vpon the face of the earth, so nigh the sinceritie of Gods trueth, as the Church of England is at this day."
These wordes with Gods helpe, he will iustifie to be true, vpon
the daunger, not of his liuing only, but of his life also, against
any man that will withstand it : and yet therein shall not shew
him selfe either " desperate Dicke," or " shamelesse, impudent
or wainscot faced Bishop," as it pleaseth the Libeller to rayle.
Neither doth he thinke, that any learned man that fauoureth the
Gospell, though he mislike some things and persons now in
present vse, will reproue it. The Papists I know in deede doe
detest the Assertion, and thinke their Synagogue blasphemed
by it : No refourmed Church can iustly take offence at it.
Where the bishop is burdened by this speech to excuse the
multitude of *Thieues, Drunkards, Murtherers, Adulterers, &c.*
that be in our Church : neither did his thought conceiue, nor
his wordes include any such matter. But what doeth not
malice, enuie, and spite vtter against the most innocent person
that is ? The bishop of Winchester hath openly more impugned the vices of this age heere in the Church of England,
then the whole broode of them that are of the Anabaptisticall
Conuenticles, and the residue of these Libellers. " Woe be
to them" (saith *Esay* the Prophet) " that speak euill   Esay. 5.
of good, and good of euill, and put light for darkenesse, and

D

darkenesse for light, sweete for sowre, and sowre for sweete."
Psal. 120. Dauid had great cause to crie, " domine libera
animam meam à labijs iniquis, et à lingua dolosa." And
Pro. 24. Salomon, " cogitatio stulti peccatum est, et abominatio
hominum Detractor." The deuise of a foole is sinne, and all
men abhorre the backbiter or Slaunderer. If any man will
reprooue the Assertion before written, God willing he shall
be answered, so that he rayle not.

This may be a sufficient aunswere to the vntruth fathered
vpon the B. of Winchesters words, and that he is not for the
same iustly tearmed " Monstrous and flattering hypocrite,
speaking against his owne conscience." But I see in these
words the reproch not only of the B. but much more a
malicious spite against this Church of England, and that so
deepely setled in their hearts, that their eares cannot, without
griefe, heare any good spoken of it. Therefore I thinke my
selfe in Christian dutie bound, somewhat farther to followe
this matter, and with some signification of thankfulnesse, to
acknowledge and confesse those excellēt blessings, which it
hath pleased God, of his great mercies, to bestowe vpon the
same, as well in King Edward the sixts dayes, as much more
in her Maiesties reigne that nowe is : and first, to beginne with
that which is the principall, that is, the sinceritie of doctrine,
and all branches of true religion receiued, professed, taught,
and established in this Realme. In which point, I thinke it
very superfluous and needles for me to recite the particular
branches, and to make a new catechisme, or to pen a new confession of the Church of England, seeing they both are so
sufficiently performed, that (without enuy be it spoken) there
is none better in any refourmed Church, in *Europe*. For a
Catechisme, I refer them to that which was made by the
learned and godly man *Master Nowel*, Deane of *Paules*,
receiued and allowed by the Church of England, and very
fully grounded and established vpon the worde of God. There
may you see all the parts of true Religion receiued, the

difficulties expounded, the trueth declared, the corruptions of the, Church of Rome reiected. But this I like not in our Church, that it is lawfull to euery man to set foorth a newe Catechisme at his pleasure. I read, that in the Primitiue church, that thing did great harme, and corrupted the mindes of many simple persons with foule errours and heresies. I see the like at this day: for thereby many honest meaning hearts are caried away to the misliking of our manner of prayer, and administration of Sacramentes, and other orders : whereby it is made a principall instrument to maintaine and increase discorde and dissention in the Church.

For a sound and true confession acknowledged by this our church, I refer them to that notable Apologie of the English church, written not many yeeres since, by that Iewel of England, late Bishop of *Sarisburie.* Wherein they shall find al partes of Christian religion confessed and proued, both by the testimonie of the canonicall scriptures, and also by the consent of all learned and godly antiquitie for the space of certain hundred yeres after Christ. For the integrity and soundnes, for the learning and eloquence shewed in the same apologie, they (that contemne that notable learned man because hee was a bishoppe) may haue very good testimonie in a little Epistle, written by *Peter Martir* vnto the said bishoppe, and nowe printed, and in the latter edition set before the same Apologie : where they shall finde that hee speaketh not for himselfe onely, but for many other learned men of the church of *Tygure,* and other places. Nowe, as this learned bishop doth acknowledge and confesse for this Church, all trueth of doctrine : so doth hee reprooue, condemne and detest all corruptions brought into the same, either by the church of *Rome,* or by any other auncient or newe heretikes, whome hee there particularly nameth : yea, and to the great comfort of all them that are members of the same church, and acknowledge the same confession, hee prooueth and euidently sheweth, that the testimonies of the Scriptures, wheron that confession is

grounded, for the true interpretation of them; haue the witnes and consent of all the learned antiquitie, as I haue saide,
for certaine hundred yeeres. Which I take to bee a very
good comfort and confirmation to all honest consciences in
these captious and quarelling dayes.

That which I meane, I will declare by some particulars.
What is more euidēt, certain and firme for the article of the
" person of Christ in his Godhead and māhood," then those
things that the auncient fathers decreed out of the canonical
scriptures in the Coūcels of *Nice, Constantinople, Ephesus,
Chalcedon,* and some others against *Arius, Samosatenus,
Apollināris, Nestorius, Eutiches,* and those heretikes that
were tearmed *Monotholetes &c ?* Therfore whosoeuer do
teach contrarie to the determination of those councels (as some
do in these daies) they do not iustly hold that principal article
and foundation of Christian religion.

Moreouer, as touching the grace and benefite of Christ, the
beginning whereof riseth from the eternall *loue* of God toward
vs, and from the free *election* to redemption and eternall saluation, and proceedeth to our vse and benefit, by the dispensation of Christ once offered vpon the crosse, by effectual
calling wrought by the holy ghost in preaching of the gospell,
by our iustification, sanctification, and the gift of perseuerance
and continuance in the faith, thereby in the end to obtaine
resurrection and eternall life : touching (I say) this free grace
of God (another principall ground of Christian religion) what
could be, or can bee more certainly or abundantly layde
downe out of the holy scriptures, then was determined in the
councels of *Carthage, Mileuitane, Aurasicane &c.* against the
Pelagians, and other enemies of the free grace of God in
Christ Iesu our Sauiour ? Especially if you adde the writings
of *August.* and other ancient fathers for defence of the same.

As to that which is necessary to bee knowen touching the
true Catholique Church (a matter of great importaunce euen
at this day) what can bee more copiously or with more

perspicuity declared, then is by that learned father *Augustine*, as well in other places, as principally in his bookes against the Donatists?

Likewise, for the matter of the Sacrament of the Lordes Supper, (if simple trueth coulde content men) what is more euident, then that doctrine, which hath bene layd down by the ancient fathers, *Iustine, Irenæus, Tertullian, Cyprian, Augustine, Theodorete,* and a number of other? For proofe whereof, I referre you to B. *Iewell,* in his worthy booke, wherein he answereth *Hardings* reply against his 27 questions, proposed at *Paules* Crosse, &c. I remēber, touching this matter of the Sacrament, *Oecolampadius,* a man of great reading and godlines, saith of S. *August.* "Is primus mihi vellicauit aurem." He did first put me in minde of the true vnderstanding of this Sacrament.

These foure principal Articles I haue laid downe for example, that the Christian Reader may the more easily perceiue what comfort it is to any Church, to haue the grounds of their faith and religion so established vpon the holy Scriptures, that for the interpretation of the same, they haue the testimonie and consent of the Primitiue Church, and the ancient learned Fathers. From which *Consent* they should not depart, either in doctrine, or other matter of weight, vnlesse it so fal out in them, that we be forced thereto, either by the plaine wordes of the Scriptures, or by euident and necessary conclusions following vpon the same, or the Analogie of our faith. Which thing if we shal perceiue, we ought, and safely may, take that liberty that themselues, and especially *Augustine* hath vsed, and requireth other to vse. "Nec Catholicis Episcopis, &c." "We must not consent (saith *Augustine,*) so much as to Catholique Bishops, if they be deceiued, and be of opinion contrary to the Canonicall Scriptures." Againe, "I am not tied with the authoritie of this Epistle. For I haue not the writings of Cyprian in like estimation, as I haue the Canonicall

De vnitate Eccle. cap. 10.

Contra Cres-con. lib. 2. ca. 32.

Scriptures, but I measure them by the rule of the holy Scriptures. If I finde any thing in his writings agreeing to the Scriptures, I receiue it with commendation and reuerence.: if otherwise, with his good leaue, I refuse it." The like you haue, *Epist.* 48. 111. & 112. *In Prooemio li.* 3. *de Trinitate,* and many other places. Otherwise, to reiect the testimonie of the ancient Fathers rashly, is a token of too much confidence in our owne wits. It was noted as a great fault in *Nestorius,* and a chiefe cause of his heresie, that contemning the Fathers, hee rested too much vpon his own iudgement. The like confidence drew many learned men, and of great gifts, to be Patrons of sundry foule and shamefull errours. How came it to passe, that after that notable Councell of *Nice,* so many detestable heresies arose against the Deitie and the Humanitie of Christ, against the vniting of both natures, and the distinction of the properties of them ? &c. but only out of this roote, that they contemned the graue sentences, interpretations, and determinations of those famous Confessors and great learned Fathers, as were in the same assembled, and had too much liking in their owne wits and learning. But " woe be unto them" (saith *Esay*) " that are ouerwise in their owne conceite." *Vigilius* in his first booke against *Eutyches* saith thus. " These cloudes of fond and vaine accusations are powred out by them chiefly, which are diseased either with the sickenesse of ignorance, and of a contentious appetite: and while they being puffed vp with confidence of a proud stomacke, for this only cause they reiect the rules of faith, laid downe by the ancient fathers, that they may thrust into the Church their owne wauering deuises, which they haue ouerthwartly conceiued." This sentence, I would our vncharitable accusers and troublers of the Church would well weigh and consider with themselues. Therfore (good reader) I protest for my selfe, and for the residue of this church, that we dare not in consciēce, nor thinke it tollerable, with contempt to reiect the testimonies of antiquity in establishing any matter of weight in the Church. We leaue that to our *hasty diuines*, that in three yeeres study thinke themselues able to controll al men, and to haue more learning then all the Bishops in England : And for this cause will they giue no credit to ancient writers against their new found equality. For with them, it is a foule fault once in a sermon to name an ancient father, or to alledge any testimony out of his works.

Nowe (good Christian Reader) seeing by the good blessing of God, we haue all parts of Christian fayth and Religion professed and taught in this Church, and the same grounded vpon the canonicall Scriptures, with the consent and exposition of the Primitiue Church and ancient Fathers : What a vaunting pride is it ? (as *Cyprian* speaketh) what an vnthankefulnesse to God ? what [an] vncharitable affection toward the Church of their naturall Countrey, that they cannot abide any good to be spoken of it ? pretending nothing but the priuate faultes and vices of some men, or the disagreeing from them in some orders and partes of Gouernement, which they will neuer be able to proue by the word of GOD to bee of necessitie. In other reformed Churches, whome they so greatly extolle, and would make paterne to vs, haue they not imperfections? Haue they not foule faults, and great vices among all sorts of men, as well Ministers as others? Surely, their worthiest writers and grauest Preachers doe note, that they haue. And if they woulde denie it, the world doth see it, and many good men among them doe bewaile it. I will not stay in the other blessings of God, wherewith hee hath adorned this Church. I shall haue occasion to speake somewhat more of it hereafter, and God send vs grace, that we may with true thankefulnesse acknowledge it. But this I may not omitte without great note of vnthankefulnesse towarde our mercifull God, which hath not only preserued, maintained and defended the State, but also appoynted this Church to be as a Sanctuarie or place of refuge for the Saints of God, afflicted and persecuted in other Countries for the profession of the Gospell : for whome I am perswaded wee doe fare the better at Gods hand. And I doubt not but in that respect, al reformed Churches in other places, feeling the blessing of God by vs, thinke reuerently of our State, and pray to God for vs, as all good men with vs ought to doe for them, that the true linke of Christian charitie may soundly knitte vs together in one bodie of right faith and Religion. If some fewe persons thinke amisse of our Church, I impute the cause therof onely to the malicious and vntrue reports made by some of our owne Countreymen vnto them. Which persons, if they did vnderstand the true State of this our Realme, would thinke farre otherwise, as diuers of the most graue and learned writers haue already euidently declared. This also is not the least blessing of God, as well in the time of *K. Edward*, as in the reigne of our gracious Souereigne, that this Church hath had as ample ornaměts of learned men, (*Rumpantur vt Ilia Momo*,) as the most reformed Churches in *Europe*, and farre more plentifully then some place, whose state they seeke to frame vs vnto. Only I except those excellēt men, whō God had prepared in the begining to be the restorers of his Trueth, and doctrine of the Gospel in those parts: Namely we haue had B. *Cranmer*, *Ridley*, *Latimer*, *Couerdale*, *Hooper*, and diuers other, which were no Bishops, as *M. Bradford*, *M. Sanders*, *M. Rogers*, *M. Philpot*, *D. Haddon*, &c. Most of which, as they haue left good proofe of their learning in writing: so did they confirme the same with their blood in the ende. The like I may iustly say of them whome God hath sent to restore his Trueth since the beginning of her Maiesties reigne, (howsoeuer it pleaseth the Broode of the *Martinists* to deface them) as Bishoppe *Coxe*, *Pilkington*, *Grindall*, *Sands*, *Horne*, *Iewel*, &c. which haue good testimonie of their learning giuen them by as graue, learned, and zealous men, as any haue liued in this age, among whome for certaine yeeres they liued. A nomber of other haue proceeded out of both our Vniuersities, which though *Martin*

Momus wil say the contrary, deserue singular commēdation for their learning, and haue declared the same to the worlde in answering and confuting the opprobrious writings of the common Aduersaries. In which their answeres (without enuie and displeasure be it spoken) there appeareth as sufficient learning as doeth in the most workes at this time published by the writers of forreine Countreies. If Englishmen at this time so greatly dispraysed, were giuen with like paines to set forth the exercises of their studie and learning, as in other places they doe: they woulde drawe as good commendation of learning to their Countrey, as most other Churches doe. To which nomber of ours, I adde also some of thē, whom certaine occasions haue caried away to the misliking of the present state of this Church: which I knowe haue receiued of God singular good giftes, which I pray earnestly they may vse to to his glory, and the procuring the vnity and peace of the Church, which our *Hastie Diuines of M. M.* his brood, seeke to breake and disturbe. This testimonie, I thought my selfe bounde in conscience to yeelde to that Church of my naturall Countrey, in which, and by which, through the mercy of our gracious God, I am that I am. The godly, I trust, will interprete all to the best: the residue I looke not to please.

The B. of Winchester is further charged in this maner, "He said that men might find fault, if they were disposed to quarrel, aswel with the Scriptures, as with the booke of common prayer. Who could heare this comparison without trembling?" Let the Libellers, whatsoeuer they are, remēber, "Os quod mētitur, occidit animam." At that time, in *S. Mary Oueries* church, in a large discourse, he did answere the obiections that many make at this day, against the booke of common praier, and toward the end vttered these words, "If it could be without blasphemy, they might picke as many and as great quarrels against the holy scriptures thēselues. For euen the best writings are subiect to the

slanderous malice of wicked mē." This assertion was found
fault withall, by a Iesuite or Massing priest at that time in
the Marshalsey, and therfore the B. the next Sunday following, expounded his meaning, and at large shewed, that that
might be done, which beforetime was done by a great number : and that he was not so far beside himself, as to compare
the booke of *common prayer* with the holy scriptures in
dignity, trueth, or maiestie : He leaueth such blasphemous
dealing to the *Papists*, the *Family of Loue*, and some other
Sectaries : but he compared them in this (as it is before said)
that the Scriptures themselues were subiect also to slaunderous
and deprauing tongues, and yet not therfore to be reiected,
whereof he recited sundry examples. *Celsus* that heathenish
Lib. 1. con-
tra Celsum. Epicure, (against whom *Origen* writeth) in his book
called *Verax*, doth powre out many railing and
slaunderous reproches, not only against the holy Scriptures,
but also against the course of Christian Religion : as that they
receiued their religiō and doctrine of the barbarous Iewes,
that is, out of the bookes of *Moses* and the Prophets. The
Euseb. lib.
6. cap. 19. like did *Porphyrius* an other Philosopher, and in his
bookes reprooued the Scriptures in many places :
for hee wrote thirtie bookes against Christian religion. That
Socr. lib. 1.
cap. 9. scoffing sophister *Libanius*, and his scholler *Iulian*
the Apostata, vsed the like blasphemies aggainst the
Christian fayth, and the Scriptures, out of which it was
prooued, as appeareth in sundrie auncient Writers. Who
knoweth not, that some Heretikes reiected the most part of
the olde Testament, as false and fabulous ? The *Valentiniane*
In Præ-
script. Ter-
tull. Euse-
bius. Euseb.
lib. 4. cap.
28. Epipha-
nius. Theo-
dor. Heretike, sayeth Tertullian, " Quædam legis et Pro-
phetarum improbat, quædam probat, id est, Omnia
improbat, dum quædam reprobat." The *Marcionists*
receiue onely the Gospell of *Matthewe*, the other
they reiect. And likewise they admitte but two
Epistles of Saint Paul, that is, to *Timothie* and *Titus*,
and (as *Hierome* sayeth) to *Philemon*. *Tatian* also depraueth

the Scriptures, reiecteth the Actes of the Apostles, and picketh
sundry other quarrels against them. There was neuer any
Heretike, but that to giue countenance to his opinion, he would
seeme to ground it vpon the Scriptures. And what is that
but wickedly to father lies vpon the Scriptures? And for this
cause you know the Papists think it no sure ground to rest
vpon the scriptures onely, affirming blasphemously, that " the
Scriptures are darke, vnperfect, and doubtfull, because they
may be wrested euery way, like a nose of waxe, or like a
leaden Rule." Wherefore, Christian charitie and modestie
woulde not thus maliciously and slaunderously wrest and
wring the words of the Bishop, tending to a good and godly
meaning.

Of like trueth it is, that he burtheneth the Bishop of Winchester, to affirme " that it was heresie to say, The preaching
of the worde was the onely ordinarie way to saluation," which
he neuer thought, or spake, either thē, or at any other time of
his life. But in handling of that controuersie, *Penrie* spake
things so strangely and obscurely, that he seemed to attribute
that effect to the preaching of the word only, and not otherwise vsed by reading: And being vrged with that question,
by occasion of reading the Scriptures in Churches, his answere
was such, as he euidently shewed himselfe to meane, that that
effect of saluatiō could not be wrought by hearing the word
of God read, with some other wordes, giuing suspition of
worse matter. And then in deede the B. rose not out of his
place, (as these honest men doe carpe) nor spake in such
cholerike maner, as they pretend : but quietly said, My Lord,
this is not farre from Heresie. What were the words that
Penry vsed, and especially moued the B. to speake, he doeth
not at this time remember: but sure he is, they were as farre
frō that, which is laide downe in the Libel, as falshood can
be from truth. I wonder that mē which professe God, yea,
or that beleeue there is a God, can with open mouth so
boldely powre foorth such heapes of vntrueths. " Detractor

abominabilis est Deo." The counsell of the Prophet is good.
Psal. 34. " He that would gladly see good daies, let him
refraine his tongue from euill, and his lippes that they speake
Epist. lib. 7. no guile." " The mouth of a malicious man" (saith
Epist. 44. Ambrose) " is a deepe or bottomles pit. The innocent that is too easie of credit, doth quickly fall, but he riseth
againe. But the backebiting railer is by his owne craft cast
downe headlong to confusion, in such sort, as he shall neuer
Super. Cont. recouer him selfe againe." And Bernard, " Let no
Serm. 24. my soule be in company of backbiting tongues
because God doth hate them, when the Apostle sayth, Back-
biters are odious to God. Euerie one that backbiteth, sheweth
himselfe voyd of charitie. Moreouer, what other thing seeketh
he by deprauing, but that he whome hee backbiteth, may
come in hatred and contempt with thē among whom he is
depraued? Wherfore the backbiter woundeth charity, in all
that heare him, and somuch as in him lyeth, doth vtterly
destroy him whome hee striketh with his tongue."

As for the reproch of " want of learning," hee will not striue
much with them. The Bishoppe hath not vsed (God bee
thanked) to vaunt himselfe of great learning. Neyther dot
he disdaine to be accounted vnlearned of these men, which
many yeares since contemned Bishoppe *Iewell* as a man of nc
deepe learning, and euen of late daies could saye that *Erasmu:*
was no Diuine. His praier is, that the small measure o
knowledge, which it pleased God to giue him in the continuance of fiftie yeeres studie, may be employed to the glori
of God, and the benefite of his Countrey. It is knowen fiu
and fourtie yeres since, that he was Master of Art, and Stu
dent of Diuinitie, and disputed in that facultie : since whic
time, hee was neuer drawen from that exercise of good learn
ing. This is his greatest comfort, that since he was a yon
man in *Magdalen Colledge* in *Oxford*, hee hath bene brough
vp in the loue of the Gospell, and was reasonablie able t
confirme his conscience, and to represse the aduersary, no

only by the holy scriptures, but also by the writings of the anciēt Fathers, and the best authors of this age since the renewing of the Gospell, as he hath many honest and learned men witnesses yet aliue. *M. Trauers,* whome they preferre before him, he knoweth not what he is. Hee neuer saw him to his remembraunce, but once, and that was at my Lord of *Canterburies,* in the presence of some honourable persons : at which time the man shewed no great learning. Doctor *Sparke* is so well knowen to the Bishoppe of *Winchester,* and the Bishoppe to him, that hee cannot bee perswaded that Doctor *Sparke* will affirme, that he did put the bishop at that time or anie other (as they terme it) to a *non plus.* But whatsoeuer hee will doe, if the one or the other, or they both, doe make anie bragge of a victorie then gotten (as I haue before sayde) surelie they doe greatlie forget themselues, and declare that *Ladie Philautie* did blear their eies, and made that they could not see the right rules of modestie : especially considering, what the witnesses were, and what report they haue made thereof to the best of this Lande, which hath not bene made vnknowen to the world. It is true that *Gregorie* sayth, " Superbia lumen intelligentiæ abscondit." Lib. epist. Pride daseleth the eies of a mans vnderstanding. 1. Epist. 3. And again, *Superbi &c.* Proud men when they thinke them selues despised, fall by and by to railing. *Cyprian,* that reuerend and learned father, sayth notably. " An Moral 8. high and swelling heart, arrogant and proud bragging Idem. 12. is not of Christ that teacheth humilitie, but springeth of the spirit of Antichrist." I pray GOD these men may remember these lessons.

As touching the Gouernement of the Church of England, now defended by the bishops, this I say. When God restored the doctrine of the Gospell more sincerely and more aboundantly then euer before, vnder that good young Prince, *King Edward* 6. at which time not the gouernours onelie of this

Realme vnder him, but a nomber of other Noblemen and
Gentlemen, were wel knowen to be zealous in the fauor o
the trueth : by consent of all the States of this Land, this
maner of gouernment that now is vsed, was by law confirmed
as good and godly.   The bishops and other of the clergy that
gaue their aduise and consent to the same, were learned and
zealous, *Bishop Cranmer*, *Ridley*, *Latimer*, and many other,
which after sealed their doctrine with their blood, all learned,
graue and wise in comparison of these yong Sectaries which
greatly please themselues.   *M. Couerdal* and *M. Hooper*,
neuer thought to be superstitious or inclining to Antichristian
corruption, were contented to vse the office, authoritie, and
iurisdiction of bishops, the one at *Exeter*, the other at *Glocester*.   *Peter Martir*, *Bucer*, and *Iohn de Alasco*, graue
men, and of great knowledge and godlinesse, did liue in that
state vnder the Archbishops and bishops that then were, and
wrote to them most reuerendly, not refusing to giue them
those Titles, that nowe bee accompted Antichristian.   The
like they did to other of late time.   Reade the Preface o
Peter Martir, set before his Dialogues against *Vbiquity*, and
see what honourable testimonie hee giueth to bishop *Iewel*,
and what titles he affoordeth him.   To condemne all these as
Reprobate and Pety Antichrists, were great rashnesse, and
such impudencie as ought not in any Christian Church or
common weale to bee borne without punishment.   When God
had marueilously preserued for vs our gratious soueraigne
Queene Elizabeth, and set her in her Fathers seat, being
brought vp from her tender yeres, in the instruction of Gods
trueth, shee tooke aduise of her most honourable Counsell
Nobles, and learned of the Realme, and especially such a
were most forward in religion, and with consent of all the
States of this Realme, by law receiued, confirmed and established the manner of Gouernment, and other orders of th
Church now obserued.   The learned men that yeelded their
advise and consent to the same, were those reuerend and godly

persons, that came lately out of banishment, from the schoole of affliction, and could not so soon forget their Lord God, and the zeale of his trueth, namely, Master *Cox*, *Grindall*, *Sandes*, *Horne*, *Pilkinton*, *Iewell*, *Parkhurst*, and a number of other, who were after chosen to be bishops, and executed those offices, without grudging or repining of any, vntill about the tenth yeere of her Maiesties raigne, the curious deuises beganne to bee more common. Since which time, by the countenauncing of some, they haue greatly increased in strange assertions, and now be come almost to the highest. The reproches therfore that are giuen to this state by these Libellers, touch not onely the bishoppes, but the Prince, the councell, and the honorable, worshipfull, wise, and learned of the Realme.

As for this question of Church-gouernement, I meane not at this time to stand much on it. For let them say what they lust, for any thing that hath bene written hitherto touching it, it is sufficiently answered. Onely this I desire, " That they will lay downe out of the worde of God some iust proofes, and a direct commaundement, that there should bee in all ages and states of the Church of Christ, one onely forme of outwarde gouernement." Secondly, " that they will note and name some certaine particular Churches, either in the Apostles time, or afterward, wherein the whole Gouernement of the Church was practised, onely by Doctours, Pastours, Elders, and Deacons, and none other, and that in an equalitie, without superioritie in one aboue an other." If this be done soundlie and truelie, without any wresting or double vnderstanding of the places of Scripture: I protest they will shake that opinion that nowe I haue of this present gouernement of the Church of *Englande*. Yet vnder correction (I will not say, that I know) but I am surelie perswaded, that they will neuer be able to doe it.

Moreouer, " I would wish them vnfaignedly to declare whether all the Churches at this day reformed in Europe,

where the light of the Gospell was first restored, and specially
of· *Saxonie* and *High Almaine*, haue this gouernement, which
by these men is nowe required, and none other." If they haue.
it is a good preiudice for their cause : if they haue not, it is
hard, that the example of two or three Churches shoulde ouer-
rule all the residue, in which the light of the Gospell beganne
before them.   And it may bee well sayde, " Did the Gospell
beginne first with you ?"   Wee may not pull downe one *Rome*
and set vp an other.   Surely as graue learned men as most
that haue written in this time, euidently affirme the contrary,
and doe make good proofe of this proposition.   " That one
forme of Church-gouernement is not necessarie in all times
and places of the Church, and that their Senate or Segniorie is
not conuenient vnder a Christian Magistrate."

In *Denmarke* they haue Bishops both in *Name*, and *Office*,
as it appeareth in certaine Epistles of *Hemingius* written to
some of them.   In which he sayth : They are greatly troubled
with continuall visitation of their Churches.   In *Saxony* they
haue Archbishoppes and Bishops in *Office*, but not in *Name*.
For proofe heereof, I alleadge the testimonies of that learned
man *Zanchius* in the Annotations vpon certaine parts of his
Pag. 272. confession.   " In the Church of the Protestants"
(saith he) " indeede they haue Bishops and Archbishops,
which chaunging the good Greeke names into ill Latine names,
they call Superintendents, and generall Superintendents. &c."

The same *Zanchius*, in the same his confession, hath these
Pag. 170.   words, " By the same reason, those thinges that were
ordained in the Church touching Archbishops, yea, and the
foure patriarches before the Counsell of Nice, may be excused
and defended."   These wordes and some other were misliked
by one famous learned man, who wrote to *Zanchius* of the
same.   But *Zanchius* was so farre from altering his iudgement
that in the foresayde *Annotations*, hee writeth a large defence
of it out of *Bucer, in. Epist. ad Ephes.* which is also founde in
a little Treatise, which the same *Bucer* hath written *De vi et*

vsu Ministerij.   And *Zanchius* in the same place shewed the reason why hee is so grounded in that opinion.   " I beleeue" (sayth hee) " that those thinges which were concluded and determined by the Godly Fathers assembled in the name of the Lord, with common consent and without contradiction to the Scriptures, proceede from the holie spirite of GOD : and therefore I dare not in conscience improoue them.   And what is more certaine by the Histories, Councels and writinges of the Fathers, then that those orders of the Ministers, of which wee haue spoken, haue bene receiued and allowed by the common consent of Christendome ?   And I pray, who am I, that I should reprooue those thinges, which the whole church hath allowed ?   Neither durst all they that bee of our time" (he meaneth the learned men of *Germany*) " reprooue the same."

In the foresayde place of his *Annotations,* when he hath spoken of the gouernement of the churches of *Saxonie,* he addeth touching other places, " Euen there where   Pag. 273. they haue neither the good Greeke names, nor the euill Latine termes : yet haue they certaine chiefe men, in whose hands well neere is all authoritie.   Seeing then we agree in the things, why should we haue controuersie about the names and titles ?"

This man vndoubtedly knewe the gouernement of all the Churches in *Germany.*   For hee had bene a reader and Teacher in diuers of them.   He had bin in *Geneua :* he taught at *Argentine* eleuen yeres : After at *Clauenna* foure yeres : Again after that, at *Heidelberge* ten yeeres : And lastly, by *Cassimire* appointed at his town at *Newstade,* where yet he liueth an olde man, if God of late hath not taken him out of this world.

Those places of high *Almaine,* wherein most zealous preachers and learned men haue remained, and with whome in doctrine wee most nighlie agree, haue not one maner Vide Gual- of gouernement, nor formes of Discipline.   In *Tygure* terum in l. it is well knowen, they haue no Senate of Elders, ad Cor. cap. 5. &c.

nor thinke it tollerable vnder a Christian Magistrate: nor the
Discipline by Excommunication, which ˌthey more mislike.
I thinke it be not much differing at *Berne* (one of the greatest
Churches) as I gather by *Aretius* in sundry places. At
Geneua, and some other places, especially such as haue had
their beginning from thence, they haue a gouernment not much
vnlike that platforme, which is desired to be with vs, and is
nowe in *Scotland*. I might say the like for some ceremonies
and outward orders. In *Saxony* and at *Basile* they kneele at
the Lords Supper. At *Tygure* they sit, and it is brought
to them : In other places they go and receiue it, for the
more expedition, as they passe.

The like libertie and diuersitie vse they in some other externall thinges, which I am not willing for some causes to lay
downe in writing. All those Churches, in which the Gospell
in these daies, after great darkenesse, was first renewed, and
the learned men whome God sent to instruct them, I doubt
not but haue beene directed by the spirite of God to retaine
this liberty, that in external gouernment, and other outward
orders, they might choose such as they thought in wisedome
and godlinesse to bee most conuenient for the state of their
Countrey, and disposition of the people. Why then should
this libertie that other Countries have vsed, vnder anie colour
bee wrested from vs? I thinke it therefore great presumption
and boldnesse, that some of our nation, and those (whatsoeuer
they thinke of themselues) not of the greatest wisedome and
skill, shoulde take vpon them to controlle the whole Realme,
and to binde both Prince and people, in necessity of conscience, to alter the present state, and to tie themselues to a
certaine platforme deuised by some of our neighbours, which
in the iudgement of many wise and godly persons is most
vnfit for the state of a Kingdome, or to be exercised vnder
a Christian Prince that defendeth the Gospell, as in part,
experience already hath taught in some. I pray God they
looke not further, and haue not a deeper reach, then

good subiectes that loue their Prince and countrey, should haue.

Lastly, I would wish them (leauing the long discourses whereunto Doctor *Bridges* was drawen by some of their strange and intricate assertions) they woulde briefly without corruption lay downe his arguments and allegations, touching the supreme authoritie of the Prince, and the superioritie of bishops, and modestly, and soundly answere the same, not reiecting the testimonie of the anciēt Writers and Historiographers, especially such as were within 400. yeeres after Christ, so farre as they may bee *Testes temporum.* For if they shall otherwise deale, and seeke to shift off the matter with reproches, scoffes, and slaunders: they wil discredit their cause, and make good men thinke, that the spirit with which they are carried, is not the milde spirit of Christ, but the spirit of him that is condemned for the father of lying, murdering and slandering from the beginning.

The reason that mooueth vs not to like of this platforme of gouernment, is, that when wee on the one part consider the thinges that are required to be redressed, and on the other, the state of our countrey, people, and commonweale: we see euidently, that to plant those things in this Church, wil drawe with it, so many, and so great alterations of the State of gouernment, and of the lawes, as the attempting thereof might bring rather the ouerthrowe of the Gospel among vs, then the end that is desired. The particulars hereof in some fewe things, in steade of many doe here follow, and hath bene opened to you before, if reasonable warning would haue serued.

First, the whole state of the lawes of this Realme will be altered. For the *Canon law* must be vtterly taken away, with all offices to the same belonging: which to supply with other lawes and functiōs, without many inconueniences, wil be very hard. The vse and studie of the Ciuill law wil be vtterly ouerthrowen: For the *Ciuilians* in this Realme liue not by

the vse of the Ciuill law, but by the offices of the *Canon law*,
and such things as are within the compasse thereof. And if
you take those offices and functions away, and those matters
wherewith they deale in the *Canon Lawe :* you must needes
take away the hope of rewarde, and by that meanes, their
whole Studie. And matters of *Tithes, Testaments, and Matrimonie, iudgements also of Adulterie, Slaunder,* &c. are in these
mens iudgements meere temporall, and therefore to bee dealt
in by the temporall Magistrate onely : Which, as yet haue
eyther none at all, or very fewe lawes touching those things.
Therefore the Temporall and Common lawe of this Realme,
must by that occasion receiue also a very great alteration.
For it will be no small matter to apply these things to the
Temporall lawe, and to appoynt Courts, Officers, and maner
of processe and proceedings in iudgement for the same.

Beside this, the Iudiciall law of the Iewes, especially for
such offences as are against the law of God, must bee brought
into this Common weale. For to this opinion doe they
playnely incline. For they say already flatly, that no Magistrate can saue the life of a blasphemer, stubborne Idolater,
murderer, Adulterer, Incestuous person, and such like, which
God by his Iudiciall lawe hath commaunded to be put to
death. The same assertion must haue like authoritie for the
contrarie, that is, that a Magistrate ought not to punish
by death those offences that God by his Iudiciall law hath
not appointed to be punished by death, and so may not
our lawes punish theft by death, nor diuers other felonies :
and so some of them haue openly preached. The lawes also
mainteining the " Queenes supremacy in gouerning of the
Church, and her prerogatiue in matters Ecclesiasticall," as
well Elections as others, must be also abrogated. Those
lawes likewise must bee taken away, whereby *Impropriations*
and *Patronages* stand as mens lawful possession and heritage.
In these *Impropriations* and *Patronages,* as I doe confesse,
there is lamentable abuse, and wish the same by some good

Statute to bee remedied : so how the thing it selfe can without great difficultie and danger be taken away, being so
generall as it is in the state of this Realme, I leaue to the
iudgement of the wise and godly.

The lawes of *Englande* to this day, haue stoode by the
authoritie of the three Estates : which to alter now, by leauing
out the one, may happily seeme a matter of more weight,
then all men doe iudge it.   If there were no more then this
one thing, which hitherto I haue spoken of, that is, the alteration of the state of all the lawes of this Realme : I thinke
there is no wise man but seeth what daunger may followe in
these perillous times, not onely by fulfilling the thing, but
also by offering to doe it.

It hath beene alwayes dangerous, to picke quarrels against
lawes setled.   And I pray God, that the very rumour hereof,
spread by these mens bookes, haue not already bred more
inconuenience, then without hurt will be suppressed : I may
not put all that I thinke, in writing.

The fourme of finding of Ministers by Tithes, must with
the Canon lawe be abolished.   For it was not vsed in the
gouernment of the Apostles time, nor a great many of yeeres
after, and therefore may seeme Papisticall and Antichristian.
There must bee some other order for this deuised.   Which,
with howe great alteration it must bee done, and how hard it
wil be to bring to good effect, I thinke there is no man but
he seeth : For the liuings of bishops and Cathedrall Churches,
(whereat they carpe) though they were all that way bestowed,
will not serue the third part.

If this gouernment, whereof they speake, be (as they say)
necessary in al places : then must they haue of necessity in
euery particular parish one Pastor, a cōpany of Seniors, and a
Deacon or two at the least, and all those to be found of the
parish, because they must leaue these occupations, to attend
vpon the matters of the church.   But there are a nūber of
parishes in *England* not able to find one tollerable minister,

much lesse to find such a company. The remedy hereof must bee, to vnite diuers parishes in one, wherof this in- conuenience wil folow, that people in the countrey must come to Church, three, foure, or fiue miles off: whereas now they that dwel in the same towne, can scarcely be forced by any penalties of Law orderly to come vnto the church, to seruice or sermons, so that they will growe to a barbarisme in many places.

Whereas it is required, that the people shoulde choose their Pastours, Elders, and Deacons: it is greatly to be feared, that it wil be matter of schisme, discord and dissension in many places : or that one or two busie heads shall leade the residue to what purpose they will, to the great disquieting both of the Church and of the common weale. Examples heereof did commonly appeare in the olde Churches, while that manner of Election did continue, as the Ecclesiasticall histories in many places doe declare. And that inconuenience caused Princes and bishops so much to intermeddle in that matter. The common people through affection and want of righ iudgement, are more easily wrought by ambitious person to giue their consent to vnworthy men, as may appeare in al those offices of gaine or dignity, that at this day remaine i the choice of the multitude, yea, though they be learned.

Men doe knowe by experience, that Parishes, vpon som priuate respect, do send their Letters of earnest commenda tions for very vnfitte and vnable persons: whereby it ma bee gathered, what they would do, if the whole choise wer in their handes, especially, being so backwardly affecte toward the Trueth of Religion, as a great part of men are They will aunswere (perhaps) that they shall bee ouerseen by the Pastours neere about them in a particular Synode, an forced both to bee quiet, and also to make more fitte election But who seeth not what matter of trouble this will bee, whe vpon the occasion almost of euery Election, they must haue particular Synode? And if the Parish will not be ruled (a surely many will not) then must they be excommunicated, and appeale made vnto the Prince and Magistrate. And that which passeth nowe with quietnesse, and with a little amendment may be well vsed, shall be continuall occasion of broile and trouble, whereto this nation is more inclined vpon light causes, then any other.

Moreouer, that which is most of all pretended for this manner of common Election, that they may knowe their Minister, and thereby haue the better liking of him, cannot possibly bee brought to passe, vnlesse they will imagine, that euery parish shall haue within it selfe a Schoole or Colledge, where those shall bee brought vp, that shall bee preferred to the Ministerie among them. But howe possible that is to bring to passe among vs let any man iudge. If their Ministers shall come vnto them from the Vniuersities or other schooles, they shall haue as little acquaintaunce with them, as nowe they haue, and farre greater occasion of partiall suites, then nowe there is. So that inconueniences by this meanes shall bee increased and not remedied.

That euery parish in England may haue a learned and discreete minister, howsoeuer they dreame of perfection, no man is able in these dayes to deuise, how to bring it to passe, and specially when by this change of the clergie, the great rewards of learning shall be taken away, and men thereby discouraged to bring vp their children in the studie of good Letters. Furthermore, who seeth not howe smal continuance there shall be in the Vniuersities, to make men of any profound knowledge, when the very necessity of places, shall drawe men away before they come to any ripenesse? the effect whereof, is partly perceiued at this day already, and much more would be, if their deuise should take place.

Touching the inconuenience of Discipline by excommunication onely, which they so much cry for, how it will bee of most men contemned, and of how small force it wil be to bring to effect any good amendment of life, some learned

men of this age in their workes set foorth to the worlde, haue
at large declared.   I let passe, that experience. teacheth,
that men of stubburnnesse will not shunne the company of
them that bee excommunicated, and then must they bee excommunicated for keeping of company with them, and so will
it fall out, that more will be excommunicated, then in Communion : whereof what deformities and inconueniences will
arise, *S. Augustine* doeth teach vs.   The loosenesse of these
dayes requireth Discipline of sharper Lawes by punishment
of body and danger of goods : which they doe, and will more
feare, then they will excommunication.   And, God bee
thanked, (if men would be contented with any moderation)
we haue a very good manner of discipline by the ecclesiastical commission, which hath done, and doth daily much
good, and would do more, if it were more common, and men
would take more pains in it.   But this is that which they be
most grieued with, because they are not doers in it themselues.

The deciding of matters in controuersie by the Pastours and
Elders of the Church, beside that it will interrupt the
course of the lawes of the realme, it will be great occasion o
partial and affectionate dealing, and thereby of further strife
and discord, and a matter of schismes and diuisions, as is to
bee perceiued aboundantly in the ecclesiasticall writers.   For
some will incline to the one part, and the residue shall bee
wrought to fauour the other : which hath bene the principal
roote of all schismes in the Church, yea, and thereby o
many heresies.   Wee must not onely looke in these corrup-
times, howe vprightly men should deale, but consider by present experience of sundrie persons and places, howe affectionately they do deale in some like matters, and thereby gathe
what they will doe, when they haue greater authoritie.   Thi
order was good, where the church was in persecution vnde
tyrants : but where the assistance may bee had of a Christiar
Prince or Magistrate, it is neither necessarie, nor so conue-

nient, as it may be otherwise. Surely common election of Ministers, and this deciding of matters in controuersie by a' multitude, will breede greater strife and contention, then without daunger will bee appeased.

Furthermore, their whole drift, as it may seeme, is to bring the Gouernment of the Church to a *Democracie* or *Aristocracie.* The principles and reasons whereof, if they bee made once by experience familiar in the mindes of the common people, and that they haue the sense and feeling of them: It is greatly to bee feared, that they will very easily transferre the same to the Gouernement of the common weale. For by the same reasons, they shall be induced to thinke that they haue iniurie, if they haue not as much to do in ciuill matters, as they haue in matters of the Church, seeing they also touch their commoditie and benefite temporally, as the other doeth spiritually. And what hereof may followe, I leaue to the iudgement of other. The way hereof is alreadie troden foorth vnto them by some that haue written and spoken in that matter: Which speeches I woulde bee loath to touch particularly, because I thinke diuers of them not to haue any meaning to indure that sequell. But men must consider, not onely what they meane presently themselues, but what other may gather vpon them hereafter. *Cyprian, Hillarie,* and other ancient writers, did not meane so ill in some things that they left written, as some Heretikes following did father vpon them, vsing their sayings, as the groundes of their false and erronious doctrines. The preachers of the Gospell in *Germanie,* at the beginning, were farre from the meaning to mooue the people to rebell against their Gouernours: but some part of doctrine vndiscreetely vttered by diuers of them, speaking against some abuses, gaue a great occasion thereof to the griefe of all good men, in such sort, as they were not able by any perswasion to quiet them, vntill it had cost a hundred thousand of them their liues. The loosenesse and boldnesse of this time in many, may iustly cause some feare that the like

E

will happen hereafter among vs. A nomber of other like
inconueniences I might lay downe in this place, and diuers o
them of as great weight as these. By these fewe, some taste
may be taken of the residue. But I will nowe returne in a
word or two to the *Martinist* againe.

Now because *M. M.* is so notable a paynter of Bishops
visages, and can purtrey them al with faces of seasoned
wainscot : it were good for him in some table to behold his
owne ougly shape, that he and his children may learne to be
ashamed of themselues. I sawe his figure drawen and se
forth in a table when I was a yong man : the paynter was one
very nigh of his kinne : His name was *Lucian*. The figur
was this, An ancient man of some authoritie sate vpon th
iudgement seate; he was like *Mydas* that couetous King : fo
hee had long cares like an Asse, and had sitting on eche sid
of him a woman : the name of the one was *Ignorance*, th
other was called *Ielous Suspition*, which two made him ver
rash in credite. Then commeth in *M. Martin M.* otherwis
called *Callumniator*, a false accuser, trimmed handsomely fo
his better credite, and not a wrinckle awry in his garment
but seemed somewhat to halte and not to goe vpright : his eye
and gesture fierce and fierie : In his left hand, he caried
flaming firebrand to note his furie. With his right hand, h
drewe by the haire of the head a young man, his name wa
Innocencie, who lifted vp his handes to heauen, protestin
before God that he was giltlesse in the cause. There folowe
two or three, much like to schollers : their names were *Dolu*
Fraus, Insidiæ. These clapped their Master on the back
to encourage him. And because Master *Martin* will be
gentleman, he had a *treader* before him, an olde fellowe : hi
eyes were fierce, his face thinne and withered, his whole coun
tenance much like to one pined away with a melancholy an
fretting furie. His name was *Liuor*, that is, *cankred malic*
or enuie : A little behinde followed *dolefull Dame repentanc*

in mourning apparell, and looking backe with shame and
teares, goeth to meete *Lady Trueth*, comming somewhat after.
In the toppe of the table this sentence was written, " Who so
euer slaundereth honest men, shall come to iust punishmēt."
In the lower part is this, " Nothing can be safe from the backebiting tongue." Rounde about was this written, " Beware
thou neyther slaunder nor giue eare vnto the Backebiter.
Flee slaundering both with thine eares, and with thy tongue.
Hee that giueth fayre countenance and light eare, encourageth
a Backebiter." If *Martin* that delighteth so much in himselfe,
woulde discreetely beholde this Table, I trust hee woulde
diminish some part of his follie. But for that it liketh *Martin*,
not onely to be a false accuser, but also a rash and credulous
Iudge with his long Asses eares receiuing euery vntrueth
that is tolde him, he may beholde himselfe in all the partes of
the Table. The best aduise that I can giue you, is out
of *Chrysostome*. " Let discretion and truth sit as Hom. Az.
Iudges ouer your owne soule and conscience. Bring Matth.
foorth before them, all thine offences. Lay downe what punishment is due for euery of them. Say continually this vnto
thy selfe, Howe durst thou do this? How durst thou do
that? &c. If thy conscience will refuse this, and prye vpon
other mens faults, say vnto her, Thou sittest not here as Iudge
of other, but to answere for thy selfe. What matter is it to
thee, if this or that man offend: looke to thine own steps,
blame thine owne doing, and not others." To the descriptiō
of a Detractor or Backebiter, are these properties. First, he
is malicious, and studieth to hurt others, and sometimes purposely doeth hurt himselfe, the sooner to hurt other. Secondly,
his soule and life is lying. Thirdly, he is an hypocrite and a
Dissembler, and pretendeth a zeale of iustice and pietie, to
colour his malice. Lastly, he is a serpent byting secretly, and
fleeth knowledge. These properties learne by the com-
plaintes of *Dauid* in sundry of his Psalmes. " Deliuer me O
Lord, from the naughtie, and from the wicked man, which

deuiseth euill in his heart. They haue sharpened their
tongues like Serpents: the poyson of Aspes is vnder their
lippes. The mouth of a backbiter is full of cursed speaking:
vnder his tongue is sorowe and griefe. He lyeth in waite in
secrete places to destroy the innocent. He lyeth lurking as a
Lyon in his denne, to rauish the poore. He falleth downe and
humbleth himselfe, that the poore may fall into his nette."
Reade the tenth Psalme, and diuers other. The residue o
their malicious and more then ruffianly railings together with
Histrionicall mockes and scoffes, too immodest for any Vice
in a Play, are not meete for any honest man to meddle with:
and therefore are returned ouer to the Libellers themselues,
as vnfallible tokens of that spirite, with which they are ledde
to these outragious dealings. But it is nowe time to answere
those quarrels that are made generally, against all Bishops.

Obiection.

But let vs see what is layde downe against the Bishops
and chiefe of the Clergie. First is, that "they are
exceeding couetous, and set to sale the libertie o
the Gospel, and the vse and Discipline of the Church
like Simoniakes and Prelates of the Church of Anti
christ: yea, that in Simonie and sale of the Gospell
they are nothing behinde the Bishop of Rome."

The objection of the couetousnesse and Simonie of Bishops.

Answere.

Surely, this is a grieuous and an horrible accusation in th
eares of any christian Magistrate: and if it be found true
the offendours not worthie to liue in this Common wealth
Or if it be false and slaunderous, the Accuser not meete
escape vnpunished. The example of the slaundering the Min
isters of the Church, is a matter more dangerous, then in thes
daies it is esteemed. But as touching the thing it selfe, I a
of opinion, that no man of meane learning, or any experience
hauing regarde of his credite, would vndertake to iustifie suc

an accusation in the hearing of any honest mā. For, this I dare say, and vpon hazard of that is most deere vnto mee in this world wil proue, that where the state of this our Church of England doth leaue to an euill disposed B. one occasion of the practise of Simony, and couetous oppressiō of the people, that the B. of Rome had fourtie. For a taste hereof, I referre the meaner learned to the common places of *Muscul.* *cap.* " Quare coniugium ministris ademptum." The better learned, I know, are better able of thēselves, to make further declaration out of their own lawes, decrees, and registers, commonly read of all them that are desirous to know the trueth, and not by ignorance, to exaggerate infamie, by false and vniust reportes. Yea, the very histories of this Realme can witnesse, that by Simony and couetous oppression, the bishops of Rome haue had yeerely out of this Realme more money, then at that time the reuenew of the Kings crowne did extend vnto, or at this day (as I thinke) al the bishoprickes in England be worth. For *Mat. Paris.* writeth, that in the time of king *Henry* the 3. the *Pope* had yerely out of this Lande 60000. markes : vnto which if you doe adde his like dealing in *Germanie* and other countreyes, you shall perceiue the value to bee inestimable. And surely I am of that hope, and in my conscience I thinke it to bee most true, that all the Bishops of this lande, by Simoniacall practise and couetous oppression, do not gaine the hundred part thereof. And if it do rise to that value, it is a great deale too much : yea, if it be one penie, it is wicked, and by no good man ought to bee defended, and much lesse by them to be practised. I hope well of all, although I wil not take vpon mee to excuse all : But for some, I assuredly knowe, and in my conscience dare depose, that since they were made bishops, they haue not wittingly gained that way, one twentie shillings. Therefore in equalling the bishops of England in the practise of Simonie with the Pope of Rome, there must needs bee great oddes in the comparison, and the whole

Musc. de minist. verbi Dei

Matth. Paris.

speech may well be called *Hyperbole,* that is, an vncharitable amplification, surmounting all likelihood of honest and Christian trueth.

Obiection.

" But somewhat to giue countenance to an euill slaunder, it will be sayde, that the Bishop of Rome practized Simonie by al meanes that he had, and our bishops, by as many as they haue."

Answere.

Oh, a worthy reason. Is this to iustifie so shameful a slaūder of the church of God, vnder a christian Princes gouernment? Is that Christian Preacher and Bishop, (if any such be) that vseth Simoniacall practise in two or three points of smal importance, and little value in grieuousnesse of offence before God and the worlde, to be equalled to the head of Antichrist, and the principal enemy of the Gospel, practizing the same in a thousand of great weight and vnestimable value? I can not but wish more charitable hearts to them that will take vpon them the zeale and profession of the Gospell. Let sinne be blamed, euē in them that fauour the word, and chiefly the Clergie: but yet so, as trueth will beare, and modestie with Christian charitie doeth require, lest in much amplifying of small offences, you become instruments, not only to discredit the parties blamed, but also to ouerthrow the doctrine that they teach. There ought to be great difference betweene Christian Preachers and writers inueighing against Antichrist and his members enemies of the Gospell, and zealous professors, blaming and reprouing the faults of their owne Bishop and Clergie in the estate of a church by authority setled. The one part is kindled with an earnest zeale and detestation of the obstinate patrones of errour and Idolatrie the other should bee mooued only with a charitable sorrowe and griefe, to see Preachers of the trueth, not to declare in life that, which they vtter to other in doctrine. They that by humane frailtie offend in blemish of life only, are not with like bitternesse to bee hated, harried, rated and defaced, as they that with obstinate and vnrepentant hearts, offend both in life and doctrine, and to the face of the worlde shewe themselues aduersaries of the truth. Christ after one maner blameth the Scribes and pharises, and after another he reproueth the ignorance, the dulnesse, the ambition and carnall affection of his owne Disciples that followed him. But I pray you, let vs consider the particular proofe of this generall accusation, and odious comparison. Surely they are so trifling, that I am ashamed to stay vpon them, and yet I must needes speake a word or two of them. The Church of England retayneth a good and necessarie order, that before the celebration of marriage, the Banes should be asked three seuerall Sabboth dayes.

Obiection.

" This order" (saith the aduersarie and accuser) "is by Dispensation abused, and by our Bishops solde for money." *The first proofe of Couetousnesse Dispensing with Banes.*

Answere.

The order I thinke very good and meete to bee obserued in a Christian Church, and not without good cause to be altered : and yet doth it not beare any necessitie in Religion and holinesse, whereby mens consciences should be wrung or wrested. But I wil demaund of the accuser, whether there be not some cases, wherein, the circumstances being considered, this matter may bee dispensed withall among Christians ? And if there be (as no reasonable man can deny) then I aske further, whether there be any lawe in this Church of England, whereby, with the authoritie of the Prince, it is granted, that a Bishop may in such conuenient cases dispense with this order ? And if there be such lawe of the Church

and of the Realme : I marueile, how it can be counted
Simonie, or couetous selling of the libertie of the Gospell, to
dispense with it.

Obiection.

" Yea, but if the order bee good, why is it not kept vnuio-
lably? if it be euill, why is it solde for money ?"

Answere.

The order is good, no man can deny it, or without good
cause alter it : but there is no external order so necessary,
but that authoritie may in some considerations lawfully dis-
pence therewith. It was a good order and commandement
of God, that none but the Priests should eat of the shew-
1 Sam. 22. bread, and yet in a case of necessitie, *Abimelech* the
hie Priest, did dispense with *Dauid* and his cōpany in eating
the same bread. The external obseruation of the Sabboth
day was a good order, and a commaundement streightly giuen
Maccab.   by God : and yet we read that the Iewes in necessity did breake it, and fought on the Sabboth day. And
Marke. 2.   Christ himselfe defended his Disciples, that on that
Math. 12.   day did bruise Corne and eat it. Therefore by lawfull authoritie, such orders may bee dispensed with, and not
deserue iust reproofe, much lesse the crime of Couetousnesse
and Simonie.

Obiection.

" Yea, but the dispensations are solde for money : for some
haue for writing, and other for sealing, and my Lord for
granting &c."

Answere.

By as good reason may they accuse any Iudge, or chiefe
officer in this Land, of extortion and bribery : because his
Clearkes and vnder officers take money for the writing and

dispatch of Processes, Writs, and other like matters, whereof happily some small portion commeth to the Iudge or chiefe officer himselfe, and the same also warranted, and made good by the lawes of this Realme. If either Ecclesiasticall Ministers or other officers and Magistrates, shall by extortion wrest more, then by order is due: there lieth lawfull remedie and sharpe punishment for the same. And in all societies and common weales that euer haue bene, aswell among Christians as other, it hath beene counted lawfull, that the Ministers to higher officers, aswell Ecclesiasticall as other, should haue lawfull portions and fees allowed them for such thinges wherein they trauell. Therefore, howe this may be imputed to Bishoppes as Simonie, and sale of Christian libertie, I see not.

Obiection.

" They will say, Dispensations for Banes, for greedinesse of money, are graunted more commonly then they shoulde be."

Answere.

If that be true, I praise it not, I defend it not, I excuse it not: and I thinke the fault more in inferiour Officers, then in bishops themselues. But in whome soeuer the fault be, that cānot be so great and hainous, that bishoppes of England may iustly be accounted " Antichristian Prelates, Petie Antichrists, Subvice-Antichrists" &c. as some in the heate of their zeale, doe tearme them. But God, I trust, in due time, will coole their heate with the spirite of mildenesse and gentlenesse. If many bishops haue gained by this kind of Dispensation, I maruaile. Surely I knowe some, that neuer receiued pennie, in that consideration, but haue giuen strait charge to their inferiour officers, neuer to dispense with that matter, but vpon great and weighty cause: and such order is now generally taken. But (good Christians) here is the griefe, that moueth all this grudge : that euill persons, when, either to cloke their whoredome, or to preuent another of his lawfull wife, or some other like purpose, will marry without orderly asking in the Church, they be for the same conuented and punished by the magistrate. This they be grieued at, and count it great ex- tremitie : for, because they see the lawfull magistrate, vpon good considerations somtime to dispense with this order, they thinke it as conuenient for them without leaue, of their owne heads to vse the same, to the satisfying of their vnlawfull lust, or other lewde affection. For such is now the state of this time, that whatsoeuer an Officer, specially Ecclesiasticall, may do by lawful authoritie, the priuate subiect thinketh he may doe the same, at his owne will and pleasure. And if he be brideled thereof, why then it is " Lordlinesse, Symonie, Coue- tousnesse, and Crueltie." And I pray God, the like bolde- nesse growe not towarde other Officers and magistrates of the Common weale also. Surely, we haue great cause to feare it : for the reasons whereon they ground their doings, may be applied as well to the one, as to the other.

Obiection.

Another Argument of couetousnesse in bishops is farre
The second worse, as it is said, then the former : " that they
proofe of prohibite marriage at certaine times, most contrary
couetousnes
forbidding to Gods worde : that is (say they) a Papisticall prac-
of Marriage. tise, to fill the Cleargies purse : yea, it is a doctrine of Antichrist, and of the deuill him selfe, prohibiting Marriage euen in Lay men, contrarie to S. Paules wordes, who sayth,
Heb. 13. Marriage is honorable in all persons."

Answere.

Surely, for my part I confesse, and before GOD and the world protest, that in my conscience I thinke, that whosoeuer forbiddeth marriage to any kinde of men, is tainted with the corruption of Antichristian doctrine, and hath his conscience

seared with an hot irō, bearing the mark of the beast spoken
of in the *Apocalypse :* but I am clerely resolued that   Apoc. 13.
the Bishoppes of England are free from anie touch of that
opinion, and doe account it no lesse then a token of Antichrist noted by *Daniel,* to prohibite lawfull Matrimonie.
Their doctrine openlie taught and preached, and the practise
of their life doth shewe it to be so, that no man vnlesse hee
bee blinded with malice, will impute that error vnto them.
Who seeth not, that by exercise of mariage in their owne
persons, they cast themselues into the displeasure and misliking of a great nomher, in that onely they be maried, contrarie to the corruption of the Popish and Antichristian
Church ? Wherefore, I pray you (good Christian readers)
weigh and consider with your selues, what vnchristian and
heathenish dealing this is toward the ministers of God, of
purpose onely to deface them, and bring them in misliking by
sinister interpretations, to cast vpon them the filth and reproch of that corrupt doctrine of Antichrist, which most of
all other they doe impugne in their teaching, and withstand
in their dooing. Is there feare of God in those hearts that
can do this ?

Obiection.

" Why ?" (they will say) " It is euident that Mariage is
prohibited by them at certaine times of the yeere, and thereby
occasion giuen to weake and fraile persons, to fall into whor-
dome and fornication, or to burne in their consciences with
great danger of their soules."

Answere.

Vndoubtedly this must needs be thought a captious and
rigorous interpretation, to say that a stay of mariage for certaine daies and weeks, is an vnchristian forbidding of mariage,
and worthy so grieuous blame, as is cast vpon bishops for it.
For then it is a *Popish disorder also, and Antichristian cor_*

ruption, to stay marriage for three weekes, vntill the Banes bee asked : for in that space, light and euill disposed mindes, may easily fall to offence.   And yet this order both is, and ought to bee accounted of them, a godly and necessary order in the Church.

Obiection.

They will answere, " that it is Popish and superstitious, to tye the order of Marriage vnto any time or season, more then other.   For the thing beeing good and lawfull by the worde of God, why shoulde it bee (say they) assigned to any time or place?   There is no place more holy then Paradise was, nor no time so good as was before Adam fell by his disobedience, &c."

Answere.

I aunswere, if any man appoint Marriage to bee vsed at this or that time and place, for conscience sake, or for holinesse, as though the time or place coulde make the thing either more or lesse holy, surely I must needs condemne him as superstitious, and cannot thinke well of the doing, though all the Bishoppes in England shoulde affirme the contrary. For to make holy, or vnholy, those things that God hath left free, and bee of them selues indifferent, is one of the chiefe groundes of all Papisticall corruption.   But I suspect no bishop in this Realme to be of that iudgement, and I dare say there is not.   A thing left by Gods lawe free and indifferent, may be accounted more conuenient, comely, and decent, at one time and place, then at another : but more holy it cannot bee.

All meats are free at all times by the law of God : " for nothing is vnclean that is receiued with thanksgiuing : neither doeth any thing that goeth into the mouth defile a man."   And yet because it is now a Positiue law in this common weale, not for holinesse, but for orders sake : it is not so comely and conuenient, for an Englishman to eate flesh on Fridayes and Saturdayes, or in the Lent, as it is at other times.

Obiection.

Heere they will crie and say, that "both the one lawe, and the other is superstitious and naught, and proceeded both out of the Popes mint, and there were coyned, and had their beginning, and therefore that the Bishops doe wickedly, and like to popish prelates, that so retain in the Church and common weale, the dregs of Antichristian corruption."

Answere.

This is the voice and opinion of them only, which think not any thing tollerable to be vsed, that hath bin vsed in the church before time, were it of it selfe neuer so good. These will haue no Font, but Christen children in basons: They wil weare no caps nor surplices: many of them wil not vse the old pulpits, but haue new made: they will not accept a collect or praier, be it neuer so agreeable to the word of God. I maruaile, that they vse the Churches them selues, thē which, nothing hath bin more prophaned with superstition and idolatrie. They should do that *Optatus Mileuitanus* writeth, that the Donatists were wōt to do, that is, when they obteyned a Church, which before had beene vsed by Catholikes, they woulde scrape the walles therof, and breake the Communion tables and cups. But it may appeare, that the learned father *August.* was not of that opinion. For in his epistle written to *Publicola*, a question was mooued vnto him, whether in destroying the idoles temples, or their groues, a Christian might vse any part of the wood, or water, or any other thing that did apperteine vnto them: His aunswere was, that men might not take those things to their priuate vse, least they run into suspicion, to haue destroyed such places for couetousnes: but that the same things might be imploied in *pios et necessarios vsus.*

But I recite not this to defend that law, whereby mariag
for a time is forbidden.   For I thinke it not a matter of suc
necessitie, neither is it so greatly pressed, as they pretend
I thinke there is no law remaining, that is so little executed
as that is.

The other law of forbearing flesh on Fridayes, in Lent, an
other dayes, for the state of our countrey I thinke very con
uenient, and most necessarie to be vsed in Christian policie
I woulde to God those men, that make so small accomp
of this lawe, had heard the reasons of the grauest, wisest, an
most expert men of this realme, not only for the maintenanc
of this Law, but also for some addition to be made vnto it
How God hath placed this land, there is no reasonable ma
but seeth : The Sea are our walles, and if on these walles w
haue not some reasonable furniture of ships, we shal temp
god, in leauing open our country to the enemy, and not vsin
those instrumēts, which God hath appointed.   There is n
state of men, that doth so much furnish this realme wit
sufficient numbers of mariners for our nauie, as fishers do
And howe shall fishers be maintained, if they haue no
sufficiēt vtterance for those thinges, for which they trauell
And howe can they haue vtterance, if euery dainty mouthe
man, without infirmity and sicknesse, shall eat flesh at hi
pleasure ?   They cannot pretend religion, or restraint o
Christian libertie, seeing open protestation is made by th
lawe, that it is not for conscience sake, but for the defenc
and safetie of the realme.   Therefore this crying out agains
this lawe, is not onely needlesse, but also vndiscreete an
factious.

Obiection.

The crime
of making
vnlearned
Ministers.

But there bee other matters that more nighl
touch the quicke, and if they be true, can receiue n
face of defence.   " They make lewd and vnlearne

Ministers for gaine : they mainteine pouling and pilling courtes : they abuse the Churches discipline, &c."

Answere.

As touching the first, if they make lewde Ministers, it is one great fault : if they do it wittingly, it is farre a more heinous offence : if they do it for gaine, it is of all other most wicked and horrible, and indeede should directly proue deuilish simonie to be in thē. That some lewd and vnlearned ministers haue bene made, it is manifest : I will not seeme to defend it : I woulde they had had more care heerein, that the offence of the godly might haue beene lesse. And yet I knowe, all their faults in this are not alike, and some haue smallie offended heerein. And in them all, I see a certaine care and determination, so much as in them lieth, to amend the inconuenience that hath risen by it. Which thing, with professours of the Gospell, shoulde cause their fault to bee the more charitably borne, least they seeme not so much to haue misliking of the offence, as of the persons them selues, for some other purpose, then they will bee openly knowen of. But if they shoulde doe, as they be (I trust) vniustly reported of, that is, to make lewde and vnlearned Ministers for lucre and gaine : truely, no punishment could be too grieuous for them. Which way that should be gainefull to Bishops, I see not.

The Clarke or Register, I knowe, hath his fee allowed for the writing of letters of Orders : but that euer Bishop did take any thing in that respect, I neuer heard, neither thinke I, that their greatest enemies be able to proue it vpon many of them. Therfore this may goe with the residue of vncharitable slanders. Or if there hath bene any one such euil disposed person that hath so vtterly forgot his duetie and calling, that eyther this way, or any such like, in making of Ministers hath sought his owne gaine and commoditie : it is hard dealing, with the reproch thereof to defame the innocent, together with the guiltie, and to distaine the honestie of them that

neuer deserued it.   There is no Magistrate in this land so
sincere and vpright in his doings, but that by this meanes his
honestie and good name may be defaced.

Obiection.

' It will be sayd that all this is but a glose or colour, to
hide and turne from you those great crimes that you are
iustly charged withall.   For the world seeth, and all men crie
out against you, that you, to the great hurt and hinderance o
the Church, vphold and maintaine an vnlearned ministerie,
and will not suffer any redresse or reformation to be made
therin.   Hereby commeth it to passe, that the people of God
be not taught their duetie, eyther to God, or to their Prince :
but, by their ignorance, are layde foorth as a pray to Sathan.
For, by that occasion, they be ledde away to euill with euery
light perswasion that is put into their heads, either against
God or their Prince, so that it may bee iustly thought that
all those mischiefes that of late haue fallen foorth, haue sprung
out of this onely roote, aswell in them that haue slid backe
and reuolted from religion, as in those that haue conceiued
and attempted the wicked murthering of our gratious Prince,
and bringing in of a stranger to sit in her royall seate. You
are therefore the principall causes of all these mischiefes."

Answere.

This is surely a grieuous accusation : but God, I trust, will
iudge more vprightly, and regard the innocencie of our hearts,
in these horrible crimes laid to our charge.   These accusers,
to satisfie their misliking affection towarde our state, not onely
suffer themselues to bee deceiued with false and captious
reasons, but dangerously also seeke to seduce other.   Logi-
cians, among other deceitfull arguments note one principally,
" A non causa vt causa," that is, when men, either to praise,
or dispraise, doe attribute the effects of either part to some
things or persons, as causes therof, which indeed are not the

true causes. Which false reasoning hath done great harme at al times, both in the Church of God, and in common weales. After the ascensiō of Christ, when God sent his Apostles and other holy men to preach the Gospell of our saluation in Christ, and the same was among men vnthankfully receiued: God did cast sundry plagues and punishments vpon them, as *dearth and scarcitie, famine and hunger, the pestilence, and sundry other diseases, warre and tumult, earthquakes and great deluges in sundry places.* The causes of al this, very slāderously and blasphemously they imputed to Christian Religion, and therby raised those dreadful persecutiōs, which at that time were exercised against the Christians.

This errour was the cause that Saint *Augustine* wrote his notable worke *De ciuitate Dei,* and that *Orosius,* by the counsell both of Saint *Hierome* and Saint *Augustine,* wrote his historie: wherein he answereth this false argument, and sheweth that God in all times, had sent the like plagues for the sinnes and offences of mankinde, and for the reiecting of his word and trueth.

In the fourtie foure Chapter of *Ieremie,* The Iewes deceiue themselues with the like argument, to confirme their conceiued superstition and idolatrie. " But we will do" (say they) " whatsoeuer thing cōmeth out of our owne mouth : as to burne incense to the Queene of Heauen, and to powre out drinke offrings vnto her as we haue done, both we and our Fathers, our Kings and our Princes in the Cities of Iudah, and in the streetes of Hierusalem : for then had we plentie of victuals, and were well, and felt no euill. But since wee left off to burne incense to the Queene of Heauen, and to powre out drinke offerings vnto her, we haue had scarcenesse of all things, and haue bene consumed by the sword and by the famine." In these words you see, to the hardening of their owne hearts, they attribute the good gifts of God to their idolatrie, and their dearth and trouble to the preaching of *Ieremie* and other Prophets, which indeede were not the true

causes therof. In like maner reason rebellious subiects in
common weales, when they seeke to make odious the Princes
and gouernors vnder whom they liue, vniustly imputing to
them the causes of such things, wherwith they finde theselues
grieued.

Walsingham. So reasoned the rebels in the time of King *Richar*
the second, against the King, against the Counsell, and chiefe
Nobilitie of the Realme, against the Lawyers, and all other
States of learning, and therefore had resolution among the
to haue destroyed and ouerthrowen them all, and to haue
suffered none other to liue in this Realme with them, but the
Gray Friers onely.

Seeing therefore this maner of reasoning is so perillous, it
behooueth all them that feare God, and loue the trueth, and
will not willingly be caried into errour, to take diligent heed
that they be not abused herewith. And so I pray God they
may doe, which at this time so earnestly seeke to make odious
the state of the Clergie of *England*, imputing to them the
causes of those things, which they most detest and abhorre.

For if they will see the trueth, and iudge but indifferently,
they shall finde that there is no such vnlearned Ministerie, as
they complaine of: neither such want of preaching, as ma
iustly prouoke the wrath of God, to send such plagues an
punishments vpon vs, as they recite. This I dare iustifie
that since *Englande* had first the name of a Christian Church
there was neuer so much preaching of the word of God
neuer so many in number, neuer so sufficient and able persons to teach and set forth the same, as be at this day, how
soeuer they be defamed and defaced. There be, I confesse
many " vnlearned and vnsufficient Ministers :" but yet I tak
it to bee captious and odious, in respect of them to name th
whole " Ministerie" vnlearned or ignorant. For the simpliciti
and charitie of Christian iudgement, doth giue the name o
any Societie, according to the better part, and not accordin
to the worse.

There were in the Church of *Corinth,* many euill persons, aswell in corruption of doctrine, as wickednesse of life : and yet Saint *Paul* noteth that Church to bee a reuerend and holy congregation. The Church of Christ militant heere in earth, hath alwayes a great number of euill mixed with them that be good, and oftentimes the worse part the greater : yet were it reprochfull and slaunderous to call the Church wicked. In like sort may it well bee thought vncharitable, to call the ministerie of the Church of *England* ignorant, when that (thankes be to God) there bee so many learned and sufficient preachers in this land, as neuer were before in any age or time, and the same adorned with Gods excellent good giftes, and comparable to anie other Church refourmed in *Europe.* If men would cast so curious and captious eyes vpon the Ministers of other countries, and note the blemishes and imperfections in them, as they doe in our owne : I am perswaded (vnder correction) they would not thinke so meanely of the state of the Ministerie of *England,* as they doe. But this is the generall disease of vs Englishmen, to haue in admiration the persons and states of other foreine countreys, and loath their owne, bee they neuer so commendable or good. I speake not this, to note with reproch any refourmed Church in forreine countries, or to diminish the commendations of those excellent gifts, which it hath pleased God plentifully to poure downe vpon them, as the first renuers and restorers of the Gospel in this latter age, to whome, in that respect, we owe great loue and reuerence : But yet they see and acknowledge, that they haue imperfections, and cannot haue churches in this world without blemishes. Notwithstanding it is not free among them, no not for the best learned, or of greatest authoritie, in publike speech or writing, to vtter those things which may tend to the generall reproche of their Church or common weale, as it is commonly vsed with vs at this day : Or if they doe, they are sharpely dealt withall for the same. For, as wise gouernours, they see, that such doings is the very seede of dissention, discorde, and faction, the verie pestilence of all Churches, commonweales, and societies. Wherefore in most Churches, they doe tollerate some imperfections setled by order, at the beginning, least by change of lawes, there should bee greater inconuenience.

Obiection.

" Yea but all their Ministers are learned and able to teach."

Answere.

Of that I doubt : and in some places, by good testimony I know it not to be true. That is easie to be had in a free Citie, that hath no more congregations, but those that be within the Citie, or within a fewe villages about, which is not possible, in so great a kingdome as this is, replenished with so many Villages almost in euery place, as scantly you haue two miles without a Towne or Village inhabited.

And yet, that men doe not conceiue euill opinion of the Bishops, for that which can not bee remedied : it behooueth the wise and godly to consider, that the state of this Church is such, as of necessitie there must be some of very meane abilitie, in comparison of that perfect rule of a Minister that S. *Paul* requireth.

It is well knowen, as it is before recited, that there be a number of parishes in this Realme, the liuings whereof are so small, that no man sufficiently learned, will content himselfe with them. In some one meane shire there bee aboue foure score Chappels to be serued, onely by Curates, with very small stipends. To place able men in them, is vnpossible : For neither sufficient number of learned men can be had, nor, if there could, woulde they be contented to be to such places appointed. And to leaue those parishes and places vnserued of common prayer, and administration of the Sacraments, were an incouenience as great on the other part : For it bringeth men to an heathenish forgetfulnes of God. To ease this matter by combinations and ioyning of many parishes together (as some deuise) besides other inconueniences, the thing is not in the bishops authoritie, nor possible for him to doe.   Euery parish hath a sundry patrone, which wil neuer bee brought to agree to that purpose, and to forgoe their patrimonie and heritage.   Now to attempt the matter, by making a law for that purpose,. would bee occasion of so great troubles and alterations, as would draw with them more inconueniences, then would stand with the safe state of this common weale, as the wiser sort doe see, and were easie for me to declare, if it were pertinent to this matter here to lay them downe in writing.   The only remedie that necessitie beareth, is, to tolerate some of the meaner sort of Ministers, hauing carefull consideration, so much as diligence can doe, that the same may be of life and behauiour, honest, and godly, and such at the least, as may bee able to instruct the parish in the Catechisme.   And surely, I hope, by the care of the bishops, that they haue already vndertaken, this thing wil be, either altogether, or in a good part brought to effect ere long time passe.

Obiection.

But some will say, that " all this is but a cloake of colourable reason to hide an vnexcusable fault.   For that no necessity can excuse a man, to breake the law of God : and Gods holy commandement is vttered by Saint Paule, 1 Tim. 3. that among other properties, a Minister should be *Aptus ad docendum*, that is, able to teach, and therefore no bishoppe can be borne with, in making an vnlearned Minister.   For he may not do euill that good may come thereof."

Answere.

For answere heereunto, it cannot be denied, but the rule which Saint *Paul* giueth, is an exact rule, and such 1 Tim. 3. an absolute description of a Minister, as is according Tit. 1.

to Christian perfection: and therefore that all Ministers ought to bee correspondent to the same : And so much as they want thereof, they lacke of their perfect state. Yea, and ecclesiasticall gouernours shoulde carefully see, so much as humane frailtie and the miserable state of this worlde wil suffer, that all Ministers of the church of God be such.   And when they doe faile heerein, they offend, and goe from that perfection that the worde of God requireth.   But yet I doubt not, but God of his great mercie in Christ our Sauiour will gratiously consider, that he hath to doe with flesh and bloud, and that euen his best children liue not here in an heauenly state, but in a miserable and wretched worlde, and specially when he seeth, that they offend not of negligence or malicious wickednesse, but are carried with the necessitie of this earthlie frailtie.   For if God shoulde measure all thinges done in his Church by the perfect rule of his word, who should be able to stand before him ?   We may not therefore, either condemne other, or esteeme our selues condemned before God, if through the frailtie of the worlde, we be not able to frame all things in his Church to such perfectnesse, as his holy word appoynteth.

As the description of a Minister, deliuered by Saint *Paul* to *Timothie* and *Titus* is perfect, so doth it containe many branches and properties to the number of (I thinke) twentie or aboue : As, that he must be vnreproueable, the husband of one wife, watching, temperat, modest, not froward, not angrie, one that loueth goodnesse, righteous, holy, harberous, apt to teach, holding fast the wholesome word according to doctrine, able to exhort with wholsome doctrine, and conuince them that say against it, not giuen to much wine, no striker, not giuen to filthie lucre, gentle, no quarreller, not couetous, one that can rule his owne house, keeping his wife and children in honest obedience, not a yong scholler least he be puffed vp with selfe liking, well reported of, graue, not double tongued, holding the mysterie of the faith in a pure conscience.

If they wil admit no Ministers as lawful, but such as shall haue fully all these properties : Surely they will cut from Churches the greatest part, or all the Ministers that they haue. Euen that one propertie which they so greatly call vpon, as of all other most necessarie, that is, that hee shoulde be apt to teach : that is, as Saint *Paul* expoundeth himselfe, to be sufficiently able to teach them that be willing, and to con- uince the aduersarie : If it be pressed to the extremitie and rigour thereof, it comprehendeth so much, as it will exclude a great many of Ministers and Preachers, which in their measure doe good seruice in the Church of God.

The best writers that euer I did reade vpon that, say, That to the performance of the same, a man must haue readie knowledge in the Scriptures, the vnderstanding of the tongues, the reading of the ancient Fathers, and histories of antiquitie. If a great many of them woulde looke into their owne bosomes, and measure themselues by this rule of sufficiencie : they would not iudge so rigorously of other, nor be so rash to condemne them.

We see in the Scriptures, that God sometime Exod. 29. beareth with breach of his cōmandemēt, falling by the ne- cessitie of our fraile life. God gaue in charge, as before is sayde, that none shoulde eate of the Shew-bread, but the Priests : And yet in necessitie *Dauid* did eate of it, 1 Reg. 21. though he were no Priest.

The *Machabies* fought on the Sabboth day contrary to this commandement, " Thou shalt keepe holy the Sabboth day :" and yet it is not read, that God was therfore displeased with them, or tooke punishment of them, though the Scrip- Num. 15. ture mention, that one without necessitie gathering stickes on the Sabboth day, was stoned to death.

Christ himselfe may seeme to giue the reason for their defence, when he saith, " The Sabboth was ordeined Mar. 3. for man, and not man for the Sabboth."

Yea, in a morall cōmandement of God touching mariage,

we see God to vse a maner of dispensation, in respect o
the frailtie of mans nature. The Scripture saith precisely,
" Quos Deus coniunxit homo ne separet :" and yet in the lawe,
Deut. 24. wee finde this dispensation or qualifying thereof.
" When a man hath taken a wife, and maried her, if she
finde no fauour in his eyes, &c. then let him make a bill o
diuorcement, and put it in her hand, and send her out o
his house."

Of this merciful bearing of God with the breach of his
commaundement, Christ sheweth the reason, *Math.* 19. saying
in this wise. " For the hardnesse of your hearts God suffered
you to put away your wiues, but from the beginning it was
not so."

Heere wee learne that our gratious and mercifull God, for
the shunning and auoiding of a greater mischiefe among stubborne people, suffered his seruaunt *Moses* to giue foorth a
more fauourable interpretation of his iust and perfect Lawe,
and to suffer diuorcements in such cases, as the right and
rigor of his iustice in it selfe, had forbidden.

This haue I written, not of purpose to incourage men to
breake and alter the Lawes and ordinances of God, but rather
to comfort those consciences, which in this case may bee
troubled, and to put away that opinion, wherewith some are
led to thinke that that Congregation is not worthie the name
of a Christian Church, not meete wherein a good Christian
man shoulde abide as Minister, where all things are not reformed, to the perfect rule of Gods holy word.

Surely the aun016cient Fathers of the primitiue Church do no
seeme to be of that iudgement. For they did all find faul
with many enormities in their time, as well in outward cere
monies, as corruption of life, yea, and in some point of doc
trine also : and yet it is not read that they did therefor
separate themselues from the Churches, or thinke that the
coulde not as faythfull Ministers serue in them.

Saint *Augustine* sheweth of himselfe, and of Saint *Cypria* very notably, as in many places, so chiefely against the *Donatists* who were infected with that errour : but Aug. de most plainely of all other places, *De Baptismo contra* baptis. con-tra Donatist: *Donatistas, Lib. 4. Cap. 9.* Where at large he dis- lib. 4. cap. 9. puteth this question : which place is worthie diligent reading and consideration.

Cyprian had blamed the Bishops and Ministers Cypr. de lap. in his time, of *Couetousnesse, Extortion,* and *Vsurie.* And yet sayth Saint *Augustine,* " *Cyprian* writeth vnto *Antonianus,* that before the last separation of the wicked and the Godly, no man ought to separate himselfe from the vnitie of the Church, because of the mixture of euill persons. What a swelling pride is it" (saith hee) ' what a forgetting of humilitie and mildenesse, what a vanting arrogancie, that he can thinke himselfe able to do that which Christ woulde not permit to his Apostles, that is, to separate the weedes from the Corne ? &c." Yea, and *S. Paul* himselfe as before I haue saide, iudgeth the Church of *Corinth,* an honorable and blessed Church of God, though there were in the same not onely some blemishes and imperfections, but many great and enormious faultes. Wherefore, to returne againe to my pur-pose, though our Bishops through the necessitie of time, neither at the beginning had, nor now can haue perfect good Ministers in euery parish within their charge : I see no cause, why they may not vse such as with their best diligence they may haue, especially if they order the matter so, as the fault be not in their owne negligence or corruption.

That you may the better conceiue, that an vn- The causes learned Ministery for want of preaching of the Gos- why an vn-learned Mi-pel, is not the cause of the backesliding and reuolting nisterie is not of so many in these dayes, nor of sundry other incon- the occasion of backe sli-ueniences imputed to the same : you shall easily ding &c. vnderstand, if you will call to your remembrance, that when there were fewer preachers and lesse teaching by great oddes, then of late yeres hath bene, the people did not reuolt as

now they doe. There is therefore some other cause, if we
will with vpright mindes looke into it. There were fewer
preachers and lesse teaching in the dayes of that King of
blessed memorie *Edward* the sixt, and yet did not the people
then reuolt, as nowe, although the reformation of the Church
was then but greenely settled. They had the same imperfection and want of Ministers, which we haue now, and that
in greater measure: in so much as they were faine to helpe
out the want with reading of Homilies, as you know. Which
deuise, although it be greatly misliked and inueighed against
in these dayes, as " intollerable :" yet did that reuerend and
learned father *M. Bucer* highly commend the same, and
shewed his good liking thereof, willing moe Homilies to bee
prepared for that purpose. And what were they that were
then Preachers, and in the state of gouernment of the Church?
Surely such persons as did diligently obserue those orders in
outwarde thinges, which the Bishops nowe, for feare of
further inconuenience, desire and studie to maintaine. In
the first ten yeres of her Maiesties most gratious reigne, there
was little or no backsliding from the Gospel, in comparison of
that now is: yet was there not then so much preaching, by the
halfe, nor so many Preachers in the Church of England by
1000. as now there are. And since that time (I speake of
good experience, and better knowledge then gladly I would)
that in diuers places where there hath bene often preaching,
and that by learned and graue men, there haue bene many
that haue reuolted, and litle good effect declared among the
residue. You wil aske me then, what I thinke to be the
true cause thereof? Surely, the causes are many: but I will
note vnto you onely two or three, that bee of greatest weight.

The first
cause why
the Gospel
prospereth
not so well
heere.
First, to haue the fruites of the Gospell setled in the
consciences of men, and declared in their liues: It
is not sufficient to haue often and much preaching,
but also to haue diligent and reuerent hearing.
Though the Preachers be neuer so learned and discreete, if it

be not heard as the worde of God, it is to no purpose. But in these dayes, as in all other, men be easily induced to disburthen themselues, and lay the whole fault vpon the Ministers and Preachers.

Obiection.

" Oh, say they, if wee had good and zealous Bishoppes, and godly Preachers, such as the Apostles were : vndoubtedly, this doctrine of the Gospell woulde haue had better successe, and would more haue preuailed in mens hearts. For they are not zealous, nor seeme to bee mooued with the spirite of God : therefore it cannot be, that they should moue other."

Answere.

Though this reason seeme somewhat plausible to some kinde of men, and to be of great force to excuse the common people : yet I aduertise all them, that haue any sparke of the feare of God in their hearts, that they take heede of it, and beware, that, to their own great dāger, they be not caried away with it. For it hath bene seldome or neuer heard or read, that the people of God among whom true doctrine hath bin preached (as the Lorde be thanked it hath bene with vs) did euer vse such allegations for their owne excuse and defence. It hath bene always the pretence of the reprobate and wicked, to colour their owne obstinacie, and contempt of Gods word, when they were offered the light of the Gospell and called to repentance. But that these kinde of men may not flatter and deceiue themselues : I let them vnderstande, that the Scriptures in no place teach them, that the offences and faults of the Ministers, are alwayes the only cause, why the word of God doth not take place in mens hearts. It is more commonly, and almost alwaies imputed to the *waywardnesse, vnthankfulnesse* and *obstinacie* of the people that heare it. Therefore it were good for all sortes of men, of what calling soeuer, to looke into their own bosomes, and

carefully to consider, whether the fault thereof be not in themselues.   For they know right well, that the master may bee
learned and diligent, and yet the scholer not thriue, by reason
of his own dulnesse.   The Physition may bee honest and
skilfull, and the obstinate Patient make light of his wholesome counsaile.   The seede may be good, and the seede
sower a painefull and skilfull husbandman, and yet the
fruite not to bee answerable to his trauel, because of the
naughtinesse and barrennesse of the ground.   This our Sauiour Christ teacheth vs in the parable of the Seede-sower.
Matth. 13. " The sower" (sayeth he) " went foorth to sowe
his seede, and some fell in the high way," that is to say, into
the hearts of them that were continually trampled with
wicked and vngodly cogitations, so that the seede could not
sinke into their hearts, but by those birds of the deuill, was
carryed away without fruite.   " Some fell into stonie ground,"
that is, into such hearts as wanted the good iuice and moysture
of Gods holy spirite : and therefore when the heate of persecution ariseth, or some great temptation assaulteth thē, their
zeale is withered, and they reuolt from the trueth.   " Some
fell into bushie ground," that is, into the mindes of them, that
were troubled with the cares of the worlde, with the loue of
riches, and with the pleasures of this life, which wholly
choked vp the good seede of the Gospell of Christ, so that
it could not in any wise prosper and bring foorth fruite.
Heere you may perceiue, that for one fourth part of good
grounde, that yeeldeth fruite of the doctrine of God, there are
three greater parts of euill ground, wherein it nothing at all
prospereth.   But in these our dayes amongst vs, we haue a
fourth sort of mē, which obstinately at al refuse to heare the
word of God, and do shut vp their eares, not only against
preaching, but against priuate exhortation also.   If there
were lesse store of these euill grounds in this land at this
day, vndoubtedly wee shoulde see more successe of the Gospell, and more ample fruite of our teaching then nowe we

doe. It were good for men to looke that these quarrellings
at other mens liues, bee not one of the *coardes of vanitie* that
Esay speaketh of. " Woe bee to them" (sayth God Esay. 5.
by his holy Prophet) " that drawe on iniquitie with coardes of
vanitie, and sinne, as it were with a Cart-rope," that is, Woe
bee to them, that imagine excuses and coulours, to nouzell
and mayntaine them selues in contempt of Gods worde, and
want of repentaunce. Let men take heede of such dealing,
that such *Coardes of vanitie* pull not on iniquitie so fast, that
it draw them to the vtter contempt of God and his trueth.
Example whereof is seene at this day, in too many, to the
griefe of all good mens hearts : For the schoole of *Epicure*
and the Atheists, is mightily increased in these daies. The
like effect *Esay* noteth to haue fallen out among the Iewes,
at that time. For this hee maketh them to say in derision of
the preaching of the Prophets, " Let God make speede, and
hasten his worke, that wee may see it. Let the counsell of
the holy one of Israel drawe neere, and come, that we may
knowe it." And in like maner dealeth the wicked in *Ieremie*
Chapter 5. " They haue denyed the Lorde, and sayde, It is
not hee. Tush, the Sworde and the Plague shall not come
vpon vs, neither shall we see it. The threatnings of the
Prophets are but winde, and the true word of God is not in
them. They vtter their owne fantasies, and these things shall
come vnto themselues." Euen with like contempt and
derision, many at this day abuse the Preachers of Gods
worde. " When we lay before them the terrible threatnings
of Gods wrath and indignation, if they reuolt from the trueth
of the Gospell, or suffer the same to be betrayed into the
bandes of the enemie, saying, that God will forsake them :
that he will take his defence from them : that he will set his
face against them : that he will bring strangers vpon them
to destroy their countrey and possesse their great lands and
goodly buildings :" Oh, say they, These Preachers make
great outcries : they put strange expectations into the peoples

heads : they are vndiscreete : they medle with matters, which
do not appertaine vnto them : if matters go amisse, the
greatest fault is in themselues. But I haue sufficiently spoken
of this maner of intertaining of Ministers alreadie, and shall
speake of the same hereafter.

The second
cause of
backsliding.

The second, and in deede a chiefe cause of back-
sliding and reuolting, is the schisme, faction and dissention, which for the space of these fifteene or six-
teene yeeres, hath exceedingly growen, betweene the Ministers
and Preachers of England. For the like hath in all ages
bene a cause to many, of falling, both from the trueth of God,
and to wickednesse of life. *Basile* speaking hereof, saith,
" Ob hæc rident increduli, fluctuant qui modicæ sunt fidei,
ambigua est fides ipsa." The effects of this schisme hath
beene (as in part I haue declared in other parts of this
treatise) First, that not only in sermons publikely, but also
in common table talke priuately, yea, and in writing and
treatises spredde abroad into all mens handes wickedly, vehement and bitter inuectiues haue beene made against the
bishops and other Preachers of the Church of England, to the
discredite not onely of their persons, but also of the doctrine
which they haue taught. Yea, the whole state and gouernment of this church, the Liturgie and booke of Common
prayer, and the administration of the Sacramentes established
by Lawe and authoritie, the externall rites and ceremonies
layde downe onely for order sake, haue beene publikely misliked, depraued and condemned, as directly contrary and
repugnant to the worde of God. Men haue not onely deliuered foorth these inuectiues against the whole state of our
Church, and all the partes thereof : but in the face of the
worlde, against Lawe, against authoritie, haue taken vpon
them to alter all thinges according to their owne pleasure :
Which dealing, you may bee sure, can not bee without great
offence of an infinite nomber, as the worlde euidently seeth
it hath beene. Moreouer, many persons, both vndiscreete

and vnlearned, because they will not bee accompted *Dumbe dogs,* haue taken vpon them to preach without license or triall : and entring into discussing of matters nowe in controuersie betweene vs and the aduersarie, haue handled them so coldly, nakedly, and vnperfectly, that many haue bene greeued to heare them, and some brought in doubt of their consciences, which neuer doubted before. Many strange Assertions, either plainly false, or as Paradoxes, true in some rare and extraordinary sense, haue beene by sundry persons, and some of them well learned, vttered and taught, to the troubling of many mens mindes, and specially such as were not able to reach to the depth of them. As for example, that it is a grieuous offence to kneele at the receiuing of the Communion. A gentleman of good countenaunce hath affirmed to my selfe, that hee woulde rather hazard all the land hee had, then be drawen to kneele at the Communion. An heauie burthen to lay vpon a mans conscience, for an external gesture. The doctrine of *the Lords Supper,* hath bene so slenderly taught by some, that a number haue cōceiued with themselues, that they receiue nothing but the external elements, in remembraunce that Christ died for thē. And these their cogitations haue they vttered to other to their great misliking. Priuate baptism, yea and publike also, if it be ministred by one that is no preacher, hath bin so impugned, as if it were no sacrament at al : whereby questiōs haue bin raised by sundry persons, what is become of them that were neuer baptised otherwise : Or whether it were not necessary, that all such persons, as are certainly knowen, not to haue receyued any other baptisme, then that was priuately done, ought not to be baptised againe, because the other is esteemed as no Sacrament ?

The article of the common Creed touching Christes descension into hell, contrary to the sense of all ancient writers, hath beene strangely interpreted, and by some, with vnreuerent speeches flatly reiected. These and a number of such other, haue vndoubtedly bred great offence, and wounded the hearts

of an infinite number, causing them partly to reuolt to Papistry, partly to Atheisme, and neglecting of all Religion, as is
seene by the liues of many, to the exceeding griefe of all them
that feare God and loue his trueth. As I haue talked with
many Recusants, so did I neuer conferre with any that would
vse any speech, but that he hath alleadged some of these
offences to be cause of his reuolting. And some haue affirmed
flatly vnto me, that in seeking to presse them to come to our
Church and seruice, we doe against our owne consciences,
seeing our most zealous preachers (as they be taken) openly
speake and write, that as well our seruice, as the administration of the sacraments, are contrary to the word of God. I
beseech Almighty God of his great mercie, that hee will open
the eies of them, which thus eagerly haue striuen against the
present state of this Church, to see what hurt and hinderaunce
hath come to the profession of the Gospell, by these vncharitable and needelesse contentions. And vndoubtedly, if
God moue not the heartes of the chiefe Rulers and Gouernours to seeke some ende of this Schisme and faction, which
nowe renteth in pieces this Churche of England : it cannot be,
but in short time for one Recusant that now is, wee shall haue
three, if the increase of that number, which I mention, be not
greater. For I doe heare and see those things, that it grieueth
my heart to consider. What hurt and trouble Satan hath at
all times raised in the Church of God by occasion of dissention and discorde, mooued not onely by heretikes and false
teachers, but also by them, which otherwise haue beene good
and godly Christians : the Ecclesiasticall Histories · doe euidently declare. What should I recite the Schisme between
the East and West Churches, for the obseruation of the
feast of Easter, which continued a great number of yeeres,
and grew to such bitternesse, that the one excommunicated
the other? What shal I say of the Schismes and grieuous
contentions in the East Church, and especially at *Antiochia,*
and *Alexandria,* betweene *Paulinus,* and *Flauianus ? Lucifer*

and *Eusebius?* the *Meletians* and *Eustathians?* all at the beginning good Christians, and imbracing true doctrine? And yet did they with great troubles, eschewe one the others Communion, as you may reade in *Epiphanius lib.* 2. *Theodor. lib.* 1. *cap.* 8. *&c. Socrat. lib.* 1. *cap.* 23. *Sozom. lib.* 2. *cap.* 18. for the space of 80. yeres and aboue. I omit the great strife betweene *Chrysost.* of the one part, and *Theophilus, Cyrill* and *Epiphanius,* on the other, for the burning of *Origens* bookes. They were all good and learned bishops, and wee doe worthily reuerence their memory: yet fell this matter so foule among them, that because *Chrysost.* woulde not consent to the burning of *Origens* bookes, *Theophilus* and *Cyrill* woulde scantly euer acknowledge him to be a lawfull Bishop. I mention not a great number of other like factiõs, which grew in the same age, to the trouble and hinderance of true Christianitie, as many godly and learned men did then complaine. And sundrie graue authours which haue written in this our time, and before, iudge, that these wayward contentions in the East Church, were the chiefe causes that brought vpon them afterward, the heauie wrath of God that tooke his Gospel from them, and cast them into the tyrannie of *Saracens* and *Turkes,* as we haue seene now these many yeeres. A notable example to vs (good Christian Readers) to take heede in time, and earnestly to pray vnto God, that he will so blesse vs with his holy Spirite, " that we may be all like minded, hauing the selfe same loue, being of one minde and of one iudgement, that nothing be done among vs, through strife and vaine glory, but that in humblenesse of minde, euery one will thinke of other better then of himselfe," that wee may grow together in one heart and minde, against the common aduersarie to the glory of God, and the promoting of his gospel, the safety of our gracious Prince, and naturall countrey. Of such discord in the church, *S. Basile* grieuously cõplaineth, " When I was growen" (saith he) " into mans age, and often going into strange Countries fel into troubles, I obserued and

found, that in other Artes there was great concord and agreement betwene them that were the chiefe of those Artes and
Sciences : Onely in the church of God, for which Christ died,
and vpon which he had plentifully powred downe his holy
spirit, I saw great and vehement discord, aswell among themselues particularly, as in things contrarie to the bolie Scriptures.   And that which is most horrible, I saw them that are
the chiefe of the Church so drawen asunder in diuersitie and
contrarietie of opinions, that without all pitie, they did most
cruelly teare in pieces the flocke of Christ, so that if euer,
now it is verified that the Apostle speaketh, From among
your selues shall rise men speaking peruerse things, that they
may draw Disciples to follow them."

The third cause and the principall of all other is,
"that the ramping and roaring Lion that goeth about
seeking whom he may deuoure," and watching all
occasions to doe mischiefe in the Church of God, hath taken
the opportunity of this Schisme and diuision among our selues.
And therefore euer since that began, he hath not ceased from
time to time, out of his scholes and Nurceries, to sende into
this realme fit instrumentes for that purpose, Iesuites, Massing-
priests, and Seminary men, and such other of our own nation,
as haue bin purposely by them corrupted : which beeing
armed with some shew of learning, but specially with readi-
nes of tongue and boldnes of speech, with some outward
shew of bolines in wordes, haue mightily preuailed against
the subiects of this realme, taking cōmonly reasons of perswasion, frō the discord that is among our selues, as by particular dealings with thē I haue learned.   The indeuours o
these men haue taken the greater effect, by one perswasiō
which they principally haue vsed: which is, that they hau
put into their minds a certain expectatiō of a speedy alteratio
and change to be, not only in religion, but also in the state o
the realme.   Their reasons haue beene, that all the Prince
Catholike in Christendom, were entred into league by al

The third cause of re-uolting.

means that might be, to depose our gracious Soueraigne Queene Elizabeth, and to set vp in her place the Queene of *Scots* when she liued : and then woe be to them that should be found in this land, to remaine in the fauour and liking of the Gospell of Christ, which they blasphemously call horrible schisme and beresie, which would bee reuenged to the vttermost.   To worke this deuise, they were let to vnderstand, what plots and meanes were made, how easie, how likely, how certaine to come to passe within few yeres, yea, moneths, yea, dayes.   For they confirmed the hearts of all them that bend to their perswasion, with all hope that might be : In so much that I knowe some, that within these two yeeres were very forward in religion, and not onely heard Sermons diligently, but also were at sundry conferences, for their better confirmation : yet within fewe Moneths, with the certaine perswasion of this expectation, were cleane caried away, and so remaine peruerse and obstinate Recusants, with the example thereof shaking the consciences of many other. In these their wicked and deuilish practises against God and his trueth, and against the state of this lande, they were not a little imboldened by slacke and remisse dealing toward them. The lawes were not executed : the aduauntage was giuen to some, that did fauourably compound with them.

Hereby I knowe by good experience, that much harme hath bene done in diuers places.   They haue also comforted and imboldened themselues in this, that mercie and fauour shoulde bee shewed them.   For this they can say, that Christian Princes and Magistrates, especially such as be Protestants, by their owne doctrine, should shewe mercie and clemencie, chiefly in matters of conscience.   But what a malicious hypocrisie is this, to call vpon Christian Magistrates for mercie and fauour, and they themselues in the meane time, breath nothing but crueltie and blood in their hearts ? I graunt mercie becommeth a Christian Gouernour, but not without seueritie of Iustice.   For seueritie stayeth a greater nomber, then mercie and fauour allureth, as (*August.* saith) De Correct. " Sicut meliores sunt quos dirigit amor : ita plures & Gratia. sunt quos corrigit Timor." The greater part is alwayes the worst : therefore Magistrates must take heede, that mercie bee not turned into crueltie : For as *August.* saith, there is " Misericordia puniens et Crudelitas parcens.

Obiection.

" Faith" (say they) " is the gift of God, it cannot be forced by any punishment : by hardnesse and extreme dealing men may be made hypocrites, but not religious : yea, they adde further, that the Apostles vsed no such helpe of Princes power to bring men to the faith, or to pull them away from errour."

Answere.

But these and such other like their Allegations, are contrary to the word of GOD, and iudgement of all the ancient learned Fathers, and specially Saint *Augustine,* who chiefly dealt against the *Donatists,* in this, and other opinions. Reade Deut. 13. the thirteenth and seuenteenth of *Deuteronomie,* and & 17. see howe straightly God giueth charge for the punishment of them that seduce other from the true worshippe of God. In *Exodus* he sayeth, " Qui immolat Dijs alienis, præterquam Domino soli, exterminetur." Hee that offereth vnto any other gods, saue vnto the Lord, &c. In the *Nombers,* he that brake the Sabboth day, was stoned to death, that his example might not seduce other. *Paul* in the *Act.* of the Apostles, by the power of God, strooke blind *Elymas* the magitian, withstanding the truth of God. *August.* in the 11. *Tract.* vpon *Iohn,* disputing against the *Donatists,* by the example of *Nabuchodonosor,* exhorteth christiā princes to vse sharp punishmēt against such persons, as contemne Christ and his doctrine. " If king Nabuchodonosor" (saith he) " gaue glory to God, because hee had deliuered the 3. yong men from the fire, and gaue vnto him so great glory, that he made a

decree throughout all his empire, which comprehēded so many
kingdoms : how should not our kings be mooued, which knowe
not onely three yong men to be deliuered out of the fire, but
themselues, and all other faithful persons deliuered from the
eternall fire of hell ? especially when they see Christ thrust
out of the minds of christians, and when they heare it saide
to a christian, Say thou art no christian. Such offences will
they commit, but yet such punishments will they not suffer.
For vnderstande you what they do, and what they suffer?
They kil mens soules, but they are afflicted but in body :
They worke to other eternal death, and they complaine that
they suffer tēporal death. &c." Againe, the same *Aug. De vi
coercend. Hæreticis ad Vincent. Epist.* 48. writeth in this
sort, " My opiniō was at the beginning, that none shold be
forced to the vnitie of the church, but that we should endeuour to deale by the worde of GOD, by disputation, by
reasoning, and perswading, least happily of those which wee
knewe to be open Heretikes, wee shoulde make counterfaite
Christians : but this mine opinion was not ouercome with the
wordes of them that reasoned against mee, but by the experience of them, which shewed mee examples to the contrarie.
For first mine owne Citie of *Hippo* was obiected against mee,
which was wholly carried away with the opinion of the
Donatistes, and yet through feare of the Emperours lawes
was turned to the Catholike vnitie. Which Citie, we now
see so to detest that pernitious errour, as if it had neuer bene
among them. And likewise diuers other cities, were namely
rehearsed vnto mee, so that by experience I learned, that my
former iudgement was not right."

The first Christian Emperour *Constantine* writing to his
Lieutenant *Taurus,* " It hath pleased mee" (sayth hee) " that
in all the places and cities, all the Temples of the idoles
·should presently be shut vp, and all wicked persons forbidden
to haue accesse vnto them. Our pleasure further is, that all
men should forbeare their sacrifices. If any such wicked-

nesse shalbe committed, let them be beaten downe with the
reuengement of the sword, and their substance to be seised
vpon, and brought into my Treasurie: And in like maner
the gouernours of Prouinces to be punished, if they neglect
to execute the same."

But I will make no longer discourse herein. Such as doe
doubt hereof, and desire to be better satisfied, I referre them
to a Treatise which Maister *Beza* hath writtē for that matter.
I haue tarried the longer in this part, for that I am desirous
to let the indifferēt christian reader vnderstand, that it is but
an affectionate iudgement of some, when they impute the
only cause to be in bishops, why there is in these daies so
great back-sliding from the Gospel, and so great mischie
deuised against the Prince and the State. It appeareth their
mindes are blinded with affection, that they cannot see the
trueth.

The quarrel   An other crime laide against Bishoppes, is, that
of maintay-   they maintayn pilling and pouling, and (as some in
ning poull-
ing Courts.   despite terme them) bawdie courtes. If they main-
tayne courtes for the administration of Iustice, in such things
as are within their charge: they doe, as I am perswaded by
Gods law they may doe, and as by the lawes of this Realme.
and state of this Church they ought to doe. But if they
mayntaine pouling in their Courtes, that (in deede) is worthy
blame, and by no pretence can bee salued. For, as al
Magistrates ought to deale vprightly, and without corruption :
so principally, such as be Spirituall, and of the Church o
God. But howe is it prooued, " that Bishops maintaine
pouling Courtes?" Surely, I knowe not: For they doe no
lay it downe in particulars. If they did, I thinke the matter
might easily be answered with good reason.

It may bee they thinke, the vnder-Officers take money and
bribes, where they should not: For that is polling and extortion. If it bee so, it is euill, and not to be suffered
and vpon proofe, the Lawe appoynteth sharpe punishment

Though it bee true that they surmise in this case, that Officers are so corrupt: it is one thing to say, The Officers vse pouling, and another to say, The bishop maintaineth a pouling Court.

A bishop may haue an euill Officer, whome yet he will not maintaine, no nor suffer, if hee knewe it, and be able to redresse it. I am in perswasion, there is no bishop in this Realme, but if it be complayned of, and proofe made vnto him, that his Officers take more then is prescribed by order and law that they may doe, but wil mislike with the thing, and doe his best to see it redressed : Or if hee will not, I fauour not their State so much, but that I could wish him to be punished himselfe. But if a bishops Officers shall be counted to poule, when they take no more then the ordinary fees and dueties by Lawe allowed, and the bishop, when he beareth with the same, shal bee called a maintainer of a poulling Court: this is a matter in a slaunderer to bee punished, and not a fault in a bishoppe to be blamed. By this meanes all the Courtes in *Englande* may bee defamed and called poulling Courtes, and the Officers or Iudges, vnder whose authoritie they stande, may be reproued as maintayners of poulling Courtes. Bee it, that there is vnlawful taking in many Courts of this Realme, as happily there is in some by greedie Officers : were it therfore the duetie of christian and godly Subiects, to spread libels against the Prince or chiefe gouernours, as maintainers of corruption, briberie, and poulling ?

An hard matter it is, in so corrupt times, for anie Magistrate, to warrant the doinges of all inferiour Officers : I pray God this making of exception to Courtes and Officers, goe no further then to the officers of bishops and of the Cleargy. Whatsoeuer they pretend, the very root of the matter is this : The whole State Ecclesiasticall, by the loosenesse of this time, is growen into hatred and contempt, and al inferiour subiectes disdaine in any point to bee ruled by them. And therfore when they be called, ꞇonuented and punished for such things, wherein they haue offended, or be brideled of that they would doe disorderly : they grudge at it, their stomackes rise against it, and thinke all that is done to be vnlawful, though it be neuer so iust. And because they are not able otherwise to be reuenged, they crie out, that they be cruel and pouling Courtes.

Obiection.

" To cut off the whole matter, it will be said, that by the word of God it is not lawfull for bishops to haue such Courtes, nor to exercise such iurisdiction."

Answere.

Yet truely I must answere, that it is lawful for christian subiects to obey it, and vnlawfull for them to kicke and spurne against it, seeing it standeth by authoritie of the Lawes, and of our christian and gracious Prince, by whom God hath sent to vs, and doeth continue with vs, the free course of his Gospell. But why may not a Bishop exercise iurisdiction, and haue a Court to iudge, determine, and ende matters ? 1. Tim. 5. Surely Saint *Paule* saieth to *Timothie*, " Against a Priest or Elder, receiue no accusation, vnder two or three witnesses." Here is an accuser : Heere is a person accused : heere are witnesses examined : here is a iudgement and deciding of the matter : therefore here is an exercise of iurisdiction, and a manner of a Court.

They will say, " It was not Timothies Court onely, but ioyntly exercised with the residue of the Elders, that had the Gouernment."

Vndoubtedly, there is no such thing there in that place The words are directed to *Timothie* onely : the adioyning o some other, is but the interpretation of some fewe : vpo which, to builde the necessity of a doctrine in the Church o Christ, is but hard dealing, and not sufficient to ground men consciences vpon. And yet here note you, that by this place it is euident, that ecclesiasticall persons may haue, and vse iurisdiction.

To proue that bishoppes may not alone exercise iuris-diction, they adde Christes saying, *Matthew* 18. " If thy brother offend thee, goe and tel him his fault between thee and him alone. If he shall heare thee, thou hast wonne thy brother: but if he will not heare thee, take yet with thee one or two : if he will not heare then, *Dic Ecclesiæ*, tell it to the Church."

Here (say they) we are willed to " tell the Church :" but " the Church" cannot be vnderstanded to be one person, as the Bishop, or such like.

First I answere, that by the consent of most Interpreters, that place speaketh not of the exercise of publique iurisdictiō, but of a charitable proceeding in priuate offences. And Christes large discourse, which immediately following he maketh vnto *Peter,* touching the forgiuing of them that doe offend vs, doth very euidently iustifie that meaning. If some . do interprete the place otherwise (as I haue before said) Christians should not build thereupon a general doctrine of necessitie.

It will be asked what Christ meant when he saide *Dic Ecclesiæ.* As some interprete it, he meant, " Tell the Gouernours of the Church :" After some other, " Tell it openly in the Church or congregation," as *Hierome* saith, " Vt qui non potuit pudore saluari, saluetur opprobriis," that is, " that hee which could not be saued by shame, might haue his saluation wrought by reproch." For a great thing it is to one that hath any feare of God, to haue reproch in the face of the Church.

And to this interpretation, the most of the ancient writers agree.

Obiection.

They will reply, that " at that time there were manie Pre-

sidents as it were, and gouernours of the Church, together
with the chiefe Ministers in euery Congregation."

Answere.

I graunt it was so : But it doth not follow thereupon, that
it is a commaundement, that for euer in all places and times,
it should be so.   I am not of that opinion, nor euer was any
of the auncient writers, no more are sundry learned men of
great credite at this time, " Quod vna semper debet esse
œconomia Ecclesiæ," that is, that the externall gouernement
of the Church, should alwaies, and in all places be one, and
specially by a College or company of Elders.   When Christ
sayd, *Tell the Church*, there was as yet no Christian church
established : but Christ tooke his speech according to the state
of the Iewes Church that then was, as in another place he
saith, " If thy brother trespasse against thee, leaue thine
offering before the altar."   If they will gather by the former
speech, *Tell the Church*, that of necessitie, they must haue
a company of Elders, as then was in the Iewes church : why,
let them make like collection of the latter, that of necessitie
there must be altars in the church of Christ : the absurditie
whereof will bee greater, then any good christian man will
easily receiue.

Obiection.

They will say, " the Apostles afterward, and the Primitiue
Church did practise the same."

Answere.

That is not yet proued : but let them struggle while they
lust, they shall neuer find a commandement in the scriptures
charging that it should for euer be so.   It were too great a
bridle of christiã liberty in things external, to cast vpon the
church of Christ.   So lõg as the church of God was in perse-
cutiõ vnder tyrants, it might well seeme to be the best and

fittest order of Gouernment: But when God blessed his Church with Christian Princes, the Scriptures doe not take away that liberty, that with the consent of their godly magistrates they may haue that outwarde forme of iurisdiction, and deciding of Ecclesiastical causes, as to the state of the Countrey and people shall be most conuenient. And that libertie haue diuers reformed churches, since the restoring of the Gospell, vsed.

Now, as when other Churches in their externall order of Gouernment, differ frō ours, we neither do, nor ought, to mislike with them: so if ours differ from theirs, retaining still the sinceritie of the gospel and trueth of doctrine, I trust they will euen as charitably thinke of vs.

If any desire further aunswere in this controuersy of Church gouernment, I referre them to the reply of D. *Bridges*, vntill they haue with modesty and grauitie answered his booke.

It is obiected also against Bishops, " that they abuse Ecclesiasticall discipline." I take " Ecclesiasticall Discipline" to consist in reprouuing, correcting and excommunicating such as be offendors in the Church. And I thinke their meaning is here, that bishops and their officers abuse *Excommunication*, in punishing therewith those persons, which obstinately and with contempt refuse, eyther to appeare, when they bee called to aunswere their offences: or when they appeare, disobey those orders and decrees by Ecclesiasticall officers appoynted. Howe this part of Church Discipline was abused by the Pope, it is well knowen: and that hee made *Excommunication* an instrument to bring the neckes of Emperors and Princes, vnder his girdle, and to make the whole world subiect to him. For this was almost the onely meane, whereby he became so dreadfull to all men, and got to himself so great autoritie. The perpetual course of the histories, euen such as were written by his owne Parasites, and chiefly of this Realme of *England*,

The crime of abusing Ecclesiasticall Discipline.

declare this to be most true. For trial hereof, reade the historie of *Thomas Becket.*

But I thinke no man is so caried with the misliking of our Bishops, that he wil accuse them, in this sort to abuse *Excommunication :* seeing by their preaching they haue bin principall instruments to ouerthrow the same in the Church of *Rome.*

They can not say, that any Bishoppe of this Church, euer since the restoring of the Gospell, indeuoured to excommunicate the Prince and gouernours, of purpose to make them subiect to their authoritie in the Church. And happily that may bee a fault, yea and a great fault that is found with them in these dayes, that they doe not so, and constraine the Prince and Rulers to doe that, which by perswasion they will not doe.

But howe expedient this maner of *Excommunication* is for this time, I leaue to the wise and godly to consider. Sure I Tygure. am, that some of the most zealons Churches reformed haue it not, nor thinke it tollerable. And yet such a maner of *Excommunication* it is, that many striue at this day to haue brought into the Church, vnder the name of *Discipline.*

But how easily it would grow to abuse, and what danger it might bring in this state of time, I thinke there is no wise man that doeth not foresee : vnlesse it be such, as to bring their purpose to passe, and to settle their deuise in the Church, thinke no danger to be shunned.

As for the *Excommunication* practised in our Ecclesiasticall Courtes, for contumacie in not appearing, or not satisfying the iudgement of the Court : if it had pleased the Prince, and them that had authoritie to make Lawes for the gouernment, to haue altered the same at the beginning, and set some other order of processe in place thereof: I am perswaded the Bishops and Clergie of this Realme would haue bene very well contented therewith.

Gualter a learned man of the Church of *Tygure,* writing vpon the first to the *Corinthians,* hauing shewed the danger of this other *Excommunication,* speaketh of a maner of ciuile discommuning, vsed in that Church : Which, or the like good order, deuised by some godly persons, if it might bee by aucthoritie placed in this Church, without danger of further innouation, I thinke it would be gladly receiued to shunne the offence that is taken at the other, and yet surely, vnder correction, the Lawe of alteration would breede some incon‐ uenience.

But the perpetuall crying of many to haue a mutation of the whole state of the Clergie, and a number of other thinges in the Church beside, (which must needes draw with it a great alteration in the state of the Realme also) maketh the Prince, and other Gouernours to bee afrayde of any mutation. For they knowe what danger may come in these perillous dayes by innouations : And if they shoulde once beginne, things are so infinite, that they can see no ende of alterations. Therefore seeing wee haue a Church setled in a tollerable maner of reformation, and all trueth of doctrine freely taught and allowed by the autoritie of this Realme, yea, and the aduersaries of trueth by lawe repressed : they thinke it better to beare with some imperfections, then by attempting great alterations, in so dangerous a time, to hazard the state both of the Church and of the Realme. And the like toleration in some meane things, I vnderstand, vpon like consideration hath bene vsed in other Churches reformed beyond the Seas.

Obiection.

An other crime is obiected, not onely against Bishops, but against all other of the Clergie, that is, " Ambition and greedie seeking after liuings and promotions. If a benefice fall voyde (say they) then rideth he, then writeth hee, then laboureth he, then inquireth hee, who can doe most with the Patrone. And if he be a Lay‐ man, then at the least, a reasonable composition will serue : And if the Bishop haue the gift, then Master Chancellor, or Master

The quar‐ rell of am‐ bition and seeking of liuings.

Steward, or my Lords Secretarie, or my Mistresse his wife, must helpe to worke the matter."

Answere.

Doe you not see, how this malicious spirite passeth ouer all the good gifts, that God hath in these dayes bestowed on a number of learned men, to the great ornament of this land? and of purpose onely to deface the Church, taketh holde o those imperfections and blemishes, which the corruption o mans nature, specially in so perillous times, and so large a Church, must needes worke in a number? Well writeth De inuidia. *Basile,* " Quemadmodum vultures &c. As vultures or carren Rauens flye alway to stinking carcasses and passe ouer many sweet medowes, and many sweete sauouring places : And as the flies shun the whole and sounde places of the body, and rest onely vpon scabs and soares, out of which they suck matter to nourish them : euen so the enuious. malitious, and backbiting spirite, passeth ouer all the orna· ments and worthy commendations of the liues of men, and carpeth and biteth at those things that he findeth worthy blame."

This Realme of *England* neuer had so many learned men nor of so excellent gift in deliuering the word of God : It is the greatest ornament, that euer this church had. For m part, surely, I doe reuerence and maruell at the singula giftes of God that I see in manie. But these thinges be wincked at, and passed with silence, and the ambitious doing of some few, brought in, as matter to discredite the whole number of Preachers.

Diogenes, seeing the cleanly furniture of *Plato* his house got vp vpon his bed, and trampled on it with his dirtie feete saying, " *Calco fastum Platonis,*" that is, " I contemne an tread vnder my feet the pride of *Plato.*" " True it is," quot *Plato,* " *sed alto fastu,* with another pride woorse then mine.' So these men, in rebuking ambition, reach at an highe authoritie and power, then any bishop in *England* hath or will vse.

Ambition, I knowe and confesse, is very wicked, and hath euer bene a perillous instrument of the deuil to make mischief. By this he drew our first parents to the disobedience of the commandement of God, perswading them not to be content with that happy state that God had placed them in. By this he incensed *Corah, Dathan,* and *Abiram* with other, to rebel against *Moses* and *Aaron*. By this he thought to ouercome Christ, when hee sawe he could not preuaile by other meanes. By this he hath alwayes raysed discorde, dissention, rebellion, warre and tumult, not onely to the troubling and disquieting, but to the shaking and ouerthowing almost of all common weales that euer haue beene, and thereby also hath wrought the murther and destruction of an infinite number of the crea-tures of God. By this he hath frō time to time raised many schismes and heresies in the Church of Christ. By this, vn-doubtedly I thinke he worketh no small euill nowe at this day, in this our church of *Englande*. But what then ? Doe they thinke, that if the bishoppes landes, and the rich liuings of the Cleargie be taken away, that they shal extinguish *Ambition* in the heartes of the Ministers ? Was there no *Ambition* in the church before that bishoppes had lands, or before Preachers had so large liuinges ? No man can so thinke, but they that are ignorant of the Ecclesiasticall his-·tories. What was the first roote of the troublesome schisme of the *Donatists?* Whereof sprang first the heresies Optat. Mi-of the *Nouatians* at *Rome?* What gaue the first oc- leu. lib. 1. casion of the pestilent beresie of the *Arians?* What hist. lib. 6. c. maintayned and continued it? was it not *Ambition,* 42. & 43. and seeking of preheminence ? But what shoulde I number vp anie more examples ? Fewe schismes and heresies in the church, but had their beginning out of this roote. And many knowe, that a repulse of a dignitie desired, was the first cause that our schisme brake foorth, and hath so eagerly continued.

Surely, though I confesse, that I see and knowe in our Church
more corruption that way, then I am gladde to beholde, and
so much especially in some kinde of Ministers, as I praie
GOD by some sharpe order may bee diminished : yet this I
dare stande to iustifie, that all the enemies of the bishoppes,
and better sort of the cleargie, shall neuer be able to proue,
notwithstanding the daunger of this corrupt time, that there
is at this day in this Realme, such heauing and shoouing, such
canuasing and woorking for bishoprikes and other Ecclesiasticall liuinges, as I will declare vnto them to haue beene in
the ancient time aboue a thousand yeeres since, in the best
state that euer was in the Church, from the Apostles age vnto
this time.   That there is no *Ambition* vsed among vs, (as I
haue saide) I dare not affirme : but surely, if there be anie,
there can be no *Ambition* on the one part, but there must bee
corruption on the other : therefore let them looke vnto themselues, that haue authoritie to bestow the liuings.   The best
sorte of the Ecclesiastical liuings are in the disposition of the
Princes authoritie.   And those honorable that haue to doe
therein, and are counsailers to her Maiestie, be not so vnwise,
but they can espy Ambition in him that sueth and laboureth
for them.   And if they doe perceiue it, they are verie greatly
to blame, if they suffer it to escape without open shame,
or other notable punishment, and thereby bring suspition,
eyther, vpon themselues, or vpon those that bee about them.

As for the corruption in bestowing other meaner liuinges,
the chiefe fault thereof is in Patrones themselues.   For it is
the vsuall manner of the most part of thē (I speake of too
good experience) though they may haue good store of able men
in the Vniuersities, yet if an ambitious or greedie Minister come
not vnto them, to sue for the benefice, if there be an vnsufficient man, or a corrupt person within two shires of them
whom they thinke they can drawe to any composition for their
owne benefit, they wil by one meanes or other finde him out
And if the bishop shal make courtesie to admitte him, some

such shift shall be found by the law, either by *Quare impedit,* or otherwise, that whether the bishop will or no, he shall be shifted into the benefice. I know some bishops, vnto whom such sutes against the Patrones haue beene more chargeable in one yeere, then they haue gained by all the Benefices that they haue bestowed since they were bishoppes, or I thinke will doe, while they bee bishoppes. They haue iniurie therefore, to bee so openly slaundered in the face of the worlde. If there bee any bishoppe that corruptly bestoweth his liuinges by sute of Maister Chauncellor, or Maister Steward, or anie other : looke what punishment I woulde haue any lay-man in that case to sustaine, I would wish to a bishop double or triple.

Obiection.

But now I must come to that which toucheth bishops most nighly, that is, " that they be carnally disposed, and not euangelically, and this their affection and corruption they shew to the worlde, by hoarding of great summes of money, by purchasing lands for their wiues and children, by marrying their sonnes and daughters with thousands, by increasing their liuings with flockes and heards of grased cattell, by furnishing their tables with plate and guilded cups, by filling their purses with vnreasonable fines and incomes, &c."

The objection, that the Bishops bee carnall and worldly disposed.

Answere.

Wee heare in this place an heape of grieuous offences, and indeed, if they be true, wel worthy such lamentable outcries, as are made against thē. But the godly must consider, that where lauishing tongues and pennes be at libertie, to lay forth reproch without feare of correction or punishment, that the best men in the worlde may be slandered and brought in danger, especially where through enuie and malice men haue conceiued displeasure against any State.

Theod. Lib.
1. cap. 20.
Eustathius, a godly and chaste Bishop, by conspiracie and false suggestion of certaine Heretikes and Schismatikes, was not accused onely, but vniustly also condemned of adulterie, and by the Emperor *Constantine* cast into banishment, into a Citie of *Sclauonie.* *Cyrillus* a good and learned father, Bishop of *Hierusalem,* and an earnest Soz. Lib. 4. patrone of the true faith of Christ, was by the cap. 26. heretike *Acasius,* and his friends in the Court, acSocr. Lib. 2. cap. 30. cused to the Emperor *Constantinus,* that he had imbezeled the Church goods, and had solde to a player of Enterludes, a rich garment, giuen to the Church by his father.

This false accusation so much preuailed, that the good Bishop was for it deposed &c. I noted you the like before Athan. of that blessed man *Athanasius* and other, and might Apol. 2. bring a great number of examples, out of the Ecclesiasticall histories and writers. For it was the vsuall practise of all such as did endeuour to further any heresie or Schismaticall faction, were they of the Clergie or Laitie, by all meanes they coulde, through infamie and discredite, to pull downe such as did withstand their euil and troublesome attempts in the Church, and not onely to raile at them, and to deface them with false and vniust reports, but also to draw to their reproch their best and most Christian doings : as the charitable dealing of *Cyrill,* was so wrested, that it brought him to great danger. And surely I cannot but feare, that the deuill is euen now in hatching of some notable heresies, or some other hid mischiefes, which hee woulde bring foorth, and thrust into the Church of England, and therfore prepareth the way for the same, by defacing and discrediting the best learned of the church, that both would and should resist them. This we see already in that peeuish faction of the *families of the loue,* which haue bin breeding in this Realme the space of these thirty yeeres, and now vpon confidence of the disgracing of the state of Bishops, and other Ecclesiasticall

Gouernours, haue put their heads out of the shell, and of late yeeres, haue shewed themselues, euen in the Princes Court. The like I might say of the *Anabaptists* and other Sectaries, as bad as they.

As touching this present point of the accusation of Bishops, I haue to admonish the godly reader, that in Christian charitie and wisedome they consider, aswell, what diuers of those persons which now be Bishops, haue bene before time : as also, in what state they are nowe in this Realme, and howe they are beset on euery side with aduersaries and euill speakers of diuers sortes, and then to weigh with themselues, whether it bee likely that all is true, which is vttered against them, or rather that for despite and displeasure, many things are spoken falsly and slanderously, and many other meane and small blemishes amplified and exaggerated to the worst, more then trueth.

That those which nowe be, or of late haue bene Bishops in this Church, shoulde be so carnally and grosly giuen ouer to the world and the cares therof, as they are by some defamed : my heart abhorreth to thinke, neither will the feare of God suffer me to iudge it to be true. I see what they are presently in all trueth of doctrine : I see how earnestly and zealously they teach and defend the same in their preachings : I see howe carefully they beate downe the grosse superstition of Antichrist and his ministers : I call to remembrance, that of late yeeres, in the time of persecution, when the most of them were in state well able to liue, that they were contented for the freedome of their consciences, and that they might enioy the doctrine and liberty of the Gospel, to forsake their liuings, to leaue their friendes, to hazard their liues, to bee accompted Traitours, and to sustaine all those miseries and troubles, that might followe vpon banishment, and casting out of their Countrey.

And I see nothing in them, if God, as wee by our vnthankefulnesse daily deserue, should cast the like scourge

vpon this Realme againe, but that they would be most readie
to do the same, although happily prosperitie in the meane
time may drawe them to some offences.   May any Christiā
heart then conceiue of them, although there be faults in them
moe then the worthinesse of their office requireth, that they
be so carnally and fleshly giuē ouer to the world, as the immodest accusations of many their aduersaries do make them?
Mans nature is corrupt and fraile, and therfore may fal to
much euil : but that so many learned men trained in the
scoole of the Crosse, and continuing in teaching and preaching
of the trueth, should be so vtterly caried away from God, I
can not beleeue, and I trust, God shall giue some euident
token of the cōtrary.   If there now be, or before time haue
bene such, as haue giuen iust occasion in such things, as they
are accused of: I cannot but blame them, and wish to the
residue more feare of God, and care of their calling.   I
neuer entred into other mens hearts to see their consciences :
I neuer looked into their Cofers to see their treasures : I
neuer was desirous to be priuie of their secret doings.   I
must therfore by that I see, heare, and know, iudge the
best.

He that shall charitably consider the state of Bishops, a
they are by the authoritie of the Prince and lawes of thi
Realme, will not thinke it impietie in them, against the time
of necessary seruice of their countrey, to haue some reasonabl
summe of money before hand, gathered in honestie, and ius
vsing of their owne.   But if they hoarde vp heapes, eithe
for greedinesse and loue of riches, or of perswasion to pu
their trust in them in time of affliction, as they are reported
surely their offence cannot be excused.

As touching their purchasing of lands, I haue not hear
much.   The greatest value that euer I heard of, doth scan
amount to one hundred pound : and that in very few, scarc
to the number of 3. persons.   Which in them, that so lon
time haue enioyed so large benefit of liuing, may seeme n

Obiection.

" They will say perhaps, that Preachers shoulde not bee so carefull for their children, nor Bishops ought not to make their wiues Ladies."

Answere.

If any looke to leaue them like Ladies in wealth and riches, they are to blame : but moderatly to prouide for their wiues and children, I thinke them bound in consciēce, especially in this vncharitable, vnkind, and vnthankfull world. For we may see the wiues and children of diuers honest and godly Preachers, yea, and of some bishops also, that haue giuen their blood for the confirmation of the Gospel, hardly to scape the state of begging, euen among vs that professe the Gospel, to our great and horrible shame. The sight whereof, I thinke, doth moue some bishops, and other Ecclesiasticall persons, to bee the more careful for their wiues and childrē, that they may haue some stay after their time, and not to bee turned to liue vppon Almes, where charitie and Christian consideration is so clean banished. Ecclesiastical persons are not as other parents are. For so soon as they depart this life, or otherwise bee put from their liuing, because they haue no state but for life, their wiues and children without consideration are turned out of the doores. And if in their husbandes time they haue not some place prouided, they hardly can tel how to shift for themselues. And surely experience teacheth mee so much, that I must needs bewaile and lament the pitiful case of diuers honest matrons, and poore infants, which in my knowledge, at the death of their husbands and fathers, haue beene driuen to great hazard and distresse. And this causeth, that most honest women, of sober and good behauiour, are loath to match with ministers,

though they be neuer so wel learned, bicause they see their
wiues so hardly bested, when they are dead.   They that are
not mooued with this, haue but cold zeale toward the Gospel.

And seeing the case is so among vs in this realme : as he
is worse then an heathen by S. *Paules* iudgemēt, that in his
life time doth not prouide for his familie : so surely hee cannot escape the blame of an vnkinde husbād, or vnnatural
parent, that hath not some care of his wife and children, after
his time.

I write not this to defend the peruerse or couetous affection of any, neyther doe I thinke that there be manie such in
this church.   Diuers I knowe, that when God shall call them,
will leaue so litle, as their children, as I think, must commend themselues only to the prouidence of God.   And therefore it is not well, that the fault of a fewe (if any such
be) should bee taken as a matter, to discredite the whole
calling.

But surely, they that murmure so greatly against the
moderate prouision of the wiues and children of Ecclesiasticall
persons, and turne that as matter of haynous slaunder vnto
them : let them pretend what they will, it may be suspected,
they scantly think wel of their marriages : Or if they doe, the
very Papistes themselues are more fauourable and charitable
Aduersaries to Preachers, then they are.   For seeing the
state of our Church alloweth Ministers to be married, they
think it to stand with godly reason also, that they should
in honestie prouide for their wiues and children.

Diuers persons of other calling, by the exercise of an office
onely in fewe yeeres, can purchase for wife and children many
hundreds, and all very well thought of : But if a bishop, that
by state of the lawe hath the right vse of a large liuing many
yeeres, doe purchase one hundred Markes, or procure a
mean Lease for the helpe of his wife and children, it is accompted greedie couetousnesse, and mistrust in the prouidence
of God.   I woulde it were not spite and enuie, with greedie

desire of bishops Liuinges, that caused this euill speeche, rather then their couetous and corrupt dealing. They feare that all will be taken from themselues.

As touching that bishops are blamed for taking of Of taking of " vnreasonable Fines, and furnishing of their Cup- Fines, &c. boardes with siluer vessel and plate," I trust euery charitable man, that hateth not the present state, may easily see what is to be answered. To take Fines for their leases and landes, is as lawful for them, by the word of God, and by the law of this Realme, as for any other christian subiect, that hath possessions. And likewise, to haue plate or siluer vessell, their condition beeing considered, is a thing indifferent, and not worthy so great reproch or biting speech as is vsed. If they had not such furniture, it is likely a great number woulde thinke euil of it, and in another sort blame them as much for it. But if they take immoderate Fines, or let vnreasonable Leases, to the grieuing and burthening of their poore and honest Tenants : or if they pompously auaunce themselues, and set their glory in the gorgious plate and gay furniture : I am so farre from defending that abuse that I will bee as ready to blame them, as any mā. And so much do I mislike such dealing in them, as I would wish those that can be found faultie in these thinges, by the Princes and Gouernours to bee examined and tryed, and vpon iust and lawfull proofe of their offences, to be punished according to their demerits : And, if the weight of matter so required, to be deposed, for the example of other, and better set in their places. But if that trial were made, as some faults perchance might be found vnworthy their calling : so I am in hope, they would not appeare so great and so grieuous, as to the discrediting of their doctrine, should deserue so heinous and bitter exclamations, and so reprochful Libels, as are giuen abroad against them. Faults, in al states, and specially of ministers, would be examined, tried, iudged and punished, by the lawe and ordinary Magistrates : and not an vnchristian loosenesse and

liberty left to vnquiet and vngodly subiects, either by euil
speeches, or vncharitable writings to slander them, and bring
thē into hatred and misliking. The example wherof may
grow to great danger, and hath bene counted perillous in all
common weales, and much more in the Church of God.

But, I pray you, what is meant by this disgracing of
bishops, and other chiefe ministers of the church? For what
purpose are their liues in such sort blazed? to what ende
are their doings so defamed? Why is their corruption,
their couetousnesse, their Simony, their extortion, and al
other vices, true or false, laide abroad before mens eyes?
Why is the perfect rule of their office and calling, according
to the patterne of the Apostles time, required at their hands
onely? Is God the God of Ecclesiastical Ministers alone?
Is he not the God of his people also? doth he require his
word to be exactly obserued of bishops and ministers alone?
doth he hate vice and wickednes in them alone? Or doth
he lay downe the rule of perfect Iustice to them only, and
not comprehend in the same all other states of his people, as
well as them? Yes truely, I thinke no Christian is otherwise perswaded.

Obiection.

Perhaps they will say, " that all other States do wel, and
liue according to their calling. The word of God is sincerely
euery where imbraced: Iustice is vprightly in all places
ministred: the poore are helped and relieued: vice is sharpely
of all other men corrected: there is no corruption, no couetousnesse, no extortion, no Simonie, no vsurie, but in the
Bishops, and in the Clergie. There are no Monopolies in this
Realme practised to the gaine of a fewe, and the vndoing of
great multitudes, that were wont to liue by those trades. All
courtes be without fault, and voyde of corruption, sauing the
Ecclesiasticall courts onely. All officers are vpright and
true dealers sauing theirs. None other doe so carefully and

couetously prouide for their wiues and children. They onely
giue the example of all euill life."

Answere.

I would to God it were so : I would to God there were
no such euils as are recited, but in them : Yea, I woulde to
God there were no worse then in them, on condition that
neuer a Bishoppe in England had one groate to liue vpon.
The want surely of the one would easily be recompensed
with the goodnesse of the other.

What then is the cause that Bishops and Preachers haue in
these dayes so great fault founde with them ? Forsooth it
followeth in the next branch of a certaine Accusation penned
against them.

Obiection.

" They haue Temporall landes, they haue great *The princi-*
liuings, They are in the state of Lordes &c. The *pall cause
wh^y the Bi-*
Prince ought therefore to take away the same from *shops be so*
them, and set them to meane Pensions, that in *depraued.*
pouertie they may bee answerable to the Apostles, and other
holy Preachers in the Primitiue Church : whereby the Queene
may bring 40000 markes yeerely to her Crowne, beside the
pleasuring of a great many of other her faithfull subiects and
seruants."

Answere.

This is the end, why Bishops and other chiefe of the
Clergie are so defaced, why their doings are so depraued,
why such cōmon obloquies is in all mens mouthes vpon them
raised, that is to say, that the mindes of the Prince and
Gouernours, may thereby be induced to take away the lands
and liuings from them, and to part the same among themselues, to the benefite (as some thinke) and to the commoditie
of their Countrey and common weale. But it behooueth all
Christian Princes and Magistrates to take heede, that they

bee not intrapped with this sophistrie of Satans schoole. This
is that Rhetorike that he vseth, when he wil worke any mischief in the Church of God, or stirre vp any trouble or alteration of a state in a common weale.

First by defaming and slandering, he bringeth the partie
in hatred and misliking, and when the peoples heads be fille
therewith, then stirreth he vp busie and vnquiet persons t
reason thus :

They be wicked and euil men : they are couetous persons
they oppresse the poore : they pill other to inrich themselues
they passe not what they doe, so they may grow to bonou
and wealth, and beare all the sway in the countrey.   Ther
fore bring them to an accompt : let them answere their faults
pul them downe : alter their state and condition : let vs n
more be ruled vnder such tyrants and oppressours : we ar
Nomb. 16. Gods people as well as they.   " Did not he deal
thus in Corah, Dathā and Abiram ? did he not by them
charge the milde and gentle Gouernour Moses, and his brothe
Aaron, the chosen Priest of God, that they tooke too muc
vpon them ? that they lifted themselues vp aboue the con
gregation of the Lord, and behaued themselues too Lordl
ouer his people ? that they brought the Israelites out of a lan
flowing with milke and honie, of purpose to worke vnto them
selues a dominion ouer the people, and to make them t
perish in the wildernesse ?"   By this meanes they so in
censed the hearts, not onely of the common people, but o
the Noblemen also, that they led a great number with the
to rebell against *Moses* and *Aaron,* and to set themselues i
their roomes and offices.   In like maner, and by like policie
hath hee wrought in all common weales, in all ages and times
as the histories doe sufficiently declare.

In this Realme of England, when the lewde and rebelliou
subiects rose against *K. Richard* 2. and determined to pul
downe the state, and to dispatch out of the way the counsellers
and other Noble and worshipfull men, together with Iudges

Lawyers, and al other of any wise or learned calling in the Realme: was not the way made before, and their states brought in hatred of the people, as cruell, as couetous, as oppressours of the people, and as enemies of the Cōmon weale, yea, and a countenance made vnto the cause, and a grounde sought out of the Scriptures and word of God, to helpe the matter?

At the beginning (say they) when God had first made the worlde, all men were alike, there was no principalitie, there was no bondage, or villenage: that grewe afterwardes by violence and crueltie. Therefore, why should we liue in this miserable slauerie vnder these proud Lords and craftie Lawyers? &c. Wherefore it behooueth all faithfull Christians and wise Gouernours, to beware of this false and craftie policie. If this Argument passe nowe, and be allowed as good at this time against the Ecclesiasticall state: it may be, you shall hereafter by other instruments, then yet are stirring, heare the same reason applied to other States also, which yet seeme not to be touched, and therefore can be content to winke at this dealing toward Bishops and Preachers. But when the next house is on fire, a wise man will take heed, least the sparkes therof fall into his owne. He that is authour of all perillous alterations, and seeketh to worke mischief by them, will not attempt all at once, but will practise by little and little, and make euery former feate that he worketh, to be a way and meane to draw on the residue. For he seeth all men will not be ouercome with all temptations, nor will not be made instruments of all euill purposes, though happily by his colours and pretenses he be able to deceiue them in some. The practise hereof, wee haue seene in this Church of England, to the great trouble and danger thereof. At the beginning, some learned and godly Preachers, for priuate respects in themselues, made strange to weare the *Surplesse, Cap,* or *Tippet:* but yet so, that they declared themselues to thinke the thing indifferent, and not to iudge

euil of such as did vse them. Shortly after rose vp other,
defending that they were not thinges indifferent, but distayned
with Antichristian idolatrie, and therefore not to bee suffered
in the Church. Not long after came forth an other sort,
affirming that those matters touching Apparell, were but
trifles, and not worthie contention in the Church, but that
there were greater things farre of more weight and importance, and indeede touching faith and religion, and therefore meete to be altered in a Church rightly refourmed : As
" the booke of Common prayer, the administration of the
Sacraments, the gouernment of the Church, the election
of Ministers," and a number of other like.

Fourthly, now breake out another sort, earnestly affirming
and teaching, that we haue no Church, no Bishops, no Ministers, no Sacraments : and therfore that all they that loue
Iesus Christ, ought with all speede to separate themselues
from our congregation, because our assemblies are prophane,
wicked, and Antichristian.

THIS haue you heard of foure degrees prepared for the
ouerthrow of this State of the Church of England.

Against the   Now lastly of all, come in these men, that make
rich Liuings
of Bishops. their whole direction against the liuing of bishops,
and other Ecclesiasticall ministers : " that they shoulde haue
no Temporal landes, or iurisdiction: that they shoulde haue
no stayed liuings or possession of goods, but onely a reasonable Pension to finde them meate, drinke, and cloth, and
by the pouerty of their life, and contempt of the world, to be
like the Apostles. For (say they) riches and wealth hath
brought all corruption into the Church before time, and so
doth it now."

Answere.

Nowe is the enemie of the Church of God come almost
to the point of his purpose. And if by discrediting of the

Ministers, or by countenance of gaine and commoditie to the Prince and Nobilitie, or by the colour of Religion and holinesse, or by any cunning he can bring this to passe (as before I haue signified) hee foreseeth that learning, knowledge of good letters, and studie of the tongues, shall decay, as wel in the Vniuersities, as other wayes, which haue bene the chiefe instruments to publish and defend the doctrine of the Gospel, and to inlarge the kingdome of Christ : And then, of necessitie, his kingdome of darknesse, errour and heresie must rise againe, and leaue this land in worse state, then euer it was before.

But to perswade this matter more pithily, to couer the principal purpose with a cloake of holinesse, it is saide, and in very earnest manner auouched, and that by the word of God, " that neyther the Prince can giue it them, nor suffer them to vse it, without the danger of Gods wrath and displeasure : nor they ought to take it, but to deliuer it vp againe into the Princes hand, or els they shal shew themselues Antichristian Bishops, vaine glorious, and lucres men, not ashamed, professing God to continue in that drossie way, and sowre lumpe of dough, that corrupteth the whole Church, and brought out the wicked botch of Antichrist, &c."

This doctrine (as it is boldly affirmed) " God himself hath vttered, Christ hath taught, his Apostles haue written, the Primitiue church cōtinued, the holy Fathers witnessed, the late writers vphold, as it must forsooth bee prooued by the whole course of the scriptures of the olde and new Testament."

But (good Christians) be not feared away with this glorious countenance, and these bigge wordes of a bragging champion. I trust you shall perceiue, that this doctrine is neither vttered by God, nor taught by Christ, nor written by his Apostles, nor witnessed by ancient writers, nor vpholden by learned men of our time : but that it is rather a bolde and dangerous assertion, vttered by some man of very small skill,

countenanced with a few wrested Scriptures, contrary to the
true meaning of God the father, Christ his sonne, and of his
holy Apostles, and a little shadowed with vaine allegations o
writers, either of no credite, or little making to the purpose.
And surely, how great and earnest zeale, how vehement and
lofty wordes so euer the vtterer of this assertion vseth : it may
be suspected, that either he is not himself soundly perswaded
in true religion, or if he be, that of simplicity, negligence or
ignorance, he was abused by some subtile and crafty Papist
that woulde sette him forth to the derision of other, to thrust
out into the world, and openly broach this corrupt and
daungerous doctrine.

Wherfore it were good, that they which wil take vpon
them to be the furtherers of such new deuises, should better
looke to their proofe and witnesses, vnlesse they will seeme
to abuse al men, and to thinke that they liue in so loose and
negligent a state, that nothing shal be examined that they
speake, but that al things shal be as easily receiued, as they
may be boldly vttered. But I trust, those that haue the
feare of God, and care of their soules, wil not be afraid o
vaine shadowes, nor by and by beleeue all glorious brags, but
take heed that they be not easily led out of the way, by such
as wil so quickly be deceiued themselues.

I do not answere their vaine Arguments, because I feare
that any discreet or learned man wil be perswaded with them :
but because I mistrust, that the simple and ignorant people,
or other that be not acquainted with the Scriptures, by the
very name and reuerence of the word of God, will be carried
away, without iust examination of them.

To descend something to the consideration of the matter
marke, I pray you, the Proposition that is to be proued. It
is not, that they may bee good bishops and ministers of the
Church, which haue neither glebe nor temporal lands to liue
on : It is not, that there were in the primitiue church, and
now are in sūdry places, churches well gouerned, which haue

not lands allotted vnto them : It is not, that the Apostles had no lands, nor any other a number of yeeres after Christ: For these points, I thinke no man wil greatly stand with them. But this is the Assertion.

Obiection.

"No prince or magistrate by Gods word may lawfully assigne lands to the ministers of the church to liue on, but ought to set them to pensions : Nor any of the Ecclesiasticall state can by the Scriptures enioy, or vse such any lands, but shoulde deliuer them vp to the Prince, &c."

Answere.

Looke, I pray you, vpon this Assertion, and consider it well. Doe you not see in it, euen at the first, euident absurditie? Doe you not see a plaine restraint of christian liberty, as bold and as vnlawfull a restraint as euer the Pope vsed any? Do you not espy almost a flat beresie, as dangerous as many branches of the Anabaptists errors? It is no better then an beresie to say, that by the word of God it is prohibited for Ministers to marry. It is no better then an heresie to affirme, that Christian men, by the lawe of God, may not eate fleshe, or drinke wine. Saint *Paule* doth con-secrate these to be *Doctrines of Deuiles*, and there- 1. Tim. 4. fore not of the Church of God: and the Primitiue church doeth confirme these to bee heresies in *Saturninus*, Theodoret. *Marcion, Tatian, Montane*, and many other. And I Epiphan. pray you, what doth this Assertion differ from the Clem. Alex. other, when it is said, It is not lawful for Ecclesiastical per-sons to haue temporall lands to liue vppon? As Gen 3. marriage is the ordinance of God, and left free by his word to all men: As meates and drinkes are the good creatures of our God, and to be vsed of all such as receiue them with thankesgiuing : so are landes, possessions, money, cattaile, the good gifts of God, and the right vse of them, not prohibited to

any of his people : For to their benefite he ordained them, as
his good blessings.   Christ by his death made vs free from
all such legall obseruations.   Therefore S. *Paul, Colos.* 2.
" If ye be dead with Christ to the iudgements of the worlde,
why are you ledde with traditions, Touch not, Taste not,
Handle not, which all doe perish in abusing?"   This boldnesse to bridle Christian libertie, and to make it sinne and
matter of conscience, to vse the creatures of God, was the
very foundation of al Papistical and Antichristian superstition.   Vpon this foundation was builded the holinesse in
vsing, or not vsing of this, or that maner of apparell : in
eating or forbearing these or those kindes of meates : in obseruing this or that day, or time of the yeere : in keeping this
or that externall forme of life, with 1000. like inuentions and
traditions of men.   Neither do I thinke euer any errour did
greater harme in the Church, or brought more corruption of
doctrine then that did.   Therefore I am sorie to see some in
these daies, to leane so much to that dangerous stay, for the
helpe of their strange opinions in things externall.   For, what
doe men when they say, It is not lawfull for a Christian man
to weare a square Cappe, to vse a Surplesse, to kneele at the
Communion?   What (I say) doe they but bridle Christian
libertie, and to the burden of consciences, make sinnes where
GOD made none ?   And in like maner, hee that sayeth, It is
wicked and not lawfull, that Bishops, Preachers, or Ecclesiasticall persons shoulde haue any temporall landes to liue
vpon, hee seemeth to finde fault with the creature of God.
For, that Bishops may haue liuing allowed them, is not
denied : but to liue by landes, that (say they) is sinne, and
prohibited, and therefore the temporall lands and glebe must
be taken from Bishops and other Ministers.

Bishops   This doctrine notwithstanding, must be proued
must have and iustified by the Scriptures, and first by the
no lands. ordinance of God himselfe in the olde testament.
Numb. 18. In the *Numbers,* when God had declared to *Aaron*

what portion he shoulde haue to liue vpon, hee addeth : " Thou shalt haue no inheritance in their land, neither shalt thou haue any part among them. I am thy part, and thy inheritance among the chil- dren of Israel. Behold, I haue giuen the children of Leui all the tenth of Israel to inherit, for the seruice which they serue in the Tabernacle." And againe after, " It shalbe a law for euer in your generations, that among the children of Israel, they possesse no inheritance." " And" in *Deut.* 10. " the Lord separated the tribe of Leui, &c. Wherefore the Leuites haue no part, nor inheritance with their Brethren, but the Lorde is their inheritance, as the Lord thy God hath promised them." In the 14. Chapter, and in the 18. and in diuers other parts of the law, and in *Iosua* 14. " Moses gaue inheritance vnto two tribes and a halfe, on the other side of Iordan, but vnto the Leuites hee gaue no inheritance among them." Vpon these testimonies, the application and con- clusion is inferred in this maner.

Obiection.

" Here it may bee seene what liuing God appoynted his Priestes to haue : not landes and possessions, but tithes and offerings. Seeing then God denied it to his Priestes, it is not lawfull for our Priestes. Whose Priestes are they? If they be Gods Priests, it is not there permitted : If they be Antichrists priests, what doe we with them ?"

Answere.

As this reason may haue some small shew or likelihoode to the ignorant : so I am sure, they that haue trauailed in the Scriptures, and any thing vnderstand the state of Christianitie, will marueile to see this application of the Texts and the conclusion inferred. Shall the Ministers of the Church of God, nowe in the time of grace, by necessitie be bound to those orders that were among the Iewes appoynted for Priestes

and Leuites by *Moses?*   Will they bring the heauie yoke and
burthen of the Law againe vpon the people of God, after that
Christ hath redeemed vs, and set vs free from it?   Will they
haue Aaronicall and sacrificing Priestes againe to offer for the
sinnes of the people?   When it is in derision asked, " Whose
Priests ours are, if they be not Gods Priests?" giuing signification that they be the Priestes of Antichrist, it may be
right well and truely answered, that they are the Priestes of
Gods holy, blessed, and true Church, and yet that they are
not such sacrificing Priests of God, as are mentioned in those
places, nor in any way bounde to those thinges that they
were, the morall Lawe of God onely excepted.

Obiection.

It is obiected to our Bishops and Ministers, " that in their
Landes and possessions, they reteine the corruption of the
Romish Church."

Answere.

The aduer-
saries build
vpon Pop¹sh
foundations.

But I marueile to see them which so boldely controll other, to builde their assertions vpon the
ruinous foundations of the Synagogue of Antichrist.
As I noted a little before, that they layde their grounde vpon
the restraint of Christian libertie : so nowe they settle it vpon
the imitation of the legall and Aaronical priesthood, as the
Church of *Rome* did.

Whence (I pray you) came the massing apparel, and almost
all the furniture of their Church in censing and singing and
burning of Tapers? their altars, their propitiatorie sacrifice,
their high Bishop and generall head ouer all the Church,
with a number of other corruptions of the Church of God, but
onely out of this imitation of the Aaronical priesthood and
legall obseruations?   Surely, while they thus vphold as
good, the wicked foundations of the Synagogue of Sathan,
they shall neuer so purely builde vp the Church of Christ, as

they woulde bee accounted to doe. They may seeme to be
in a hard streight, that to batter down the state of the Church
of *England*, must craue ayde of Antichrist, to set vp a fort
vpon his foundation.

The learned fathers of the primitiue Church, did, so much
as they coulde, striue to be furthest off from the imitation of
the Iewes, and of the Aaronicall priesthood, in so much that
they woulde needes alter not onely the Sabboth day, but also
the solemnizing of the feast of Easter : And shall the Lawe
of the Leuites, and maner of their liuing bee layde downe to
vs as a patterne of necessitie, which the Prince must followe
in reforming her Church, or else the priestes thereof shall not
be the priestes of God, but of Antichrist? Is there no more
reuerence and feare of the maiestie of Gods Prince and
sacred Minister, then by such grosse absurdities to seeke to
seduce her ? If this bee a conclusion of such necessitie, then
let them goe further : for by as good reason they may.

God sayeth to *Aaron*, " Thou shalt not drinke Leuit. 10.
wine, nor strong drinke, thou, nor thy sonnes that are with
thee, when yee goe into the Tabernacle of the Congregation,
least yee dye. Let it bee a Lawe for euer throughout your
generations."

In another place commaundement is giuen to the Leuit. 22.
Priestes, " That they may not eate of that which is rent of
wilde beastes." And in the same chapter, " If the Priests
daughter be marryed to any of the common people, shee may
not eate of the hallowed offerings : but if shee be a Widowe,
or diuorced from her husbande, and haue no childe, and is
returned into her fathers house againe, she may eate of her
fathers meate, as she did in her youth, but there shall no
stranger eate thereof." In the 21. of Leuiticus it is sayde,
" Speake vnto the Priests the sonnes of Aaron, and say, Let
none bee defiled by the dead among their people." And a
litle after, " Let them not make baldnes vpon their head, nor
shaue off the locks of their beard." And againe, " Let him

take a Virgine to wife : but a widowe, a diuorced woman, or
a polluted &c. shall he not marry."

Now if the obseruation of the orders appointed by God to
the Priests and Leuites of the olde Law, be a thing so
necessary in the church of God : Why, " then the Ministers
of the Gospell may not drinke wine or strong drinke : they
may not suffer their daughters married forth, if they come
vnto their houses, to eate any of the tenths and oblations,
whereby they liue : they may not come nigh a dead body, nor
burie it : they may marry no widowes, but maydes onely."
And so likewise shall you bring in by as good authoritie,
infinite numbers mo of Leuiticall orders into the Church, and
make it rather like a superstitious Synagogue, as the Popes
church was, then like a sincere and vndefiled Church of
God, as you would pretend to doe.

But let vs descende further into this allegation, and see
howe they ouerthrowe themselues in their owne purpose.
If vpon this proofe it be so necessarie, that bishops and other
Ministers shoulde not liue by Lands : then, as the negatiue is
necessarie in the one branch, so is the affirmatiue in the other.
When God hath sayd, " Thou shalt haue no inheritance in
their land," he addeth : " Beholde, I haue giuen the children
of Leui all the tenth of Israel to inherite for the seruice,
which they doe. &c." Then it is of necessitie by the Lawe
of God, that bishops and Preachers shoulde liue vpon
Tenthes and offerings, neither may this order be altered by
any authoritie.

And here is another errour of the Papists, that Tenths and
offerings are in the Church *Iure diuino*, by the lawe of God,
and not by any positiue Law of the Church. Thus we see
that these men are not able to stand to their positions, but
they must ioyne arme in arme with the Papists, in their
greatest and grossest errors. And if it be of necessitie, that
Ministers must liue by Oblations and tithes, and no otherwise : how can the Prince by Gods Lawe take away their

Landes, and set them to meere pensions in money? Or if Princes haue libertie by the Lawe of God, according to their discretions, to appoynt the liuings of Ministers, by pensions of money, contrary to the order that God hath prescribed to his Priests in his law: why haue they not like authoritie by the same worde of God, (if they see it conuenient for the state) to allot vnto them some portion of temporall Landes, and much more, to suffer and beare with that order, beeing already setled in the Church? By this it appeareth, that the assertion of the aduersaries doeth not hang together in it selfe, but that the one part impugneth and ouerthroweth the other.

But mee thinkes these men deale not directly, but seeme to hide and conceale that which maketh against them. For in the same place of *Iosua*, by which they will prooue, Iosh. 14. that bishoppes and Ministers may not haue any possession of Landes, because hee sayth, " To the Leuites he gaue no inheritance among them," Immediately he addeth, " Sauing Cities to dwell in, and the fieldes about the Cities, for their beastes and Cattell." And in like manner, " The Nom. 35. Lorde sayde to Moses, Commaund the children of Israel, that they giue vnto the Leuites of the inheritance of their posses- sion, Cities to dwell in. And yee shall giue also vnto the Cities suburbes harde by their Cities rounde about them, the Cities they shall haue to dwell in, and the Suburbes or fieldes about their Cities for their cattell, and all manner beastes of theirs. And the Suburbes of the Cities which you shall giue to the Leuites, shall reache from the wall of the Citie rounde about outwarde a thousande cubites. &c. And you shall measure on the East side two thousande cubites, and on the West side two thousande cubites. &c." In the twentie one Chapter of *Iosua*, The number of these Cities is mentioned, ' And the lot came out of the kinred of the Caathites, the children of Aaron the Priest, which were of the Leuites, and giuen them by lot out of the tribe of Iuda, Simeon, and Ben- iamin, thirteene Cities. And the rest of the children of

Caath had by lot of the kinreds of the tribe of Ephraim, Dan, and halfe the tribe of Manasses, tenne cities. And the children of Gerson, had by lotte out of the kinred of the cities of Isachar, Aser, Nepthaly, and the other halfe of the tribe of Manasses in Basan, thirteene cities. And the children of Merari, by their kinreds, had out of the Tribes of Ruben, Gad and Zabulon, twelue cities. The whole number therefore of the cities assigned to the Leuites in the lande of Iurie, amounted to fortie eight."

Nowe I would demaund of indifferent Christians, that were not obstinately set to maintaine an euill purpose, Whether the state of inheritance without rent, of fortie eight Cities in one Region, no bigger then England, with the fieldes almost a mile compasse, may bee thought in trueth, to bee temporall possessions or no? Surely I thinke there is no man so wayward, that will denie it to be most true.

Wherefore, eyther the worde of God must bee found vntrue, (which is blasphemie to thinke) or els that boulde assertion, that is made of the contrary, is found vaine, and the argument to prooue it, false and deceitfull. They that had to their portions fortie eight Cities, with the fields thereof, did not liue by tithes and oblations onely.

You see therefore (good Christians) how they vnderstand the Scriptures, that in such immodest and confident maner, take vpon them to be masters and controllers of other: and by how sleight allegations and absurde arguments they seeke to leade men into error, euen in great and weighty matters, without feare of God himselfe, or reuerence of his people with whome they deale. God blesse them with more grace of his true, milde, aud humble spirite, that they runne not so headlong, to the daunger of their owne soules, and the trouble of the Church of Christ.

And for the better vnderstanding heereof, let vs consider, what state the Leuites had in this Lande that was allotted vnto them. They might sell, and alienate it, but not to any other Tribe or familie, but to some of the same familie, whereof they were. The Lawe therein saith, Leuit. 25. " Notwithstanding, the Cities of the Leuites, and the houses of the cities of their possession, may the Leuites redeeme at all seasons. If a man purchase of the Leuites, the house that was soulde shall goe out in the yere of Iubile. But the fields of their Cities may not be soulde, for it is their possession for euer."

And yet we read that the Prophet *Ieremie* bought   Iere. 32. a peece of land of *Hananael* his Vncles sonne, which I take to bee, because *Ieremie* was his next of kinne, to whome by Lawe after him it shoulde come : So that *Hananael* soulde onely the interest of his life time.

Thus, by the way you may note, that buying and purchasing of such ground as was lawfull to them, was not prohibited to Gods Priests in the olde law.

Obiection.

Happilie they will say, " That although they had some temporall Landes, yet it was in comparison of the large inheritaunce of the other Tribes, but a small portion : And as the Ministers of God, they liued meanely and porely vpon it."

Answere.

But they that rightly consider and weigh the quantitie and largenesse of the Lande of Promise, not being (as I thinke) so large as this Realme of *England,* shall perceiue, that the same being diuided into twelue partes, according to the twelue Tribes, that eight and fourtie Cities, with the fieldes about them, onely for the tribe of *Leui,* was a portion, although not so big, yet not much inferiour to the residue, although the one part had their liuing together, and the Leuites had theirs disparkled in sundry partes of the Countrey. To which, if you adde Gods part, that is, the oblations, the first fruits and the tenthes of their fruites, and cattell beside,

you shall perceiue, that the Priestes, Leuites, and Ministers
of the Temple of God were not left in meaner or poorer, but
rather in as good or better state, then any of the other Tribes.
Which thing vndoubtedly God did of his gratious prouidence,
not that his ministers should by wealth wax wantō and proud,
but that by that meanes, they might be of more authoritie
with his people, and not beeing drawen away by the necessitie
of care howe to liue, they might more freely and quietly
attend vpon the seruice of God in the Temple and other
places.   Wherefore these places of the Law of *Moses*, were
not fitly alleadged to prooue, either, that the Ministers of
the Church should haue no temporall possessions, or that
they should by stipends of money liue in poore or base
condition.

It pleased God, that the Leuites shoulde not haue their
portion lying together, as the other had, but to bee sparkle
among all the Tribes of that nation, that they might the
better instruct the people of all partes, in the Lawe and
Ordinaunces of almightie God, as their office and and duetie
was.   But if the value of their portion, together with the firs
fruites and tenths bee considered, you shall perceiue it was
nothing inferiour to any of the best.

They that had not some peculiar drift and purpose in their
heades, which by all meanes, right or wrong, they wil
further and confirme, but did sincerely, and with good con
science, seeke the true meaning of the spirit of God in th
holy scriptures, out of these testimonies of the Lawe of God
might haue gathered a right and wholesome instruction, pro
fitable not onely to Ministers of the Church, but to all othe
good and faythfull Christians, to whom these places appertain
as well as to bishops and Ministers.

The right For as *Aaron* the high Priest in the Lawe, wa
vnderstand- the figure of the true high Priest Christ Iesus ou
ing of the
places of the Sauiour : so the inferiour Priestes and Leuites seruin
olde Lawe. in the temple of God, represent vnto vs all othe

faithfull and elect of God, whome hee hath chosen vnto him, to serue him as his peculiar heritage, and in steed of the first begotten of mankinde. To this interpretation alludeth S. *Peter*, speaking, not to Priests alone, but to the whole Church of God, and number of the faithfull. " You are" (saith he) " a chosen generation, a royall priesthood, 1. Pet. 2. an holy nation." This exposition S. *August.* confirmeth, " As for the Priesthoode" (saith he) " of the Iewes, Lib.2.quest. there is no faithfull man that doubteth, but that Euan. c. 40. it was a figure of the roiall Priesthood that should be in the Church. Whereunto all they are consecrated, which appertaine to the mysticall body of the most high and true Prince of Priestes, as Peter also witnesseth."

Bede also writeth very euidently to the same pur- Li. de. temp. pose. " By the name of Priesthood in the Scrip- Salom. cap. 16. tures, figuratiuely is vnderstoode, not onely Ministers of the Altar, that is, Bishops and Priestes : but all they which by high and godly conuersation, and by excellencie of wholesome doctrine, are profitable, not to themselues onely, but to many other, while they offer their bodies as a liuelie and holy Sacrifice well pleasing God. For *Peter* spake not to Priests onlie but to the vniuersall Church of Ood." Nowe, if this bee true, the right and sincere doctrine, that is to be taken out of the testimonies of the law of God, is this, that as the Preestes and Leuites had not a like portion of inheritance allotted vnto them, as the residue of their brethren had, but God onely whome they serued, was their portion : so all faithful Christians, being of the true Priesthoode of God, must not thinke they haue any allotted portion in this worlde, but God onely is their portion, to whome they must cleaue, and heauen to bee their inheritaunce after which they must seeke, according as S. *Paul* saieth, " Wee haue heere no Heb. 13. abiding Citie, but wee seeke for one in Heauen. Wee be as pilgrimes and straungers in this earth. Therefore if Col. 3. wee bee risen with Christ, wee shoulde seeke those things

H

that be aboue, where Christ our portion sitteth at the right
hand of God the Father, and our whole heart shoulde be
fastened vpon thinges aboue, and not on earthly thinges."
This instruction, as nighly and as deepely toucheth all
Christians, as it doth Bishops and Ministers of the Church
of God.

But countenaunce must bee giuen to this quarrell against
bishops, and this strange Assertion must bee confirmed by
the Prophets also, euen as aptly alledged as the other places
before mentioned.

AND first they beginne with Esay. " His watchmen are all blinde, they haue altogether no vnderstanding, they are all dumbe dogges, not being able
to barke, they are sleepie, sluggish, and lie snorting,
they are shamelesse dogges that neuer are satisfied, the
shepheards also haue no vndrstãding, but euery man turneth
his owne way, euery one after his couetousnesse with all his
power." Out of *Ieremie* also, are alledged these wordes.
" I wil giue their wiues vnto aliens, and their fields
to destroyers : for from the lowest vnto the highest, they followe filthie lucre, and from the Prophet to the Priest, they
deale all with lies." The Prophet *Ezechiel* also is brought
in, to helpe this matter, where hee terribly thundreth against
negligent, naughtie and corrupt shepheards, that deuoure the
flocke and feed it not. " Thou sonne of man, prophecie against the Shepheards of Israel, woe bee vnto the
Shepheardes of Israel, that feede themselues : shoulde not
the Shepheardes feede the flockes ? yee eate vp the fat, ye
clothe you with the wooll, the best fedde doe you slay, but
the flocke doe you not feede, the weake haue you not
strengthened, the sicke haue you not healed, the broken haue
you not bound together, &c. but with force and crueltie haue
you ruled them." Wise and discreete christians, that in
iudging of things feare to be deceiued, and looke to the direct
proofe of that which is in controuersie, will marueile to see

Margin notes:
Esai. 56.
Allegations out of the Prophets for the same purpose.
Ierem. 8.
Ezech. 34.

these testimonies alleadged, to the end before prefixed : that is, that bishops may not enioy any temporall Landes. For there is nothing in these places of the Prophets that toucheth it. But if the ende were onely to make an inuectiue against the negligent, corrupt, and couetous liues of bishops, or other Ministers : indeede these allegations might seeme not altogether to be vnfit for the purpose : And happily that is it that is especially intended, by such meanes to make them contemptible and odious. And yet this is no sincere handling of the Scriptures, to apply those places to the particular blaming of some one sort of men, which the spirite of God directeth against many. Who being acquainted with the Scriptures, knoweth not, that by the words *Watchmen* and *Shepheards*, in the Prophets, are meant not only bishops, Priests, and Leuites : but also Princes, Magistrates and Rulers? Vpon the place of *Ezechiel* aboue recited, *Hierome* saith : " The speech is directed to the Shepherds of   Hierome. Israel : by which we ought to vnderstand, the Kings, the Princes, the Scribes and Pharises, and the Masters of the people." And againe vpon these words, " The fat they did eate, by a metaphore" (saith hee) " the Prophet speaketh to the Princes, of whom it is said in another place, Which deuoure my people as it were bread." Yea, when Psalm. 32. God himselfe saith in this same place of *Ezechiel*, " with force and crueltie haue ye ruled them :" It may euidently appeare, that he speaketh not there to ecclesiastical ministers only, but to Princes, Iudges, and rulers also, which sucke the sweete from the people of God, and do not carefully see to their defence, and godly gouernment, but suffer them to bee spoyled of their enemies, and to wander from God, and his true worship. But what should I seeme to proue that, which all learned knowe to bee most true ? The spirite of God speaketh to the same purpose by these Prophets vnder figuratiue wordes, that he doeth by other Prophets in playne speeche. " O yee Priestes" (sayeth *Osee*) " heare this O yee   Osee. 5.

house of Israel, giue eare O thou house of the King: Iudgement is against you, because you are become a snare in
Mispath, and a spread nette in Mount Thabor," that is, you,
as hunters lay wayte to snare the people, and to oppresse
them by couetousnesse, extortion, and briberie: and your
corrupt manners is as a nette to take other in, by your euill
example.   And likewise sayth *Micheas.* "Heare this O yee
heads of the house of Iaacob, and yee Princes of the house
of Israel: they abhorre iudgements and peruert equitie: They
build vp Sion with blood, and Hierusalem with iniquitie.
The heads thereof iudge by rewardes, and the Priestes
thereof teache for hire, and their Prophets prophecie for
money."   These bee the ordinarie voyces of the holy Ghost,
vttered by the Prophets, in sharpe and earnest reproouing,
not onely for the people for their wicked reuolting from God,
but also, yea and that chiefly, for the Princes, Rulers Magistrates, Iudges, Bishops, Pristes, ministers and other, whome
God hath set in place of gouernment.   For God hath appoynted them, as Shepheards, as guiders, and Patrons of his
people, to direct them, to keepe them, to defend them in his
true worship, and right seruice, and, if they will bee wander-
ing from him, eyther by errour in Religion, or by wickednesse
in life, to instruct and teach them, and by all meanes that may
bee, to call them home againe: or if they will not bee ruled,
by authoritie to bridle and restraine them, yea, and by punishment to correct them.   Now if the watchmen and Shepheards,
that is, the guiders and rulers of the people, whether they bee
Ciuill or Ecclesiasticall, shall waxe ignorant, and vnskilfull of
their dueties, shall become negligent and carelesse of their
charge, shall be giuen ouer to voluptuousnesse and pleasure
of the world, or to couetousnesse, bribery, and extortion, to
iniurie, violence and oppression, and in their gouernment
seeke their owne pleasure and commoditie, and nothing regarde, either the benefite of the people, or the glory of God:
then (I say) these speeches of the Prophets lie directly against

them, and may well bee vsed to declare the wrath of God towards them. But what maketh this to the purpose pretended? how hangeth this reason together? God by the Prophets earnestly reproueth the gouernours, aswell of the Church as of the commonweale, for their wickednesse, couetousnesse, and extortion: therefore bishops, and ecclesiasticall ministers may not by the word of God enioy temporall lands and possessions. Or this, God blameth the priestes of the olde lawe for couetousnesse: therefore the bishops of the church of Christ may haue no Landes and possessions. They that wil be perswaded with such reasons, wil easily be caried away into error. If it were certaine, and did of necessitie followe, that all they, which haue great liuings and possessions, must needes bee couetous: then happily this reasoning might bee of some force. But I thinke there is no reasonable man that wil graunt it, and therefore this reasoning is without all reason. The Priests and Leuites, as themselues confesse, had no great lands and lordships, and yet wee finde them often in the Prophets accused and blamed for couetous- nesse: therefore it is not the want of temporall lands and liuings, that can bring a poore heart and contented minde, voide of couetousnes. We see often as couetous and greedie hearts in meane mens bosoms, as in the greatest landed Lordes in a whole Country. And on the contrary part, wee finde in them that haue veric great possessions, as humble, and as contented mindes, and as farre from the affection of couetousnesse, as in the meanest man that is.

Neither doth pouerty bring a contented mind: neither great possessions causeth couetousnes.

Iob was of great wealth and possessions, and yet wee reade not that hee was euer blamed for couetousnesse: Yea hee beareth witnesse of his owne free heart and liberality, and sayth, "Hee neuer set his heart vpon Gold, nor saide   Iob. 31. to the wedge of Golde, Thou art my hope, nor reioyced of beeing rich, nor because his hande had founde abundance, &c." *Abraham* also was rich, and God had blessed him with great

possessions, and yet surely his heart was farre from the loue
of money.

Ioseph had no small possessions, and was in place of honour,
and yet fewe in the meanest state or degree did euer keepe a
more humble heart, or put lesse delight in honour and riches
then hee did.   I might say the same of *Dauid,* though a king,
and of *Daniel,* though in very high estate, and in great authoritie, and as it may bee thought, in liuing proportionable to the
same.   When Christ in the gospell had saide, that it was " as
vnpossible for a rich man to enter into heauen, as for
a Camell to goe through the eie of a needle," and
his Disciples had wondered at that saying, hee aunswered :
" That which is with man impossible, is possible with
God."   Albeit mans corrupt nature, as it is generally giuen
to all ill, so it is chiefely inclined to couetousnesse, and
delight of the worlde : Yet the good grace of Gods holy
Spirite doeth so guide the hearts of his faythfull, that in the
midst of greatest abundaunce of his plentifull blessings, they
can retaine the feare of God, and contempt of the worlde.
Wherefore, it is great rashnesse and presumption, to condemne all them to bee giuen ouer to couetousnesse and delight
of the worlde, whom they see by the state of the Commonweale, or by the goodnesse of the Prince, or by any other
lawfull and iust meanes to haue landes and possessions, or
wealth and riches, according to their state.   Such persons as
so rashly deeme of other, may seeme rather to bewray the
sicknesse and ill disposition of their owne mindes, then to
iudge truely of them, whome in such case they condemne.
It is the pouertie and humblenesse of Spirite and minde, it
is not the pouertie and basenesse of outwarde estate
and condition, vnto the which Christ imputeth Gods blessings.
If couetousnesse be " a desire to haue, for feare of want and
scarcitie," as some learned men haue defined it : then is a poore
estate to a corrupt minde a greater spurre to couetousnesse,
then lands and plentie of liuing can bee.   Before that bishops

Matt. 19.
Mar. 10.

Luke 13.

Matth. 5.

and Ministers had any Landes assigned vnto them, yea, when they were yet vnder the Crosse of persecution in the time of *Cyprian :* ^wee^ reade that hee findeth great fault with many bishops, which leauing the care of their charge, went from place to place, vsing vnlaw- full meanes to get riches, practising vsurie, and by craft and subtiltie getting other mens lands from them.

Serm. de. lapsis August. de bap. lib. 2. Not much more then 200. yeeres after Christs ascension.

In like manner complaine *Hierome, Augustine, Chrysostome, Basile,* and other auncient Writers, and Histories of their time. Yea, in the Apostles time wee see some giuen ouer to the worlde, and ledde away with couetousnesse, when Ministers as yet liued onely vpon the free beneuolence of the people. Wherefore, it is not pouertie, or a lowe and con- temptible state in the face of the worlde, that can bring a satisfied and contented Spirite. And surely I am of this opinion, that a poore and straight state of liuing in the Minis- terie, especially in these dayes, woulde bee a greater cause of euill and inconuenience in the church, and a more vehement temptation to carry away their mindes from the care of their Office, then nowe their ample and large liuings are. I coulde, and will (when God shall giue occasion) declare good reason of this my opinion : which for some considerations I thinke good at this time to lette passe.

If our bishops and other chiefe of the Cleargie, beeing nowe in the state of our Church, by the prouidence of God, and singular goodnes of our Prince so amplie prouided for, be so vnthankfull vnto God, and so giuen ouer to the worlde, as they are bitterly accused to bee : surely their fault must needes bee the greater, neyther will I, or any other that feareth God, in that poynt excuse them, but pray to God (if there bee any such) that these odious reportes spredde vpon them, may bee a meanes to put them in remembraunce of their duety, and to amend. But vndoubtedly (good Chris- tians) I speak it with my heart, mee thinketh I doe foresee

at hand those dayes, and that time, when GOD of his iustice
will both condignly rewarde our vnthankfull receiuing of his
Gospell, and contempt of his Ministers, and also giue to them
iust occasion to declare vnto their aduersaries and cuill
speakers, that they are not such bond-slaues of the world, nor
bee so lead away captiue with the lusts of the flesh, as they
are defamed. Yea, I thinke, this crosse of contempt, slaunder
and reproch, that nowe is layd vpon them, is Gods fatherlie
admonition to warne them : and as it were a meane to prepare them to that day that is comming : which day vndoubtedly will bee " a day of wrath, a day of trouble and
heauinesse, a day of vtter destruction and misery, a darke and
gloomy day, a cloudie and stormie day, a day of the trumpet
and of the alarme against the strong cities. On that day will
Sophon. 1.2. the Lord search Hierusalem with Lanthorns, and
visite them which continue in their dregges, and say, Tush,
the Lorde will doe no euill. Therefore their goods shall be
spoiled, their houses shall bee laid waste, they shall build
gay houses, and not dwell in them, they shall plant vineyardes
but not drinke the wine thereof. In that day the Lorde will
visite the Princes, and Kinges Children, and all such as weare
gay cloathing, and all those that leape ouer the thresholde so
proudly, and fill their Lordes houses with robberie, and false-
hoode. On that day God will bring the people into such
vexation, that they shall goe about like blinde men, and all
because they haue sinned against the Lord, and contemned
his worde." Wherefore, I most heartily pray vnto God, that
we altogether, both Prince and people, honourable and worshipfull, ecclesiasticall and lay persons, preachers and hearers,
may ioine together in the faythfull remembrance of that day,
and to consider that it can not bee farre from vs, and therefore that it is full time, and more then time, to turne vnto
God by hearty repentance, and faithfull receiuing of his worde.
For surelie the sentences of the Prophets, of some men par-
tially and affectionately applied to the Clergy and ministers

only, do in right and true meaning touch vs all, of al states
and conditions. But I wil returne to my matter againe.

The testimonie of *Malachy* vsed of some to like effect, as
the other before, I haue purposely left to this place : because
it speaketh particularly of priestes, and therefore will they
haue it more nighly to touch our bishops &c. " And now
O yee Priestes" (sayth the Prophet) " this com- _{Mala. 2.}
mandement is for you, &c." And a litle after, making comparison betweene *Leui* and the Priests of that time, " The
Law of trueth was in his mouth, and there was no iniquitie
founde in his lippes, he walked with me in peace and in
equitie, and hee turned many from their iniquitie : but yee
haue gone out of the way, yee haue caused many to fall by
the Lawe, ye haue corrupted the couenant of Leui, sayth the
Lord of hosts : therefore haue I made you despised, and vile
before the people." These wordes of the Prophet doe so
touch our bishops and clergie men, if they be so euill as they
are made, as all sentences wherein the Prophets blame the
Priests of their time, doe touch euill Ministers of the Church :
but howe they eyther specially nippe our bishoppes, as it is
thought, or any thing pertaine to the proofe of the principall
matter, or reproouing of Preachers liuings by Landes, I see
not. In deede this sentence of *Malachi* might bee rightly
vsed against the Pope and his Prelates, which neglecting the
whole dutie of Gods ministers, both in preaching and liuing,
stayed themselues vpon the authoritie of Saint *Peter*, and of
succession, as though the Spirite of God had beene bounde
to their succession, though they taught and liued neuer so
corruptly. For so in deede did these priestes whom *Malachi*
reprooueth : they neglected the true worshippe of God, and
yet woulde they bee accompted his good and true Priestes,
because they were of the tribe of *Leui*, with whom _{Num. 25.}
God had made his couenant, that hee and his seede shoulde
haue the office of the high priesthood for euer. But *Malachi*
sayth they haue broken the couenant on their part.

That our Bishops and Ministers doe not challenge to holde
by succession, it is most euident: their whole doctrine and
preaching is contrary: they vnderstand and teach, that neither
they, nor any other can haue Gods fauour so annexed and
tyed to them, but that, if they leaue their dueties by Gods
worde prescribed, they must in his sight leese the preheminence of his Ministers, and bee subiect to his wrath and
punishment.   They knowe, and declare to all men, that the
couenant on the behalfe of *Leui*, that is, on the behalfe of the
Ministers of God to be perfourmed, consisteth in these three
branches: by preaching to teache the right way of saluation,
and to sette foorth the true worshippe of God: to keepe peace
and quietnesse in the Church of God: and thirdly, by honest
life to bee example vnto others.

These branches of the couenant, if our Bishops and Preachers haue corrupted and broken, they haue to answere for it
before God, and their punishment will be exceeding grieuous.

As for their doctrine, I am right sure, and (in the feare of
GOD I speake it) will hazarde my life to trye it, that all their
enemies shall neuer bee able so to prooue it, but that it shall
bee founde sincere and true: so that I doubt not, but GOD
him selfe will beare witnesse with them, as hee did with *Leui*,
that *trueth is in their mouth*, and (as touching their doctrine)
no iniquitie founde in their lippes.   For they doe both teache
the trueth according to the Scriptures, sincerely, and confound
the errours of the Antichristian Church, learnedly and truely.

They therfore that speake so much against them, may
seeme lesse to regarde this part of their obseruing the couenant of *Leui*, then the duetie of Christians requireth.   But I
trust, our mercifull God will fauourably consider it, and
beare with some other their imperfections in them.   I pray
God wee be not lighted into that time, that men haue itching
eares, and can like no Preachers, but such as clawe their
affections, and feede their fantasies in vanities and newe
deuises.   The couenant of peace they keepe also, liuing in

vnitie and peace among themselues, and studying (so much as they can) by teaching, and by good order, to keepe it among other. And that is no small cause of their misliking at this time, because they, being in some place of gouernment, according to their dueties striue to represse those, which by vntemperate zeale seeke to disturbe the Church, and to giue cause of faction and disorder, by altering things externall in a setled and refourmed state.

As touching their liues and conuersations according to the Lawe of God, (as before I haue said) if I must iudge according to that I knowe, I must thinke the best, because I know no ill. Though there be imperfections in some things: if men woulde charitablie consider, in what time wee liue, and whose Messengers they are, and somewhat withall descend into their owne bosomes, and lay their owne dueties before their eyes: I thinke surely they would iudge of them more christianly then many doe.

Obiection.

" But they will say, that according to the wordes of Malachie, God sheweth his iudgement against them for their wickednesse, because hee hath made them so contemptible, so vile and despised before all the people: for (say they) wee may see howe all men loath and disdaine them."

Answere.

It must needes be true (I confesse) that *Malachi* spake of the Priests of his time: but I doe not take it to be alwayes an vnfallible token of euill Priests and Ministers, or a certaine signe of Gods displeasure towarde them, when the people doe hate, disdaine, and contemne them. I see more commonly in the Scriptures, that it is a token of vnthankefull, stubborne, and hard-hearted people, which smally regarde the worde of God, and therefore also mislike his Ministers. *Elias, Micheas, Amos,* and other Prophets were smally esteemed, you

knowe, among the Israelites, *Esay, Ieremie, Ezechiel*, were
euen of as small credite and estimation among the Iewes.   It
may appeare so to bee, seeing *Esay* signified, that they lilled
out their tongues, in mocking of him, and other of his time.
And I am sure, you knowe the fauour and entertainement that
the Apostles had also among the same people.   I trust then
you will not say it was a token of naughtie and corrupt Ministers, or of Gods iust iudgement against them: for they were
the right and true Prophets, Apostles, and Messengers of
God, and yet were in great hatred and misliking of them
that thought themselues to be the people of God.

It may be surely, and in deede I thinke it to be very true,
that God hath touched our bishops and Preachers with this
scourge of ignominie and reproch, for their slackenesse and
negligence in their office: And I pray God they may take
this mercifull warning, and shunne his greater plagues.   But
I must say withall, as Christ sayth of the *Galileans*, whose
Luke 13.   blood *Pilate* mixed with their sacrifice, and of them
vpon whome the Tower of *Siloe* fel: "Doe you thinke, that
they onely are sinners? nay I say vnto you, if you do not
repent, you shall all taste of the same sharpe iustice."   If
God punish his Ministers, hee will not suffer the other
vntouched.   "Nowe the time is come that the iudgement
1 Pet. 4.   beginneth at the house of God," and if God punish
those that hee sent with his worde, what will hee doe to them
that vnthankfully receiue his worde ?

Proofes out
of the Newe
Testament
against the
rich liuings
of Bishops.   THAT this matter of Eeclesiasticall mens liuings
may seeme to be of great importance, and such in
deede as God hath had much care of in all times: as
before it hath beene countenanced by the Lawe and
Prophets, so must it nowe bee drawen also through the whole
course of the newe Testament.   Yea, whatsoeuer is vsed,
eyther of Christ himselfe or of his Apostles, against couetousnesse, or the loue and care of this worlde, and delight- of

this life; all that, either by fayre meanes or foule, is brought into this fort, to batter and shake the lands and possessions of Bishoppes, and other of the Cleargie.

And first men are willed, to call to remembrance the example of Christ our Sauiour, his birth, the state of his life, the choise of his apostles, and his perpetuall doctrine, exhorting to pouerty and contempt of the worlde. "His parents" (say they) "were poore, and liued by an bandie craft, descended of a stocke and kinred growen altogether out of credite in the worlde: insteede of a princely chamber, born in an Oxe stall, wrapped in poore clothes, in steede of white and fine linnen: layed in a cribbe for want of a rich cradle: and in place of worthie seruitours, hee had the presence of an Oxe and an Asse. And that hee might shewe himselfe to delight in pouertie and contempt of the worlde, his natiuitie was first reuealed vnto poore Shepheards watching their flockes. As hee was borne, so was hee bredde, in the poore and contemptible Towne of *Nazareth*, out of the which *Nathaniel* thought nothing worthy credite coulde come: in which Towne, as it may bee thought, by the exercise of an bandie craft, hee liued in obedience of *Ioseph*, and of his Mother. Such as his birth and breeding was, such was the state of his liuing, when the full time of his dispensation came: for hee was not borne to any Landes or possessions, neyther had hee any great wealth and riches to susteine him selfe, yea, not so much as an house to put his heade in, but was maynteined by the almes as it were, and by the charitable deuotion of certaine wealthie women of Galiley, and other godly persons. His Apostles that he chose to followe him, and to bee the Ministers of his kingdome, he tooke not out of the state of Princes, noble men, or great and rich Lordes, with Landes and dominions: but out of the pore state, and condition of fishers, Tent-makers, and toule-gatherers. And thus may wee see our Lorde and Christ altogether wrapped in pouerty, and besette on euery side with the base and contemptible state of the world."

But to what purpose is all this alleaged ?   Forsooth, that wee may vnderstande, that it is not lawfull for such as bee guides of the Lordes flocke, to liue in any other state, then in that the Lorde gaue example of : " For whosoeuer seeketh Christ" (say they) " in other state and sort, then hee gaue example of, seeketh not Christ, but Antichrist and the pompe of the world."   So that the sense and effect of the reason is this : Christ was borne, bredde, and liued in pouertie, and chose vnto him Apostles of poore condition : therefore bishoppes and Ministers of the Church must haue no Landes or possessions, but stay them selues in like poore state, as Christ and his Apostles did.   I doe not. frame this argument (good Reader) of purpose to cauill, but to admonish thee o the principall state, and that considering the proofe to bee naked in it selfe, thou mayest the better iudge of the strength thereof.

Surely, I will hencefoorth cease to marueile at the wrested and violent interpretations that Hermites, Monkes and friers haue made vpon the scriptures, to iustifie and set foorth their superstitious life of voluntarie pouertie and forsaking the world : seeing professors of the gospel, to maintaine their new doctrines, take vpon themselues the like liberty and boldnesse, in abusing the holy Scriptures and worde of God : And yet surely it doth grieue mee, and make my heart bleede to see it.   What shall the aduersarie thinke of our dealing with the Scriptures ?   Surely, that wee doe in so earnest manner pull them from the interpretation of the Fathers and of the Church, to the ende that by applying them according to our owne fantasies, we may set foorth and seeme to iustifie to the worlde, what doctrine soeuer we shall thinke good our selues : And so shall this bee an occasion to discredite all the particular doctrines of the Gospell, which hitherto, as well this Church of England, as other Churches reformed haue taught.   But to vnderstand the weight of this reason before vsed against the wealthie liuings of our Clergie, wee must

trie it by a right and iust balance : that is, by the true meaning of the holy Ghost.   First therefore, let vs consider the
causes of Christes pouertie, and of the choyce of such Apostles, which in mine opinion are two :   The one is the The right
causes of
necessitie of our redemption : the other is an ex- Christes po-
ample and iust instruction set foorth vnto Christians. uertie and
his Apos-
As touching the first, when the certaine purpose of tles.
God had determined that his sonne shoulde come into the
worlde, to worke the redemption of mankinde, and his
deliueraunce from sinne : necessarie it was for him to satisfie
the iustice of God, in sustaining all those difficulties and
punishmentes, that were due to man for sinne : that is to
say, affliction, ignominie, reproch, contempt, pouertie, and
all worldly troubles and miseries, and last of all, death.
This is it that the Prophet *Esay* spake of long before.
Hee is despised and abhorred of men, hee is such a   Esai. 53.
man as hath good experience of sorowes and infirmities: we
reckned him so vile that we hidde our faces from him.   Howbeit hee onely hath taken our infirmities on him, and borne
our paynes.   Yet wee did iudge him as though he were
plagued and cast downe of God."   This is that humiliation
and debasing of himselfe that *Paul* speaketh of, when hee
sayth, " Hee being in the forme of God, thought it   Phil. 2.
no robberie to bee equall with God, but made him selfe of no
reputation, taking on him the forme of a seruant, and made in
the likenesse of men, and founde in figure as a man, hee
humbled himselfe, made obedient vnto death, euen to the
death of the Crosse."   These places (good Christians) declare
vnto vs, both the pouerty and contemptible state of Christ
here in earth, and also the very roote and principall cause
thereof: that is, the saluation of mankinde.   The sonne of
God became the sonne of man, that he might make vs the
children of God : he was borne a weake and tender babe, that
hee might make vs strong men in him : hee was tied in
swadling bands, that hee might loose and deliuer vs from the

bondes of the fraile and sinfull flesh : he was wrapped in
poore clowtes, that with the garment of his innocencie, he
might hide our nakednes : he was borne and liued poorly,
that he might make vs rich and plentiful in him : he was a
stranger in the worlde, and had not an house to put his head
in, that he might purchase for vs a citie and heritage in
heauen : he was borne vnder bondage, and payed tribute to
Cæsar, that hee might deliuer vs from the tyranny of Hel :
he was debased euen to the company of bruite beasts, that
hee might bring vs to the glorious company of Angels : he
laye in hay in a Crib, that hee might procure euerlasting
food for our soules : finally, hee was accused of sin and put
to most cruel death, that we being iustified by his merite,
might appeare innocent in the sight of God. These be the
sweete and comfortable cogitations that good Christians should
conceiue vpon the consideration of Christs poore and base
state in this life. For pouerty in Christ was not so much
for exāple of life, as to satisfie a punishment due to sinne.
Riches is the good blessing and gift of God : but pouerty
came in at the same doore that death did, that is, by the disobedience of our first father. We may not therefore thinke
with Monks and Friers, that pouertie in it self is a more holy
state of liuing, then wealth and riches is. But of that more
hereafter. Now let vs consider what maner of pouerty this
was in Christ. Christ was in himself exceeding rich, both
as the son of God, and as the sonne of man. As God, he
Ioh. 16.   had al things common with his father. " All things
that my father hath" (saith he) " are mine." And againe,
Iohn 17.   " All thine are mine, and mine are thine." As
touching his humanitie, hee is likewise of great possessions.
Psal. 2.   For his Father sayth vnto him, " Desire of me, and
I shal giue thee the heathen for thine inheritance, and the
vttermost parts of the earth for thy possession." How hapned
it then, yᵗ Christ being in right Lord of so great possessions,
became in the time of his dispensation, almost in the state of

a beggar? certainly, *quia ipse voluit*, because he would himself. For he that filleth heaue and earth, was born in an
Oxe stale in *Bethleem :* he that had al power in the whole
world, was a banished person for a certaine time in *Egypt :*
he that feedeth with sustenance man and beast, foule and fish,
partly by labor gate his liuing, partly was fed with the
liberalitie of other. He that prouideth apparel for al things,
hung naked vpon the Crosse : he that sitteth in heauen as his
throne, and hath the earth for his footestoole, at an other
mans charge was buried and layde in a strange Sepulchre.
Christes pouertie therfore was willing, not of any necessitie
of holynesse, as I haue said, but to beare that which for sinne
was due to vs. Nowe, I pray you, marke the strength of the
former reason. Christ, to sustaine the punishment due to our
sinnes, liued in great pouertie and humilitie in this worlde :
therefore Bishops and Ministers of the Church, of necessitie,
must liue in pouerty, and not haue any wealthy liuings, by
landes or otherwise. I trust they that haue care of their
consciences, will not easily be led to any perswasion by such
reasons. They will say, Christ did this also for our example.
I graunt, in some respect he did so : By his example he
teacheth vs humblenesse and modestie, that we may not bee
loath to doe those things, that he did, for the benefit and
commoditie of our christian brother. If we so swel with
pride, that in respect of our Noblenesse, or birth, or great
estate in the worlde, wee disdaine other, and thinke our poore
neighbour doeth vs iniurie, if hee in respect of christian
brotherhood require of vs a benefit for his better reliefe : then
is it time for vs, to behold the Sonne of God lying poorly
in a cribbe or manger, betweene beastes : who, although he
were God eternall with his Father, and by his mother borne
of the most noble family of manie Kinges and Prophets : yet
for our sake hee did so humble and debase himselfe, that he
came in so poore and vile condition before men. Furthermore, Christ by his example, hath as it were consecrated

pouertie, trouble, miserie, and affliction, that they may not
be accompted tokēs of the wrath of God, or such things as
doe hinder true piety and bolines, or let the saluation of our
soules.   For as mans nature doeth abhorre al afflictions : so
chiefly doe men thinke pouertie and neede, to be not onely
one of the greatest miseries that can happen to man, but also
hatefull to God himselfe.   Thus we see men commonly to
think of such, as are any way fallen into pouerty and misery.
Let *Iob* hereof be an example.   In this cause also it is expedient for vs to looke vpon our poore Christ, and to set him
before our eyes, that wee may both more patiently beare
these thinges, when for Gods cause they light vpon vs, and
more charitably iudge of other, whom God therewith toucheth :
yea, it is good to teach vs to pull downe our brissles, when we
waxe proude of those giftes of plenty and riches, that God
hath giuen vs.   Thus you see what profit the example of
Christes pouerty bringeth : but I pray you, to whō is Christ
an example ? to bishops and Ministers only ? did he liue in
poore and miserable state for Ministers only ? did he die for
their sinnes onely ? God forbid.   He was borne, he liued, he
died for all mankind, and all faithful haue the fruit of this
his birth, his life, and his death.   Therefore the example of
Christs life must stretch further thē to Bishops and Ministers.
It is a farre truer argument to say, Christ liued a simple and
poore life, while he was here on earth : therefore all Christians ought to liue in the same manner that he did, then to
apply the same onely to Ministers and Ecclesiasticall persons,
Therefore I will all Christians to beware of this hereticall and
Anabaptisticall assertion :

  " Whosoeuer seeketh Christ in other state and sort then
hee gaue example of, seeketh not Christ, but Antichrist, and
the pompe of the world."

  For if this sentence be applied to the example of the poore
state of Christ, it is the very ground of Anabaptisticall communitie, and that none can be saued, but such as renounce

all their goods and possessions. Albeit the example of Christ in this place be applied to Ministers onely : yet in trueth it appertaineth to all other faithfull, as wel as to them. And if the Argument shal be counted good now : hereafter, with as good likelihood, and farre truer interpretation, it may be vsed against al that shal truely professe Christ. As touching that Christ chose so simple Apostles, and of so poore estate, *Saint Paul* sheweth the reason and cause thereof. " Brethren" (saith hee) " you see your calling, howe 1. Cor. 4. that not many wise men after the flesh, not many mightie, not many Noble are called : but God hath chosen the foolish things to confound the wise, and the weake things to confounde the mightie, and vnnoble things of the world, and things that are despised, God hath chosen, and things which are not, to bring to nought things that are, that no flesh shoulde glorie in his presence." If Christ in the entrance of his Kingdome, going about to subdue the world to his knowledge, shoulde haue vsed the seruice and ministerie of Princes, Noblemen, great, wealthie, and rich men : or of such as had bene wise, learned, and eloquent, and politique : the glorie of his mightie conquest would haue bene attributed to the power and might, to the wealth and riches, to the wisdome and learning, to the eloquence and policie of those, which had bene his ministers, and so the glorie of God in that worke of mans saluation, should haue bene diminished. Therefore God, to shewe his power in heauenly things, ouerthwarted the wisedome of the world, and chose his Apostles poore, vnnoble, simple, vn-learned, without eloquēce, farre from the cunning, wisedome, and policie of the world, and by them and by their preaching in fewe yeeres wanne the whole worlde to his knowledge, and defaced the kingdome of Sathan, consisting in superstition, idolatrie, and wickednesse. And in deede, this order of Gods woorking by these poore and vnlearned men, preuailed against all the Nobilitie, the honour, the power, the might, the wisedome, the policie, learning, the eloquence of the

worlde, so that it might bee truely sayde, " Non est potentia;
non est prudentia, non est consilium aduersus Dominum."
But what hereof is to bee concluded to this purpose? forsooth, " that as Christ thought it fittest to chuse onely poore
men to his Apostles, and sent them abroade without any stay
of Liuing in the worlde : so hee thinketh it meetest, that his
Ministers in his Church in all times and places should be in
poore estate, and not to haue any wealth or riches."

It is good to consider this reason also, that you be not
more ledde with it, then the weight and force of it requireth. The office of the Apostles was, to goe from
Countrey to Countrey, from place to place, to plant Churches
vnto God, so that they could not haue any certaine stay of
Liuing : It is not therefore like reason, that in a setled
Church where the Gospel is receiued, the Ministers and
Preachers thereof may haue no certaine forme of Liuing appoynted them, eyther by land or otherwise. As Christ chose
his Apostles poore, so hee chose them simple, and vnlearned,
without eloquence, or any kinde of knowledge, that his glorie
thereby might the more be set foorth : Shall we therefore inferre thereupon, that it is fittest alwayes for the Ministers of
the Church, to bee simple, without learning, eloquence, and
knowledge? It is well knowen that the Anabaptists, and
some other phanaticall spirits troubling the reformed Churches
beyond the seas, vpon the same example of the Apostles haue
gathered, that learning and knowledge is not to bee respected
in the choyce of Ministers : because God needeth no such
helpes to set forth his Gospel, yea they say that learning and
eloquence are perillous instruments, to corrupt the simplicitie
of the Gospel, and to giue countenance to errour. Wherefore
such persons doe vsually admit among them to the Ministerie handicrafts men, and such as challenge to themselues the
spirite of God onely, without further knowledge. But the
godly, I doubt not, vnderstand that all things neither can, nor
ought to be like in the state of the Church beginning and

vnder persecution, and in the Church setled and liuing in peace and quietnesse.

The Ministers and Preachers of our Church, beside the example of Christ and his Apostles liuing in pouertie, are willed diligently to looke into the perpetual doctrine, which Christ in all the Euangelists doeth teach them, touching the state of their liuing, namely against riches, couetousnesse, the glorie of the world, and care of this life. To this doctrine apperteyneth that which Christ teacheth. *Matth.* 6. That they " shoulde not hoarde vp treasure for themselues Matth. 6. vpon earth, where thieues breake through and steale Luke 12. them, but that they should lay vp treasures in heauen &c. That they can not serue two masters, God and Mammon :" That they shoulde not " bee carefull for their life, what they shoulde cate, what they shoulde drinke, or what apparell they shoulde put on : but cast all their care vpon God, and seeke his kingdome, and the righteousnesse thereof," for that it is heathenish carefully to seeke after those other things, which God of himselfe will plentifully cast vpon his : that riches, and the pleasures and cares of this life, are resembled to *thornes* which choake vp the good seede of Gods Matth. 13. word, and make that it cannot prosper : " That it is Mar. 4.
Luk. 8.
as vnpossible for a rich man to enter into the king- Matth. 19. dome of God, as for a Camell to goe through the eye Luk. 6. of a needle :" That hee cryeth out, " woe to them Luk. 12. that are full, for they shall bee hungrie : and to them that bee rich, because they haue alreadie their comfort and consolation :" yea, he willeth them to "sell all that they haue, and giue vnto the poore," with a number of other places : wherein hee instructing his disciples and followers, vtterly willeth them to renounce this world and the treasures thereof. Whereupon it is thought it may be very well concluded, that the Ministers of the Church may not haue any wealthy liuings and especially by landes and lordships : and therefore that our Bishops bee not the true followers of Christ, but walke in the steps of

Antichrist. Surely our Sauiour Christ did see, that as the
perpetuall enemie of mankinde did continually seeke by all
wayes to drawe men from God : so he did not vse any meane
more commonly, then by honour, glorie, riches and wealth.
And therefore when he saw that Christ coulde not by other
temptations bee ouercome, he assaulted him with ambition and
desire of principalitie, honour, and lordship.   This temptation
is therefore the more dangerous, because mans corrupt nature
is of it selfe greatly inclined to the loue of the world and
earthly pleasures.   Wherefore I cannot denie, but that our
carefull and louing sauiour did often and in many places warne
his disciples, and by them all vs, to beware of this working of
Sathan, and so much as they could, to shunne his snares.   But
shall wee thinke therefore, that hee condemneth principalitie,
lordship, dominion, wealth, riches, landes, in them that bee
his true and faithfull followers ? No surely : for that is the
full grounde of the Anabaptists doctrine, to be shunned of al
right christians.   And yet before I begin to answere this, I
must needes protest it is a queisie and dangerous matter, to
speake of wealth and riches of the world, for feare of mistaking, either on the one part, or on the other.   For whatsoeuer a man shall say in that case, among the vngodly will
bee drawen according to their priuate affections.

The rich, when they heare the possession of riches and the
right vse of them defended, by and by if Gods special grace
stay them not, waxe more confident and secure, and with contempt and disdaine of other, thinke themselues free maisters
and Lordes of Gods giftes, to vse them euen at their owne
pleasure, and to the fulfilling of their own fleshly fantasies.
On the cōtrary part, when they that bee poore and destitute
of those giftes, shall heare the rich blamed for the abuse ol
their wealth, and signification giuen, that what soeuer is aboue
the sufficient maintenance of their own state, is due vnto the
poore : they also as rashly enter into iudgement, and condemne al rich men as couetous, as greedy gatherers, as thieues

and extortioners, and cruel detainers of that which by Gods
law is due to others. Some there be also, that thinke all vse
and administration of riches to be dangerous, and to bring no
smal hinderance to the saluation of mens soules. Vnto which
perswasion, the phanaticall spirites of the Anabaptists adde
more difficultie, not onely taking away al possession and
property, and allowing a *Platonicall* community of al things:
but also denying superioritie, and Lordship and dominion,
and bringing in a general equalitie, most dangerous tò the
societie of man. Wherefore, it behooueth mee so to speake
of riches and possessions, that (so neere as I can) none of
these offences may be iustly taken.

First therefore to begin, we may not thinke that Christ
in them that be his, condemneth either the possession or the
right vse of Lordship, dominion, lāds, riches, money and such
like: for they are the good gifts of God, wherewith he
blesseth his people, as the whole course of the Scriptures
declare. " The blessing of the Lord" (saith *Salo-* _{Pro. 10.}
mon) " maketh rich, and bringeth no sorowe of heart with it."
" Blessèd is the man" (sayth *Dauid*) " that feareth _{Psal. 112.}
the Lord &c. his seede shall be mightie vpon earth, the
generation of the faithfull shall be blessed, riches and plente-
ousnesse shall be in his house &c." And againe, " His horne
shall bee exalted with honour: the vngodlie shal see it, and it
shall grieue them." Therefore wee see many of the good
saints of God, that haue bene indued with great riches and
possessions, as *Abraham* the Father of the faithful, *Iob*,
Ioseph, Dauid, Salomon, Daniel. And in the new Testament,
*Nicodemus, Ioseph of Arimathea, Lazarus of Bethania, Mary
Magdalene, Sergius Paulus* Proconsul of *Cypres*, the *Centurion*,
and manie other. Wee may not thinke therefore, that Christ
condemneth the giftes and blessinges of God, or the vse of
them, in his seruauntes. And that the trueth taken out of
the Scriptures may be of more authoritie with you, I wil
let you vnderstand it by the wordes of the ancient and

learned Fathers : so shal you perceiue, it is not my inter-
Hierom ad pretation, but theirs.   And first *Hieroms,* " *Ioseph,*
Saluinam. which both in pouertie and riches, gaue triall of his
vertues, and was both a seruant and a maister, teacheth vs the
freedome of the minde.   Was hee not next vnto *Pharao,*
adorned in royal furniture? and yet was he so beloued of
God, that aboue al the *Patriarkes,* hee was a Father of two
Tribes.   *Daniel,* and the three young men, had such rule
ouer the power and riches of Babylon, that in apparell they
serued Nabuchodonosor, but in minde they serued God.
Mardocheus and Hester, in the middest of their purple, silke,
and precious iewels, ouercame pride with humilitie, and were
of such worthinesse, that they being Captiues, bare rule ouer
Conquerours.   My speech tendeth to this end, that I may
declare that this young man that I speake of, had kinred of
royall blood, aboundance of riches, and ornamentes of honour
and power, as matter and instrumentes of vertue vnto him."
S. *Augustine* disputeth this question, writing to *Hillarius.*
Epist. 89. " Thou writest vnto me," (saieth hee) " that some say,
that a rich man remaining in his wealth, cannot enter into the
kingdome of God, vnlesse that hee sell all that he hath, and that
it shal not profit, though in his wealth he keep the commandements of God.   Our fathers, Abraham, Isaac and Iacob, vnderstood not this reasoning : for they all had no smal riches, as
the holy Scriptures witnesse, &c."

And least that some might say, that those holie men were
vnder the old Testament, and vnderstood not the perfect law
that Christ giueth, when he sayeth, " Goe and sel al that thou
Matt. 19.   hast, and giue it vnto the poore, and thou shalt haue
treasure in heauen," the same *Augustine* addeth, " If they
will say so, they may speake with some reason : but let them
heare the whole, lette them marke the whole : they may not
in one parte open their eares, and in an other part stoppe
them.   Hee spake that to one that asked him, What shall
I doe to obtayne euerlasting life ? and Christes aunswere is

not, If thou wilt obtaine euerlasting life, sell all that thou hast : but, if thou wilt haue euerlasting life, keepe the Commaundementes, &c. And a little after, our good Maister doeth make a distinction betweene the keeping of the Commandements, and that other rule of perfectnesse." For in the one part he saide, " If thou wilt enter into life, keepe the Commaundements :" And in the other hee saide, " If thou wilt bee perfect, sell all thou hast, and come and followe me." " How therefore can we denie, that rich men, although they haue not the perfection, shall come into euerlasting life, if they keepe the Commaundementes, and giue, that it may be giuen vnto them ?" And in the ende he concludeth his reason in this manner, after hee hath spoken of the vncharitable minde of the riche glutton. " This pride" (sayeth hee) " wherewith this riche man did contemne the poore iust *Lazarus* lying before his gates, and that trust that hee did put in his riches, whereby he thought himselfe a blessed man, because of his purple, silke, and sumptuous feastes, did bring him to the tormentes of hell, and not his riches." By which wordes of *Augustine*, it may appeare, it is not riches, Landes and possessions, that GOD condemneth in his seruauntes, but the euill vse of them. Wherefore the same *Augustine* sayeth, " When the Lorde had sayde, It is easier for a Psal. 51. Camell to passe thorowe the eye of a needle, then for a riche man to enter into the kingdome of GOD : and the Apostles maruailing thereat, answered, Who then can bee saued ? What respected they I pray you ? surely, *non facultates, sed cupiditates* : not great substaunce, but greedie desire of them."

Immediately hee sheweth, that riche Abraham had preheminence in heauen, before poore Lazarus. " Reade the Scriptures," (saieth hee) " and thou shalt find riche Abraham, that thou maiest knowe, it is not riches that is punished. Abraham had great store of golde, siluer, cattell and housholde. Hee was rich, and yet was poore Lazarus brought into his bosome : the poore man in the bosome of the rich, or rather both rich before God, and both poore in spirite &c. Marke this, that you do not commonly blame rich men, or put trust in poore estate. For if a man should not put his trust in riches, much lesse in pouertie." To the like effect speaketh *Hierome*, " Is it euill to haue riches iustly gotten, so that a man giue thankes to God that gaue them? No, but cuil it is to put a mans trust in riches. For in another Psalme it is sayde, If riches come vnto thee, set not thine heart vpon them. A man may haue riches for his necessitie, but hee may not possesse them to delight in them." Well therefore

Homil. 2. saith *Chrysostome*, " As I haue said, wine is not ill, ad popul. Antioch. but drunkennesse is ill : so say I, riches are not ill, but couetousnesse is ill. A rich man is one thing, and a Homil. 13. couetous man is another. A couetous man cannot ad popul. Antioch. be a rich man." And to the same meaning in another place : " Let vs not falsely accuse either riches or pouertie : for both riches and pouertie are such, as, if we will our selues, bring instruments of vertue. Let vs therefore so frame our selues, that we iudge not so, as we may seeme to blame Gods giftes, but the euill affections of men." The Homil. ad. same *Chrysostome*, " Riches" (saith hee) " killeth popul. Antioch. 58. not : but to be a slaue to riches, killeth, and to loue couetousnesse. And againe, the rich glutton was punished, not because he was rich, but because he wanted mercie. For it may be, that one hauing riches, ioyned with mercie, may attaine to all goodnesse." By these testimonies of the ancient learned Fathers, grounded vpon the examples and doctrine of the Scriptures, you may perceiue, that riches are the good gift and blessing of God : that the Saintes of God haue vsed and enioied them : that wealth and possessions of them selues are not hinderous to pietie and godlinesse, but rather instruments of vertue and meanes to come to heauen : that God doeth not condemne them in his seruants : that it is not a man voyde of lands and possessions, but a heart voyd of couetousnesse that Christ desireth : that it is not riches, but the

sinfull affections of men that he reproueth. How then can
it bee prooued by Christes doctrine, that any state of his disciples or faithfull seruants and followers, ought not to haue
landes, possessions, or ample and large liuings? or that they
be by his word so expresly prohibited, that neither Prince
may suffer it without danger, nor faithfull Minister with good
conscience inioy them? Let vs somewhat better consider
the particular places of this doctrine of Christ, whereon
this assertion is grounded. Where Christ saith, " Hoarde not
vp treasures for your selues on earth," he saith not, Matth. 6.
you shall haue no treasures. To haue treasures, and to hoarde
treasures, be diuerse. Hee that hoardeth vp treasures, sheweth that hee hath a carefull minde to keepe them : but a man
may possesse treasures, and yet with free heart bee willing to
imploy them to godly purposes : like as *Iob* did, who had his
riches alwayes readie to pleasure other. When Christ affirmeth, that " where a mans treasure is, there is his heart:" by
treasure, he meaneth not the possession of riches simply, but
hee meaneth that, wherein a man reposeth his chiefe treasure
and felicitie to consist. And in deede it cannot be, but that
hee that esteemeth his chiefe felicitie in any thing, doeth set
his heart also vpon it. Hee that setteth his felicitie in honour
and dignitie, hath his heart possessed with ambition. Hee
that thinketh it to bee in worldly pleasure, hath his whole
minde on playing, banqueting, feasting and riot. He that reposeth his felicitie in building, giueth ouer his cogitations vnto
that. So hee that iudgeth his blessednes in this life to be in
possession of riches and lands, vndoubtedly cannot but haue
his heart fastened vpō them. And seeing that God chalengeth
vnto himselfe all our whole heart, and our whole soule and
minde, they that so do, must needs offend God most grieuously, and make of their riches their God, and so as *S. Paul*
saith, become very idolaters. Therfore if either Ecclesiastical persons, or lay men, do so set their minds on riches,
this place nighly toucheth them. When Christ saith, " No

man can serue two masters &c. and ye cannot serue God and
Mammon," Marke, I pray you, that he saith not: " No man can
serue God and get riches." For godly men both haue before
time, and now may get lands and riches, procured either by
heritage or by gift, or by any other lawfull meanes. Con-
Gene. 32. sider the Patriarch *Iacob :* who passed *Iordane* onely
with a staffe in his hand, and in the time of his liuing in a
strange Countrey, gate so great riches, as he returned with
two great cōpanies of seruants and cattel. And yet vndoubtedly this Patriarch was a good Christian, being saued by the
same religion that his Grandfather *Abraham* was, the father of
the faithfull, who with reioycing sawe the day of Christ.
Neither doth Christ say, " No man can serue God and possesse
riches." For as it is said before, *Abraham, Iob,* and *Ioseph,*
possessed great wealth and riches, and yet vndoubtedly, truely
and sincerely serued God. Riches are the blessings of God,
neither may any more rightly or with better title possesse
them, then the good and faithfull seruants of God. What
saith Christ then? forsooth, "No man can serue two masters :"
or " No man can serue God and Mammon." Getting or pos-
sessing is one thing, and *seruing* is another. *Seruing* pre-
supposeth a mastership or dominion in him that is serued.
Hee that *serueth riches,* acknowledgeth them to be his Lord
and Master. *Seruitude* or bondage hath this condition, that
hee wholly obey his master: that night and day he doe
nothing but that pleaseth his master : that hee shall be contented to haue the displeasure of al other, so that he may haue
the good will of his master : Finally, whatsoeuer a seruant
doth, what labour soeuer he taketh, whatsoeuer by his paines
he getteth, he doth it to the vse and behalfe of his master.
Whosoeuer is such a bondslaue to riches, is a traitour
reuolted from God, neither can it be possible for him to serue
God. Such a seruing of *Mammon* it is that Christ in this
place rebuketh, with which seruice, the seruice of God cannot
be joyned.

But it were great rashnesse to thinke all that possesse lands, lordships, and riches, of necessitie to be subiect to this slauish seruice of *Mammon*, as some men vncharitably iudge of the Bishops and Clergie of England. Ioseph of *Arimathea* was a rich man, and yet in time of great perill did more seruice to Christ, then all his poore Apostles which had so little to leese. It is written in the Euangelists, " When euen was come, there came a rich man from Arimathea named Ioseph, Matt. 27. which also himselfe was Iesus his disciple. He went to Pilate and begged the body of Iesus. Then Pilate commanded the bodie to bee deliuered, and when Ioseph had taken the body, hee wrapped it in a cleane linen cloth, and layde him in a newe tombe &c." Consider the circumstances of the historie : weigh the danger of the time : call to remembrance how many thinges might haue hindered, and staied *Ioseph* from this doing, and you shall perceiue that possession of landes and riches, may be ioyned with a free and faithful seruice, yea, often times more faithful, then pouerty and base estate in the worlde. Good Christians therefore may not condemne as slaues and seruants to Antichrist, al such as haue lands and possessions. Experience in England (God be thanked) hath taught, whē a number of poore Priests and Ministers reuolted frō Christ to the *Mammon* their Masse, that many which had the greatest liuing in this lād, were most readie not onely to bee banished their countrey, but also to shead their blood, and giue their liues to serue faithfully their Lord and maister Christ: and I doubt not, wil doe againe, if euer God giue the occasion. Iudge therefore more charitably of your Ministers and Preachers, (O ye English professours) which haue seene these things with your eies, and know not how soon, to the sorow of your own hearts, ye may see the same againe. But they which at this day mislike the state of bishops, and doe write or speake against them, are those persons, which in the time of affliction, eyther were not borne, or els were very yong, and therfore haue no sense of that temptation, which that persecution did then bring. As God of his goodnes granteth

vs now some *Halcion* dayes : so I beseech him against that
day to giue vs the grace of his mighty spirit, so that we may
haue the like constancie.

It is further alledged out of Christs doctrine, that when he
Matth. 22. answered the Pharisees, *Matt.* 22. he giueth a plaine
cōmandement, that landes and possessions should be at the
pleasure of the Prince, and that Ministers of the church ought
to giue them vp vnto him. For this he saith, " Giue to
Cæsar, that which is Cæsars, and to God, that is Gods."
" But" (say they) " all temporall landes are *Cæsars*, therefore
they ought to giue them vnto *Cæsar :* and our *Cæsar* is our
gracious Prince and Soueraigne."

Truely it woulde make any Christian heart to lament in
these dayes, to see Gods holy word so miserably drawen,
racked, and pulled in sunder from the true meaning thereof.
If the Bishops, and other of the Cleargy of England did
grudge or murmure to haue their landes and Liuinges to bee
tributarie to the Prince, and subiect to all taxes and seruices,
that by the lawes of this realm may be, either to the maintenance of her person, or to the defence of our countrey : Or
if they did challenge such an immunitie or exemption from the
authoritie of the Prince, as the Pope and his Cleargy did : Or
if they did finde themselues grieued to bee punished by the
Prince for the breach of her Lawes, as the *Donatists* in old time
did, and some now in our age doe : If they were such enemies to
Princes and Gouernours, as they woulde exempt thē out of the
state of true christianitie, and of the Church of God, and make
them onelie to serue their turne in euill affaires : then in deede
did this place make strongly against them. But I trust the
Clergie of Englande, are with all good men out of the suspition of these pointes. They are as willing and readie at all
times to bee contributarie, as any other subiectes are : they
claime no exemption from her authoritie : they willingly sub-
mitte themselues to her correction : they humbly acknowledge
their obedience in all thinges, that anie Christian prince may
require : and this doe they principally for conscience sake,

because it is the ordinaunce and commaundement of God : but much moued thereto also, as men, in consideration of their owne state, which next vnder God dependeth of her Maiestie. Seing therfore the hand of God hath more straightly bounde them vnto her, then other common subiects : I doubt not, but she willingly hath, and shall haue all dueties of obedience at their handes, that any Christian subiects by the word of God are bound vnto. Neither are they in any feare that her Maiestie will presse them to any thing, which shall not stande with the glorie of God, and furtherance of the Gospel. But how these words of Christ before mentioned, doe commaund them presently to yeeld vp into her Maiesties hands sueh lands and possessiōs, as by the graūt of her goodnes, and by the law of this realm they nowe inioy, indeede I see not. If such a prince shall come (as I trust in my daies neuer to see) that shal put them to this choise, either to forgo their landes and liuings, or to loose the free course of the Gospell : it is before declared, what their duty is to do therin. And I doubt not, but in the late time of persecutiō, there were many of them that would haue bin glad with al the veines in their heartes, by that choice to haue enioyed in this Realme the freedom of their consciences, though they had bin put to as pore estate, as possibly men might haue liued in. But how that christiā princes are warranted, either by this place of the gospel, or by any part of the worde of God, so hardly to deale with the state of the ministery, I haue not as yet learned, though it be in these daies by some boldely affirmed. *Amb.* hath a worthy saying, wherin he plainly noteth both what a christiā prince may do in these things that appertain vnto the church, and how a godly bishop should in that case behaue himselfe. " When it was proposed vnto me" (saith Epist. lib. 5. he) " that I should deliuer the plate or vessel of the in Orat. contra Auxentium. church, I made this answeare: If there were any thing required that was my owne, either land, house, gold or siluer beeing of my owne priuate right, that I would willingly

deliuer it: but that I coulde not pull anie thing from the
Church of God. And moreouer I said, that in so doing I
had regard to the Emperours safetie, because it was not profitable either for me to deliuer it, or for him to receiue it.
Let him receiue the wordes of a free Minister of God: If he
will do that is for his own safetie, let him forbeare to doe
Christ iniurie." By these words yee may perceiue, both that
Ambrose woulde not deliuer the Church-goods, nor that he
thought it safe for the Emperour to require it. The mening
of Christ is in those words, to teach his to put a differēce
between the duty that they owe to the Prince, and that they
owe to God: and to declare, that within their due boundes,
they may both stand together. Therfore they that will
rightly follow Christ in this doctrine, must cōsider, in what
consisteth the duety towards a Prince or Magistrate, and
wherein resteth our duetie towards God. Wee˙ owe to the
Prince, honour, feare, and obedience: obedience (I say) in al
those things that are not against the worde of God and his
commandementes. Those things that God commaundeth, a
Christian Prince can not forbid: Those things that God forbiddeth, no Prince hath authority to command. But such
things as be external, and by Gods word left indifferent, the
Prince by his authoritie may so by lawe dispose, either in
cōmanding, or forbidding, as in wisedome and discretion he
shall thinke to make most to the glory of God, and to the
good and safe state of his people. Among these things external, I think lands, goods, and possessions to bee, and therefore that the same ought to be subiect to taxe and tribute in
such sort, as the lawes and state of the country requireth: yea,
and if there shall happen in any country a magistrate, which
by violence and extortion shall wrest more vnto him of the
lands and substance of the people, then law and right requireth: I see no cause warranted by Gods worde, that the
inferiour subiects can rebell, or resist the prince therein, but
that they shal euidently shew thēselues to resist the ordi-

nāce of God. For they haue not the sworde of correction committed into their hande, and often times God by euil princes correcteth the sinnes of the people. Wherefore, if subiects resist the hard dealings euen of euill Magistrates, they doe in that respect striue against God himselfe, who will not suffer it vnpunished. Wherefore *Ieremy* willeth the Iewes to submit themselues to the obedience of *Nabuchodo-* Ierem. 28. *nosor*, a wicked and cruell king: and *Baruch* teacheth Baruc. 1. them to pray for the good estate of the saide *Nabuchodonosor* and his nephewe *Balthasar*. And Saint *Peter* and 1. Pet. 1. saint *Paul*, will Christian subiects not onely to bee Rom. 13. obedient to the heathen tyrants, which were in their 1. Tim. 2. time, as *Nero*, and such other: but also to make most humble and heartie praiers for them, that his people might liue vnder them a quiet and peaceable life, with all godlinesse and honestie. *Tertullian* also sheweth the same to haue Tertulli. ad beene the practise of the primitiue Church, euen Scapulam. toward the enemies and cruell persecutours of the faith of Christ.

"A Christian" (saith he) "is enemie to none, and least of all to the Emperour, whome hee knowing to be ordeined of God, must of necessitie loue, reuerence, and honour, and wish to be in safetie together with the whole Romaine Empire." And againe, "We pray for all Emperours, that God Tertul. woulde graunt vnto them long life, prosperous Apolog. reigne, strong armies, faithfull Counsell, obedient Subiects. &c."

We may learne then by this, that Christian duetie of a subiect consisteth in louing, in reuerencing, in obeying the Prince and Magistrate in all things, that lawfully he command- eth: and in those things that he commandeth vnlawfully, not by violence to resist him, though the same touch our goods, our lands, yea and our life also. As touching our duetie toward God, wee owe vnto him, our selues whollie, both bodie and soule, and all thinges and partes to the same appertaining, according to that his Lawe requireth, "Thou shalt loue God with all thy heart, with all thy soule, with all thy minde, and with thy whole power." For wee are his creatures, and hee is our Lorde and maker. But forasmuch as Princes, Magistrates, Rulers, Parents, Masters, and all superiours, haue a portion of Gods authoritie ouer vs, as his officers and Lieutenants in their callings: therefore God doeth permit vnto them some part also of his honour, but so farre, and in such things, and such maner as before is declared, retaining vnto himselfe our faith and religion, with all the partes of his diuine worship consisting in Spirite and in trueth, the calling vpon his blessed name, the confession of his holy trueth, and the obedience of his morall Lawe: which thinges hee doeth not make subiect to any Princes authoritie. And if any Prince or Magistrate by violence and crueltie shall breake into the boundes of our duetie towardes God, I say not that priuate subiects may by violence resist it: but surely they may not obey it, but rather yeelde into his hands, goods, Lands, Countrey, and life too. For so did the Prophet *Daniel :* so did the yong men his companions : so did the whole number of the martyrs of GOD, by whome the Church of Christ _{August de} increased as *Augustine* sayeth, *Non resistendo sed* _{Agon. Chri.} *perferendo*, not by resisting but by suffering. And _{Hierom. ad} *Hierome :* " The Church of Christ was founded by _{Theophil.} suffering reproch, by persecutions it increased, by martyrdomes it was crowned." To this end sayth *Tertullian* also, *Semen Euangelij Sanguis Martyrum.* This is the true doctrine of the wordes of Christ before mentioned, by which wee are taught to put a difference betweene our duetie towards God, and that we owe toward the Prince, yeelding to each that which is his : A doctrine most profitable and necessary to all Christian Churches and common weales. But who can gather of this, that the Ministers of the Church of Christ, liuing vnder a Christian Prince fauouring and defending the Gospell, must of necessitie giue vp into the Princes hands those landes and possessions, which by the graunt of the same

Prince and the Lawe of the Land is assigned vnto them ? For if the land be *Cæsars,* and therefore must be deliuered to *Cæsar:* then are all goods, *Cæsars,* and must be also yeelded into his hands.

God saue vs from Princes that will vse like violence and tyrannie toward our Landes, goods, and bodies, as these men vse to the word of God. I haue not as yet noted vnto you (good Christians) the very grounde of this corrupt interpretation of the doctrine of Christ, and the mischiefe that is hid vnder it. I pray you therefore consider, to whome doth Christ speake in al those places of his doctrine before mentioned ? Whome doth he teach ? whom doth he instruct, " that they shoulde not hoarde vp treasure vpon earth ? that they may not serue God and Mammon ? that they may not bee carefull what to eate and what to drinke ? that they must sell all that they haue and followe him ? that they must renounce all that they haue if they wil be his true Disciples? and lastly that they must yeelde to Cæsar that which is Cæsars ?" Are these things spoken to Ministers onely ? doeth Christs doctrine pertaine to Bishops and Ministers onely ? Is it his will that they onely shoulde followe his godly instructions and commaundements ? Then of likelihoode, as hee came onely to teach Ministers, and to be example of life to them alone : so hee came to saue Ministers onely. But what a wicked vanitie were it so to speake or thinke ?

Now if Christes doctrine be generall to all the faithfull, as in deede it is: (that beeing the true interpretation that they woulde haue to bee) it must of necessitie followe, that no true Christian can keepe lands and possessions, nor abide in any wealthie or rich estate: which is the very ground of the *Anabaptistes* doctrine, as all learned men doe knowe. In so much, that all the famous men, that in this our age haue expounded the Scriptures, or written against the *Anabaptistes,* doe note, that by this interpretation of the speeches of Christ before mentioned, they do ground their cōmunitie, and taking away

of proprietie and possession of goods, with sundry like other
doctrines.   We may see therefore, and it is time to take heed
of it, how Sathan, vnder pretences seeketh to thrust the Spirit
of the *Anabaptistes* and the groundes of their learning into this
Church of *England.*   The inconuenience then of this kinde of
reasoning is, either, that these sentences of the Gospel touch
bishops and Ministers onely, and all other are left free, which
is a very great absurdity: or else that the same doctrine
gathered out of these places in the same sense that they vse,
doth belong to all Christians, which with the *Anabaptists*
taketh away all proprietie and possessions of lands and goods,
and (as I haue before saide) bringeth in a Platonicall communitie.   I say not, that they which vse these places doe meane
it: but surely that inconuenience and daunger followeth vpon
it.   Therefore, they that haue any feare of God, ought to take
heed, that their immoderate stomack and affections against
bishops and other Ministers, doe not ouermuch blind them,
and carrie them away, eyther to the affirming, or to the main-
tayning of corrupt and daungerous doctrines, both to the
Church and common wealth.   If this their doctrine spread in
libelles, shall once become familiar vnto the common people
of this Realme: it may happily breed such a scab and daungerous sore, as al the cunning in this lande wil scant bee able
to beale it.   God send grace, that heede may be taken thereo
in time.

  They will say (I knowe) " That this is but a shift of Logike
that the false Sophisters the Bishops doe vse, to turne the
matter from themselues, when they say, that this doctrine o
Christ pertaineth to al Christians, aswel as to them: and wi
aske me howe they will auoyd those plain and euident word
that Christ speaketh to his Apostles and disciples onely, whe
hee sendeth them abroad two and two, to preach the kingdom
of God.   This (say they) doth belong to Ministers an
Preachers onelie."

Matth. 10.   " As ye goe, preach, saying, that the kingdome o

beauen is at hand: heale the sicke, clense the leapers, raise
the dead, cast out deuils, freely ye haue receiued, Mar. 3.
and freely giue you. Possesse not gold, nor silver, nor Luke 9.
money in your purses, nor scrip toward your iourney, neither
two coates, neither shoes, nor yet a staffe. For the workman
is worthy of his meate." These wordes, I must confesse, doe
not appertaine generally to all Christians, no more doe they
generally to al ministers and preachers of all times and places.
Is it euill in it selfe to haue golde or siluer? or to haue a
staffe on the way to walke with? or to weare shooes to saue
his feete in iourneying? I thinke there is no Christian that
will so iudge. Christ himselfe had a purse, wherein *Iudas*
carried money for his prouision, and hee suffered certaine rich
women to goe with him, and to minister to him and to his Disciples. *Peter* also bare a sworde, and ware sandalles on his
feete, when the Angell bade him put on his sandalles. And
Paule writing to *Timothie*, willeth him to bring his cloake
with him, although vndoubtedly hee had another garment
before. Wee must consider then what it is that Christ in this
place meaneth, seeing neither himselfe nor his Apostles did
obserue it according to the strictnesse of the letter.

There bee some that say these precepts bee personall, and
for a time onelie, not generall or perpetuall: for that which
goeth before may seeme to take away the continuance of these
precepts, " Go not in the way of the Gentiles, but to the lost
sheepe of the house of Israel." Which precept the Apostles
at this time obserued, but afterward they preached the Gospel
vnto al the nations of the earth: so doe they thinke, that
Christ, for the time of this message onelie, commaunded them
to possesse no golde nor siluer, &c. and from thencefoorth
that this commaundement was abrogated. This interpretation
I can not reiect as euill, or not pertinent to the meaning of
Christ. There bee also some hypocrites, and Pope-holie
persons, which will haue these preceptes perpetuall, and
builde thereon friery and monkish superstitiō: They wil not

touch any money: They wil weare no whole shooes: They
wil not haue a staffe to walke with, thinking that they shew
themselues the holy seruaunts of God therein. To this interpretation verie nighly commeth that, which these men vse tc
proue, that bishoppes and preachers may haue no landes noi
possessions, nor riches, no nor money, further then will barelj
prouide them meat, and drinke, and cloth, and whatsoeuei
is aboue, to be of superfluitie. Some other thinke, that Chrisi
in those woordes onely compareth the Ambassadours of othei
princes with his: as if he had sayde, I sende you foorth to
preach the kingdome of God: and the state of an ambassade
or message doeth require, that I shoulde deliuer vnto you
money, and all other like thinges conuenient for this voyage,
as princes vse to their Ambassadours: but deceiue not youi
selues: the maner of this message is diuers from such mes-
sages as ciuil princes vse. In ciuill ambassades, great furniture (I know) is thought co̅uenie̅t: but this message of mine
is such, as needeth no such matter to set it out. For th
maiestie of the thing it selfe, and the myracles that you shall
worke, shall sufficiently giue authoritie vnto it. This interpretation also I think not amisse: but in my opinion, and
that by the iudgement of some other learned men also, the
true and simple meaning of Christ was, to teach his Apostles
to put their trust and whole confidence vpon the prouidence
of God onelie, and for the better perswasion, would haue them
at this time to make triall thereof, and by experience to learne,
that though they haue nothing in the sight of the world tc
feede them, to helpe or to defend them: yet that hee wil sc
prouide for them, if they continue in their vocation and calling faithfully, that they shall want nothing: yea, that the
fowles of the aire shall rather feede them, then that they
shoulde lacke sustenance. That this was Christes meaning,
Luke 22.   it may appeare in Saint *Luke*, where he sayeth tc
his Apostles, "When I sent you forth without wallet oi
scrippe, or shooes, lacked you any thing? and they saide,

No. Then saide he vnto them, But nowe hee that hath a wallet, let him take it vp, and hee that hath none, let him sell his coate and buy a sworde." The Apostles vndoubtedly had great need of this instruction, and to be taught to put their whole trust in the prouidence of God, and to depende vppon that onelie. For he did see that in the execution of their office they shoulde bee cast into all the difficulties of this world, which either Satha or his ministers were able to raise against them. This lesson is very necessary also for all other Christians, but principally for the Ministers and preachers of the Gospel, whensoeuer God for the profession and teaching of his trueth shall cast them into the like difficulties. For if they doe not rest vpon that onely, they shall finde lands, possessions, power, authoritie, kinred, friendshippe, and al other helpes of this world, to be but as a broken staffe to leane vnto.

But what maketh this against that, that Ministers of the Church in the calme times of quietnesse, may enioy the benefites and liberalitie of good and gratious Princes, whome he hath appoynted as fosterers and nourishers of his Church and people, wherein soeuer those benefites of their liberalitie shall be imployed, bee it landes, possessions, goods, money, or any other maner of prouision ?

For further proofe of this matter against the wealthie state of the Cleargie, the example of S. *Peter* also is brought in, who sayeth in the *Actes* to the poore lame man, Actes 3. *Siluer and golde haue I none, &c.* Loe (say they) Sant *Peter* was a right Apostle, and was in so poore case, that hee had neither siluer nor gold, no not so much as he could bestowe a meane reliefe vpon a poore begger. His example should our rich Bishops and Preachers follow. And Saint *Paul* to *Timothie, Hauing foode and rayment, we shoulde therewith be content.*

" Here wee may learne (say they) what maner of liuing Ministers of the Church should haue, that is, so much onely, as will prouide them meate, drinke, and cloth: whatsoeuer is aboue, that is superfluity, and more then Gods word requireth." Who seeth not (good Christians) whereat these men shoote, and what state of the Ministerie, this earnest zeale that nowe is pretended, woulde settle in this Church? that is, more miserable and worse prouided for, then any other state of the lande beside. Those heartes wherein is true deuotion, and the right loue of the Gospell, are rather ouer bountifull toward the Preachers thereof, then too sparing. For they are thus affected, that they thinke nothing too deare for thē, yea, if it were possible, they would giue their eyes vnto them out of their heads, as *Paul* saith to the *Galathians*.

What spirite this is therefore that woulde so hardly pinch and wring the Ministers of the Church, it is euidently to be gathered. The principall purpose at the beginning was, to prooue that the Ministers might not by the word of God inioy any temporall landes: but nowe forsooth, through the goodnesse of their cause, in the vehemencie of their reasoning, and fulnesse of their proofe, it falleth out so, that Ministers may not haue so much as any peny in their purse to prouide them sustenance: but must liue vpon the charitable almes of the people, and content themselues with meate, drinke, and apparell onely, as the Apostles did. "For they are no spirituall men (say they) that haue temporall liuing." Yea, of the very tithes they ought to claime no more, then may serue them to meate, drinke, and cloth. And if the same be denied them, they may not by lawe sue for it. "For if their coate be _{Matth. 5.} taken from them, they should deliuer their cloake also."

This doctrine doeth very well iustifie the couetous and vncharitable dealings of many Parishioners, which partly by violence, partly by craftie meanes detaine from the Ministers their portion of tithes appoynted by the lawe. This doctrine giueth good countenance to corrupt patrons, who will not bestow their benefices, but by composition of a good part of the fruites to their owne vse and commoditie. And when the liuing shall be worth 100. poundes by the yeere, they will aske, whether thirtie or fourtie pounds be not a sufficient portion for the Parson? This dealing before time hath bene accounted little better, then sacrilege or simonie: but now it may be thought (if this doctrine be good and allowable) that it is lawfully done, and according to the word of God: yea, and that the Minister is a couetous worldling, and worthy great blame, that will not content himselfe with such a rate, as they willingly shall allowe him. What care they which thus reason haue, I will not say of the preaching of the Gospel, but of the state of learning and knowledge in the Church of Christ, all men may euidently perceiue. Either they iudge, as I haue before written at large, that men bee Angels without corruption, and will followe the course of learning for conscience sake, though there bee no hope of rewarde to allure them: or els they thinke, that God will miraculously giue knowledge to such as he shall incline to the Ministerie, as he did in the primitiue Church to his Apostles and other.

As touching the example of Saint *Peter,* it is before declared, what cause Christ respected in the choosing of so poore Apostles, and leauing them in so base state and condition of life: that is, that the worke of winning the whole world to the doctrine of saluation by so simple and poore instruments, as in the iudgement of men they seemed, might be the greater glorie to God, as Saynt *Paul* sayeth: Especially seeing hee did set them foorth, and furnish them with the heauenly riches of his holie spirite, that is to say, extraordinary knowledge, rare giftes of vertue, and power to worke myracles.

But vpon this extraordinarie dealing of God in the founding of his Church, to grounde a generall and perpetuall rule, to binde the Ministers of al places and times, is such maner vsing the Scriptures, as must needes breede great inconueniences among the people of God.

1. Tim. 6.   As for the words of Saint *Paul*, there is no man I thinke, but that hee may perceiue they are spoken generally, and not to Ministers onely, as they are in this place applied. Remember the place: viewe the circumstances: consider what goeth before, and what commeth after, and you shall vnderstand it to bee true. For Saint *Paul* there, speaketh to Matth. 6. the same purpose, that Christ doth *Matth.* 6. when he willeth men not to be carefull what to eate, what to drinke, or what to put on, but that they shoulde seeke the kingdome of GOD and the righteousnesse thereof, and all other things shoulde by the prouidence of God bee cast vnto them. So, I say, Saint *Paul* exhorteth men not to be in loue with the riches of this world, which they shall neuer cary away with them: that they shoulde not practise wicked waies to gaine, but account godlines their chief gaine and cōmoditie, holding themselues contented with those things that the necessity of nature requireth, that is, foode, and apparell: For whatsoeuer is aboue that, may seeme to bee superfluous. This wholesome doctrine, the spirit of God in the Scriptures doth often cast vpon the consciences of Christians, as a necessarie bridle, to stay the wicked affection of couetousnesse and greedie desire of the world, wherto the corruptiō of our nature is giuen. And yet he doeth not condemne riches, or a more plentifull life, as euill in it selfe. It is the heart, the minde, and the affection, that God would haue staied and kept vnder in his obedience, and not the forbearing of the externall creatures as before is at large declared. *Iob* in the middes of his greatest wealth had as poore and as contented a heart, as he that had a small liuing, and did no more exceede in gluttonie, or other riotous excesse, then hee did, which had not a peny more then to prouide meate, drinke and cloth. This doctrine, as it doeth generally pertaine to all Christians: so I denie not, but it very nighly and chiefly ought to touch Preachers and Ministers of the Church. Wherefore I must and doe confesse, that so much as our Bishops and Clergie

want of the perfourmance heereof, they want of that perfection
that by the worde of God they shoulde haue. But howe can
it bee prooued heereby, that they may not haue more ample
or large allowance then shall suffice them for necessarie foode
and apparell? In deede that contentation of mind they
should haue, whensoeuer God calleth them to that necessitie,
yea and when they be in their wealthiest state that any condition of a Christian common weale doth giue them, they ought
not in those things to exceed, but to keepe that moderation
that godlines requireth: and whatsouer is aboue that, they are
bound in conscience to see godly and honestly bestowed, or
else they grieuously offende God, and giue euill example to
other. This rule (as I haue said) pertaineth in like maner to
all christians: and therefore it can no more follow vpon this,
that the lands and liuings of ministers must be taken from
them, because it bringeth superfluitie vnto them and more then
the necessitie of nature requireth, then you can conclude the
same against all other Christians that haue more ample lands
and liuings then will suffice them to the like purpose. As I
haue said before, so say I now again, If our bishops and other
clergy men, imploy the ouerplus of their large and plentifull
liuings vnto euill and naughty vses, neither I nor any other can
therein defend them.

For the better vnderstanding of my aunswere to these
places, and of the imperfect manner of reasoning vsed by the
aduersary: it behoueth to consider, that God in his worde
layeth downe a perfect measure of his iustice, and an absolute
rule of that life that Christians shoulde leade. As for example, when hee sayth in the Law, "Thou shalt loue the Lorde
thy God with all thy heart, with all thy soule, with all thy
minde, with all thy power, and thy neighbour as thy selfe:"
This commaundement requireth, that all the parts and members of our soule inwardly, and our bodie and goods outwardly, should be bent and giuen ouer to the setting foorth of
the glory of God. Our *heart* is the roote of our affections:

therefore we are commaunded to loue or hate nothing, to feare or hope for nothing, to desire or shun nothing, not to be sory for any thing, nor reioyce in any thing, but onely in God and his glory. By our *soule*, is meant all the course of our life: our infancie, our young age, our middle age, and our old age. Wherefore in this it is required, that the whole time of our life, from the beginning of our birth to the houre of our death, shoulde bee imployed to the seruice of God. Our *minde* comprehendeth our reason and vnderstanding: so that by that branche, wee are taught that our vnderstanding, our reason, and all the cogitations of our minde should bee occupied in nothing, but in the loue of God. Our *power* noteth all the strength and sences of our body, and the abilitie of worldly substance and outwarde giftes of God. So that there is nothing apperteining to vs, eyther inwardly, or outwardly, (as I haue saide) but God wholly requireth the same fo his seruice: and if wee doe fayle therein, wee offend his iustice, and want of that perfect rule of life that is prescribed vnto vs: Insomuch that if the mercie of God in Christ our Sauiour helpe not, wee deserue for the same euerlasting damnation. To the declaration of the latter part of this rule, " that wee should loue our neighbour as our selfe," apperteineth the doctrine of Christ, *Matth.* 5. " that we should not so much as once bee mooued with anger toward our neighbour, that wee should not looke vpon a woman to lust after her, that wee should not onely loue our neighbour as our selfe, but that we should loue our enemies, blesse them that curse vs, doe good to them that hate vs, pray for them that persecute vs, &c."

As for our money, lands, goods and possessions, wee should haue our mindes so litle giuen to them, and our hearts so smally set vpon them, that we nothing at all should care for them further, then that they may bee vnto vs, either instruments of vertue, or necessary helps of our fraile life. Yea, there is nothing so nigh, nothing so deere vnto vs by Christes rule, eyther eye, or hande, or foote, or whatsoeuer it bee, but we should cut it off, and cast it from vs, if it be a let or hinderance vnto vs to enter into the kingdom of God. Finally, our bodies being here in this vale of miserie, our minds, and hearts and conuersations should be in heauen: "they that haue wiues, as though they had none: they that weepe, as though they wept not: they that reioyce, as though they reioyced not: they that buy, as though they possessed not: they that vse this worlde, as though they vsed it not." 1. Cor. 7.

To this rule of Christian perfection, appertaine all those sentences and exhortations of Christ and of his Apostles, which before you haue heard alledged, tending all to this ende, to pull away the hearts of men from the loue of riches and care of this worlde, that they may set the same wholly vpon God. This rule is layde downe not onely for Ministers of the Church, as though they onely were the seruants of God, but also for all other faithful Christians, whom it bindeth as streightly as it doeth the Ministers. For it is a marke, vnto which they both should direct their whole indeuours.

They therefore that will apply this rule to some one state of men, and not to other, fal into like error as Monkes and Friers did, dreaming a more straite order by God to be appoynted to one, then to another. The Minister so much as he lacketh of this perfection, so much is hee indebted and in daunger vnto God: And if he flye not to the mercie of God purchased by the merite of Christ to wash away that want and imperfection, vndoubtedly there resteth nothing, but eternall damnation.

Nowe, as I haue sayde of the Minister, so must I say of all Christians beside. Therefore out of this doctrine is no particular application to bee made more to one state then to another, but onely this, that ministers, because of their calling, should shew themselues to come neerer to this marke, then other. Where the errour in reasoning is, you may nowe by this perceiue, which consisteth in two points. First, that the branches of the rule of Christian perfection generally

giuen to all, are applied onely to Ministers of the Church, as
speciall precepts to binde them: And secondly, that the per-
forming of this rule is more imputed (as the Monkes and
Friers did) to the outwarde refusing of Gods creatures, then
the brideling of the affections and humble contentation of the
mind before God.

By this corrupt manner of reasoning in these dayes, are
framed sundry daungerous arguments against the state of the
Ministerie heere nowe with vs in England.   As for example,
"Our Bishops and Ministers are euill men: they aunswere
not the perfect rule, that is prescribed vnto them by the worde
of God: therefore they shoulde bee deposed, their state
altered, and their Lands and liuings taken into the Princes
hands, or be otherwise imploied as it shall be thought good."

The daunger of this argument will be easily perceiued, if
you apply the same to other states, as thus: "Princes, Magistrates and noble men are euill, they do not fulfill that rule
of right and perfect gouernment that the worde of God
requireth: therefore pull them downe, set other in their
places, or alter their state cleane."

This is a seditious and perillous argument, especially when
common and inferior subiects, not hauing authoritie, shall
take vpon them to bee iudges in such cases, as nowe they doe
against bishops.

With this manner of reasoning (as I haue before noted) the
Deuill filleth the heads and hearts of his troublesome instru-
ments, when hee intendeth to worke mischiefe, eyther in the
Church of God, or in the state of any common weale.

This manner of arguments they alwayes vse, which for
priuate respects, pretend generall reformations or alterations
in the state of a Church or Countrey, wherein they liue.   Let
the bishops and Cleargie of England haue such iudges and
triall, as the word of God requireth, and euer hath beene vsed
in the Church of Christ: yea, or such as other states woulde
thinke reasonable and indifferent for them selues in their

calling: and then, on Gods name, let them abide the hazard of the sentence eyther with them or against them, and the daunger of such penaltie as in iustice and equitie may be assigned. Another daungerous Argument is this: "Bishops and Preachers by Christ are commaunded not to bee careful for the world, not to hoord vp treasures in earth, yea to renounce all they haue and follow Christ: therefore they ought not to haue any lands or Lordships, or great and weal‑thie Liuings, but to be contented with meate, drinke and cloth. &c." The hardnesse of this reason will be the better vnder‑standed, if the like bee applyed to some other persons.

" Noble men and gentlemen, if they wil bee right and true Christians, by Gods worde are commaunded not to be care‑full for the worlde, not to hoord vp riches heere on the earth, yea to renounce all that they haue, and followe Christ: there‑fore they may not haue so great and ample liuings more then other, but shall content themselues with such a moderate por‑tion, as may tollerably maynteine them, in seeing the ad‑ministration of iustice in their countreyes, and the residue that nowe is spent in gaming and vnnecessarie pompe, and vanitie of the worlde, to be imployed to the maintenance of a great nomber of the Princes subiects, and people of God, that are not able in meane estate to liue." For in such case were the noble men and Gentlemen of the Israelites called *Principes familiarum*, the Princes and chiefe of each tribe and familie among the people of God.

A many of such factious and seditious arguments may in like manner be framed, more meete for rebels, then for good subiects or faithfull Christians, which I do in this place for good considerations omitte. For if they shoulde bee so countenaunced with particular allegations of the Scriptures, and furnished with such learning and examples of histories, as factious heades are able to deuise: happily they woulde carrie as much credite, and drawe as great a number of followers and mainteiners, as nowe the like dealing doeth against the

Clergie. I will not therefore tarrie any longer in this point.
I haue set foorth vnto you an example or two nakedly and
barely, to this ende onely, if it might bee possible, to open the
eyes of some, which seeme in part to bee blinded eyther with
affection against bishops, or with a desire to worke and bring
to passe some speciall drift and purpose that they haue deuised : for what cause, it may be more easily by wise men
coniectured, then safely by mee layde downe in writing.

For the further examining of this matter, and that it may
be the better vnderstanded, whether ecclesiasticall men may
How Mini- with safe consciences enioy the state of their liuings
sters were by landes or no, Let vs briefely consider the condi-
maintained
from the tion of the Church, and howe Ministers haue beene
beginning. mainteined from the beginning, euen to this day.
And heere I must protest, that the Histories and writers,
especially such as bee of credite, are so imperfect in this
point, as the trueth must bee gathered by coniecture of certaine braunches, rather then by any discourse in their writing.

For the space of the first three hundred yeeres after Christ,
it is well knowen to all such as haue looked into the Ecclesiasticall Histories, that it was almost in continuall persecution
vnder heathen tyrantes, which with all indeuour sought meanes
to oppresse Christian Religion, and the true professours thereof. Wherefore in all that time it was not possible for the
church to haue any setled state, by Landes or certaine
reuenewe to maintaine the Ministers thereof : but they were
sustained onely by the liberall contribution of godlie persons,
collected at certaine times for that and other like Christian
vses.

Lib. 4. epi. 5. For Saint *Cyprian* signifieth, that to certaine persons appointed to the office of readers, hee distributed the
measure of gifts and distributions, as were assigned to the
Canon. 5. Priestes. The Canons attributed to the Apostles,
make mention of oblations and the first fruites to bee brought
home to the house of the bishoppe, beside such thinges as

were offered in the Church. *Origen* somewhat more straightly
seemeth to require the tenthes and first fruites of such increase as Christians haue by the blessing of God : his wordes
bee these. "It is comely and profitable, that the first fruits
should be offered to the Priests of the Gospell also, Homil. 11.
for so the Lord disposed, that he that preacheth the in Numer.
gospell, should liue by the Gospell. And as this is good and
comely : so contrariwise, it is euill and vncomely, that one that
worshippeth God, and commeth into the church, knowing that
the Priestes attend on the Altar, and serue the worde of
God, and ministerie of the Church, should not offer vnto the
Priests the firstlings of those fruites that God giueth by bringing foorth his sunne and seasonable showers vpon them. For
such a soule seemeth not to mee to haue any remembrance of
God, or to thinke, that it is God that giueth those fruites."

It may appeare also, that euen in this time the Church had
certaine houses allotted to their Bishops. For when *Paulus
Samosatenus*, after his deposition, would not depart out of the
house that belonged to the Church, it was appoynted by
the authoritie of the Emperour *Aurelius*, that he Euseb. ec-
should bee remoued from it, and the house assigned clesiast.hist.
lib. 7. cap.
vnto him, to whom the Bishops of *Italie* did agree 30.
in doctrine. *Origen* also mentioneth certaine rentes and
reuenues to the Church. "Many of vs" (sayeth he) " haue
neede of this warning, that wee bee both faithfull, Orig. tract.
and also wise," *ad dispensandos Ecclesiæ redditus,* in Matt. 31.
" to bestowe the rents of the Church."

And one *Petrus de Natalibus* writeth, that in the time of
Vrbane bishop of *Rome*, about two hundred twentie and sixe
yeeres after Christ, the Church first beganne to possesse landes
towarde the finding of the Ministers. Certaine it is, that many
godly disposed persons, notwithstanding they were letted by
the crueltie of tyrantes, euen in that time gaue large and ample
giftes vnto the Church, not onely in money and plate, but as it
is to bee gathered, in reuenue also. For *Optatus Mileuitanus*

K

Opt. lib. 1. writeth, that *Mensurius* Bishop of *Carthage* before *Cecilianus*, when hee was sent for to the Emperour, fearing that hee should returne no more agayne, left in the custodie of certaine persons *Ornamenta plurima et aurea et argentea,* " many ornaments of gold and siluer." The restoring of which ornamentes and iewels afterwarde, was one great occasion of the schisme of the *Donatists*, as the same *Optatus* sheweth. Wherefore it may appeare, the Church was not in those dayes so poore and needie, as some men woulde haue vs thinke it was : though it were then vnder heathenish and cruel tyrants, with all extremitie forbidding, that any persons should giue eyther goodes or Landes to the releefe of it.   *Sabellicus*

Ennead. 7. writeth, that in the time of *Maxentius* the Emperour,
lib. 8.   one *Lucina* a noble and rich gentlewoman of *Rome,* appoynted the Church of *Rome* to bee heire vnto all her substance and possessions.   Which, when that cruell tyrant vnderstoode, hee for the time banished her out of the Citie.   But when *Constantine* that good and first Christian Emperour, vn-

Lib. 1. de   dertooke the defence and maintenance of Christian
sacrosancto religion, he not only liberally bestowed vpon the
eccles.   Church himselfe, but by lawe made it free, to all that woulde giue any thing vnto the Church, were it in Landes

Lib. 16. Cod. or otherwise.   Which lawe *Valentinianus, Theodosius,*
Theod.   and other afterwarde confirmed, nor euer was it abridged but by *Iulian* the Apostata.   A copie of one decree of

Lib. 10. cap. *Constantine* is in *Eusebius*.   " Those thinges that be-
5.   long to the right of other, we will not onely not to haue retayned, but plainly to be restored.   Wherefore our will and pleasure is, that so soone as thou shalt receiue these our letters, if there be any goods belonging to the Catholike Church of Christians, eyther in cities, or other places, taken in possession by the eitzens, or by any other, that the same presently be restored in like right, as before they had it.   See therefore that all things, eyther houses, or gardens, or whatsoeuer, bee with speede restored to the Church againe."   By this meanes,

not only the Emperors themselues gaue both lands and many other riche giftes, but also sundry other rich and godly persons. *Constantine* gaue lands in the countrey about *Sabine*, and an house and a garden at *Rome*. The same *Constantine* out of the tribute of euery citie, gaue a portion to the Churches for the maintenance of their Ministers, and established them to continue as a Law for euer. _{Sabell. Ennead. 7. lib. 8.} _{Sozom. lib. 1. cap. 8.}

Eusebius writeth, that beside many other benefites (as contribution of corne, building of Churches, &c.) he graunted to all Ecclesiastical persons, free immunitie of all seruices and taxes, sauing only for their lands. For the lands of the Church were subiect to tribute, as other were, by an ordinance made by the sonnes of the forenamed *Constantine*. This may appeare also by *Ambrose*, writing of the second *Valentinian*. "If he require tribute, we denie it not : the lands of the Church do pay tribute." The Church then had lands, and that a good while before *Ambrose* his time, which was about the yeere of our Lord three hundred sixtie and eight. Yea, *Ambrose* himselfe liued by his owne lands being Bishop. Therefore it may appeare hee did not thinke it to be against the worde of God, for a Bishoppe or Minister of the Church to liue vpon the reuenewe of landes. _{Euseb. ecles. hist.13. ca. 7.} _{Lege tertia Cod. de episc. & clericis.} _{Lib. epist 5. in orat. cont. Auxentium.}

After the time of *Constantine*, the wealth of the Church increased, as well in landes as other substance and prouision, not only by the gifts of Emperors, Kings, and Queenes, but partly also (as I haue said) by the deuotion of other godly persons, who oftentimes left to the vse of the Church, eyther a great part, or their whole substance and possessions, partly by the gift of Bishops themselues, partly by other Ecclesiasticall persons, which, because they were not maried, nor had issue or heires, were by order bound to leaue vnto the church, all their possessions, both lands and goods. _{Basil. epist. 140.}

Sometime also by the punishment of offendors.   For it is read
that one *Bassus* a gentleman falsely accused *Sixtus* bishoppe
of *Rome*, and when *Sixtus* had cleared himselfe in a
synode of Bishops, *Bassus*, for his slaunderous accusation, was banished, and his landes giuen vnto the
Church.   The same *Sixtus* gaue landes vnto the Church himselfe also.   *Crescentius* a noble man gaue vnto the Church o
Rome all his substance, and a manour in *Sicilie* called *Ar-
gianum*.   *Eudotia* the Empresse, wife to *Theodosius,*
adorned the Bishops house at *Constantinople*, and
gaue vnto it a yeerely reuenue.   By the counsell at *Berythe*
it may appeare, the Church of *Edessa* had rentes, manours
woods, and plate set with pretious stones, &c.   This state of
wealth the church grewe vnto, not much more then in the
space of one hundred yeeres after it pleased God to giuc peace
vnto it from outwarde and Heathenish enemies : and yet in the
meane time had it other tempestes and bitter stormes of ad-
uersitie, that did more hinder deuotion and godlinesse, then the
bloody persecutions of the Emperors did : as namely the troubles raysed by the *Arian* heretikes, by the space of many
yeres, and especially in *Asia*, *Greece*, and all the East parts of
the world.   And shortly thereupon folowed the horrible inuasion of the *Goths*, *Vandals*, *Herules*, and other barbarous people, which as swarmes came out of the north parts, and with
maruellous cruelty ouerwhelmed all the west Countreyes of
Europe, to the great hindrance, daunger, and vnquietnesse of
the Church of God.   After these stormes and tempests were
somewhat ouerblowne, the riches of the Church did very much
increase, both in lands and otherwise, by such meanes as before
I haue rehearsed.   And this generally I obserue in all histories, and in all times, that the wealth thereof vnder Christian
Princes was neuer diminished, but rather increased : nor euer
did they murmure at it, or thought it too much, vntill the Pope
chalenged his vsurped dominion, and did seeke to bring the

Platina.

Sabell. en-
nead.8.lib.1.

Niceph. lib.
14. cap. 5.

neckes of Princes vnder his girdle, and to alter Empires, Kingdomes, and Principalities at his will and pleasure, saying, that he had *Ius vtriusque gladij,* the power of both swords.

"Heere (I knowe) some will say, that by my owne confession, I am fallen to acknowledge that botch that first bredde Antichrist, and set him vp into his throne aboue Kings and Princes, that is to say, the immoderate wealth of the Ecclesiasticall men, which then did corrupt religion, and so, say they, doth it now with vs." No, no (good Christians) they that so say, eyther are blinded with ignoraunce, or looke into thinges with partiall eyes, and seeke rather a secrete furthering of priuate purposes, then the knowledge of the true causes of that, whereof they speake. For they that will indifferently consider the states of times, and with true iudgement weigh the circumstaunces of them, may easily discerne, that it was not the wealth of the Cleargie, but other causes of greater weight and importaunce, that sette vp Antichrist aloft in his throane, and wrought him the dominion of the Church, which I pray God may bee more carefully looked vnto among vs, then yet I perceiue that they haue beene: especially if we meane so earnestlie to keepe away from vs the returne of his corruption, as many now woulde seeme to doe.

The first cause that aduaunced Antichrist, was *Schisme and heresie in the Church,* for the space of two hundred yeeres and more, together with the barbarous irruptions which before I spake of. The second cause was, *the generall decay of learning,* and especially of *the knowledge of the Scriptures, and of the tongues.* Thirdly, *the vsurpation of Ecclesiasticall Discipline,* practised against Emperours and Princes, by which hee conquered more then by all other meanes. The helping causes to these principall, were these two: first, the negligence, the vnskilfulnesse, the vnworthinesse of many emperours and gouernours, giuen ouer rather to wantonnesse and voluptuous pleasures, then to the care of their charge: and secondly, the superstitious deuotion

The true causes that set vp Antichrist.

of the people, maintained by corrupt doctrine. But the graund
cause of all causes was, *the iust iudgement of God*, for the
generall vnthankfulnesse of the world, in receiuing the knowledge of his gospell, which he sent among them.

And this cause was vniuersall in all estates and kindes ol
persons, as well ecclesiasticall as other. The bishoppes and
Ministers were giuen ouer to maintaine factions and hereticall
doctrines : Princes looked more to their sensuall pleasure, then
to the godly gouernment of their subiects : the people were bent
wholly to superstition and wickednes of life, so that (a small
number onely excepted) none did studie howe in life and godly
conuersation, to frame themselues to the good and wholesome
doctrine of the Gospell, which at the hande of many godly
men, they at the beginning had receiued. Sundry of these or
the like causes haue we now also growing and encreasing
among vs : and therefore haue we great cause to fear the like
iust iudgement of God, that eyther shall cast vs againe vnder
the tyranny of Antichrist, or bring vpō vs some plague no
lesse greuious then that is.

Our ministers and Preachers breake out to Schismaticall
factions and curious Doctrines. The people, in steede of
superstitious deuotion, haue conceiued an heathenish contempt
of Religion, and a disdaynefull loathing of the ministers
thereof. Vice and wickednesse ouerwhelmeth all states and
conditions of men. None almost, vnlesse it bee some that
God reserueth to his secrete knowledge, studie to shewe themselues thankfull to God, and in life to expresse that, which in
doctrine they will seeme to approoue. I pray God, that by
abusing this long suffering of the Lorde, wee heape not vp
wrath for our selues against the day of wrath. God hath
dealt as mercifullie with this land, as euer hee did with any.
I beseech him, that in time we may repent with *Niniue*, and
turne to him in sackcloth and ashes, while hee may bee founde,
and while hee stretcheth vnto vs the hande of his gratious
goodnesse, least when it is too late, and hee hath turned his

face from vs, wee crie vnto him with vaine gronings, and mourne
with vnprofitable sighings. Hee sent the light of his trueth
into this realme, first in the time of K. *Henry* the eight, and
brake the power of Antichrist among vs : but because hee
sawe neyther thankfull receiuing of the Gospell, nor any thing
studied for by men generally, but the benefite of Abbey lands,
and possessions, to enrich them-selues : hee by and by cut
off the comfortable sweetenesse of his word, with the bitter
sauour of the sixe articles, and sharp persecution of them that
professed true religion.

His iustice indeede coulde no longer abide the full ripenesse
of the superstition, idolatrie, and wicked life of the Monkes
and Friers, and such other swarms of Antichristian impietie :
but our vnthankfulnesse deserued not to haue the same turned
to our benefite, nor the freedome of his Gospell to be continued among vs to our further comfort.

In the time of that gratious Prince King *Edward* the sixt
hee gaue vs a larger taste of his word and a greater freedome
of all points of sound and true christian doctrine, to our vnestimable benefite, if wee could haue receiued it accordingly.
But euen then also, hee perceiued, that wee sought not so
much the increase of his glory, or to frame our liues according to our profession, as wee did studie vnder countenance of religion, by al meanes we could, to work again our
owne worldly benefit and commoditie. And therefore did hee
the second time take from this realme his fatherly blessing, and
cast vpon vs that heauie scourge of persecution, which im-
mediatly followed, keeping vs vnder the rodde of his correction by the space of certaine yeeres.

Neuerthelesse, as a mercifull Father, declaring that by his
chastening he sought not our confusion but our amendment,
euen for the glory of his names sake onely, beyonde all hope
and expectation, hee shewed vs againe the light of his countenance, and that more fauourably and bountifully then euer
hee did before, raysing for vs as it were out of the dust of

death, a Noble Queene, a gratious Prince, as a nurse or pro
tectresse of his church : Vnder the shadow of whose wings, al·
though but a Virgine, he keepeth vs in great safetie and quiet
nesse, against al the ancient enemies both of his Church, and o
our natutall countrey.   Notwithstanding all this, our olde vn·
thankfulnesse and forgetfulnesse of our duetie still continueth
and we shew our selues the same men that euer we did before

   And therefore beside the earnest preaching of his worde
calling vs continually to repentance, who seeth not, that diuers
times he hath shaken the rod of his displeasure ouer vs ? as ir
the Northren rebellion, and in many signes and tokens from
heauen, thereby, if it were possible, to waken vs out of our sin·
full securitie, wherein wee sleepe so confidently ?   Yea, and
the more to keepe vs in feare, hee hath made vs to nourish in
our bosomes the apparent instrument of his wrath, by whome
wee coulde not choose but see, that in a moment hee might
haue taken from vs both the comfort of his Gospell, and
the freedome and happinesse of our state.   Here must I put
you in minde againe of his exceeding mercies shewed toward vs
euen in these fewe Moneths, deliuering vs from the bloody
crueltie of our enemies.

   But to what effect, I pray you, commeth all this carefull
working of our mercifull God, by fayre meanes and foule
meanes thus labouring to drawe vs vnto him ?   Doth it
quicken in vs the care of our saluation ? doth it increase the
feare of his displeasure ? doth it stir vp any more zeale and
loue of his Gospell ? hath it any thing diminished our vncharitable strife and contentiō ? doth it any thing abate the
obstinacie of the aduersary ? hath it any way diminished the
loosenes of our liuing ? hath it taken from vs our pride in apparell ? our daintines in feeding ? our wastfull and pompous
building ? hath it made lesse any euill among vs, and not
rather encreased euery thing, to an higher degree then euer it
was before ? Shall we thinke then, that this our vnsensible dul-
ness and vnthankfulnesse, can be without imminent punishment.

Surely, me thinketh the song of *Esay* the Prophet painteth
out our state and condition with the euent that will follow of it.
"The Lord hath chosen this lande, as his beloued vineyard,
hee hath mounded it" with his gratious fauour and   Esay. 5.
diuine protection, "hee hath stoned it" by casting out the
rubble of the Synagogue of Antichrist, the broken stones
I meane, of idolatrie, superstition, false doctrine, and corrupt
worship of God : hee hath planted among vs the sweete grape
of his most wholesome Gospel, and the true vine Christ Iesu :
he hath *set up a watch Tower* of Christian gouernment, *and a
wine presse* of earnest preaching of repentance, to presse and
wring mens hearts, if it were possible, to yeelde foorth the
sweete iuice of the fruits of the gospel to the glorie of God.
And he long hath looked, (for these his great benefites) that
wee should haue brought foorth *sweete grapes*, and wee
haue yeelded nothing but sowre and stinking fruite, discord
and dissension among our selues, couetousnesse, oppression,
extortion, drunkennesse, banquetting, voluptuous pleasure,
whoredome, adulterie, securitie in sinne, contempt of God,
disdaine of his Ministers, despising of his worde, selfe-liking
in our owne doings, confidence and trust in our owne wisedome
and policie &c. I pray God therefore in time wee may take
heede of that heauie iudgement that followeth, I meane, that
hee will "take away the hedge, and breake downe the wall"
of his mightie protection, whereby onely wee haue hitherto
remayned safe, and that hee will lay vs waste that the beastes
of the fielde may ouertrample vs : that hee will take from vs
the teaching and preaching of his Gospell, wherewith in vayne
hee hath so long digged and delued in our barraine heartes :
that hee will forbidde the cloudes of his heauenly prouidence
to rayne downe vpon vs his great and manifolde blessings,
which beforetime hee hath giuen vs, so that wee shalbe left as
a desolate ground, breeding nothing but bushes and brambles
of ignorance, errour, idolatrie, superstition, heresie and wicked
life, and bee made subiectes and slaues vnto our greatest ene-

mies. The Lorde turne away that, which our vnthankfull
hearts may iustly feare to be at hand, &c.

By this that I haue written, as I doubt not but the godly may
perceiue it was not riches and wealth of the Cleargie that first
set vp Antichrist in the vsurped throne of his dominion ouer
the Church, but that there were other more true and right
causes that bredde that mischiefe: so likewise that conscience,
that feareth God, and without affection looketh into the state
of this time among vs, and rightly weigheth and considereth
things, may easily iudge, that it is not the Landes and great
liuings of bishop and Ecclesiasticall persons, but other matters,
more heynous and more greuious, that will hasten the wrath and
displeasure of God against this Realme, which in deede, it
behooueth bishops principally, and all other in their states and
conditions to haue care of, and in time, while wee may, by all
godly meanes to preuent it.

The affection of them, which at this day speake so much
against the Landes and liuings of bishops, and other Cleargie
men, is much like the dealing of those persons, that murmured
against *Marie* of *Bethania*, which in the house of *Simon* the leper,
in testimonie of her thankefulnesse, for the great mercies that
shee had receiued of Christ, powred vpon his head the precious oyntment of Spikenard. For euen in like manner our
gracious Queene, when God had deliuered her out of the
iawes of the greedie lyons, and cruell wolues that sought her
blood, and by his mightie hand had set her in the throne
of this her Fathers kingdome: to testifie her thankefull minde,
and to shewe her liberall and bountifull heart towarde the
Church of God, shee powred vpon it this plentifull gift,
towarde the maintenance of the Ministers and Preachers of his
worde, that shee might declare to the worlde, that in imbracing the Gospell, and restoring the same to this Realme,
shee had not that minde and affection, which some other
haue shewed, that is, vnder colour thereof, to make the increase of her owne benefite, and the commoditie of her

Crowne. But as then *Iudas* and some other Disciples murmured at *Marie,* and vnder pretence of holinesse and charitie toward the poor, founde great fault with that superfluous
excesse (as they thought it) euen so nowe, many Disciples
among vs, with like colour of religion and holinesse, and
of zeale toward the perfection of the Church (forsooth)
murmure at the liberal benefit of our prince, which she
hath bestowed vpon the Church, and think the same a great
superfluitie, that might bee better imployed sundry wayes, to
the benefite of the common weale. Whatsoeuer is pretended,
I pray God the cause of the griefe bee not the same that *Iohn*
mentioneth to haue beene that, which first began   Iohn. 12.
the murmuring at that time. But whatsoeuer is the cause of
this reproouing of the liberalitie of our gracious Prince and
soueraigne : if the time did now serue, I coulde with better
reason and authoritie prooue the Contrary Proposition to that
which they take vpon them to maintaine : that is, " That it is
not lawfull to bestow such liuings vpon Lay men, as are
appointed by godly lawes for Ministers and Preachers of the
worde of God." But the shortnesse of the time will not now
serue to followe that course.

IMPRINTED AT LON-
don by the Deputies of Christopher Barker, Printer to the
Queenes most excellent
Maiestie.
1589.

Puritan Discipline Tracts.

HAY ANY WORKE FOR COOPER;

BEING

A REPLY

TO THE

"ADMONITION TO THE PEOPLE OF ENGLAND."

BY

MARTIN MAR-PRELATE.

Re-printed from the Black Letter Edition.

WITH

AN INTRODUCTION AND NOTES.

LONDON:

JOHN PETHERAM, 71, CHANCERY LANE.

1845.

INTRODUCTION.

"HAVE you any work for John Cooper" appears to have been one of the cries of London, according to a print in that scarce and curious volume, "Tempesta's Cries of London," folio 1711.

There are two or three allusions in the present Tract to its author, which, though they afford us no means of judging who he was, will satisfy us that he was the author also of the "Epistle" and the "Epitome." "I haue onely published a Pistle, and a Pitomie, wherein also I graunt that I did reasonably Pistle them," says he at p. 60 ; and again at p. 41, "*I am alone.* No man vnder heauen is priuy, or hath bin priuie vnto my writings against you, I vsed the aduise of non therein. You haue and do suspect diuers, as master Paggett, master Wiggington, master Udall, and master Penri, &c. to make Martin." It has been inferred, with very great probability, that John Penri was the author of the Epistle, and it is remarkable that the author here puts Penri last, against whom and Udall a much stronger suspicion existed than against Eusebius Paget and Giles Wiggington.

The "More Work for Cooper," so often referred to, was never wholly printed, for it was during the printing of it that the press was seized, together with several unfinished pamphlets, and the persons engaged on it; but whether the whole work exists in any form is very doubtful.

The original of the present Tract is in black letter, altogether consisting of 58 pages. It was, without doubt, printed with the same types as those used for the Epistle and the Epitome; and the date of publication may be referred, with some degree of certainty, to the earlier part of the year 1589, because he speaks in the beginning of the pursuivants who were sent about the country to seek for him, which was towards the latter end of the year 1588, and a little further on he says, "I loue not the ayre of the Clinke or Gatehouse *in this colde time of Winter.*"

J. P.

London, February 10, 1845.

Hay any worke for Cooper:

Or a briefe Pistle directed by Waye of an

hublication to the reverende Byshopps, counselling them,
if they will needs be barrelled vp, for feare of smelling
in the nostrels of her Maiestie and the State, that they would
vse the aduise of reuerend Martin, for the prouiding of their
Cooper. Because the reuerend T. C. (by which misticall
letters, is vnderstood, eyther the bounsing Parson of
Eastmeane, or Tom Coakes his Chaplaine)
[*hath shewed himselfe in his late Admo-*
nition to the people of England]
to bee an vnskilfull
and a beceytfull
tubtrimmer.

Wherein worthy Martin quits himselfe like a man

I warrant you, in the modest defence of his selfe and his
learned Pistles, and makes the Coopers hoopes
to flye off, and the Bishops Tubs to
leake out of all crye.

Penned and compiled by Martin the Metropolitane.

Printed in Europe, not far from some
of the Bounsing Priestes.

A man of Worshipp, to the men of Worship, that is, Martin Marprelate gentleman, Primate, and Metropolitane of all the Martins whersoeuer. To the Iohn of al the sir Iohns, and to the rest of the terrible priests : saith have among you once againe my cleargie masters.　　For

O BRETHREN, there is such a deale of loue growne of late I perceiue, betweene you and me, that although I would be negligent in sending my Pistles vnto you: yet I see you cannot forget me. I thought you to bee verye kinde when you sent your Purcivaunts about the countrie to seeke for me. But now that you your selues haue taken the paines to write, this is out of all crie. Why it passes to thinke what louing and carefull brethren I haue, who although I cannot be gotten, to tell them where I am, because I loue not the ayre of the Clinke or Gatehouse in this colde time of Winter, and by reason of my busines in Pistlemaking, will notwithstanding make it knowne vnto the world, that they haue a moneths mind towards me. Now truly brethren, I find you kinde, why ye do not know what a pleasure you haue done me. My worships books were vnknowne to many, before you allowed T. C. to admonishe the people of England to take heed, that if they loued you, they woulde make much of their prelates, and the chiefe of the cleargie. Now many seeke after my

B 2

bookes, more than euer they did.   Againe, some knew
not that our brother Iohn of Fulham, was so good vnto
the porter of his gate, as to make the poore blinde
honest soule, to be a dum minister.   Many did not
know, eyther that Amen, is as much as by my fayth,
and so that our Sauiour Christe euer sware by his fayth :
or that bowling and eating of the Sabboth, are of the
same nature : that Bb. may as lawfully make blinde
guydes, as Dauid might eate of the Shew bread : or
that father Thomas tubtrimmer of Winchester, good old
student, is a master of Arts of 45. yeares standing.
Many I say, were ignorant of these thinges, and many
other prettie toyes, vntil you wrote this prettie booke.
Besides whatsoeuer you ouerpasse in my writings, and
did not gainsay, that I hope wilbe iudged to be true.
And so Iohn a Bridges his treason out of the 448. page
of his booke, you graunt to be true.   Your selues you
denie not to bee pettie popes.   The B. of sir Dauids in
Wales, you denie not to haue two wiues, with an hundred other thinges which you do not gainsay : so that
the reader may iudge that I am true of my worde, and
vse not to lye like Bb.   And this hath greatly commended my worshipps good dealing.   But in your confutation of my book, you haue shewed reuerende Martin
to be truepenie in deede : For you haue confyrmed,
rather then confuted him.   So that brethren, the pleasure which you haue done vnto me, is out of all scotche
and notche.   And shoulde not I againe be as readie to
pleasure you ?   Naye, then I shoulde be as vngrateful
towards my good brethrē, as Iohn of Cant. is to Thomas

Cartwright. The which Iohn, although he hath bin greatly fauored by the said Thomas, in that Thomas hath now these many yeares let him alone and said nothing vnto him, for not answering his books, yet is not ashamed to make a secrete comparison, betweene himselfe and Thomas Cartwright. As who say, Iohn of Lambehith, were as learned as Thomas Cartwright. What say you old deane Iohn a Bridges, haue not you shewed your selfe thankfull vnto hir Maiestie, in ouer-throwing hir supremacie in the 448. page of your booke. I will lay on load on your skincoat for this geare anon.

And I will haue my penyworths of all of you brethrē ere I haue done with you, for this pains which your T. C. hath taken with me. This is the puritans craft, in procuring me to be confuted I knowe: Ile be euen with them to. A craftie whoresons brethren Bb. did you thinke, because yᵉ puritans T. C. did set Iohn of Cant. at a *nonplus*, and gaue him the ouerthrow, that therefore your T. C. alias Thomas Cooper bishop of Winchester, or Thomas Cooke his Chaplaine, could set me at a *nonplus*. Simple fellowes, me thinkes he should not.

I gesse your T. C. to be Thomas Cooper (but I do not peremptorily affirme it) because the modest olde student of 52. yeres standing, setteth Winchester after Lincolne and Rochester in the contents of his booke, which blasphemy, would not haue bin tollerated by them that saw and allowed the book, vnlesse mistres Coopers husband had bin the author of it.

Secondly, because this T. C. the author of this booke

is a bishop, and therefore Thomas Cooper, he is a Bishop, because he reckoneth him selfe charged amongst
others, with those crimes whereof non are accused but
bishops alone, pag. 101. lin. 26. Ka olde Martin yet
I see thou hast it in thee, thou wilt enter into the
bowels of the cause in hand I perceue. Nay, if you
wil commend me, I will giue you more reasons yet.
The stile and the phrase is very like her husbands,
y^t was sometimes woont to write vnto doctor Day of
Welles. You see I can do it in deed. Again, non
would be so groshead as to gather, because my reuerence telleth Deane Iohn, that he shall haue twenty
fists about his eares more then his owne (whereby I
meant in deede, that manye would write against him,
by reason of his bomination learning, which otherwise
neuer ment to take pen in hand) that I threatned him
with blowes, and to deale by stafford law: Whereas
that was far from my meaning, and could by no means
be gathered out of my words, but only by him that
pronounced *Eulojin* for *Eulogein* in the pulpit: and by
him whom a papist made to beleeue, that the greek
word *Eulogein*, that is to giue thanks, signifieth to make
a crosse in the forhead: py hy hy hy. I cannot but laugh,
py hy hy hy. I cannot but laugh, to thinke that an
olde soaking student in this learned age, is not ashamed
to be so impudent as to presume to deale with a papist,
when he hath no grue in his pocked. But I promise
you Sir, it is no shame to be a L. bishop if a man could,
thogh he were as vnlerned as Iohn of Glocester or
William of Liechfeld. And I tel you true, our brother

Westchester, had as liue playe twentie nobles in a night, at Priemeero on the cards, as trouble him selfe with any pulpit labor, and yet he thinks him self to be a sufficient bishop. What a bishop such a cardplaier? A bishop play 20. nobles in a night? Whie a round threpence serueth the turn to make good sport 3. or 4. nights amongst honest neighbours. And take heede of it brother Westchester: it is an vnlawfull game if you will beleeue me. Foe, in winter it is no matter to take a litle sport, for an od cast braces of 20. nobles when the wether is foule, that men cannot go abroad to boules, or to shoote? What would you haue men take no recreatiō? Ye but it is an old said saw, inough is as good as a feast. And recreations must not be made a trade and an occupation, ka master Martin Marprelate. I tel you true brother mine, though I haue as good a gift in pistle making, as as you haue at priemeero, and far more delight then you can haue at your cards, for the loue I beare to my brethren, yet I dare not vse this sport, but as a recreation, not making any trade thereof. And cards I tel you though they bee without hornes, yet they are parlous beasts. Be they lawful or vnlawful take heed of them for al that. For you cannot vse them but you must needs say your brother T. C. his Amen, that is, sweare by your faith, many a time in the night, wel I will neuer stande argling the matter any more with you. If you will leaue your card playing so it is, if you wil not, trust to it it wil be the worse for you.

I must go simply and plainly to worke with my

brethren, that haue published T. C. Whosoeuer haue
published that booke, they haue so hooped the bishops
tubbs, that they haue made them to smel far more
odious then euer they did, euen in the nostrels of all
men. The booke is of 252. pages. The drift thereof
is, to confute certaine printed and published libelles.
You bestowe not full 50. pages in the answeare of any
thing that euer was published in print. The rest are
bestowed to maintaine the belly, and to confute : what
think you? Euen the slanderous inuentions of your
owne braines for the most part. As y^t it is not lawfull
for her Maiestie to allot any lands vnto the mainte-
naunce of the minister, or the minister to liue vpō
lands for this purpose allotted vnto him, but is to content him selfe with a smal pention, and so small, as he
haue nothing to leaue for his wife and childrē after him
(for whom he is not to be careful, but to rest on gods
prouidence) and is to require no more but foode and
raiment, that in poverty he might be answerable vnto
our Sauiour Christ and his apostles. In the confutation
of these points, and the scriptures corruptly aplied to
proue them, there is bestowed aboue an 100. pages of
this book, that is, from the 149. vnto the end. Well
T. C. whosoeuer thou art, and whosoeuer Martin is,
neither thou, nor any man or woman in England shal
know while you liue, suspect and trouble as many as
you wil, and therefore saue your mony in seeking for
him, for it may be he is neerer you then you are ware
of. But whosoeuer thou art I say, thou shewest thyself
to be a most notorious wicked slanderer, in fathering

these things vppon those whome they call puritans, which neuer any enioying common sense would affirme. And bring me him, or set downe his name and his reasons that holdeth any of the former points confuted in thy book, and I wil proue him to be vtterly bereaued of his witts, and his confuter to be either stark mad, or a stark enemy to al religion, yea to her Maiestie and the state, of this kingdome. No no, T. C. puritans hold no such points. It were well for bishops, that their aduersaries were thus sottishe. They might then iustly insence her Maiestie and the state against them, if they were of this minde. These obiections, in the confutation whereof, thou hast bestowed so much time, are so farre from hauing any puritane to be their author, as whosoeuer readeth the book, were he as blockheaded as Thomas of Winchester himselfe, hee may easily knowe them to be obiections onely inuented by the authour of the booke himselfe. For although hee bee an impudent wretch, yet dareth he not set them downe, as writings of any other : for then he woulde haue described the author and the booke by some adient.

The puritans in deede, holde it vnlawfull for a minister to haue such temporall reuenews, as whereby tenne ministers might be well maintained, vnlesse the sayd reuenews come vnto him by inheritance.

They holde it also vnlawfull, for any state to bestowe the liuings of many ministers vpon one alone, especially when there is such want of ministers liuings.

They holde it vnlawfull for anye minister to be Lorde ouer his brethren. And they holde it vnlawfull for

anye state to tollerate such vnder their gouernment.
Because it is vnlawfull for states, to tollerate men in
those places whereinto the word hath forbidden them to
enter.

They affirme that our Sauiour Christe, hath forbidden all ministers to be Lords, Luke 22. 25. And the
Apostle Peter, sheweth them to be none of Gods
ministers, which are Lords ouer Gods heritage, as
you Bishopps are, and woulde bee accounted. These
thinges T. C. you should haue confuted, and not
troubled your selfe, to execute the fruites of your owne
braines, as an enemie to the state. And in these points,
I do challenge you T. C. and you Deane Iohn, and you
Iohn Whitgift, and you doctor Coosins, and you doctor
Capcase (Copcoat I think your name be) and as many
else, as haue or dare write in the defence of the established church gouernment. If you cannot confute my
former assertions, you do but in vain thinke to maintaine your selues by slaunders, in fathering vppon the
puritanes, the ofspringes of your owne blockheads.
And assure your selues, I wil so besoop you if you
cänot defend your selues in these points, as al the world
shal cry shame vppon you, you think pretely to escape
the point of your Antichristian calings, by giuing out
that puritans hold it vnlawfull for her maiestie to leaue
any lands for the vse of the ministers maintenance. I
cannot but commend you, for I promise you, you can
shift of an haynous accusation very pretily.

A true man bringeth vnanswerable witnesses against
a robber by the high way side, and desireth the iudge,

that the lawe may proceede against him. O no my
Lord saith the thiefe, in any case let not me be dealt
with. For these mine accusers haue giuen out, that
you are a drunkard or they haue committed treason
against the state: therefore I pray you beleeue my
slander against thē, that they may be executed: so when
I come to my trial, I shalbe sure to haue no accusers.
A very prety way to escape, if a man could tel howe
to bringe the matter about. Now bretheren bishops,
your manner of dealing, is euen the very same. The
puritans say truly, that al Lord bishops are pety Antichristes, and therefore that the magistrates ought to
thrust you out of the common welth. Nowe of all
loues say the bishops, let not our places be called in
question, but rather credit our slanders against the
puritans, whereby, if men would beleeue vs when we
lie, we would beare the world in hand, that these our
accusers are Malcontents and sottish men, holding it
vnlawful for the maiestrat to alott any lands for the
ministers portion, and vnlawful for the minister to prouide for his family. And therefore you must not giue
eare to the accusations of any such men against vs.
And so we shall be sure to be acquited. But brethren
doe you thinke to be thus cleared? why the puritans
hold no such points as you lay to their charg. Though
they did, as they do not, yet that were no sufficient
reason, why you being pettye popes, shoulde be maintained in a christian commonwealth. Answeare the
reasons that I brought against you: otherwise, Come
off you bishops, leaue your thousandes, and content

your selues with your hundreds, saith Iohn of London.
So that you do plainly see, that your Cooper T. C.
is but a deceitful workeman, and if you commit the
hooping of your bishopricks vnto him, they wil so leake
in a short space, as they shalbe able to keepe neuer a
Lord bishop in them.   And this may serue for an
aunswere vnto the latter part of your
booke, by way of an Interim, vntil
more worke for Cooper
be published.

Hay any worke for Cooper.

AND now reuerend T. C. I am come to your epistle to
the reader, but first you and I must go out alone into
the plaine fields, and there we wil try it out, euen by
plaine syllogismes, and that I know bishops cannot
abide to heare of.

The reuerend T. C. to the reader. page 1.

I draw great danger vpon my selfe, in defending our
bishops and others the chiefe of the clargy of the church
of England. Their aduersaries are very eger : the
saints in heauen haue felt of their tongs, for when they
speake of Paule, Peter, Marye, &c. whome others iustly
call saints : they in derision call them sir Peter, sir
Paule, sir Marie.

Reuerend Martin.

Alas poore reuerende T. C. Be not afraid. Heere
be non but frends man. I hope thou art a good fellow,
and a true subiect, ye but I defend the bishops of the
church of England saith he, then in deed I maruell not
though thy conscience accuse thee, and thou art sure to
be as wel fauoredly thwacked for thy labour, as euer

c

thou wast in thy life. Thy conscience I say, must needs make thee feare in defending them. For they are petty popes, and petty Antichristes as I haue proued, because they are pastor of pastors, &c. thou hast not answered my reasons, and therefore swadled thou shalt be for thy paynes, and yet if thou wilt yeeld I will spare thee. Thou canst not be a good and a sound subiect and defend the hierarchy of Lorde bishopps to be lawful, as I will shewe anone. Concerning Sir Paul, I haue him not at all in my writings. And therefore the reader must know, that there is a canterbury trick once to patch vp an acusation with a lye or two.

Sir Peter was the ouersight of the printer, who omitted this Marginal note vz. He was not Saint Peter which had a lawfull superiour authority ouer the vniuersal body of the church. And therfore the priest wherof Deane Iohn speaketh was Sir Peter.

And good reuerend T. C. I pray thee tel me, what kin was Saint Mary Oueries, to Mary the Virgin. In my book learning, the one was some popish Trull, and the other the blessed virgine. But will you haue all those, who are saints in deed, called saints ? Why then why doe you not call saint Abraham, saint Sara, saint Ieremie. If Iohn of Canterbury should marie, tell me good T. C. dost thou not thinke that he would not make choyse of a godly woman. I hope a would. And T. C. though you are learned, yet you go beyond your bookes if you saide the contrary : being a godly woman, then she were a sainte. And so by your rule, her name

being Marie, you would haue her called sainte Marie
Canterburie.   But I promise thee, did his grace what
he could, I would call her sir Marie Canterburie as
long as he professed himselfe to be a priest, and this
I might do lawfully.   For he being sir Iohn, why should
not his wife be sir Marie.   And why not sir Marie
Oueries, as well as sir Marie Canterburie ?   I hope
Iohn of Canterburie whom I knowe, (though I know no
great good in him) to be as honest a man as M. Oueries
was, whom I did not know.   Neither is there any
reason why you T. C. should holde M. Oueries and
his Marie, because they are within the diocesse of Winchester, to bee more honest then M. Canterburie and
his wife.   Naye there is more reason, why M. Canterburie and his wife dwelling at Lambehith, should be
thought the honester of the two, then Oueries and his
wife, because they dwel O the bankes side.   But good
Tom tubtrimmer, tell me what you meane by 'the chiefe
of the cleargie in the Churche of England ?   Iohn Canterburie I am sure.   Why good T. C. this speache is
either blasphemous or traiterous, or by your owne confession an euident proofe, that Iohn of Canterburie is
Lord ouer his brethren.   He that is chiefe of the
cleargie, is chiefe of God's heritage, and that is Iesus
Christ only, and so to make the pope of Canterburie
chiefe of Gods heritage, in this sence is blasphemous.
If you meane by cleargie, as Deane Iohn doeth page
443. of his booke, both the people and ministers of the
Churche of England : in this sence her Maiestie is
chiefe of the cleargie in the Church of England, and so

your speach is traiterous.   Lastly, if by cleargie you
mean the ministers of the Churche of England, none in
this sense can be chiefe of the cleargie, but a pettie
pope.   For our Sauiour Christe flatly forbiddeth anye
to be chiefe of the cleargie in this sence, Luke 22. 26.
And none euer claimed this vnto him selfe but a pettie
pope.   Therefore T. C. you are either by your owne
speach, a blasphemer or a traitor, or els Iohn of Cant.
is a pettie pope.   Here is good spoonemeat for a Cooper.
Take heede of writing against Martin, if you loue your
ease.

Reuerend T. C. page 2. Epistle.

But I feare them not, while I go about to maintain
the dignitie of priests.

Reuerend Martin.

Well fare a good heart yet, stand to thy tackling, and
get the high commission to send abroad the purciuants,
and I warrant thee thou wilt do something.   Alas good
priests, that their dignitie is like to fall to the ground.
It is pitie it should be so, they are such notable pulpit
men.   There is a neighbour of ours, an honest priest,
who was sometimes (symple as he nowe standes) a vice
in a playe for want of a better, his name is Gliberie of
Hawsteade in Essex, he goes much to the pulpit.   On
a time, I think it was the last Maie, he went vp with a
full resolution, to do his businesse with great commendations.   But see the fortune of it.   A boy in the
Church, hearing either the sommer Lord with his Maie
game, or Robin Hood with his Morrice daunce going

by the Church, out goes the boye. Good Gliberie, though he were in the pulpit, yet had a minde to his olde companions abroad (a company of merrie grigs you must think them to be, as merie as a vice on a stage) seeing ye boy going out, finished his matter presently with Iohn of Londons Amen, saying, ha, ye faith boie, are they there, then ha w^t thee, and so came down and among them hee goes. Were it not then pittie, that the dignitie of such a priest should decaie. And I would gentle T. C. that you would take the paines to write a treatise against the boie with the red cap, which put this Gliberie out of his matter at another time. For Glibery being in the pulpit, so fastened his eyes vpon a boye with a red cap, that he was cleane dasht out of countenaunce, in so much that no note could be hard from him at that time, but this. Take away red cap there, take away red cappe there: it had bene better that he had neuer bin borne, he hath marred suche a sermon this day, as it is woonderfull to thinke. The Queene and the Counsell might well haue heard it for a good sermon, and so came down. An admonition to the people of England, to take heed of boies with red caps, which make them set light by the dignitie of their priests, would do good in this time, brother T. C. you know well.

Reuerend T. C.

The cause why wee are so spighted, is be- *You may herby perceiue that T. C. is a bishop.* cause we doe endeuor to maintaine the lawes which her Maiestie and the whole state of the

c 3

Realme haue allowed, and doe not admit a new platforme of gouernment, deuised I know not by whom.

Reuerend Martin.

Why T. C. saye *Eulojin* for *Eulogein* as often as you
will, and I wil neuer spight you, or the Bishop of Winchester eyther for the matter.   But doe you thinke our
Churche gouernement, to be good and lawfull, because
hir Maiestie and the state, who maintaine the reformed
religion alloweth the same?   Why the Lorde doth not
allow it, therefore it cannot be lawfull.   And it is the
falt of such wretches as you bishops are, that her Maiestie and the state alloweth the same.   For you should
haue otherwise instructed them.   They know you not
yet as thorowly as I doe.   So that if I can prooue,
that the Lord disliketh our Church gouernement, your
endeuors to maintaine the same, shew that thereby you
cannot chuse, but be traytors to God and his worde,
whatsoeuer you are to her Maiestie and the State.
Nowe T. C. looke to your selfe, for I will presently
make all the hoops of your bishoppricks flie assunder.
Therefore
Our Churche gouernement, is an vnlawfull Churche go-
uernment, and not allowed in the sight of God.   Because
That church gouernment is an vnlawful church gouernment, the offices and officers whereof, the ciuil
maiestrate may lawfully abollish out of the church,
marke my craft in reasoning brother T. C.   I say the
offices and officers for I grant that the maiestrate may
thrust the officers of a lawful church gouernment out of

the church if they be Diotripheses, Mar-elmes, Whitgifts, Simon Maugustes, Coopers, Pernes, Renoldes, or
any such like Iudases, (though the most of these must
be packing, offices and al) but their offices must stand,
that the same may be supplied by honester men. But
the offices of Archbishops and bishopps, and therefore
the officers much more, may be lawfully abollished out
of the church by her Maiestie and our State. And
truely this were braue weather to turne them out : it is
pitty to keepe them in any longer. And that would do
me good at the hart, to see Iohn of London, and the
rest of his brethren so discharged of his busines, as he
might freely runn in his cassocke and hose after his
bowle, or florish with his 2. hand sword. O tis a
sweete trunchfiddle.

But the offices of Archbishops and bishops, may be
lawfully abollished out of the church by her Maiestie,
and the state. As I hope one day they shalbe. Therefore (marke now T. C. and cary me this conclusion to
Iohn O Lambehith for his breakefast) our church gouerment by Arch. and bishops, is an vnlawful church
gouerment. You see brother Cooper, that I am very
courteous in my minor, for I desire therein no more
offices to bee thrust out of the church at one time, but
Archb. and Bishops. As for Deanes, Archdeacons and
Chancellors, I hope they wilbe so kind vnto my Lords
grace, as not to stay, if his worship and the rest of the
noble clergie Lords weare turned out to grasse. I wil
presently proue both maior and minor of this sillogisme.
And hold my cloake there sombody, that I may go

roundly to worke. For ise so bumfeg the Cooper, as he had bin better to haue hooped halfe the tubbes in Winchester, then write against my worships pistles.

No ciuil maiestrat may lawfully either maime or deforme the body of Christ, which is the church, but whosoeuer doth abollish any lawful church officer, out of the church gouernment, he doth either maime or deforme the church. Therefore T. C. no ciuil magistrate, no prince, no state, may without sinn abollishe any lawfull officer, together with his office, out of the gouernement of the church, and *per consequence*, the offices of Archbishops and Lord bishops, which her Maiestie may without sinn lawfully abollish out of the church, are no lawful church officers, and therefore also, the church gouernment practised by Iohn Whitgift, Iohn Marelme, Richard Peterborow, William of Lincolne, Edmond of Worcestor, yea and by that old stealecounter masse priest, Iohn O Glossester, with the rest of his brethren, is to be presently thrust out of the church. And me thinks this geare cottons in deed my masters. And I tould you T. C. that you should be thumped for defending bishops. Take heed of me while you liue. The minor of my last sillogisme, that whosoeuer doth abollish the office of any lawfull church officer out of the church, he either maimeth or deformeth the church, I can proue with a wet finger. Because euery lawful Churche officer, euen by reason of his office, is a member of the bodye of Christe Iesus, whiche is the church, and being a member of the body, If the maiestrate doth displace him by abollishing his office, and leaueth the

place thereof voide, then the maiestrate maimeth the
body. If he put another office vnto an officer in stead
thereof, he deformeth the same. Because the maiestrate
hath neither the skil nor the commission, to make the
members of the body of Christ. Because he cannot tel
to what vse, the members of his making may serue in
the church. Do you think T. C. that the maiestrat may
make an eie for the visible body of the church. (For
you must vnderstand, that wee al this while speake of
the visible body) can he make a foote or a hand for
that body? I pray you in what place of the body
would you haue them placed? If our Sauiour Christ
hath left behind him a perfect body : surely he hath left
therein no place, or no vse for members of the maies-
trates making and inuention : if an vnperfect and maimed
body, I am wel assured that the maiestrate is not able
to perfect that which he left vnfinished. But I hope
T. C. that thou wilt not be so mad, and wicked, as to
say that our Sauiour Christ, left behind him heere on
earth an vnperfect and maimed body. If not, then
where shal these offices, namely these members inuented
by the maiestrate be placed therein.

Would you haue the naturall eies put out (as your
brethren the bishops haue don in the church of England,
euer since Iohn of Canterbury vrged his wretched subscription) and vnnatural squint gogled eies put in their
steede : when the body cannot see with any eies, but
with the natural eies thereof, displace them howsoeuer
you may seme to help the matter, by putting others in
their steed, yet the body shalbe stil blind and maimed.

What say you T. C. may the Maiestrate cut of[f] the true
and natural legges, and handes of the body of Christe,
vnder a pretence to put woodden in their steed.   I hope
you wil not say that he may.   How then commeth it to
passe T. C. that you hold Iohn of Canterbury his office,
and Iohn Mar-elms to be true and natural members of
the body, that is true officers of the church, and yet
hold it laweful for her Maiestie to displace them out of
the church.   I cannot tel brother what you hold in this
point.   Me think I haue disturbed your sences.   Do
you thinke that the maiestrat may displace the true
members of the body of Christ, and place woodden in
their steed?   Why this is to hold it lawful for the maiestrate to massacre the body.   Do you thinke he may
not?   Then may not her maiestie displace Iohn of Canterburies office out of our church : if shee may not displace his office, then either he by vertue of his office, is
a lawfull Pope aboue all ciuill magistrates, or els the
Church gouernment is so prescribed in the word, as it
is not lawfull for the magestrate to alter the same.   But
Puritans Iohn of Canterburie, as the puritans their
confes Iohn selues confesse, is no Pope.   Then either the
Cant. to be
no Pope. church gouernment is so prescribed in the
word as it may not be altred, or els the magestrat
may abolish a lawful church gouernement, and place
another in stead thereof.   If the Church gouernment be
so prescribed in the worde, as it cannot be altered, then
either our gouernment is ye same which was therein
prescribed, or our Church gouerment is a false Church
gouerment.   If ours be the same which is mentioned in

the word: Then Paule and Peter were either no true Church gouernours, or els Paul and Peter, and the rest of Church gouernors in their time were Lordes, for all our Church gouernours are Lordes. But Paule and Peter, &c. were no Lords, and yet true church gouernours. Therefore our church gouernment is not that which is prescribed in the word: and therfor a false and vnlawfull church gouernement. If you thinke that the magistrate may displace the lawful offices of the bodie, then as I said before, you hold it lawfull for the magistrate to maime or deforme the bodie. Because whatsoeuer he pulleth in the roome of the true and right members, must needs be a deformitie, and what place soeuer he leaueth vnfurnished of a member, must needes be a maime. And this is the onely and sole office of Christe onely, to place and displace the members of his bodie: to wit, the officers of his Church, he may lawfully do it, so cannot man. And therefore the sots (of which nomber you T. C. and you Iohn Whitgift, and you Deane Iohn, and you D. Coosins, and you D. Copcot, with the rest of the ignoraunt and wretched defendors of our corrupt church gouernement are to be accounted) which thinke that the offices of pastors, doctors, elders and deacons, or the most of them, may be as well nowe wanting in the Church, as the offices of Apostles, prophets and Euangelists: do notably bewray their vile ignorance, but the cause they doe not hurt. For the beastes do not consider that the offices of Apostles, Euangelists and Prophets, were remoued out of the church, not by man, but by the Lord, because

hee in his wisdome did not see any vse of such members
in his body, after the time of the first planting of the Churche.   I say they were remooued by the Lord himselfe and not by
man: because, partly the giftes wherewith
they were endued, partly the largenesse of
their commission, with certaine other essen-
tiall properties to them belonging, were by
him abrogated and taken away, which no man
could do.   Againe, the Apostolicall, Euan-
gelical and propheticall callings, were either
lawfully or vnlawfully abolished out of the
Churche, if lawfully, then they were abolished by the
Lord: and therefore they are neither to be called backe
vntill he sheweth it to be his pleasure that it shoulde be
so, neither can the church be truely said to be maimed
for want of them: because he which could best tell,
what members were fitte for his Churche did abolishe
them.   If vnlawfully, then those callings may be lawfully called backe againe into the church, and the
church without them is maimed, that is, wanteth some
members.   For if their callings were iniuriously abrogated, they are as iniuriously kept out of the churche:
and being members of the church, the church is maimed
without, vnlesse the Lorde hath shewed, that the time
of their seruice in the bodie is expired.   But they are
not iniuriously kept out (for so her Maiestie shoulde be
said to iniurie the church, vnlesse she would see Apostles, prophets and Euangelists, planted therein) neither
can the church be saide to be maimed for want of them,

*The apos-
tles chose
non in sted
of James
being be-
headed as
they did in
steed of Ju-
das, Act. i.
which they
would haue
don if the
apostolicall
calling had
been per-
manent.*

because the Lorde by taking them away hath declared, that now there can be no vse of them in the bodie: therefore the Lorde abrogated them. Therefore also they may be wanting, and the churche neither maimed nor deformed thereby. Whereas the keeping out of eyther of the former offices of pastors, doctors, elders and deacons, is a maiming of the churche, the placing of others in their steed, a deforming. Now reuerend T. C. I beseech you entreat mistris Cooper, to write to M. D. Day, somtimes of magdalins, that he may procure D. Cooper, to know of him that was the last Thomas of Lincolne, whether the now B. of Winchester be not perswaded, that reuerend Martin hath suffi[ci]ently prooued it to be vnlawful, for the ciuill magestrate, to abolishe any lawfull churche officer out of the church. Because it is vnlawfull for him to maime or deforme the bodie of Christe, by displacing the members thereof. But it may be, your Coopers noddle, profane T. C. doubteth, (for I knowe you to be as ignorant in these points, as Iohn Whitgift, or dean Iohn their selues.)

Whether a lawfull Church officer, in regard of his office, be a member of the bodie of Christ, which is the Church.

Therefore looke Rom. 12. vers. 4. 5. &c. and there you shall see, that whosoeuer hath an office in the bodie, is a member of the bodie. There also you shall see, that he that teacheth, which is the Doctor: he y^t exhorteth, which is the Pastor: he that ruleth, which is the Elder: he that distributeth, which is the Deacon

D

(as for him that sheweth mercie that is there spoken off,
he is but a church seruant, and no church officer).
There I say, you shall also see, that these 4. offices, of
Pastors, Doctors, Eleders and Deacons, are members of
the bodie: and 1. Cor. 12. 8. & 28. you shal see that
God hath ordained them.   Out of al, which hitherto
I haue spoken T. C.   I come vpon you, and your
bishopprickes, with 4. or 5. (yea halfe a dozen and
neede be) suche drie soopes, as Iohn of London with his
two hand sword neuer gaue the like.   For they aunswere your whole profane booke.   First, that the platforme of gouernment, by Pastors, Doctors, Elders and
deacons, which you say was deuised you knowe not by
whom, is the inuention of our Sauiour Christ.   For
God ordained them, saith the apostle, 1. Cor. 12. 8. 28.
And therefore vnlesse you will shew your selfe, either
to be a blasphemer, by terming Iesus Christ to be you
cannot tell whom, or els to be ignorant who is Iesus
Christ: you must needs acknowledge the platforme of
gouernment, which you say, was inuented by you know
not whō, to haue Christ Iesus for the author thereof.

This T.
Cooper
gainsaieth
pag. 2. of
his Epistle.
Secondly, that the word of God teacheth,
that of necessitie, the gouernment by Pastors,
doctors, elders, &c. ought to be in euery
Churche, which is neither maimed nor deformed.   Because that Church must needs be maimed
which wanteth those mēbers, which the Lorde hath
appointed to be therein: vnlesse the Lord himselfe
hath, by taking those members away, shewed that nowe
his bodie is to have no vse of them.   But as hath bene

sayde, God hath ordained pastors, doctors, elders and deacons to be in his Church, proued out of Rom. 12. 6. 7. 8. 1. Cor. 12. 8. 28. Ephe. 4. 12. And he hath not taken these officers away out of his church, because the Church hath continuall need of them. As of Pastors to feed with the word of wisedome: of the Doctors, to feede with the worde of knowledge, and both to builde vp his bodie in the vnitie of fayth: of Elders, to watch and ouersee mens maners: of Deacons to looke vnto the poore, and church treasurie. Therefore, where these 4. officers are wanting, there the Church is imperfect in her regiment.

Thirdly that this gouernement cannot be inconuenient for any State or kingdom. For is it inconuenient for a State or kingdome, to haue the bodie of Christ perfect therein ? *T. Cooper saith it is, pag. second, Epist.*

Fourthly that euery christian magestrate is bound to receue this gouerment, by Pastors, Doctors, Elders and deacons into the church, within his dominions, whatsoeuer inconuenience may be likely to follow the receuing of it. Because no likelyhood of inconuenience ought to induce the magistrate willingly to permit the church vnder his gouernment, to be maymed or deformed.

Fiftly that the gouerment of the church by Lord Archbishops and bishops, is a gouerment of deformed and vnshapen members, seruing for no good vse in the church of God. Because it is not the gouerment by pastors, doctors, elders and deacons, which as I haue shewed are now the only true members, that is the only true officers of the visible body.

Sixtly and lastly. That they who defend this false and bastardly gouernment of Archbishops and bishops, and withstand this true and natural gouernment of the church, by Pastors, Doctors, Elders and deacons, are likely in awhile to become, Mar-prince, Mar-state, Mar-lawe, Mar-magestrate, Mar-common wealth. As for Mar-church, and Mar-religion, they haue long since proued them selues to be.

These six points doe necessarily follow, of that which before I haue set downe, namely that it is not lawfull for any to abollish or alter, the true and lawful gouernment of the church, because it is not lawfull for them to maime or deforme the body of the church.

And I chaleng you T. C. and you Deane Iohn, and and you Iohn Whitgift, and you D. Coosins: and you D. Copcot, and al the rest that wil or dare defende our established Churche gouernement, to be tried with me in a iudgement of life and death, at any barre in England in this point. Namely,

That you must needs be, not onely traytors to God and his word, but also enemies vnto her Maiestie and the land, in defending the established Church gouernment to be lawfull.

You see the accusation which I lay to your charge, and here followeth the proofe of it : They who defend that the prince and state, may bid God to battel against them, they are not only traitors against God and his word, but also enemies to the Prince and state. I thinke Iohn of Glocester himselfe, wil not be so sensles as to deny this.

But our Archbishops and bishops, which hold it lawful for her maiestie and the state, to retain this established forme of gouernment, and to keep out the gouernment by pastors, doctors, elders and deacons, which was appointed by Christ, whom you profane T. C. cal you know not whome, hold it lawful for her maiestie and the state to bid God to battel against them. Because they bid the Lord to battel against them which maime and deforme the body of Christ, vz. the church. And they as was declared maime and deforme the body of the church, which keep out the lawful offices, apointed by the Lord to be members thereof, and in their steed, place other woodden members of the inuenteon of man. Therefore you T. C. and you Deane Iohn, and you Iohn Whitgift, and you the rest of the beastly defendors of the corrupt church gouernment, are not only traytors to God and his word, but enemies to her maiestie and the state. Like you any of these Nuts Iohn Canterbury. I am not disposed to iest in this serious matter. I am called Martin Marprelat. There be many that greatly dislike of my doinges. I may haue my wants I know. For I am a man. But my course I knowe to be ordinary and lawfull. I sawe the cause of Christs gouernment, and of the Bishops Antichristian dealing to be hidden. The most part of men could not be gotten to read any thing, written in the defence of the on[e] and against the other. I bethought mee therefore, of a way whereby men might be drawne to do both, perceiuing the humors of men in these times (especially of those that are in any place) to be giuen to mirth. I

tooke that course. I might lawfully do it. I, for
iesting is lawful by circumstances, euen in the greatest
matters. The circumstances of time, place and persons
vrged me thereunto. I neuer profaned the word in any
iest. Other mirth I vsed as a couert, wherin I would
bring the truth into light. The Lord being the authour
both of mirth and grauitie, is it not lawfull in it selfe
for the trueth to vse eyther of these wayes, when the
circumstances do make it lawful ?

My purpose was and is to do good. I know I haue
don no harme howsoeuer some may iudg Martin to mar
al. They are very weake on[e]s that so think. In that
which I haue written I know vndoubtedly, that I haue
done the Lord and the state of this kingdom great
seruice. Because I haue in som sort discouered the
greatest enemies thereof. And by so much the most
pestilent enemies, because they wound Gods relligion,
and corrupt the state with Atheism and loosnes, and so
cal for Gods vengance vppon vs all, euen vnder the
coulor of relligion. I affirm them to be the greatest
enemies that now our state hath, for if it were not for
them, the trueth should haue more free passage herein,
then now it hath. All states thereby would be amended :
and so we should not be subiect vnto Gods displeasure,
as now we are by reason of them.

Nowe let me deale with these that are in authority.
I do make it knowne vnto them, that our bishops are
the greatest enemies which we haue. For they do not
only go about, but they haue long since, fully perswaded our state, that they may lawfully procure the

Lord, to take the sword in hand against the state : if this be true, haue I not said truly, that they are the gretest enemies which our state hath.   The papistes work no such effect, for they are not trusted.   The Atheistes haue not infected our whol state, these haue. The attempts of our forraine enemies may be pernicious. But they are men as wee are.   But that God, which when our bishops haue, and doe make our prince, and our gouernors to wadge war, who is able to stand against him ?

Wel to the point, many haue put her maiestie, the parliament and counsell in minde, that the church officers now among vs, are not such as the Lord aloweth of : because they are not of his owne ordaininge. They haue shewed that this falt is to be amended, or the Lords hand to be looked for.   The bishops on the other side, haue cried out vpon them, that haue thus dutifully mooued the state.   They with a loud voice gaue out, that the maiestrat may lawfully maintaine that church gouerment, which best fitteth our estate, as liuing in ye time of peace.   What do they else herein, but say that the magestrat in time of peace, may maime and deforme the body of Christ his church.   That Christ hath left the gouerment of his own house vnperfect, and left the same to the discretion of the magestrate, wheras Moses before whome in this point of gouernment, the Lord Christ is iustly preferred, Heb. 3. 6. made the gouernment of the legal politie so perfect, as he left not any parte thereof, to the discretion of the magestrate.   Can they deny church officers, to be mem-

bers of the church.   They are refuted by the expresse
text. 1. Cor. 12. will they affirme Christ to haue left
behinde him an vnperfect body of his church, wanting
members at the lest wise, hauing such members as were
only permanent at the magestrates · pleasure.   Why
Moses the seruant, otherwise gouerned the house in his
time.   And the sonne is commended in this point for
wisdome, and faithfulnes before him. Heb. 3. 6.   Either
then, that commendation of the sonn before the seruant,
is a false testimony, or the sonne ordained a permanent
gouernment in his church.   If permanent, not to be
changed.   What then, do they that hold it may be
changed at the magestrates pleasure, but aduise the
maiestrate by his positiue lawes, to proclaime that it is
his will, that if there shalbe a church within his dominions, he will maime and deforme the same.   He wil
ordaine therein, what members he thinketh good.   He
will make it knowne, that Christ under his gouernment,
shalbe made lesse faithfull then Moses was.   That he
hath left the placing of members in his body vnto the
magestrate.   O cursed beastes, that bring this guilt
vppon our estate.   Repent Caitifes while you haue time.
You shal not haue it I feare when you wil.   And looke
you that are in authority vnto the equity of the controuersie, betwene our wicked bishops, and those who
woulde haue the disorders of our Churche amended.
Take heed you be not caried away with slaunders.
Christs gouerment is neither Mar-prince, Mar-state, Mar-
law nor Mar-magistrate.   The liuing God whose cause
is pleaded for, will bee reuenged of you, if you giue eare

vnto this slander, contrary to so many testimonies as are
brought out of his word, to prooue the contrary. He
denounceth his wrath against all you, that thinke it lawfull for you, to maim or deform his church: he accounteth his Churche maimed, when those offices are
therein placed, whiche hee hath not appointed to be
members thereof: he also testifieth that there be no
mēbers of his appointment in the Churche, but such as
he himselfe hath named in his word, and those that he
hath named, man must not displace, for so he shoulde
put the bodie out of ioynt. Nowe our bishops holding
the contrary, and bearing you in hande, that you may
practize the contrary, do they not driue you to prouoke
the Lorde to anger against your owne soules? And
are they not your enemies? They hold the contrary
I say, for they say that her Maiestie may alter this
gouernment now established, and thereby they shew
either this gouerment to be vnlawfull, or that the magistrat may presume to place those members in Gods
Church, which the Lord neuer mentioned in his word.
And I beseech you marke howe the case standeth
betweene these wretches, and those whom they call
puritans.

1 The puritans (falsely so called) shew it to be
vnlawfull for the magistrate, to goe about to make any
members for the bodie of Christ.

2 They hold all officers of the Church, to be members of the bodie, Rom. 12. 6. 1. Cor. 12. 8. 28.

3 And therfore they hold the altering, or the abolish-

ing of the offices of church government, to be the altering
and abolishing of the members of the Church.

4 The altering and abolishing of which members,
they holde to be vnlawfull, because it must needs be a
maime vnto the bodie.

5 They hold Christ Iesus to haue set downe as exact,
and as vnchaungeable a churche gouernement, as euer
Moses did. Heb. 3. 6.

These and such like are the points they holde, let
their cause be tried, and if they hold any other points in
effect but these, let them be hanged every man of them.

Now I demand, whether they that hold the contrary
in these pointes, and cause the State to practize the contrary, be not outragious wicked men, and dangerous
enemies of the state, it cannot be denied but they are.
Because the contrarie practize of any of the former
points, is a way to worke the ruine of the state.

Now our Bishopps holde the contrary vnto them al,
saue the 3. and 2. points, whereunto it may be they
will yeeld, and cause our estate to practize the contrary:
whence at the length our destruction is like to proceed.
For

1 They denie Christ Iesus to haue set downe as
exact, and as vnchangeable a forme of church gouernment as Moses did. For they say, that the magistrat
may change the church gouernment established by
Christ, so could he not do that prescribed by Moses.

2 In holding all offices of the Church to be members
of the bodie, (for if they be not members, what shoulde

they do in the body) they hold it lawful for the magistrat to attempt the making of new members for that bodie.

3 The altering or abollishing of these members by the magistrates, they holde to be lawfull. And therefore the maiming or deforming.

Now you wretches (Archb. and L. Bishops I mean) you Mar-state, Mar-law, Mar-prince, Mar-maiestrat, Mar-commonwealth, Mar-church, and Mar-religion. Are you able for your liues, to aunswere any part of the former syllogisme, whereby you are concluded, to be the greatest enemies vnto her Maiestie and the State? You dare not attempt it I know. For you cannot denie, but they who holde it and defend it lawfull, (yea enforce the magistrate) to maime or deforme the bodie of Christ, are vtter enemies vnto that magistrat, and that state, wherin this disorder is practized. You cãnot denie your selues to do this, vnto our magistrate and State: because you beare them in hand, that a lawfull church gouernment, may consist of those offices, which the magistrate may abollishe out of the church without sinne: and so, that the magistrate may lawfully cut off the members of Christ from his body, and so may lawfully massacre the body. You are then the men by whome our estate is most likely to be ouerthrowne, you are those that shal answere for our blood which the Spaniard, or any other enemies are like to spil, without the Lords great mercy: you are the persecutors of your brethren, (if you may be accounted brethren) you and your hirelings are not only the wounde, but the very plague and pestilence of our church. You are those

who maime, deforme, vex, persecute, greeue, and wound
the church.   Which keepe the same in captiuity and
darknes, defend the blind leaders of the blind, slander,
reuile and deforme Christes holy gouernment, that such
broken and woodden members as you are, may be still
maintayned, to haue the romes of the true and natural
members of the body.   Tel me I pray, whether the true
and natural members of the body may be lawfully cut
of[f] by the magestrate.   If you should say they may,
I knowe no man would abide the spech.   What?   May
the maiestrat cutt of[f]˙ the true and naturall members,
of the body of Christ?   O impudency, not to be tollerated.   But our magestrate, that is her maiestie, and
our state, may lawfully by your owne confession, cut
you of[f], that is displace you and your offices out of
our church.   Deny this if you dare.   Then in deed it
shal appeare, that Iohn of Canturbury meaneth to be a
Pope in deede, and to haue the soueraignty ouer the
ciuill magestrate.   Then will you shewe your selfe in
deed, to be Mar-prince, Mar-law and Mar-state.   Now
if the magestrate may displace you as he may, then you
are not the true members.   Then you are (as in deed
you ought) to be thrust out, vnlesse the magestrate
would incur the wrath of God, for maiming and de-
forminge the body of the church, by ioyning vnnatural
members thereunto.

Answere but this reason of mine, and then hang those
that seeke reformation, if euer againe they speke of· it,
if you doe not, I wil giue you litle quiet.   I feare you
not.   If the magestrate wil be so ouerseene as to beleeue,

that because you which are the maim of the church
are spoken against, therefore they, namely our prince
and state, which are Gods lieftenaunts, shal be in like
sort, dealt with, this credulity wil be the magestrates
sinne. But I know their wisdome to be such as they
wil not. For what reason is this, which you profane
T. C. haue vsed. pag. 103.

The sinful, the vnlawful, the broken, vnnatural, false
and bastardly gouernors of the church, to wit archb. and
bishops, which abuse euen their false offices, are spoken
against. Therefore the true, natural and lawful, and
iust gouernors of the common welth, shalbe likewise
shortly misliked. Ah sencelesse and vndutifull heastes,
that dare compare your selues with our true magestrates,
which are the ordinaunces of God, with your selues,
that is, with Archbishops and bishops, which as you
your selues confesse (I will by and by proue this) are
the ordinances of the Diuell.

I knowe I am disliked of many which are your enemies, that is of many which you cal puritans. It is
their weaknes, I am threatened to be hanged by you.
What though I were hanged, do you thinke your cause
shalbe the better. For the day that you hange Martin,
assure your selues, there wil 20. Martins spring in my
place. I meane not now you grosse heastes, of any
commotion as profane T. C. like a sensles wretch, not
able to vnderstand an English phrase, hath giuen out
vpon that which he calleth the threatning of fistes.
Assure your selues, I wil proue Marprelat ere I haue
don with you. I am alone. No man vnder heauen is

E

priuy, or hath bin priuie vnto my writings against you,
I vsed the aduise of non therein. You haue and do
suspect diuers, as master Paggett, master Wiggington,
master Udall, and master Penri, &c. to make Martin.
If they cannot cleare their selues their sillinesse is piti-
full, and they are worthy to beare Martins punishment.
Well once againe answere my resons, both of your
Antichristian places in my first epistle vnto you, and
these nowe vsed against you. Otherwise the wisdome
of the magistrate must needs smel what you are. And
cal you to a reckoning, for deceauing them soe long,
making them to suffer the church of Christ vnder their
gouernment to be maimed and deformed.

Your reasons for the defence of your hierarchie, and
the keeping out of Christs gouernment, vsed by this
profame T. C. are already answered. They shew what
profane beastes you are. I wil heere repete them.
But heere first the reader is to know what answere this
T. C. maketh vnto the syllogismes, whereby I prooue
all L. bishops to be petty popes, and petty Antichristes.
I assure you no other then this, he flattly denieth the
conclusion, wheras he might (if he had any learning in
him, or had read any thing) know, that euery dunstical
logician, giueth this for an inuiolable precept, that the
conclusion is not to be denied. For that must needs be
true, if the maior and minor be true, he in omitting
the maior and minor, because he was not able to answere thereby, granteth the conclusion to be true. His
answeare vnto the conclusion is, that al lord Bb. were
not pety popes. Because pag. 74. Cranmer, Ridly,

Hooper, were not petty Popes. They were not pety
popes, because they were not reprobates. As though
you block you, euery petty pope and petty Antichrist
were a reprobate. Why no man can deny Gregory the
great, to be a pettye Pope, and a petty and petty Antichrist. For he was the next immediate pope before
Boniface the first, that knowne Antichrist: and yet this
Gregory left behind him, vndoubted testimonies of a
chosen childe of God: so might they, and yet be petty
Popes, in respecte of their office. Profane T. C. his
1. and 2. reason, for ye lawfulnes of our church gouerment. And what though good men gaue their consent
vnto our church gouernement, or writing vnto bishops,
gaue them their lordly titles? Are their offices therefore lawfull, then soe is the popes office. For Erasmus
was a good man you cannot deny, and yet he both
alowed of the popes office since his calling, and writing
vnto him, gaue him his titles. So did Luther, since his
calling also, for he dedicated his booke of christian
liberty vnto Pope Leo the tenth. The booke and his
Epistle vnto the Pope, are both in Englishe. Here I
would wish the magistrat, to marke what good reasons
you are able to afford for your hierarchie.

Thirdly, saith profane T. C. page 75. All Churches
haue not the gouernment of Pastors and Doctors: but
Saxoni and Denmark, haue L. bishops. You are a
great State man vndoubtedly T. C. that vnderstand, the
state of other Churches so well. But herein the impudencie of a proude foole appeareth egregiously. As
though the testimonie of a siely Schoolemaster, being also

E 2

as vnlearned, as a man of that trade and profession can
be, with any honestie, would be belieued against knowne
experience.   Yea, but Saxonie and Denmarke haue
Superintendents, what then? ergo L. Archb. and bishops?
I deny it.   Though other Churches had L. Archb. and
Bb. this prooueth nothing els, but that other Churches
are maimed and haue their imperfections.   Your reason
is this, other good Churches are deformed, therefore
ours must needes be so to.   The kings sonne is lame,
therefore the children of no subiects must go vpright.
And these be all the good reasons which you can bring
for the gouerment of Archb. and bishops, against the
gouerment of Christ.   You reson thus.   It must not be
admitted into this kingdome, because then Ciuillians
shal not be able to liue, in that estimation, and welth,
wherein they now do.   Carnal and sensles beastes,
whoe are not ashamed to prefer, the outward estate of
men, before the glory of Christs kingdom.   Here againe,
let the magestrate and other readers consider, whether
it be not time, that such brutish men, should be looked
vnto.   Which reason thus.   The body of Christ which
is the church, must needes be maimed and deformed in
this common welth, because otherwise ciuillians should
not be able to liue.   Why you enemies to the state, you
traytors to God and his worde, you Mar-prince, Mar-
law, Mar-magestrate, Mar-church, and Mar-common
welth : do you not know that the worlde should rather
go a begging, then that the glory of god by maiming
his church, should be defaced?   Who can abide this
indignity.   The prince and state, must procure god to

wrath against them, by continuing the deformity of his church, and it may not be otherwise, because the ciuilians els must fall to decay. I wil tel you what, you monstrous and vngodly bishops, though I had no feare of God before mine eies, and had no hope of a better life, yet the loue that I owe, as a natural man, vnto her maiestie and the state would inforce me to write against you: her maiestie and this kingdome, (whome the Lord blesse, with his mighty hand, I vnfainedly beseech) must endanger them selues vnder the peril of Gods heauy wrath, rather then the maime of our church gouernment must be healed, for we had rather it should be so, say our bishops, then wee should be thrust out, for if we should be thrust out, the studie of the ciuil lawe, must needs goe to wrack. Well, if I had liued sometimes a citizen, in that olde and auncient (though heathenish) Rome, and had heard kinge Deiotarus, Cesar, yea or Pompei himself giue out this spech, namely: that the citty and empire of Rome must needes be brought subiect vnto some danger, because otherwise, Catelin, Lentulus, Cethegus, with other of the nobilitie, could not tell how to liue, but. must needs go a begging. I woulde surely, in the loue I ought to the safetie of that state, haue called him that had vsed such a speech, *in judicium capitis*, whosoeuer he had bin: and I woulde not haue doubted to haue giuen him the ouerthrow. And shal I being a christian English subiect, abide to heare a wicked crue of vngodly bishopps, with their hangones and parasites, affirme that our Queene, and our State, must needs be subiect vnto the greatest

daunger that may be, vz. the wrath of God, for deforming his Church, and that Gods Church must needes be
maimed and deformed among vs, because otherwise, a
few Ciuillians shal not be able to liue.   Shall I heare
and see these thinges professed and published, and in
the loue I owe vnto Gods religion and her Maiesty, say
nothing.   I cannot, I will not, I may not be silent at
this speech : come what will come of it.   The loue of a
christian Church, prince and state, shal I trust, worke
more in me, then the loue of a heathen Empire and
state should do.   Now iudge good reader, who is more
tollerable in a commonwealth, Martin that would haue
the enemies of her Maiesty remoued thence, or our
bishops which would haue her life, and the whole kingdomes prosperitie hazarded, rather then a few Ciuillians
should want maintenance.   But I praye thee tell me
T. C. why should the gouernment of Christ impouerish
Ciuillians ?   Because saith he, pag. 77. the Canon law
by which they liue, must be altered, if that were admitted.   Yea but Ciuillians liue by the court of Amraltie,
and other courts as well as by·the Arches, vz. also the
probatts of Testaments, the controuersies of tythes,
matrimonie, and many other causes, which you bishops
Mar-state, do vsurpingly take from the ciuill magistrate,
would be a means of Ciuillians maintenance.   But are
not you ashamed, to professe your whole gouernment,
to be a gouernment ruled by the Popes Canon lawes,
which are bannished by statute out of this kingdome ?
This notably sheweth that you are Mar-prince and
Mar-state.   For howe dare you retaine these lawes,

vnles by vertue of them, you meane eyther to enforce the supremacie of the prince to go again to Rome, or to come to Lambeth. It is treson by Statute, for any sub-iect in this land, to proceed doctor of the Canō law, and dare you professe your church gouerment to be ruled by that law. As though one statute might not refer all matters of the Canon law, vnto the temporall and common law of this Realme: and this is all you can say, T. C.

Yes sayth he, the gouernment of Christe, would 2 bring in the iudiciall law of Moses. As much as is morall of that law, or of the equitie of it, would be brought in. And do you gainesay it. But you sodden headed Asse you, the most part of that law is abrogated. Some part thereof is in force among vs, as the punishment of a murtherer by death, and presumptuous obstinate theft by death, &c. Hir Maiesties prero- 3 gatiue in ecclesiastical causes, should not be a whit diminished, but rather greatly strengthened by Christs gouernment. And no lawe should be altered, but such as were contrary to the lawe of God, and against the profit of the common wealth : and therefore there can be no danger in altering these.

The ministers maintenance by tythe, no puritane 4 denieth to be vnlawfull. For Martin (good M. Parson) you must vnderstand, doth account no Brownist to be a puritane, nor yet a sottish Cooperist.

The inconuenience which you shew of the gouer- 5 ment which is, that men would not be ruled by it, is answered afore. And I praye you, why should they

not be better obedient vnto Gods law, if the same also
were established by the lawe of the lande, then to the
Popes lawe and his Canons. You think that all men
are like your selues : that is, like bishops, such as cannot chuse but breake the laws and good orders of God
and her Maiestie.

7   The lawes of England haue bene made, when
there was neuer a bishop in the Parliament, as in
the first yere of her Maiestie. And this reason as al
the rest, may serue to maintaine poperie, as well as the
hierarchie of Bb.

8   The gouerment of the church of Christ, is no
popular gouernement, but it is Monarchicall, in regarde of our head Christ, Aristocraticall in the Elder-
ship, and Democraticall in the people. Such is the
ciuill gouernement of our kingdome : Monarchicall in
her Maiesties person: Aristocraticall in the higher house
of Parliament, or rather at the Councell table : Democraticall in the bodie of the commons of the lower
house of Parliament. Therefore profane T. C. this
gouernment seeketh no popularity to be brought into
the Church : much lesse entendeth the alteration of the
ciuill state, that is but your slaunder, of which you
make an occupation. And I will surely paye you for
it. I must be brief now, but more warke for Cooper
shall examine your slaunders. They are nothing else
but prooffes, that as by your owne confessions you are
bishops of the Diuell, so you are enemies vnto the
state. For by these slaunders, you go about to blinde
our state, that they may neuer see a perfect regiment of

the Church in our dayes. I saye, that by your owne
confession, you are bishops of the Diuell. I will prooue
it thus. You confesse that your Lordly gouernment,
were not lawfull and tollerable in this cōmonwealth,
if her Maiesty and the state of the land did disclaime
the same. Tell me, doe you not confesse this. Denie
it if you dare. For will you say, that you ought lawfully to be here in our commonwelth whether her Maiesty and the Counsell wil or no: Is this the thankes
that her Maiestie shall haue, for tollerating you in her
kingdome all this while, that nowe you will saye, that
you and your places stand not in this kingdome by her
curtesie, but you haue as good right vnto your places, as
she hath vnto her kingdome. And by this meanes your
offices stande not by her good liking, and the good
liking of the state, as do the offices of our L. high Chancellor, high Treasurer, and high Steward of Englande.
But your offices ought to stand and to be in force, in
spight of her Maiestie, the Parliament, Counsell, and
euerie man els, vnles they woulde doe you iniury. Soe
that I know, I, you dare not deny but that your offices
weare vnlawfull in our common wealth, if her Maiestie,
the Parliament, and the Counsell woulde haue them
abollished. If you grant this, then you doe not hold
your offices as from God, but as from man. Her maiestie she holdeth hir office, and her kingdome, as from
God, and is beholding for the same, vnto no prince nor
state vnder heuen. Your case is otherwise, for you
hold your offices as from her Maiestie, and not from
god. For otherwise, you needed not to be any more

beholding vnto her Maiestie for the same in regarde of right, then she is bounde to be beholding vnto other states in regarde of her right : and so you in regarde of your Lordly superioritie, are not the bishops of god, but as Ierom sayth, the bishops of man. And this the most of you confes to be true, and you see how dangerous it woulde be for you, to affirme the contrary : namely, that you holde your offices as from god. Well sir, if you say that you are the bishops of man. Thē

T. C. 38. tell me whether you like of Dean Iohn his booke. O yes sayth T. C. For his grace did peruse that book, and we know the sufficiencie of it to be such, as the Puritans are not able to answere it. Well then, whatsoeuer is in this booke is authenticall. It is so, saith T. C. otherwise his grace would not haue alowed it. What say you then to the 140. page of that booke, where he saith (answering the treatise of the bishop of God, the bishop of Man, and the bishop of the Diuell) that there is no bishopp of man at all, but euerie B. must be either the Bishopp of God, or the Bishop of the the Diuel. He also affirmeth, none to

Deane Iohn, lib. 4. page 340. line 7. be the bishop of god, but he which hath warrant, both inclusiuely and also expresly in gods word. Now you Bishops of the Diuell, what say you now, are you spighted of the Puritans, because you like good subiects defend the lawes of her Maiestie, or els because like incarnate Diuells, you are bishops of the Diuells, as you your selues confesse.

Here againe, let the Magistrate once more consider,

what pestilent and daungerous beasts these wretches are vnto the ciuill state. For either by their owne confession, they are the Bishops of the Diuell (and so by that means will be the vndoing of the state, if they be continued therin) or else their places ought to be in this commonwealth, whether her Maiestie and our state wil or no: because they are not (as they say) the bishops of man, that is, they haue not their superioritie, and their Lordly callings ouer their brethren by humane constitution, as my LL. Chancellor, Treasurer, and other honorable personages haue, but by diuine ordinance. Yea, and their callings, they holde (as you haue heard) not onely to be inclusiuely, but also expreslie in the word. What shifte will they vse to auoyde this point? Are they the Bishopps of men, that is, holde they their iurisdiction as frō men. No saith Deane Gridges, no sayth Iohn of Canterburie and the rest of them, (for all of them allowe this booke of Iohn Bridges) for then we are the bishops of the deuill, we cannot auoid it? Are they then the bishops of God, that is, haue they such a calling as the Apostles, Euangelists, &c. had: that is, such a calling as ought lawfully to be in a christian common wealth (vnlesse the magistrate woulde iniurie the Church, yea maime, deforme, and make a monster of the Church) whether the magistrate will or no. We haue say they. For our callings are not onely inclusiuely, but also expressely in the worde. So that by Deane Bridges his confession, and the approbation of Iohn Canterburie, either our bishops are bishops of the diuel, or their callings cannot be defended lawful, with-

out flat and plaine treason, in ouerthrowing her Maiesties supremacie.   And so Deane Bridges hath written,
and Iohn Whitgift hath approoued and allowed, flat
treason to be published.

Is Martin to be blamed for finding out and discouer-
ing traitors ?   Is he to be blamed for crying out against
the Bb. of the Diuel.   If he be, then in deed haue I
offended in writing against bishops ?   If not, whether is
the better subiect Martin or our bishops : whether I be
fauored or no, I wil not cease, in the loue I owe to her
Maiestie, to write against traitors, to write against the
Diuels bishops.   Our bishops are such by their owne
confession.   For they protest them selues to be bishopps
of the Diuel.   If they should holde the preheminence
to be from man, If they hold it otherwise then from
man, they are traytors.   And vntil this beast Docter
Gridges wrote this booke, they neuer as yet durst presume to claim their Lordships any otherwise lawful
then from her maiestie, yea and D. Bridges about the
60. page saith the same.   But they care not what con-
trariety they haue in their writings, what treason they
hold, as long as they are perswaded that no man shalbe
tollerated to write against them.   I haue once already
shewed treason to be in this booke of the Deane of
Sarum, page 448.   I shew the like now to be pag. 340.
Because Deane Bridges durst not answeare me.   They
haue turned vnto me in his stead, a beast whome by
the length of his eares, I gesse to be his brother, y^t is,
an Asse of the same kinde.   But I wil be answered of
the Deane him selfe in this and the former point of

treason, or else, his cloister shal smoake for it. And thus profane T. C. you perceue what a good subiect you are, in defending the established gouernment. Thus also I haue answered all your booke in the matters of the lawfulnes of the gouerment by Pastors, Doctors, Elders and Deacons, and the vnlawfulnes of our bastardly Church gouernment, by archbishops and bishops, where also the reader may see, that if euer there was a church rightly gouerned, that is a church without maime or deformity, the same was gouerned by Pastors, Doctors, elders and deacons.

Whau, whau, but where haue I bin al this while. Ten to one among some of these puritans. Why Martin? Why Martin I say, hast tow forgotten thy selfe? Where hast ti bene, why man, cha bin a seeking for a Samons nest, and cha vound a whol crue, either of ecclesiasticall traitors, or of bishops of the Diuel, of broken and maimed members of the church: neuer winke on me good fellow, for I will speke the truth, lett the puritans doe what they can. I say then that they are broken members, and I say Iohn of Canterbury if he be a member of the church, I say he is a broken member, and that Thomas of Winchester is a Cholerick member. Yea and cha vound that profane T. C. is afraid lest her Maiestie shoulde giue Bishops liuings away from them. And therefore shutteth his booke with this position, vz. That it is not lawful to bestow such liuings vppon lay men, as are appointed by Gods law vppon ministers. But hereof more warke for Cooper shal learnedly dispute.

F

Reuerend T. C. Admonition page 1. 2. 3.

We vse the Ministers most vile nowe a dayes.   God
will punish vs for it, as hee did those which abused his
prophets.

Reuerend Martin.

Look to it T. C. then.   For out of thine own mouth
shalt thou be iudged, thou vnrighteous seruant.   Our
bishops are they which abuse the ministers.   Our bishopps were neuer good ministers as yet, and therefore
they are not to be compared with the prophets.

Reuerend T. C. Page 4.

Some men will say, that I do great iniurie to the
prophets and apostles, in comparing our Bishops vnto
thē.   But we may be happie if we may haue tollerable
ministers in this perilous age.

Reuerend Martin.

I hope T. C. that thou dost not mean to serue the
church with worse then we haue: what worse then Iohn
of Canterburie? worse then Tom Tubtrimmer of Winchester? worse then the vickers of Hell, syr Jefferie
Jones, the parson of Micklain, &c. I pray thee, rather thē
we should haue a change from euil to worse, let vs haue
the euil stil.   But I care not if I abide yᵉ venture of
the change.   Therfore get Iohn with his Canterburinesse, remooued, &c. (whome thou acknowledgest to be
euill) and I doe not doubt, if worse come in their stead, .
but the diuell wil soon fetch them away, and so we
shalbe quickly rid, both of euill and worse.   But good

T. C. is it possible to find worse then we haue. I do not maruel though thou callest me libeller, when thou darest abuse the Prophets farre worse, then in calling thē libeliers: for I tel thee true, thou couldest not haue anye way so stayned their good names, as thou hast done, in comparing them to our bishopps. Call me Libeller as often as thou wilt, I do not greatly care: but and thou louest me, neuer liken me to our bishops of the diuell. For I cannot abide to be compared vnto those. For by thine owne comparison, in the 9. page, they are iust Balaams vp and downe.

Reuerend T. C. page 8. 9. 10.

Though our bishops be as euil as Iudas, the false Apostles, and Balaam, yet because they haue sometimes brought vnto vs Gods message, wee must thinke no otherwise of them, then of Gods messengers. For God will not suffer diuellishe and Antichristian persons, to be the chiefe restorers of his gospell.

Reuerend Martin.

First T. C. I haue truly gathered thine argument, thogh thou namest neither Iudas nor the false apostles. Prooue it otherwise. Then hast thou reuerend Martin, prooued thy selfe a lyar. Now secondly then seeing it is so, I praye thee good honest T. C. desire our Iudasses (who was also one of the first Apostles) not to sell their master for money, desire our false Apostles (who preached no false doctrine for the most part) not to insult ouer poore Paule, and desire our good Balaams, not to followe the wages of vnrighteousnes. The coun-

F 2

sell is good. For Iudas, thogh one of the first pub-
lishers of the gospell (so were not our bishops in our
time) yet hung himself. The false apostles had their
reward, I doubt not. And Balaam, as soon as euer the
Israelites tooke him, was iustly executed for his wickednes. The forced blessing wherewith he blessed thē
saued him not.

Reuerend T. C. page 10. 11. 12. 13.

Ma[n]y coniecturall speeches flye abroad of bishops,
as that they are couetous, giue not to the poore, hinder
reformation, Simoniacks, &c. but the chiefe gouernours
ought to take heede, that they giue no credit to any
suche things. I trust neuer any of them, commited
idolatrie as Aharon did.

Reuerend Martin.

Yea, I beseeche you that are in authoritie in any
case, not to beleeue any trueth against our bishops.
For these puritans (although the bishops grant themselues, to bee as euill as Balaam) coulde neuer yet
prooue the good fathers, to haue committed idolatrie as
Aharon did. And as long as they bee no worse then
Balaam was, there is no reason why they should be
disliked. You know this is a troublesome worlde,
men cannot come vnto any meare liuing without friendes.
And it is no reason why a man should trouble his
friende and giue him nothing, a hundred poundes and a
gelding, is yet better then nothing. To bowle but
seuen dayes in a weeke, is a very tollerable recreation.
You must knowe, that Iohn of London, hath sometimes

preached (as this profane T. C. hath giuen out to his no
small commendations) thrise in a yeare at Paules crosse.
A sore labor, it is reason that he should bestowe the
rest of the yeare, in maintaining his health by recreation,
and prouiding for his family: giue him leaue but to
keepe out the gouernment of the Church, to swear
like a swag, to persecute, and to take some small ten in
the hundred : and truely he will be loath euer to commit idolatrie as Aharon did. I hope, though Iudas sold
his master, yet that it cannot be prooued since his calling, that euer he committed idolatrie.

Reuerend T. C. page 16. 17.

Though bishops should offende as Noah did in drun-
kennes, yet good childrē should couer their fathers falts.
For naturall children, though they suffer iniuries at their
fathers hands, yet they take their griefes veric mildely.

Reuerend Martin.

Bishop Westphaling. But what then ? Parson *Grauat*
parson of sir Iohn Pulchres in London (one of dumbe
Iohns bousing mates) will be drunke but once a weeke.
But what then ? good childrē should take linkes in a
cold morning, and light them at his nose, to see if by
that means some part of the fire that hath so flashed his
sweete face, might be taken away : this were their
dutie, sayth T. C. and not to crie redde nose, redd nose.
But T. C. what if a man shoulde find him lying in the
kenill, whether shoulde he take him vpp (all to be
mired like a swine) in the sight of the people, and cary
him home on his backe, or fling a couerled on him, and

let him there take his rest, vntill his leggs woulde be
aduised by him to carie him home. But me thinks
brother T. C. you defend the bishops but euilfauoredly
in these pointes. For you doe, as though a thiefe
should saye to a true man, I must needs haue thy purse,
thou must beare with me, it is my nature, I must needes
playe the thiefe. But yet thou dealest vncharitably
with me, if thou blasest it abroad : for though I make
an occupation of theft, yet charitie would couer it. So
saye you, though our bishops make a trade of perse-
euting and depriuing Gods ministers, though they make
a trade of continuing in Antichristian callings, yet charitie woulde haue their faltes couered, and haue them
mildely delt with. As though T. C. there were no
difference, betwixt those that fall by infirmitie into
some one sinne, not making it their trade, and not
defending the same to be lawfull, and our bishops
which continue in an Antichristian calling, and occupation, and defend they may do so. But wil they
leaue think you, if they be mildly and gently delt with.
Thē good Iohn of Canterbury, I pray thee leaue thy
persecuting : good Iohn of Canterbury leaue thy Popedome : good father Iohn of London, be no more a
bishop of the Diuell : be no more a traytor to God and
his worde. And good sweet boyes, all of you, become
honest men : maim and deforme the church no longer :
sweet fathers now, make not a trade of persecuting :
gentle fathers keep the people in ignoraunce no longer :
good fathers now, maintaine the dumb ministerie no
longer. Be the destruction of the Church no longer,

good sweete babes nowe : leaue your Nonresidencie, and your other sinnes, sweete Popes now : and suffer the trueth to haue free passage. Lo T. C. nowe I haue mildely delt with the good fathers, I will now expecte a while, to see whether they will amende by faire means, if not, let them not say but they haue bin warned.

Reuerend T. C. from the 20. *to the* 30.

Though the bishops be faltie, yet they are not to be excused that finde falt with them for synister ends. And the prince and magistrates, is to take heed that by their suggestions, they be not brought to put downe L. bishops, to take away their liuings, and put them to their pensions. For the putting of them to their pensions, would discourage young students from the study of diuinity.

Reuerend Martin.

I thought you were a fraide to loose your liuings, by the courtier Martins meanes. But brethren feare it not. I woulde not haue any true minister in the land, want a sufficient liuing. But good soules, I commend you yet, that are not so bashful, but you will shew your griefes. Is it the treading vnder foote of the glory of God, that you feare good men. No no say they, we could resonably wel bear that losse. But we dye if you deminish the alowance of our Kitchin. Lett vs be assured of that, and our Lordly callings, and we do not greatly care, how other matters go. I will when more worke is published, helpe these young students vnto a means to liue, though they haue none of your Bishop-domes, if they will be ruled by me.

Reuerend T. C. page 35. 36.

There haue bene within these fewe weekes 3. or 4. pamphlets published in print, against bishops. The author of them calleth him selfe Martin, &c.

R. Martin.

But good Tom Tubtrimmer, if there haue bin 3. or 4 published, why doth bishop Cooper name on[e] only, why doth he not confute all? why doth he inuent obiections of his owne, seeing he had 3. books more to confute, or 2. at least then he hath touched, nay, why doth he not confute one of them thoroughly, seeing therein his Bishopdome was reasonably caperclawed. I haue onely published a Pistle, and a Pitomie, wherein also I graunt that I did reasonably Pistle them. Therefore T. C. you begin with a lye, in that you say that I haue published either 3. or 4. bookes.

Reuerend T. C. page 38.

His grace neuer felt blow as yet, &c. What is he past feeling, wilt thou tel me that T. C. he sleepeth belike in the top of ye roust. I would not be so wel thwacked for the popedome of Canter. as he hath borne poore man. He was neuer able to make good syllogisme since I am sure. Hee alowed D. Bridges his booke quoth T. C. I pray thee what got he by that, but a testimony against him selfe, that either he hath allowed treason, or confessed him selfe to be the bishop of the Diuell.

T. C. page 38. He that readeth his grace's answere,
and M. Cartwrights reply, shal see which is the better
lerned of the twoe. So he shal in deed T. C. and he
were very simple which could not discerne that. And
there is soe much answered already as thou saist, that
his grace dare answere no more for shame. And T. C.
you your selues grant T. Cartwright to be learned, so
did I neuer thinke Iohn Whitgift to bee, what comparison cann you make betwene them? But Thomas
Cartwright, shall I say, that thou madest this booke
against me, because T. C. is sett to it, wel take heed
of it, if I find it to be thy doing, I will so besoop thee,
as thou neuer bangedst Iohn Whitgift better in thy life.
I see 'heere that they haue quarrelled with thee Wa[l]ter
Trauerse, Iohn Penri, Thomas Sparke, Giles Wiggington, Master Dauison, &c. Nay it is no matter, you are
een wel serued, this wil teach you I trow to become
my chaplaines. For if you were my chaplains once, I
trowe Iohn Whitgift, nor any of his, durst not once say
blacke to your eies. And if I had thy learning Thomas
Cartwright, I would make them all to smoak. But
though I were as verye an Assehead as Iohn Catercap
is, yet I coulde deale well inough with cleargie men:
yea with olde Winken de word, D. Prime his selfe.
And ile bepistle you D. Prime, when I am at more
leasure, though in deede I tell you true, that as yet
I doe disdaine to deale with a contemptible trencher
chaplaine, such as you, D. Bankcroft, and Chaplaine
Duport are. But ise be with you all three to bring one
day, you shall neuer scape my fingers, if I take you

but once in hande. You see how I haue delt with
Deane Iohn, your entertainement shalbe alike. But
Thomas Cartwright, thou art T. C. so is Tom Cooper
too. The distinction then, betweene you both, shall be
this : he shalbe profane T. C. because he calleth Christ
Iesus, by whom the gouernment by Pastors, Doctors,
Elders and Deacons was commanded, to be he knowes
not whom : and thou shalt be simple T. C.

Concerning Mistresse Lawson, profane T. C. is it not
lawfull for her to go to Lambeth by water, to accom-

Qui pergit panie a preachers wife, going also (as com-
quod vult monly godly matrons in London do) with her
dicere quæ
non vult man : No saith T. C. I doe not like this in
audiet. women. Tushe man, Thomas Lawson is not
Thomas Cooper, he has no suche cause to doubt of
Dame Lawsons going without her husbande, as the
bishop of Winchester hath had of dame Coopers gadding. But more worke for Cooper, will say more for
mistresse Lawson.

From whom soeuer Charde had his protection, his
Face is glad of it, for otherwise he knoweth not how to
get a printer, for the established gouernment, because
the bookes will not sell.

T. C. pag.   Touching the Premunire, let the Libeller
40.   and his, doe what he dare. Why brethren,
what wisedome is this in you to dare your betters ? doe
you not know that I can sende you my minde by a
Pistle, and then prooue you to be pettie Popes, and
enemies to the State. And how can you mend your
selues. It is certain you are in a premunire. If her

Maiestie will giue me leaue to haue the law, I will be bound to bring 10000. poundes into her coffers vpon that bargain. And therefore foolish men, dare your betters no more. And here I pray thee mark how I haue made the bishops to pull in their hornes. For whereās in this place, they had printed the word *dare*, they bethought themselues, yᵗ they had to deale with my worship, which am fauoured at the Court, and being afraide of me, they pasted the word *can* vpon the word *dare*, and so, where before they bad me and mine doe what we durst: now they bid vs do what we can, hoping thereby to haue a frinde in a corner, whoe woulde not suffer vs to doe what wee ought and durst: and so our abilitie shoulde not be according vnto their demerit. Marke now, ye bishopps of the Diuell, whether you be not afraide of me: I will see you iolled with the Premunire one day.

The like thing you shall finde in the 135. page. For there hauing said, that they will not denie the discipline to haue bene in the Apostles time, they haue now pasted there vpon that, That is not yet proued. So that although their consciences do tell them, that the discipline was then, yet they will beare the world in hand, that that is not yet proued. Here you see that if this patch T. C. had not vsed two patches to couer his patcherie, the bishops woulde haue accounted him to be as very a patch as Deane Iohn.

A, but these knaue puritans are more vnmannerly before his grace, then the recusaunts are, and therefore the recusants haue more fauor. I cannot blame them,

for wee ought to haue no popes. The papists liketh
the Archiepiscopall Pall, and therefore reuerenceth a
petty Pope therein. And though the recusant come
not to heare the sermons, yet he is an informer very
often, vppon other mens information.

His grace denieth that euer he hard of any such
matter, as that the Iesuit should say, he would becom a
braue Cardinal, if popery should come againe. I knowe
T. C. that long since he is past shame, and a notorious
lyer, otherwise how durst he deny this, seeing Cliffe an
honest and a godly cobler, dwelling at Battell bridg,

page 41.   did iustifie this before his grace his teethe,
             yea and will iustifie the same againe if he be
page 46.   called. So will Atkinson too. Send for them
page 44.   if he dare. Ministers of the Gospel ought to
be called priests, saith his grace, what say you by that?
Then good sir Iohn Ò Cant. when wilt thou say Masse
at our house. His grace is also perswaded, that there
ought to be a Lordly superioritie among ministers. So
was Iudas perswaded to sell his master. If you woulde
haue these thinges prooued, profane T. C. referreth you
to his grace his answer vnto simple T. C. and to doctor
Bridges. That is, if you woulde learne any honestie,
you must go to the stewes, or if you would haue a good
sauour, you must go to the sincke for it. Why thou
vnsauorly snuffe, dost tow thinke that men know not
D. Bridges and Iohn Whitgift. Yea but his grace also
firmely beleeueth, that Christ in soule descended into
Hell. This is the 3. point of his catholike perswasion:
but tell him from me, that he shal neuer be saued by

this beliefe, and my finger in his mouth. Let him tell what our sauiour Christ should do, if he did not harrow Hell. Where thou saiest M. Yong had onely the dealing with Thakwel the popish printer, without his graces priuitie, thou liest in thy throat: M. Yong him selfe brought him to his grace, who ordered the matter as it is set downe in my Pistle. But did not I say truely of thee, y^t thou canst cog, face and lye, as fast as a dog can trot, and that thou hast a right seasoned wainscoate face of ti nowne, chwarnt tee, ti vorehead zaze hard as horne.

Concerning Walde-graue, its no matter how you deal with him, heez a foolish fellow, to suffer you to spoyle his presse and letters: an a had bin my worships printer, ide a kept him from your clouches. And yet it is pitie to belye the diuell: and therefore you shall not belye him and goe scotfree. As for the presse that Walde-graue solde, he did it by order, vz. He solde it, to an allowed printer, I. C. one of his owne companie, with the knowledge of his Warden, Henry Denham, &c. And cal you this fauor, in releasing him after long imprisonment? But I will giue you a president of great fauour in deede, wherein you may see what an vngrateful fellow Walde-graue is to his grace, who hath bin so good vnto him from time [to] time. There being a controuersie betweene another printer and Walde-graue (all matters of printing being committed by the LL. of the Counsell to his grace) Walde-graue made one of his company his friende (who could do much with his grace) to deale for him, who brake the matter to his

G

worship, being at Croydon in his Orcharde: so soone as
the partie named Walde-graue, he sweetely aunswered
him, saying: if it had bin any of the cōpany saue him,
he would haue graunted the suite, but in no case to
Walde-graue.   Well Walde-graue, obtained the R. H.
Lord Treasurers letter in his behalfe to his grace, who
when he had read it, said, I wil answer my L. Treasurer:
with that Walde-graue intreated for his fauorable letter
to the Wardens of his companie, which in the end
through D. Coosins he obtained (though late) yet went
home at night, thinking to deliuer it in the morning:
but before he was readie, the Wardens were with him,
and rested him with a Purciuant vpon his graces commandement, Walde-graue telling them there was a letter
from his grace, which he receiued late the last night at
Croidon: who answered, they knew it well inough, but
A new re- this is his pleasure now: so they caried Walde-
uenge for graue to prison, and in this, his grace was so
an old
grudge. good vnto him, as to help him with an hundred marks ouer the shulders.   If this be your fauour,
God keepe me from you, ka M. Marprelate.   Bishops
haue iustly receiued according to their desertes, hauing
found greater fauour at my worships hands thē euer
they deserued, being notorious, disobedient and godlesse persons, vnthrifty spenders and consumers of the
fruits, not of their own labors, (as you say Walde-graue
was) but of the possessions of the church, persons that
haue violated their faith to god, his church, hir maiesty,
and this whol kingdom, and wittingly bring vs al without the great mercy of god to our vndoing: so that our

wiues, children and seruants, haue cause to curse al
L. Bb. Lo T. C. you see that I haue a good gift in
imitation, and me thinkes I haue brought your wordes
into a marueilous good sense, wher as before in the
cause of Walde-graue, they were ilfauoredly wrested:
and as for his wife and children, they haue iust cause
to curse Iohn of London, and Iohn of Canterburie, for
their tyrannizing ouer him: by imprisoning and spoyling
his goods, and vexing his poore wife and children, with
continuall rifeling his house with their purciuants: who
in Nouember last, violently rusht into his house, breaking through the maine wall thereof after midnight, taking
away his goods, for some of the purciuants solde his
books vp and downe the streats, to watchmen and
others. Ah you Antichristian prelats, when will you
make an ende of defending your tyrannie, by the blood
and rapine of her maiesties subiectes? You haue bin
the consumers of the fruits of Walde-graues labors: for
haue you not sent him so often to prison, that it seemed
you made a common occupation thereof? For as soon
as any book is printed in the defence of Christs holy
discipline, or for ye detecting of your Antichristian dealings, but your rauening purciuantes flye citie and countrie to seeke for Walde-graue, as though he were boūd
by statute vnto you, either to make known *O the*
who printed seditious books against my L. *greatnes of his graces*
Face, or to go to prison himselfe, and threat- *fauor.*
ned with the racke. And are you not ashamed to say,
that he euer violated his fayth? you know wel inough,
that he is neither Archb. nor L. B. The case thus

G 2

stood, after he had remained a long time in prison, not
that time when Hartwell his graces secretary wisht that
his grace might neuer eat bit of bread after he released
him.   Nor at that time when you profane T. C. told
him, that all puritans had traiterous hearts.   Nor at
that time Wald-graue tolde his grace, that he was worse
thē Boner in regard of the time.   Nor that time when
he was straungely released by one of the Lorde of good
Londons Swans.   Neither was it at yᵗ time, when his
grace (good conscionable noble man) violated his promise, in that he told the wardens of the stacioners, that
if Walde-graue woulde come quietly to him, and cease
printing of seditious bookes, he would pardon what was
past, and the wardens promised his wife, that if he were
committed, they would lye at his graces gate til he were
released, and for al this, yet he was committed to the
white Lyon, where he laye sixe weekes.   Nor it was
not at that time, when his grace allowed Watson the
purciuant, to take of Walde-graue, 13. s. 4. pence, for
cariyng of him to the white Lyon.   But it was that
time, when his grace kept him 20. weekes together in
the white lyon, for printing the Complaint of the com-
minaltie, the Practize of prelats, A learned mans iudgment, &c.   Means being vsed for his liberty, his frend
who was bound for him told him, his liberty was obtained
in maner following.   You must be bounde saith he,
in a 100. pounds, to print no more books herafter,. but
such as shalbe authorized by hir Maiesty or his grace,
or such as were before lawfully authorized : wherunto
he answered, that it was not possible for him to containe

himselfe within the compasse of that bond, neither should his consent euer go to the same (the *Whereby it may appeare he swore not to his friend.* same wil D. Coosins witnes (that maidenly Doctor, who sits cheek by ioll with you) if he will speake a trueth, which words Walde-graue vttered to him, going in the old pallas at westminster with his keeper before he was released) yet he woulde gladly haue his libertie if he might lawfully. For saide he, I being a poore workeman to my companie, cannot possibly obserue it. For many bookes heretofore printed, had *cum priuilegio*, and yet were neuer authorized : and againe, that it were but a folly for him to sue to her Maiestie, the office were very base and vnfit for her. And he might be wel assured that Caiphas of Cant. would neuer authorize any thing for his behoofe, and so it fell out. And thus Martin hath prooued you in this, as in all other things, to be lyars. And what is it that you Bb. and your hangones will not saye by Walde-graue, whom you would hang if you could. I will be briefe in the rest, but so, as reader may perceiue that T. C. was hired to lye by commission.

I wil stand to it, that his grace accounteth the preaching of the word, being the only ordinary page 46. meanes of saluation to be an heresie, and doth mortally persecute the same : his appellation to the page 47. obedient cleargie shall stand him in no steed, when more worke for Cooper is published. And there I will pay thee for abusing M. Wiggington, and Master Dauison, whose good names can take no staine, page 47. from a bishops chopps. If his grace reiected Master

Euans for want of conformity, why is the *quare impedit*
gotten against the bishopp of Worcester, by the noble
Earl of Warwick his patron.   I hope he wil see both
the *quare impedit*, and the premunire to, brought vppon
the bones of father Edmond of Worcester.   It is a common bragge with his grace his parasites, and
with him selfe, that he is the second person in

page 48. 49.

the land.   More work shall pay his grace for com-
mending the Apocripha, a profane and a lying
storye in many places, to be vnseparably
ioined with the holy word of God.   You grant

2 Esdras 14. 21-37. &c.

D. Spark to haue set his grace and your selfe T. C. at
a *non plus*, for the *septuaginta* is contrary to

page 50.

the Hebrew, and therefore, you maintain contrary translations, and require men to aproue both.   Martin hath
marred Richard patriks market, for otherwise he was in
good hope to haue a benefice at his grace his hand, and
to be made a minstrell.   Shamelesse and impudent
wretches that dare deny Iohn of Căt. to haue bin at any
time vnder D. Perne, but as a fellowe of the house,
where he was master, whereas all the world knoweth
him to haue bin a poore scholler in that house, yea and
his grace hath often confessed, that hee beinge there a
poore scholler, was so poor as he had not a napkin to
wipe his mouth, but when he hadd gotten some fatte
meat of O the fellowes table, would go to the skrine,
and first wipe his mouth on the on[e] side and then O
the other, because he wanted a napkin, iudge you whether this bee not a meaner state, then to cary a cloakbag,
which is not spoken to vpbraide any mans pouerty, but

to pull the pride of Gods enemy an ase lower. Although
wee cannot beleeue D. Perne in the pulpit, yet in this
point wee will not refuse his testimony. I am gladd
Iohn of London you will not deenie, but you page 51.
haue the Diars cloth, make restitution then : 52. 53. 54.
thou madest the porter of thy gate a minister Iohn, and
thou mightest do it lawfully. Why so I pray thee, why
man, because he was almost blinde, and at Paddington
being a small people, hee could not starue as many
soules, as his master doth, which is a great page 55.
charge. I hope M. Madox will thinke scorne, 56.
to ask Iohn of London forgiuenesse. The substance of
the tale is true. I told you that I had it at the second
hand. Are you not ashamed, to deny the elmes to be
cut downe at Fulham ? Why her maiesties taker tooke
them from Iohn of London. And simple fellowes, are
you not able to discern between a plesant frump giuen
you by a counsellor, and a spech vsed in good earnest.
Alas poore Iohn O London, doest thou thinke, that M.
Vicechamberlain spake as he thought. Then it is time
to begg thee for a swagg. And so it is if thou thinkest
wee will beleeue the turncoate D. Perne speaking vnto
vs in his owne name, who like an Apostate, hath out of
the pulpit, tolde so many vntruthes. And as it is as
lawfull to boule, O the Sabboth, as it is to page 57.
eat, and for you to make dumbe ministers, as 58.
it was for Dauid to eat of the shew bread, pag. 110. or
for the Machabees to fight on the Sabboth, or for Moses
to grant a bil of diuorcement? I perceiue these men
will haue the good diuinity, if it be to be page 62.

gotten for money.   Yea and our Sauiour Christ, sware
by his faith very often.   How so good Iohn.   I neuer
hard that before, why saith T. C. he sayd Amen Amen
very often, and Amen, is as much as by my faith, page
62. horrible and blasphemous beastes, whither will your
madnes growe in a while, if you be not restrained.   M.
page 58.   Allen the Grocer is paid all saue 10. pound :
for the vse of that, the executors haue Iohn O Londons
blessing.   And I thinke they are reasonably wel serued.
page 59.   If the tale of Benison be not true, why was
Iohn of London alotted by the counsel, to pay him (I
think) 40. pounds for his false imprisonment.   Iohn of
London is not dumb, because he preacheth somtimes
thrise a yeare at Pauls crosse.   Then we shall neuer
page 6.   make our money of it I see.   But I pray thee
61. 62.   T. C. howe canst thou excuse his blaspeemie, of
Eli, Eli, lama sabackthani : there haue bin 2. outragious facts amongst others committed in the world, by
those that professe true religion, the on[e] was the
betraying of our sauiour by Iudas an apostle, the other
was the horrible mocking of his agonie and bitter passion, by Iohn Elmar a bishop in this speeche.   If he
had bene in some reformed Churches, the blaspheemer
woulde haue hardly escaped with his life.   And is it
true sweete boy in deed ?   Hath Leicestorshiere so
embraced the Gospell without contention, and that by
Dumb Iohns meanes ?   Litle doest thou know what
thou hast done nowe, howe if Martin be a Leycester
shiere man, hast not thou then sett out the praise of
thine owne bane ?   For martin I am sure, hath wroght

your Caiphas Chaire more wracke and misery, then all
the whole land beside. And therefore thou seest, a
man may be so madd somtimes, that he may praise he
cannot tel what. The bishop of Rochester in page 63.
presenting him selfe to a parsonage, did noe more then
lawe allowed him. And do so againe good Iohn of
Rochester, and it will be for thy credit. Fo, these
puritans woulde finde fault I thinke with Iohn of Cant.
(if he beleeuing that Christe in soule went to Hell)
should holde it vnlawfull for a man to pray vnto Christe
being in hell. And sweet Iohn of Cant. if euer thou
praiedst in thy life for any bodies souls, now pray for
thy brother D. Squire and Tarletons soules. They
were honest fellows, though I think dean Iohns
ears be longer. For why good sweet Iohn, may not
your worship do this, as well as William of page 63.
Lincolne might pray, that our soules should 64.
be with the soules of professed traiterous papists.

The good B. of Winchester did not protest, that at
sir M. Oueries which was laid to his charge, page 14.
but he spake som things that way. Wel bro- 65. 66. &c.
ther Winchester, you confesse the most part, and we
wil beleeue the rest for your sake without witnes.
The B. of Winchester neuer said that it was page 71.
an heresie, to holde that the preaching of the worde was
the only ordinarie means to saluation, but inasmuch as
Penri helde that the effect of saluation coulde not be
wrought by the word read, he said that was not far
from heresie: why brother Cooper, what is this els but
open confession. For Iohn Penri as appeareth in his

writings holdeth the word read, to be no ordinary means
of saluation at al.   This I know you wil accoūt an
heresie, otherwise your case is damnable, that cause the
people to content themselues with reading, and hold
that they may ordinarily be saued thereby.   Yea but
page 72.   T. of Winchester disputed a M. of Art, 45.
75.   yeare· ago in diuinitie.   Here is an old lad
once.   I hope that disputation was very cholerickly
performed.   And he did once as prety a thing as that
came to.   For once preaching at Canter. he was disposed to note out T. C. I meane simple T. C. in his
sermon, his part he plaid after this sort.   He noted 4.
great Hidraes of the gospell in his sermon.   1. Carnall
security.   2. Heathenish gentility.   3. Obstinat papistrie.   4. saith he, when I looke in his forehead, I finde
T. C. written therein, which I cannot otherwise interpret, then thankles curiositie, thanklesse for the benefits
already receiued, and more curious than needs in vain
and needles questions.   The old studēt did not know
himselfe to be T. C. when he thus spake, and 'this is
yᵗ thankles curiosity yᵗ hath answered Martin.   Yea
and he saw martins picture drawn when he was a yong
man.   I perceiue then he was not blind, as the old
porter of Paddington, whom Iohn of London bedeaconed
and beminstrelled.   Lucian of Winchester himselfe was
the painter.   Mydas of Cant. the iudge.   The one of
the 2. womē caled ignorance, was the goodwife of Bath,
D. Culpable warden of new colledge, yᵉ other called
ielious suspicion, was yᵉ fox Iohn of Exetor.   Thē came
in Winkendeword, alias D. Prime callumniator.   This

Winken and his L. of Winchester, drew innocencie : to
wit, Martin Marprelat gentleman by the haire of the
head. Then followed *Dolus fraus insidiæ*. To wit,
D. Perne, D. Renold and D. Cosins. The treader was
cankered malice, his eyes were fierie, his face thinn and
withered, pined away with melancholi, and this was D.
Copcoat. Then followed dolfull repentance, y^t is, dean
Iohn repenting that euer he had writtē in the Bb. behalfe
because his grace is not as good as his worde. T. C.
consider this picture vntill we meet againe. Now my
busines calleth me away, I am trauelling towards Ban-
bury, for I here say that there hath bin old adoe. For
bakers daughters wold haue knights whether they would
or no. I wil learne the trueth hereof, and so I will post
to Solihill, and visiting som parts of Stafford, Warwick,
and Northampton shires, I will make a iourney backe
againe to norfolke and suffolke : I haue a register at
Burie, and by that time my visitors will be come out of
Cornwall, Deuon and Hampshire. And now fare thee
well good profane T. C. I cannot now meddle with the
long period which thou hast in the 33. 34. pag. of thy
book, it is but 38. lines : thou art longer wi[n]ded then
Deane Iohn is I see, though he hath longer periods then
that which I set downe. Whereas thou dost complaine
that the liuings of our bishopps are so small, that some
of their children are like to go a begging. There is a
present remedy for that. For to what end els, is Iohn of
Cant. vnmaried, but to prouide for the bishops children
who shalbe poorly left. Though in deed, I neuer said in
my life, that there was euer any great familiaritie (though

I know there was some acquaintaunce) betweene mistris
Toye and Iohn Whitgift. And ile befie em, ile befie
em that will say so of me. And wherfore is Richard of
Peterborowe vnmaried, but to prouide for other mens
children. O now I remember me, he has also a charge
to prouide for, his hostesse and cosin of Sibson. The
peticoat which he bestowed vpon her, within this six
moneths was not the best in England, the token was not
vnmeete for hir state. Farewell, farewell, farewell olde
Martin, and keepe thee out of their handes for all that.
For thou art a shrewd fellowe, thou wilt one day ouerthrow them Amen. And then thou swearest by thy
faith, quoth Iohn of London.

Martin the Metropolitane to Iohn the Metropolitane
sayth, *Nemo confidat nimium secundis.*

Martin to his troubled sonnes sayth,
Nemo desperet meliora lapsus.

Anglia Martinis disce favere tuis.

NOTES.

TITLE.] The words inserted in parenthesis, form, in the original, an erratum at the end.

P. 7, l. 4. *sir Iohns.*] *Sir* was a title formerly applied to priests and curates in general. *Dominus*, the academical title of a bachelor of arts, was, at the Universities, usually rendered by *sir* in English; so that a bachelor, who in the books stood *Dominus* Brown, was in conversation called *Sir* Brown. In the use of the word by our old dramatists and writers, the Christian name appears to have been generally used, although at the Universities it was omitted. In the " Epistle to the Terrible Priests," *Reprint,* p. 53, we have the amusing story of *sir* Iefferie Iones, in which he is also styled *sir* Iones. Sir Hugh Evans, in the *Merry Wives of Windsor;* Sir Topas, *Twelfth Night;* Sir Oliver, *As You Like It;* of Shakspeare; and the Sir Hugh Pancras, in Ben Jonson's *Tale of a Tub,* will readily occur to most readers. Whether it was from the general prevalence of the Christian name John, that we find so many Sir Johns, I cannot tell; but it would appear from many instances, that it was applicable to all such as had proceeded to the first degree at the Universities, that of bachelor of arts. The author has in the present instance used the term generically, in which sense the following illustration from Latimer may be quoted:—

" Instead of a faithfull and painefull teacher, they have a *Sir John,* who hath better skill in playing at tables, or in keeping a garden, than in God's word."—*Latimer's Sermons, Dedication.*

The reader who is curious in the matter may consult the Notes to Reed's Shakspeare, ed. 1813, v. 7. 229; viii. 117; xiv. 390. 482.

H

P. 7, l. 13. *out of all crie.*] This expression, which is to be met with in the title also, is one of a numerous class of expressions, meaning, out of all measure, beyond measure.

" Sirrah, serjeant and yeoman, I should love these maps *out of crie* now, if we could see men peep out of door in 'em."—*Puritan,* iii. 5.

·' And then I am so stowt, and take it upon me, and stand upon my pantofles to them *out of all crie.*"—*Six Old Plays,* i. 174.

So also in Martin's Month's Mind, " he knew not which way to turn himselfe, and at length [was] clean Marde [marred], the greefe whereof vext him *out of all crie.*"—*Sign.* E 3, verso. Shakspeare has *out of all whooping,* As You Like It, iii. 2. In Greene's Fryer Bacon, " For he once loved the fair maid of Fresingfield *out of all hoe.*" In Martin Mar-Prelate's Epitome, *Reprint,* p. 49, l. 3, " This is put home I trow, and ouerthroweth the Puritans *out of all cesse :* and in Shakspeare, I. Hen. IV. " the poor jade is wrung in the withers *out of all cesse.* In page 8 we have *out of all scotche and notche.*

P. 7, l. 20. *moneths mind.*] This expression has nothing to do with the office of the Romish Church for the repose of the dead, formerly used in England, although it is possible the expression might have originated from it. Here it expresses the meaning of a strong desire, and just in the same sense it is used in the western counties to this day. Shakspeare, in the following quotation, has used it in this sense, although the Commentators have given some most strange illustrations :—

" *Julia.* I see you have a *month's mind* to them."
> *Two Gent. of Verona,* i. 3.

Fuller has the expression, " The king had more than a *moneth's mind* to procure the pope to canonize Henry VI. for a saint."—*Ch. Hist.* b. iv. § 23. So Hall,

" And sets a *month's mind* upon smiling Mary."
> *Satires,* b. iv. § 4.

And Butler,

> " For if a trumpet sound, or drum beat,
> Who hath not a *month's mind* to combat."

Hudibras, Part i. Cant. ii. ver. 3.

Nares has given, from Croft's Excerpta Antiqua, a different origin to the expression, but which does not on examination appear very tenable.

P. 8, l. 4. *dum minister.*] This story is to be found in Martin's Epistle.

P. 8, l. 25. *true penie.*] Hamlet uses this expression to the Ghost: " Ha, ha, boy ! say'st thou so ? art thou there *true-penny* ?" It also occurs in the Malcontent, 1604: " Illo, ho, ho, ho; art thou there old *True-penny* ?" See also Forby's Glossary.

P. 10, l. 7. *stafford law.*] *i. e.* club law.

P. 10, l. 20, l. 22. *Eulogein.*] *Enlogeni* in the original, but corrected by the author in the errata.

P. 10, l. 27. *no grue in his pocked.*] Nares, in glossing the word *grew*, says that it "seems to be put for the Greek term γρυ ; *i. e.* any trifling or very worthless matter." The allusion in the text having evident reference to the moderate knowledge of Greek which Martin's adversary possessed, may therefore mean, when he hath *very little or no learning wherewith to answer him.*

P. 11, l. 1 and 8. *our brother Westchester.*] *i. e.* Winchester.

P. 11, l. 2. *Priemeero on the cards.*] Primero was a game at cards, very fashionable in the reign of Elizabeth. This word occurs in Pap with a Hatchet, in the Note to which, p. 46, l. 24, I must request the reader to correct an error inadvertently committed, for Greene to read Cooke, the latter being the author of the play of " Tu Quoque."

P. 11, l. 15. *ka.*] *i. e.* quoth. It is remarkable that the word does not appear in Nares' Glossary. It is frequently used by this writer in his Epistle.

P. 11, l. 26. *argling.*] *i. e.* arguing.

H 2

P. 13, l. 21. *adient.*] Adjoint, adjunct. It refers to the then general custom of placing in the margin, or "margent," such notes as were necessary to elucidate the text, whether in reference to the author or the title of his book.

P. 14, l. 21. *besoop.*] To belabour.

P. 15, l. 13. *of all loues.*] A tender expression frequently used instead of *by all means.* Coles renders the phrase by *amabo.* Shakspeare has some instances :—

" But Mrs. Page would desire you to send her your little page *of all loves;* her husband has a marvellous infection to the little page."—*Merry Wives of Windsor,* ii. 2.

" For *all the loves on earth,* Hodge let me see it."
Gammer Gurton, O. P. ii. 76.

" Alack where are you ? speak an if you hear;
Speak, *of all loves;* I swoon almost with fear."
Mids. N. D. ii. 3.

P. 16, l. 8. *vntil more worke for Cooper be published.*] The allusion to this intended tract, in the printing of which some short time afterwards the press was seized, is frequent in the present work.

P. 17, l. 10. *haue felt of their tongs.*] Meaning, I suppose, their tongues covered with felt. Shakspeare has the word :—

" It were a delicate stratagem, to shoe
A troop of horse with *felt.*"—*Lear,* iv. 6.

See Reed's Shakspeare, xvii. 550, ed. 1813, for other instances.

P. 23, l. 15. *O tis a sweete trunchfiddle.*] Nares has the word *Trunchefice,* with the following illustration, which, as the *running* qualifications of Bishop Aylmer are referred to, may not be inappropriate :—

" Or say'st thou this same horse shall win the prize,
Because his dam was swiftest *Trunchefice,*
Or Runcevall his sire."
Hall's Satires, ed. 1753, iv. 3. p. 65.

P. 24, l. 1. *bumfeg.*] *i. e.* belabour; I see no reference to it in any Glossary: *bumbaste*, a word of similar meaning, sometimes occurs.

"I will so codgell and *bombaste* thee, that thou shalt not be able to sturre thyself."—*Palace of Pleasure*, sign. K 6.

"I will *bombaste* you, you mocking knave."

Damon and Pithias, O. P. i. 209.

P. 24, l. 17. *stealecounter.*] Counters were small circular pieces of base money used for reckoning; and, according to Dr. Farmer, were introduced from France towards the latter part of the seventeenth century. A *stealecounter*, therefore, must be one of the pettiest of thieves.

P. 24, l. 20. *this geare cottons.*] *i. e.* succeeds, prospers.

"Still mistress Dorothy! the *geer will cotton.*"

Beaumont & Fletcher, Mons. Tho. iv. 8.

"Now Hephestion, doth not this matter *cotton* as I would."

Lyly's Alex. & Camp., O. P. ii. 122.

P. 24, l. 26. *proue with a wet finger.*] *i. e.* great ease. Nares seems to think it is derived from the custom of wetting the finger to turn over the leaves of a book with more ease, and quotes the following:—

"I hate brawls with my heart, and can turn over a volume of wrongs with a *wet finger.*"

Gabriel Harvey's Pierce's Superer. 21, *Reprint.*

P. 27, l. 12. *pulleth.*] Evidently an error for putteth.

P. 30, l. 9. *soopes.*] *i. e.* blows.

P. 33, l. 18. *Nuts.*] The expression "that's nuts," when any thing witty is said, and especially in reply to another, is very common in the West of England.

P. 40, last line. *so ouerseene.*] *i. e.* guilty of oversight.

P. 43, l. 26. *Denmark.*] In the original in one copy is Denmake, and in another Denmark, a fact hardly worth noticing but for the purpose of stating that the variation occurs in the same edition, nor can I trace but one edition, although it is stated by more than one authority that there were at least two about this time; there was a reprint I believe in 1641.

P. 44, last line. *procure god to wrath.*] The sense requires *provoke*, unless wrath is used as a verb.

P. 45, l. 23. *ought.*] *i. e.* owed. It occurs in the Mirror for Magistrates, p. 420 :—

"The trust he *ought* me, made me trust him so."

P. 45, l. 29. *hangones.*] A word still in use in some counties, frequently joined to rascal, and probably means a person who deserves hanging. It occurs again at page 69. A friend has, however, suggested that it might only be another form for *hangers-on.*

P. 46, l. 20. *court of Amraltie.*] *i. e.* Admiralty. Amral occurs in Paradise Lost.

P. 47, l. 26. *Brownist.*] Robert Brown, from whom the Independents or Congregationalists date their origin, was a gentleman of Rutlandshire, who suffered several imprisonments for adherence to his opinions. He was a violent opponent of the Church of England discipline and ceremonies. The Brownists were for a long time the subject of popular satire. "I had as lief be a *Brownist* as a politician," says Shakspeare in Twelfth Night.

P. 48, last line. *regiment.*] *i. e.* government. It appears to have been in general use amongst our old writers to the time of James I.

P. 51, l. 16. *Deane Gridges.*] *i. e.* Bridges, probably an error of the printer. It occurs again in the next page.

P. 63, l. 14. *tow.*] *i. e.* thou; it occurs again at page 64, line 26.

P. 53, l. 15. *Where hast ti bene, &c.*] *i. e.* thou been, why man I have been seeking for a salmon's nest, and I have found a whole crew. See Note, page 65, line 10.

P. 53, l. 16. *Samons nest.*] Of the meaning of this expression I must confess my ignorance.

P. 63, l. 25. *patch.*] *i. e.* fool.

P. 65, l. 2. *harrow Hell.*] Harrow; to plunder, spoil, lay waste, subdue. The *harrowing of hell* is an expression constantly applied to our Lord's descent into hell, as related in the Gospel of Nicodemus. There were several early Miracle-plays on the subject, one of which, of the age of Edward II., has recently been edited by Mr. Halliwell, from a MS. in the British Museum. Spenser, in one of his Sonnets, addressing Christ, says,

> " And having *harrowed hell* didst bring away
> Captivity thence captive."—*Sonnets,* 68.

P. 65, l. 8. *cog, face and lye, as fast as a dog can trot.*] This proverb I do not recollect having seen in any collection, although " to lie as fast as a dog can trot" is still in use in Somersetshire.

P. 65, l. 10. *ti nowne, chwarnt tee, ti vorehead zaze hard as horne.*] *i. e.* in plain English, " thine own, I warrant thee, thy forehead is as hard as horn." Steevens, in his Notes on Lear, says, " When our ancient writers have occasion to introduce a rustick, they commonly allot him the Somersetshire dialect. Mercury, in the second Book of Ovid's Metamorphoses, assumes the appearance of a clown, and our translator Golding has made him speak with the provinciality of Shakspeare's Edgar." See Golding's Ovid, ed. 1603, b. ii. One of these peculiarities is in the various forms which the personal pronoun I is made to assume. Mr. Jennings, in his Somersetshire Glossary, says, that it is variously pronounced, Ise, Ich, Iché, Utchy. Whenever the word occurs in composition, the mark of elision should be put before instead of after the *ch;* thus in the text, *chwarnt* should be *'ch warnt.* Without extending this note further, it may be worth while to remark, that in the present instance, in Lear, in Gammer Gurton's Needle, and in every instance which I have met with, the sense requires this mark of elision before the *ch.*

P. 70, l. 26. *skrine.*] Screen?

P. 71, l. 17. *frump.*] *i. e.* a jest : it sometimes means a con-temptuous speech.

P. 74, l. 22. *martins picture, &c.*] The description which fol-lows is evidently an allusion to the exhibition of Martin on the stage, some particulars relating to which will be found in the Notes to the Reprint of Pap with a Hatchet.

P. 76, l. 16. *Richard af Peterborowe.*] Bishop Howland held the see of Peterborough at this time.

THE END.

LONDON :
HUGH WILLIAMS, Printer, Ashby-street, Northampton-square.

Puritan Discipline Tracts.

PAP WITH A HATCHET;

BEING

A REPLY

TO

MARTIN MAR-PRELATE.

Re-printed from the Original Quarto Edition.

WITH

AN INTRODUCTION AND NOTES.

LONDON:

JOHN PETHERAM, 71, CHANCERY LANE.

1844.

INTRODUCTION.

In presenting the following tract to the public, I offer no apology for the sharpness of its sarcasm, or the coarseness of its language. The comparatively few persons into whose hands it may fall, will, I trust, appreciate that which I can assure them they possess, an accurate reprint of a very rare, and by no means an uninteresting tract.

The original edition is in small quarto, printed in Roman letter, without date, but evidently in the latter half of the year 1589. It is mentioned with much commendation by Nash, in his "First Part of Pasquils Apologie," which bears the date of 1590; "I warrant you the cunning *Pap-maker* knew what he did when he made choice of no other spoon than a *hatchet* for such a mouth, no other lace than a halter for such a necke." And the allusion at page 36, "I drew neere the sillie soule, whom I found quiuering in two sheetes of protestation paper," shows that it was printed after "The Protestacyon of Martin Mar-Prelate," dated 1589.

In the copy which I possess, in the handwriting of Isaac Reed, is the following note:—" Collier, in his Ecclesiastical History, ii. 606, gives this pamphlet to Thomas Nash, but Gabriel Harvey ascribes it to John Lyly. *Pierce's Supererogation,* 69." To this statement respecting the authorship very little can be added. It has been attributed to Nash chiefly from the similarity which it bears to his style; and this opinion is somewhat strengthened by the fact that he wrote more than one tract on the same side. On behalf of Lyly it may be said, that the testimony of Gabriel Harvey is that of a contemporary, and therefore more likely to be true. Mr. J. P. Collier, in his " Annals of the Stage," attributes it to Lyly; and Mr. D'Israeli, in his " Calamities of Authors," to Nash. To these authorities might be added others, which, however, afford no additional evidence, and therefore we must be content to leave the discovery to future research.

Some letters will be found at the end amongst the Notes, which show us that the exhibiting of Martin on the Stage led to the interference of Lord Burghley, and the then Master of the Revels, Tylney, issued his orders " to staie all plaies within the cittie, utterlie misliking the same:" it is evidently to the period of this inhibition that the facts mentioned at page 32 must be referred.

J. P.

London, Nov. 4, 1844.

Pappe with an hatchet.

Alias,

A figge for my God sonne.

Or

Cracke me this nut.

Or

A Countrie cuffe, that is, a sound boxe of the
eare, for the idiot *Martin* to hold his peace,
seeing the patch will take no
warning.

Written by one that dares call a dog, a dog,
and made to preuent *Martins* dog daies.

Imprinted by *Iohn Anoke,* and *Iohn Astile,* for the
Bayliue of Withernam, *cum priuilegio perennita-
tis,* and are to bee sold at the signe of the
crab tree cudgell in thwack-
coate lane.

A sentence.

Martin hangs fit for my mowing.

To the Father and the two Sonnes,
Huffe, Ruffe, and Snuffe,

the three tame ruffians of the Church, which take pepper

in the nose, because they can not

marre Prelates :

grating.

Roome for a royster ; so thats well sayd, itch a little
further for a good fellowe. Now haue at you all my
gaffers of the rayling religion, tis I that must take you
a peg lower. I am sure you looke for more worke,
you shall haue wood enough to cleaue, make your tongue
the wedge, and your head the beetle, Ile make such a
splinter runne into your wits, as shal make thē ranckle
till you become fooles. Nay, if you shoot bookes like
fooles bolts, Ile be so bold as to make your iudgements
quiuer with my thunderbolts. If you meane to gather
clowdes in the Commonwealth, to threaten tempests,
for your flakes of snowe weele pay you with stones of
hayle ; if with an Easterlie winde you bring Catterpillers

into the Church, with a Northerne wind weele driue barrennes into your wits.

We care not for a Scottish mist, though it wet vs to the skin, you shal be sure your cockscombs shall not be mist, but pearst to the skuls. I professe rayling, and think it as good a cudgell for a Martin, as a stone for a dogge, or a whippe for an Ape, or poyson for a rat.

Yet find fault with no broad termes, for I haue me- sured yours with mine, and I find yours broader iust by the list. Say not my speaches are light, for I haue weighed yours and mine, and I finde yours lighter by twentie graines than the allowance. For number you exceede, for you haue thirtie ribauld words for my one, and yet you beare a good spirit. I was loath so to write as I haue done, but that I learnde, that he that drinkes with cutters, must not be without his ale dagger; nor hee that buckles with Martin, without his lauish termes.

Who would currie an Asse with an Iuorie combe? giue the beast thistles for prouender. I doo but yet angle with a silken flye, to see whether Martins will nibble; and if I see that, why then I haue wormes for the nonce, and will giue them line enough like a trowte, till they swallow both hooke and line, and then Martin beware your gilles, for Ile make you daunce at the poles end.

I knowe Martin will with a trice bestride my shoulders. Well, if he ride me, let the foole sit fast, for my wit is verie kickish; which if he spurre with his copper replie, when it bleedes, it will all to besmeare their consciences.

If a Martin can play at chestes, as well as his nephewe the ape, he shall knowe what it is for a scaddle pawne, to crosse a Bishop in his owne walke. Such dydoppers must be taken vp, els theile not stick to check the king. Rip vp my life, discipher my name, fill thy answer as full of lies as of lines, swell like a toade, hisse like an adder, bite like a dog, and chatter like a monkey, my pen is prepared and my minde; and if yee chaunce to finde any worse words than you brought, let them be put in your dads dictionarie. And so farewell, and be hangd, and I pray God ye fare no worse.

Yours at an houres warning
Double V.

INDIFFERENT READER.

It is high time to search in what corner of the Church the fire is kindled, being crept so far, as that with the verie smoke the consciences of diuers are smothered. It is found that certaine Martins, if no miscreants in religion (which wee may suspect) yet without doubt malecōtents (which wee ought to feare) haue throwen fire, not into the Church porch, but into the Chauncell, and though not able by learning and iudgement to displace a Sexton, yet seeke to remooue Bishops. They haue scattered diuers libels, all so taunting and slanderous, as it is hard to iudge, whether their lyes exceed their bitternesse, or their bitternesse their fables.

If they be answered by the grauitie of learned Prelates, they presentlie reply with railings; which argueth their intent to be as farre frō the truth of deuotion, as their writings from mildnes of spirit. It is said that camels neuer drinke, til they haue troubled the water with their feete, and it seemes these Martins cannot carouse the sapp of the Church, till by faction they make tumults in religion. Seeing thē either they expect no graue replie, or that they are settled with railing to replie; I thought it more conuenient, to giue them a whisk with their owne wand, than to haue them spurd with deeper learning.

The Scithian slaues, though they bee vp in armes, must bee tamde with whippes, not swords, and these mutiners in Church matters, must haue their mouthes bungd with iests, not arguments.

I seldome vse to write, and yet neuer writ anie thing, that in speech might seeme vndecent, or in sense vn-honest; if here I haue vsed bad tearmes, it is because they are not to bee answered with good tearmes: for whatsoeuer shall seeme lauish in this Pamphlet, let it be thought borrowed of Martins language. These Martins were hatcht of addle egges, els could they not haue such idle heads. They measure conscience by their owne yard, and like the theeues, that had an yron bed, in which all that were too long they would cut euen, all that were too short they would stretch out, and none escapte vnrackt or vnsawed, that were not iust of their beds length: so all that are not Martins, that is, of their peeuish mind, must be measured by them. If he come short of their religion, why he is but a colde Protestant, hee must bee pluckt out to the length of a Puritane. If any be more deuout than they are, as to giue almes, fast, and pray, then they cut him off close by the workes, and say he is a Papist. If one be not cast in Martins mould, his religion must needes mould.   He saith he is a Courtier, I thinke no Courtier so peruerse, that seeing the streight rule of the Church, would goe about to bend it.   It may be he is some Iester about the Court, and of that I meruaile, because I know all the fooles there, and yet cannot gesse at him. What euer he be, if his conscience be pind to his cognizance, I will account him more politicke than religious, and more dangerous for ciuill broyles, than the Spaniard for an open warre.   I am ignorant of Martin and his maintainer, but my conscience is my warrant, to care for neither.   For I knowe there is none of honour so carelesse, nor any in zeale so peeuish, nor of nature any so barbarous, that wil succour those that be suckers of the Church, a thing against God and policie ; against God, in subuerting religion ; against policie, in altering gouernment, making in the Church, the feast of the Lapithees, where all shall bee throwne on anothers head, because euerie one would be the head.   And these it is high time to tread vnder foote : for who would not make a threshold of those, that go about to make the Church a barne to thresh in.   *Itaque sic disputo.*

FINIS.

Pappe with an Hatchet.

Good morrow, goodman Martin, good morrow : will ye
anie musique this morning?   What fast a sleepe?   Nay
faith, Ile cramp thee till I wake thee.   *O whose tat?*
Nay gesse olde knaue and odd knaue : for Ile neuer
leaue pulling, til I haue thee out of thy bed into the
streete ; and then all shall see who thou art, and thou
know what I am.

Your Knaueship brake you fast on the Bishops, by
breaking your iests on them : but take heed you breake
not your owne necke. Bastard Iunior dinde vpon them,
and cramde his maw as full of mallice, as his head was
of malapertnesse.   Bastard Senior was with them at
supper, and I thinke tooke a surfet of colde and raw
quipps.   O what queasie girds were they towards the
fall of the leafe.   Old Martin, neuer entaile thy wit to
the eldest, for bee'le spend all he hath in a quire of
paper.

Now sirs, knowing your bellies full of Bishops bobbs,
I am sure your bones would be at rest : but wee'le set
vp all our rests, to make you all restie.   I was once
determined to write a proper newe Ballet, entituled
Martin and his Maukin, to no tune, because Martin was

Hee sweares by his maz^er, that he will make their wits wet-shod, if the ale haue his swift current. out of all tune. Elderton swore hee had rimes lying a steepe in ale, which should marre all your reasons: there is an olde hacker that shall take order for to print them. O how hee'le cut it, when his ballets come out of the lungs of the licour. They shall be better than those of Bonner, or the ierkes for a Iesuit. The first begins, Come tit me come tat me, come throw a halter at me.

Then I thought to touch Martin with **Logick,** but there was a little wag in Cambridge, that swore by Saint Seaton, he would so swinge him with Sillogismes, that all Martins answeres should ake. The vile boy hath manie bobbes, and a whole fardle of fallacies. He begins,

Linquo coax ranis, cros coruis, vanaque vanis.

Ad Logicam pergo, quæ Mart'ins non timet ergo.

And saies, he will ergo Martin into an ague. I haue read but one of his arguments.

> *Tiburne stands in the cold,*
> *But Martins are a warme furre :*
> *Therefore Tiburne must be furd with*
> *Martins.*

O (quoth I) boy thou wilt be shamed ; tis neither in moode nor figure: all the better, for I am in a moode to cast a figure, that shall bring them to the conclusion. I laught at the boye, and left him drawing all the lines of Martin into sillogismes, euerie conclusion beeing this, Ergo Martin is to bee hangd.

Nay, if rime and reason bee both forestalde, Ile raile, if Martin haue not barrelde vp all rakehell words : if he haue, what care I to knock him on the head with his owne hatchet. He hath taken vp all the words for his obscenitie : obscenitie? Nay, now I am too nice ; squirrilitie were a better word : well, let me alone to squirrell them.

Martin, thinkst thou, thou hast so good a wit, as none can outwrangle thee? Yes Martin, wee will play three a vies wits : art thou so backt that none dare blade it with thee? Yes Martin, wee will drop vie stabbes. Martin sweares I am some gamester. Why, is not gaming lawful? I know where there is more play in the compasse of an Hospitall, than in the circuite of Westchester. One hath been an old stabber at passage : the One that I meane, thrust a knife into ones thigh at Cambridge, the quarrel was about cater-tray, and euer since he hath quarrelled about cater-caps.

I thought that hee which thrust at the bodie in game, would one daie cast a foyne at the soule in earnest. But hee workes closelie and sees all, hee learnd that of old Vydgin the cobler, who wrought ten yeares with spectacles, and yet swore he could see through a dicker of leather. He hath a wanton spleene, but wee will haue it stroakt with a spurne, because his eies are bleard, he thinkes to bleare all ours; but let him take this for a warning, or else looke for such a warming, as shall make all his deuices as like wood, as his spittle is like woodsere. Take away the Sacke, and giue him some Cinamom water, his conscience hath a colde stomacke.

Cold? Thou art deceiued, twil digest a Cathedral
Church as easilie, as an Estritch a two penie naile.

But softe Martins, did your Father die at the Groyne?
It was well groapt at, for I knewe him sicke of a paine
in the groyne. A pockes of that religion, (quoth Iulian
Grimes to her Father) when al his haires fell off on the
sodaine. Well let the olde knaue be dead. Whie are
not the spawnes of such a dog-fish hangd? Hang a
spawne? drowne it; alls one, damne it.

Ye like not a Bishops rochet, when all your fathers
hankerchers were made of his sweete harts smocke.
That made you bastards, and your dad a cuckold, whose
head is swolne so big, that he had neede sende to the
cooper to make him a biggin: and now you talke of a
cooper, Ile tell you a tale of a tubb.

At Sudburie, where the Martin-mōgers swarmd to
a lecture, like beares to a honnie pot: a good honest
strippling, of the age of fiftie yeares or thereabout, that
could haue done a worse act if companie had not been
neere, askt his sweete sister, whether lecherie in her
conscience were a sinne? In faith (quoth she) I thinke
it the superficies of sinne, and no harme if the tearmes
be not abusde, for you must say, vertuously done, not
lustily done. Fie, this is filthie ribaldry. O sir, ther
is no mirth without ribaldrie, nor ribaldrie without
Martin, ask mine hostesse of the iuie bush in Wye for
the one, and my old hostesse of the Swanne in Warwicke
for the other. She is dead: the diuell she is. You
are too broad with Martins brood: for hee hath a
hundred thousand that will set their handes to his

Articles, and shewe the Queene. Sweeter and sweeter: for wee haue twentie hundred thousand handes to withstand them. I would it were come to the grasp, we would show them an Irish tricke, that when they thinke to winne the game with one man, wee'le make holde out till wee haue but two left to carrie them to the gallowes: well followed in faith, *They are not so many, thei are all Centimani, an hundred hands a peece: so that in all they are but one thousand.*

for thou saidst thou wert a gamester. All this is but bad English, when wilt thou come to a stile? Martin hath manie good words. Manie? Now you put me in minde of the matter, there is a booke cōming out of a hundred merrie tales, and the petigree of Martin, fetchte from the burning of Sodome, his armes shal be set on his hearse, for we are prouiding his funerall, and for the winter nights the tales shall be told *secundum vsum Sarum:* the Deane of Salisburie can tell twentie. If this will not make Martin mad, malicious and melancholie (ô braue letter followed with a full crie) then will we be desperate, and hire one that shall so translate you out of French into English, that you will blush and lie by it. And one will we coniure vp, that writing a familiar Epistle about the naturall causes of an Earthquake, fell into the bowells of libelling, which made his eares quake for feare of clipping, he shall tickle you with taunts; all his works bound close, are at least sixe sheetes in quarto, and he calls them the first tome of his familiar Epistle: he is full of latin endes, and worth tenne of those that crie in London, *haie ye anie gold ends to sell.* If he giue you a bob, though he drawe no bloud, yet are you

c

sure of a rap with a bable. If he ioyne with vs, *perijsti*
Martin, thy wit wil be massacred : if the toy take him
to close with thee, then haue I my wish, for this tenne
yeres haue I lookt to lambacke him.   Nay he is a mad
lad, and such a one as cares as little for writing without
wit, as Martin doth for writing without honestie ; a
notable coach companion for Martin, to drawe Diuinitie
from the Colledges of Oxford and Cambridge, to Shoomakers hall in Sainct Martins.   But we neither feare
Martin, nor the foot-cloth, nor the beast that wears it,
be he horse or asse ; nor whose sonne he is, be he Martins, sonne, Iohns, sonne, or Richards, sonne ; nor of
what occupation he be, be a ship-wright, cart-wright, or
tiburn-wright.   If they bring seuen hundred men, they
shall be boxt with fourteen hundred boyes.   Nay we
are growing to a secret bargaine.   O, but I forgate a
riddle ; *the more it is spied, the lesse it is seene.*   Thats
the Sunne : the lesse it is spied of vs, the more it
is seene of those vnder vs.   The Sunne ? thou art an
asse, it is the Father, for the old knaue, thinking by his
bastardie to couer his owne heade, putteth it like a
stagge ouer the pale.   Pale ? nay I will make him blush
as red as ones nose, that was alwaies washt in well water.

What newes from the the Heraldes ? Tush, thats
time enough to know to morrow, for the sermon is not
yet cast.   The sermon foole ? why they neuer studie,
but cleaue to Christ his *dabitur in illa hora.*   They
venter to catch soules, as they were soles ; Doctors are
but dunces, none sowes true stitches in a pulpet, but a
shoomaker.

Faith, thou wilt bee caught by the stile. *Martin Iu-*
What care I to be found by a stile, when so *nior saies,*
hee found
many Martins haue been taken vnder an hedge? *his fathers*
papers vn-
If they cannot leuell, they will roue at thee, *der a bush,*
and anatomize thy life from the cradle to the *the knaue*
was started
graue, and thy bodie from the corne on thy *from his*
Fourme.
toe, to the crochet on thy head. They bee as
cunning in cutting vp an honest mans credit, as Bull
in quartering a knaues bodie.   Tush, (what care I) is
my posie; if hee meddle with mee, Ile make his braines
so hot that they shall crumble, and rattle in his warpt
scull, like pepper in a dride bladder.

I haue a catalogue of al the sheepe, and it shall go
hard, but I will crosse the bel-weather.   Why shuld I
feare him that walkes on his neats-feete. Neither court,
nor countrie that shal be free, I am like death, Ile spare
none.   There shall not misse a name of anie, that had a
Godfather; if anie bee vnchristened, Ile nicke him with
a name.

But whist; beware an action of the case.   Then put
this for the case, whether it bee not as lawfull to set
downe the facts of knaues, as for a knaue to slander
honest men.   Alls as it is taken; marie the diuell take
al, if truth find not as many soft cushions to leane on,
as trecherie.

Theres one with a lame wit, which will not weare a
foure cornerd cap, then let him put on Tiburne, that hath
but three corners; and yet the knaue himselfe, hath a
pretie wench in euerie corner.

I could tickle Martin with a true tale of one of his

c 2

He calls none but the heavens to witnesse. sonnes, that hauing the companie of one of his sisters in the open fieldes, saide, hee would not smoother vp sinne, and deale in hugger mugger against his Conscience. In the hundred merrie tales, the places, the times, the witnesses and all, shall be put downe to the proofe, where I warrant you, the Martinists haue consciences of proofe. Doost think Martin, thou canst not be discouered? What foole would not thinke him discouered that is balde? Put on your night cap, and your holie day English, and the best wit you haue for high daies, all wil be little enough to keep you from a knaues penance, though as yet you bee in a fooles paradice. If you coyne words, as *Cankerburie, Canterburines,* &c. whie, I know a foole that shall so inkhornize you with straunge phrases, that you shall blush at your owne bodges. For Similes, theres another shal liken thee to anie thing, besides he can raile too. If Martin muzzle not his mouth, and manacle his hands, Ile blabb all, and not sticke to tell, that pewes and stewes are rime in their religion.

Scratch not thy head Martin, for be thou Martin the bird, or Martin the beast; a bird with the longest bill, or a beast with the longest eares, theres a net spread for your necke. Martin, Ile tell thee a tale woorth twelue pence, if thy witt bee woorth a pennie.

There came to a Duke in Italie, a large lubber and a beggerlie, saying hee had the Philosophers Stone, and that hee could make golde faster, than the Duke could spend it. The Duke askt him, why hee made none to mainteine himself? Because, quoth he, I could neuer get a secret place to worke in; for once I indeuoured, and the Popes holinesse sent for me, whom if he had caught, I should haue been a prentice to mainteine his pride. The Duke minding to make triall of his cunning, and eager of golde, set him to worke closely in a vault, where it was not knowen to his neerest seruants. This Alcumist, in short time consumed two thousande pound of the Dukes gold, and brought him halfe a ducket: whie (quoth the Duke) is this all? All quoth he my Lord, that I could make by Art. Wel said the Duke then shalt thou see my cunning: for I will boile thee, straine thee, and then drie thee, so that of a lubber, that weighed three hundred weight, I will at last make a dram of knaues powder. The Duke did it.

Martin, if thou to cousen haue crept into the bosome of some great mē, saying thou hast the churches discipline, and that thou canst by thy faction and pollicie, pull down Bishops and set vp Elders, bring the lands of the Clergy, into the cofers of the Temporaltie, and repaire Religion, by impairing their liuings, it may bee, thou shalt bee hearkened too, stroakt on the head, greasd in the hand, fed daintelie, kept secretlie, and countenaunst mightelie. But when they perceiue, that all thy deuices bee but Chymeraes, monsters of thine owne imaginations, so farre from pulling downe a Cathedrall Church, that they cannot remooue a corner of a square cap, thē will they deale with thee, as the Duke did with the Alcumist, giue thee as many bobs on the eare, as thou hast eaten morsels of their meate, and make thee an ex-

Martin and his mainteiner are both sawers of timber,

c 3

but Martin ample of sedition to be pointed at, that art now
stands in
the pit, all so mewde vp, that none can point where thou
the dust art.   All this tale, with the application, was
must fall
in his eies, not of my penning, but found among loose
but he shal papers; marie he that did it, dares stand to
neuer walke
on the it.   Now, because I haue nothing to doo be-
boards.
tweene this and supper, Ile tell you another
tale, and so begin Winter by time.

There was a libeller, who was also a coniurer, so that
whatsoeuer casting of figures there was, he deceiued
them; at the last, one as cunning as himself, shewed,
wher he sate writing in a fooles coate, and so he was
caught and whipt.   Martin, there are figures a flinging,
and ten to one thou wilt be found sitting in a Knaues
skinne, and so be hangd.

Hollow there, giue me the beard I wore yesterday.
O beware of a gray beard, and a balde head: for if
such a one doo but nod, it is right dudgin and deepe
discretion.   But soft, I must now make a graue speach.

There is small difference between Swallowes and
Martins, either in shape or nature, saue onely, that the
Martins, haue a more beetle head, they both breed in
Churches, and hauing fledgde their young ones, leaue
nothing behind them but durt.   Vnworthie to come into
the Church porch, or to be nourished vnder anie good
mans eues, that gnawe the bowels, in which they were
bred, and defile the place, in which they were ingendred.

They studie to pull downe Bishopps, and set vp
Superintendents, which is nothing else, but to raze out
good Greeke, and enterline bad Latine.   A fine period;

but I cannot continue this stile, let me fal into my olde vaine. O doost remember, howe that Bastard Iunior complaines of brothells, and talkes of long Megg of Westminster. A craftie iacke, you thoght because you twitted Mar-martin, that none would suspect you; yes faith Martin, you shall bee thresht with your owne flaile.

It was one of your neast, that writt this for a loue letter, to as honest a womā as euer burnt malt. "Grace, mercie, and peace to thee (O widow) with feruent motions of the spirit, that it may worke in thee both to will and to doo. Thou knowest my loue to thee is, as Paules was to the Corinthians; that is, the loue of co-pulation."

Hee thought Lais had still lien at Corinth as wel as Paul.

How now holie Martin, is this good wooing? If you prophane the Scriptures, it is a pretie wit; if we but alledge Doctors to expound them, wee are wicked. If Martin oppresse his neighbor, why hee saith, it is his conscience; if anie else doo right, it is extremitie. Martin may better goe into a brothell house, then anie other go by it; he slides into a bad place like the Sunne, all others stick in it like pitch. If Martin speake broad bawdrie, why all the crue saies, your worship is passing merrie. Martin will not sweare, but with indeede, in sooth, and in truth, hee'le cogge the die of deceipt, and cutte at the bumme carde of his conscience. O sweetelie brought in, at least three figures in that line, besides, the wit ant.

One there was, and such a one as Martin would make the eldest of his Elders, that hauing fortie angels sent

him for a beneuolence, refusde to giue the poore fellowe
a quittance for the receipt, saying, Christ had giuen his
master a quittance, the same howre he told it out: and
this was at his table, where he sate with no less than
fortie good dishes of the greatest dainties, in more pompe
than a Pope, right like a superintendant.

Now to the two bastards, what were you twins? It
shuld seeme so, for there wēt but a paire of sheeres
betweene your knaueries. When the old henne hatcht
such eggs, the diuell was in the cocks comb. Your
father thrusts you forward, remember pettie Martins
Aesops crab, the mother going backward, exhorted her
sonnes to goe forward; doo you so first mother quoth
they, and we will follow. Now the old cuckold hath
puld in his hornes, he would make you creepe cleane
out of the shell, and so both loose your houses, and
shewe your nakednesse. You go about impossibilities,
wele no such chāge, and if ye had it, ye would be
wearie of it.

There was a man like Martin, that had a goose, which
euerie daie laid him a golden egge, he not content with
the blessing, kild his goose, thinking to haue a myne of
golde in her bellie, and finding nothing but dung, the
gāder wisht his goose aliue. Martinists that liue well
by the Church, and receiue great benefites of it, thinke
if all Churches were downe, they should be much better,
but when they shall see cōfusion instead of discipline,
and atheisme to be found in place of doctrine, will they
not with sighs wish the Churches and Bishops in their
wonted gouernmēt? Thou art well seen in tales, and

preachest Aesops fables. Tush, Ile bring in *Pueriles*,
and *Stans puer ad mensam*, for such vnmannerlie knaues
as Martin, must bee set againe to their A.B.C. and
learne to spell Our Father in a Horne booke. Martin
Iunior giues warning that none write against reuerent
Martin: yes, there are *a tribus ad centum*, from three
to an hūdred, that haue vowed to write him out of his
right wittes, and we are all *Aptots*, in all cases alike, till
we haue brought Martin to the ablatiue case, that is, to
bee taken away with Bulls voyder.

O here were a notable full point, to leaue Martin in
the hangmans apron. Nay, he would be glad to scape
with hanging, weele first haue him lashte through the
Realme with cordes, that when hee comes to the
gallowes, he may be bleeding new.

The babie comes in with *Nunka, Neame*, and *Dad*:
(Pappe with an hatchet for such a puppie) giue the
infant a bibbe, he all to beslauers his mother tongue, if
he driuell so at the mouth and nose, weele haue him
wipte with a hempen wispe *Hui?* How often hast thou
talkt of haltring? Whie it runnes still in my minde
that they must be hangd. Hangde is the Que, and it
comes iust to my purpose.

There was one endited at a Iaile deliuerie of felonie,
for taking vp an halter by the high way. The Iurie
gaue verdit and said guiltie. The Iudge an honest man,
said it was hard to find one guiltie for taking vp a penie
halter, and bad them consider, what it was to cast awaie
a man. Quoth the foreman, we haue enquired throughly,
and found there was a horse tied to the halter. I marie

(quoth the Iudge) then let him be tied to the halter, and let the horse goe home. Martin, a Monarch in his owne moyst conceit, and drie counsell, saies he is enuied onelie, because he leuelleth at Bishops; and we say as the Iudge saith, that if there were nothing else, it were hard to persecute them to death; but when we finde that to the rule of the Church, the whole state of the Realme is linckt, and that they filching away Bishop by Bishop, seeke to fish for the Crown, and glew to their newe Church their owne conclusions, we must then say, let Bishops stand, and they hang; that is, goe home. Looke howe manie tales are in this booke, so manie must you abate of an hundred in the next booke, reckon this for one.

There came by of late a good honest Minister, with a cloake hauing sleeues: ah (quoth a Martinist, sitting on a bulke in Cheapside) he is a knaue I warrant you, a claspe would become one of his coate to claspe his cloak vnder his chinne. Where tis to be noted, that they come in with a sleeuelesse conscience, and thinke it no good doctrine, which is not preached with the cloak cast ouer each shoulder like a rippier.

Twas a mad knaue and a Martinist, that diuided his sermon into 34 parts for memorie sake, and would handle but foure for memorie sake, and they were, why Christ came, wherefore Christ came, for what cause Christ came, and to what end Christ came; this was all for memorie sake. If that Martin could thatch vp his Church, this mans scabship should bee an Elder, and Elders they may bee, which being fullest of spungie

pith, proue euer the driest kixes. For in time you shall
see, that it is but a bladder of worldlie winde which
swells in their hearts, being once prickt, the humour
will quicklie be remoued. O what a braue state of
the Church it would be for all Ecclesiasticall causes to
come before Weauers and Wierdawers, to see one in a
motlie Ierkin and an apron to reade the first lesson.
The poore Church should play at vnequal game, for it
should loose al by the *Elder* hand. Nay Mas Martin,
weele make you deale, shuffle as well as you can, we
meane to cut it.

If you had the foddring of the sheep, you would make
the Church like Primero, foure religions in it, and nere
one like another. I cannot out of his gaming humour.
Why? Is it not as good as Martins dogged humour,
who without reuerence, regard, or exception, vseth such
vnfitting tearmes, as were hee the greatest subiect in
England hee could not iustifie them.

Shut the doores (sirs) or giue me my skimmer, Martins mouth had sod vnskimde these twelue months, and
now it runnes ouer; yet let him alone, he makes but
porredge for the diuell.

His Elderberines though it be naught worth, yet is it
like an elderberrie, which being at the ripenes of a perfect black, yet brused staines ones hands like bloud.
They pretending grauitie in the rottennes of their zeale,
bee they once wrung, you shall finde them lighter than
feathers. Thats a simile for the slaues. Nay, Ile touch
them deeper, and make them crie, O my heart, there is
a false knaue among vs.

Take away this beard, and giue me a pickede vaunt, Martin sweares by his ten bones: nay, I will make him mumpe, mow, and chatter, like old Iohn of Paris garden before I leaue him.

If Martin will fight Citie fight, wee challenge him at all weapons, from the taylors bodkin to the watchmans browne bil. If a field may be pitcht we are readie: if they scratch, wee will bring cattes: if scolde, we will bring women: if multiplie words, we will bring fooles: if they floute, we will bring quippes: if dispute the matter, we will bring schollers: if they buffet, we will bring fists. *Deus bone*, what a number of we will brings be here? Nay, we will bring Bull to hang them. A good note and signe of good lucke, three times motion of Bull. Motion of Bull? Why, next olde Rosses motion of Bridewell, Buls motion fits them best. *Tria sequuntur tria*, in reckoning Bull thrise, methinkes it should presage hanging. O bad application; Bad? I doo not thinke there can be a better, than to applie a knaues necke to an halter. Martin cannot start, I am his shadowe, one parte of the day before him, another behinde him; I can chalke a knaue on his backe thrice a weeke, Ile let him bloud in the combe.

Take heed, he will pistle thee. Pistle me? Then haue I a pestle so to stampe his pistles, that Ile beate all his wit to powder. What will the powder of Martins wit be good for? Marie blowe vp a dram of it into the nostrels of a good Protestant, it will make him giddie; but if you minister it like Tobacco to a Puritane, it will make him as mad as a Martin.

Goe to, a hatch before the doore, Martin smels thee, and wil not feare thee ; thou knowest how he deales with the Archbishop and a Counseller, hee will name thee and that broadlie. Name me ? Mary he and his shall bee namefied, that's it I thirst after, that name to name, and knowing one another, wee may in the streetes grapple ; wee except none : wee come with a verse in our mouthes, courage in our hearts, and weapons in our hands, and crie

Discite iustitiam moniti, et non temnere diuos.

Martins conscience hath a periwig; therefore to good men he is more sower than wig : a Lemman will make his conscience curd like a Posset. Now comes a biting speach, let mee stroake my beard thrice like a Germain, before I speak a wise word.

Martin, wee are now following after thee with hue and crie, and are hard at thy heeles ; if thou turne backe to blade it, wee doubt not but three honest men shall bee able to beate sixe theeues. Weele teach thee to commit sacriledge, and to robbe the Church of xxiiij. Bishops at a blowe. Doost thinke that wee are not men Martin, and haue great men to defend vs which write ? Yes, although with thy seditious cloase, thou would'st perswade her Maiestie, that most of the Gentlemen of account and men of honour, were by vs thought Puritañes. No, it is your poore Iohns, that with your painted consciences haue coloured the religion of diuers, spreading through the veynes of the Commonwealth like poyson, the doggednes of your deuotions ;

D

which entring in like the smoothnes of oyle into the flesh, fretteth in time like quicksiluer into the bones.

When children play with their meate, tis a signe their bellies are full, and it must be taken from them; but if they tread it vnder their feete, they ought to be ierkt. The Gospell hath made vs wantons, wee dallie with Ceremonies, dispute of circumstances, not remembring that the Papists haue been making roddes for vs this thirtie yeares; wee shall bee swing'd by them, or worse by Martin, if Martins be worse.   Neuer if it, for they bee worse with a witnesse, and let the diuell be witnesse. Wee are so nice, that the Cap is a beame in our Church, the booke of Common Praier a milstone, the *Pater noster* is not well pend by Christ.   Well, either religion is but policie, or policie scarce religious.

If a Gentleman riding by the way with twentie men, a number of theeues should by deuise or force binde all his seruants; the good Iustice of Peace would thinke he should be robd.   When Martinists rancke robbers of the Church shall binde the legges and armes of the Church, me thinkes the supreme head of the Church should looke pale.

They that pull downe the bells of a steeple, and say it is conscience, will blow vp the chauncell to make it the quintessence of conscience.   Bir Ladie, this is a good settled speech, a Diuine might haue seemed to haue said so much.   O sir, I am nor al tales, and riddles, and rimes, and iestes, thats but my Liripoope, if Martin knock the bone he shall find marrow, and if he looke for none, we'le knock the bone on his pate, and bring him on his marie bones.

I haue yet but giuen them a fillip on the conceipt, Ile fell it to the ground hereafter. Nay, if they make their consciences stretch like chiuerell in the raine, Ile make them crumple like parchment in the fire.

I haue an excellent balme to cure anie that is bitten with *Martin mad-dog.*

I am worth twentie Pistle-penners; let them but chafe my penne, and it shal sweat out a whole realme of paper, or make thē odious to the whole Realme.

O but be not partial, giue them their due though they were diuels, so will I, and excuse them for taking anie money at interest.

There is a good Ladie that lent one of these Martinists fortie pounds, and when at the daie shee required her money, Martin began to storme, and said, he thought her not the child of God, for they must lend, looking for nothing againe, and so to acquite himselfe of the blot of vsurie, he kepte the principall.

These Martins make the Scriptures a Scriueners shop to drawe conueyances, and the common pleas of Westminster to take forfeitures. Theyle not sticke to outlaw a mans soule, and serue it presently with an execution of damnation, if one denie them to lie with his neighbours wife. If they bee drunke, they say, they haue Timothie his weake stomacke, which Saint Paule willeth to warme with wine.

They haue sifted the holie Bible, and left vs nothing as they say, but branne; they haue boulted it ouer againe

and againe, and got themselues the fine meale ; tis
meale indeede, for with their wresting and shuffling
holie Writ, they find all themselues good meales, and
stand at liuerie as it were, at other mens tables.

Sed heus tu, dic sodes, will they not bee discouraged
for the common players? Would those Comedies might
be allowed to be plaid that are pend, and then I am sure
he would be decyphered, and so perhaps discouraged.

He shall not bee brought in as whilom he was, and
yet verie well, with a cocks combe, an apes face, a
wolfs bellie, cats clawes, &c. but in a cap'de cloake,
and all the best apparell he ware the highest day in the
yeare, thats neither on Christmas daie, Good fridaie,
Easter daie, Ascension, nor Trinitie sundaie, (for that
were popish) but on some rainie weeke-daie, when the
brothers and sisters had appointed a match for particular praiers, a thing as bad at the least as Auricular
confession.

A stage plaier, though he bee but a cobler by occupation, yet his chance may bee to play the Kings part.
Martin, of what calling so euer he be, can play nothing but
the knaues part, *qui tantum constans in knauitate sua est.*

If it be shewed at Paules, it will cost you foure pence : at the Theater two pence : at Sainct Thomas a Watrings nothing. Would it not bee a fine Tragedie, when
Mardocheus shall play a Bishoppe in a Play,
and Martin *Hamman,* and that he that seekes
to pull downe those that are set in authoritie
aboue him, should be hoysted vpon a tree
aboue all other.

Though he play least in sight now, yet we
hope to see him stride from Aldgate to Lud-

gate, and looke ouer all the Citie at London Bridge.
Soft swift, he is no traytor. Yes, if it bee
treason to encourage the Commons against the *Reade Martin Se-*
chiefe of the Clergie, to make a generall re- *niorsLibell, and you*
uolt from the gouernment so wel established, *shall per-*
so wisely maintained, and so long prospering. *ceiue that he is able*

Because they say, *Aue Cæsar*, therefore *to teach Gracchus*
they meane nothing against Cæsar. There *to speake*
may bee hidden vnder their long gownes, short *seditiouslie.*
daggers, and so in blearing Cæsars eyes, conspire Cæsars death. God saue the Queene ; why it is the Que
which they take from the mouthes of all traytors, who
though they bee throughly conuinced, both by proofe
and their owne confessions, yet at the last gaspe they
crie, God saue the Queene. GOD saue the Queene
(say I) out of their hands, in whose hearts (long may
the Queene thus gouerne) is not engrauen.

Her sacred Maiestie hath this thirtie yeares, with a
setled and princelie temper swayed the Scepter of this
Realme, with no lesse content of her subiects, than
wonder of the world. GOD hath blessed her gouernment, more by miracle thā by counsaile, and yet by
counsaile as much as can come from policie. Of a
State taking such deepe roote, as to be fastened by the
prouidence of God, the vertue of the Prince, the wisedome of Counsellers, the obedience of subiects, and the
length of time; who would goe about to shake the
lowest bough, that feeles in his conscience but the least
blessing. Heere is a fit roome to squese them with an
Apothegme.

There was an aged man that liued in a well ordered
Common-wealth by the space of threescore yeares, and
finding at the length that by the heate of some mens
braines, and the warmnes of other mens bloud, that
newe alterations were in hammering, and that it grewe
to such an height, that all the desperate and discontented
persons were readie to runne their heads against their
head; comming into the midst of these mutiners, cried
as loude as his yeares would allow; Springalls and vn-
ripened youthes, whose wisedomes are yet in the blade,
when this snowe shall be melted (laying his hand on his
siluer haires) then shal you find store of durt, and
rather wish for the continuance of a long frost, than the
comming of an vntimely thaw. Ile moralize this.

Ile warrant the good old man meant, that when the
ancient gouernment of the state should be altered by
faction, or newe lawes brought in that were deuised by
nice heads, that there should followe a foule and slip-
perie managing; where if happelie most did not fall,
yet all would bee tired. A settled raigne is not like
glasse mettal, to be blowne in bignesse, length or fashion
of euerie mans breath, and breaking to be melted
againe, and so blowne afresh; but it is compared to the
fastning of the Cedar, that knitteth it selfe with such
wreaths into the earth that it cannot be remooued by
any violent force of the aire.

Martin, I haue taken an inuentorie of al thy vnciuill
and rakehell tearmes, and could sute them in no place
but in Bedlam and Bridewell, so mad they are, and so
bad they are, and yet all proceedes of the spirit. I

thinke thou art possest with the spirites of Iacke Straw
and the Black-smith, who, so they might rent in peeces
the gouernment, they would drawe cuts for religion.

If all be conscience, let conscience bee the foundation
of your building, not the glasse, shew effects of conscience, mildnesse in spirit, obedience to Magistrates,
loue to thy brethren. Stitch charitie to thy faith, or
rip faith from thy works.

If thou wilt deale soberlie without scoffes, thou shalt
be answered grauely without iests, yea and of those,
whom thou canst not controll for learning, nor accuse for
ill life, nor shouldst contemne for authori [ti] e. But if
like a restie Iade thou wilt take the bitt in thy mouth,
and then runne ouer hedge and ditch, thou shalt be
brokē as Prosper broke his horses, with a muzroule,
portmouth, and a martingall, and so haue thy head runne
against a stone wall.

If thou refuse learning, and sticke to libelling; if
nothing come out of those lauish lips, but taunts not
without bitternesse, yet without wit; rayling not without
spite, yet without cause, then giue me thy hand, thou
and I will trie it out at the cuckingstoole. Ile make
thee to forget Bishops English, and weep Irish; next
hanging there is no better reuenge on Martin, than to
make him crie for anger; for there is no more sullen
beast, than a he drab. Ile make him pull his powting
croscloath ouer his beetle browes for melancholie, and
then my next booke, shall be Martin in his mubble
fubbles.

HERE I was writing *Finis* and *Funis*, and determined
to lay it by, till I might see more knauerie filde in:
within a while appeared olde Martin with a wit worn
into the socket, twinkling and pinking like the snuffe of
a candle; *quantum mutatus ab illo*, how vnlike the knaue
hee was before, not for malice but for sharpnesse.

The hogshead was euen come to the hauncing, and
nothing could be drawne from him but dregs: yet the
emptie caske sounds lowder than when it was ful; and
protests more in his waining, than he could performe in
his waxing. I drew neere the sillie soule, whom I
found quiuering in two sheetes of protestation paper.
O how meager and leane hee lookt, so creast falne, that
his combe hung downe to his bill, and had I not been
sure it was the picture of enuie, I shoulde haue sworne
it had been the image of death, so like the verie Anatomie of mischiefe, that one might see through all the
ribbes of his conscience, I began to crosse my selfe, and
was readie to say the *Pater noster*, but that I knewe he
carde not for it, and so vsed no other wordes, but *abi in
malam crucem*, because I knewe, that lookt for him. I
came so neere, that I could feele a substantiall knaue
from a sprites shadowe.

I sawe through his paper coffen, that it was but a
cosening corse, and one that had learnde of the holie

maid of Kent, to lie in a trance, before he had brought
foorth his lie; drawing his mouth awrie, that could
neuer speake right; goggling with his eyes that watred
with strong wine; licking his lips, and gaping, as though
he should loose his childes nose, if he had not his
longing to swallowe Churches; and swelling in the
paunch, as though he had been in labour of a little
babie, no bigger than rebellion; but truth was at the
Bishoppes trauaile: so that Martin was deliuered by
sedition, which pulls the monster with yron from the
beastes bowells. When I perceiued that he masked in
his rayling robes, I was so bolde as to pull off his
shrowding sheete, that all the worlde might see the olde
foole daunce naked.

Tis not a peniworth of protestation that can buy thy
pardon, nor al worth a penie that thou proclaimest.
Martin comes in with bloud, bloud, as though hee
should bee a martir. Martins are mad martirs, some of
them burnt seauen yeares agoe, and yet aliue. One of
them lately at Yorke, pulling out his napkin to wipe
his mouth after a lie, let drop a surgeans caliuer at his
foote where he stood; these fellowes can abide no
pompe, and yet you see they cannot be without a little
squirting plate: rub no more, the curtall wrinches.

They call the Bishops butchers, I like the Metaphore
wel, such calues must be knockt on the head, and who
fitter than the Fathers of the Church, to cut the throates
of heresies in the Church. Nay, whē they haue no
propertie of sheepe but bea, their fleece for flockes, not
cloath, their rotten flesh for no dish, but ditches; I

thinke them woorth neither the tarring nor the telling,
but for their scabbednes to bee thrust from the pinfolde
to the scaffold, and with an *Habeas corpus* to remooue
them from the Shepheards tarre-boxe, to the hangmans
budget.

I but he hath sillogismes in pike sauce, and arguments that haue been these twentie yeres in pickle. I,
picke hell, you shall not finde such reasons, they bee all
in *celarent*, and dare not shewe their heads, for wee will
answere them in *ferio* and cut their combes. So say
they, their bloud is sought. Their bloud? What should
wee doo with it, when it will make a dogge haue the
toothach to eat the puddings.

Martin tunes his pipe to the lamentable note of
Ora whine meg. O tis his best daunce next shaking
of the sheetes; but hee good man meant no harme by it.
No more did one of his minions, that thinking to rap
out an oath and sweare by his conscience, mistooke the
word and swore by his concupiscence; not vnlike the
theefe, that in stead of God speede, sayd stand, and so
tooke a purse for God morowe.

Yet dooth Martin hope that all her Maiesties best
subiects will become Martinists; a blister of that tongue
as bigge as a drummes head; for if the Queenes Maiestie haue such abiects for her best subiects, let all true
subiects be accompted abiects.

They that teare the boughs, will hew at the tree,
and hauing once wet their feete in factions, will not care
how deep they wade in treason.

After Martin had racked ouer his protestation with a

Iades pace, hee runnes ouer his fooleries with a knaues
gallop, ripping vp the souterlie seames of his Epistle,
botching in such frize iestes vppon fustion earnest, that
one seeing all sortes of his shreddes, would thinke he
had robd a taylors shop boord; and then hee concludes
all doggedlie, with Doctor *Bullens* dogge *Spring*, not
remembring that there is not a better Spanniell in England to spring a couie of queanes than Martin.

Hee sliues one, has a fling at another, a long tale of
his talboothe, of a vulnerall sermon, and of a fooles
head in souce. This is the Epistle which he woonders
at himselfe, and like an olde Ape, hugges the Vrchin
so in his conceipt, as though it should shew vs some
new tricks ouer the chaine, neuer wish it published
Martin, we pittie it before it comes out. Trusse vp
thy packet of flim flams, and roage to some countrey
Faire, or read it among boyes in the belfrie, neuer
trouble the church with chattering; but if like dawes,
you will be cawing about Churches, build your nests in
the steeple, defile not the quier.

Martin writes merely, because (hee saies) people are
carried away sooner with iest than earnest. I, but
Martin neuer put Religion into a fooles coate; there is
great oddes betweene a Gospeller, and a Libeller.

If thy vaine bee so pleasaunt, and thy witt so nimble,
that all consists in glicks and girds; pen some play for
the Theater, write some ballads for blinde *Dauid* and
his boy, deuise some iests, and become another *Scogen*,
so shalt thou haue vēt inough for all thy vanities, thy
Printer shall purchase, and all other iesters beg.

For to giue thee thy due, thou art the best died foole in graine that euer was, and all other fooles lacke manie graines, to make them so heauie.

There is not such a mad foole in Bedlam, nor such a baudie foole in Bridewell, nor such a dronken foole in the stockes, nor such a scolding foole on the cucking-stoole, nor such a cosening foole on the pillerie, nor such a roaging foole in the houses of correction, nor such a simple foole kept of alms, nor such a lame foole lying in the spittle, nor in all the world, such a foole, all. Nay for fooles set down in the scriptures, none such as Martin.

What atheist more foole, that saies in his heart, *There is no God?* What foole more proud, that stands in his own cōceit? What foole more couetous than he, that seekes to tedd abroad the Churches goods with a forke, and scratch it to himselfe with a rake.

Thou seest Martin with a little helpe, to the foure and twentie orders of knaues, thou maist solder the foure and twentie orders of fooles, and so because thou saist thou art vnmarried, thou maist commit matrimonie, from the heires of whose incest, wee will say that which you cannot abide, *Good Lord deliuer vs.*

If this veyne bleede but sixe ounces more, I shall proue a pretie railer, and so in time may growe to bee a proper Martinist. Tush, I doo but licke ouer my pamphlet, like a Beares whelpe, to bring it in some forme ; by that time he replies, it will haue clawes and teeth, and then let him looke to bee scratcht and bitten too.

Thou seest Martin Moldwarpe, that hetherto I haue
named none, but markt them readie for the next market: if thou proceed in naming, be as sure as thy shirt
to thy knaues skinne, that Ile name such, as though
thou canst not blush, because thou art past shame, yet
they shall bee sorie, because they are not all without
grace.

Pasquil is coming out with the liues of the Saints.
Beware my Comment, tis odds the margent shall be as
full as the text. I haue manie sequences of Saints, if
naming be the aduantage, and ripping vp of liues make
sport, haue with thee knuckle deepe, it shall neuer bee
said that I dare not venter mine cares, where Martin
hazards his necke.

Now me thinkes Martin begins to stretch himselfe
like an old fencer, with a great conscience for buckler
and a long tongue for a sword. Lie close, you old
cutter at the locke, *Nam mihi sunt vires, et mea tela
nocent.* Tis ods but that I shal thrust thee through the
buckler into the brain, that is through the conscience
into the wit.

If thou sue me for a double maime, I care not though
the Iurie allow thee treble damages, it cannot amount
to much, because thy cōscience is without wit, and thy
wit without conscience, and therefore both, not worth a
penie.

Therefore take this for the first venew, of a yonger
brother, that meanes to drie beate those of the *Elder*
house. Martin, this is my last straine for this fleech

E

of mirth. I began with God morrowe, and bid you God night. I must tune my fiddle, and fetch some more rozen, that it maie squeake out Martins Matachine.

FINIS.

Candidissimi Lectores, peto terminum ad libellandum.

Lectores.

Assignamus in proximum.

NOTES.

TITLE. *Pappe with an hatchet.*] According to Mr. Park, in his Notes on the following quotations, "to give pap with a hatchet" is a proverbial phrase for doing a kind thing in an unkind manner.

"They give us pap with a spoone before we can speake, and when we speake for that we love, *pap with a hatchet.*"—LYLY's Court Comed. Z 12 b.

"He that so old seeks for a nurse so young, shall have *pap with a hatchet* for his comfort."—Disc. of Marr. Harl. Misc. ii. 171.

So the author of the present tract, at p. 25: "The babe comes in with Nunka, Neame, and Dad: *(Pappe with an hatchet for such a puppie)*." But it must be admitted that these illustrations are anything but satisfactory.

P. 7, l. 1. *royster.*] i. e. rioter.
"If he not reeke what ruffian *roisters* take his part."
                                    Mirror for Magist. p. 484.

P. 7, l. 3. *gaffers.*] A contemptuous term applied to old men. "Gaffer" and "gammer" are still used amongst the common people.

P. 7, l. 9. *fooles bolts.*] "A fool's bolt is soon shot" is a common proverb. "Bolt" is an arrow; for which explanation see R. Holmes' Academy of Armory: so also Shakspeare,
"Yet mark'd I where the *bolt* of Cupid fell."
                                    Mids. N. D. ii. 2.

P. 8, l. 15. *he that drinkes with cutters, must not be without his ale dagger.*] "Cutter" is a cant term for a swaggerer, bully, or cutpurse: what an "ale-dagger" is I am unable to explain; but as a "dag," or "dagge," is the old term for a pistol, it is not unlikely that something of this kind is meant, instead of a stabbing instrument.

P. 9, l. 6. *copper replie.*] This may be an allusion to some kind of spurs. We have, in Webster's Malcontent, "Your knight courts your city widow with jingling of his gilt spurs." Works by Dyce, iv. 48. See also many authorities quoted in Nares' Glossary, p. 483.

P. 9, l. 10. *scaddle pawn.*] An allusion to some move in the game of chess which I am unable to explain. "Dydoppers," in the following line, is a common name for the dab-chick.

P. 10, l. 13. *If they be answered by the grauitie of learned Prelates.*] This refers to the grave reply of Cooper, bishop of Winchester, entitled "An Admonition to the People of England," to Martin Mar-Prelate's "Oh! read ouer D. Iohn Bridges" and "Epitome."

P. 13, l. 10, 12. *Bastard Iunior—Bastard Senior.*] These allusions are to two tracts by Martin Junior and Martin Senior.

P. 13, l. 18. *Bishops bobbs.*] Here the word appears to mean blows, as also in p. 17, last line, "if he give you a *bob*, though he draw no bloud;" and in p. 21, "give thee as many *bobs* on the eare, as thou hast eaten morsels of their meate." Skelton has

"And, whan I fayle, *bobbe* me on the noll."

The Bowge of Courte, Works by Dyce, i. 40.
In this sense the word "bob" does not appear in Nares' Glossary.

P. 14, l. 1. *Elderton swore.*] Elderton's company of players is mentioned, under the year 1572, in Collier's Annals of the Stage, i. 205.

P. 14, l. 3. *hacker.*] In Nares it is "haxter," and "hackster," a hacknied person. "For to bring an old *haxter* to the exercise of devotion, is to bring an old bird to sing prick-song in a cage."

CLITUS's [i. e. BRATHWAIT's] Whimzies, p. 61.

P. 14, l. 7. *Bonner's ballets—ierkes for a Iesuit.*] Probably old songs with these titles.

P. 14, l. 13. *The vile boy hath manie bobbes.*] That is, taunts or scoffs : "fardle" is bundle.

"I have drawn blood at one's brains with a bitter *bob.*"

Alex. and Campaspe, O. P. ii. 113.

P. 15, l. 10. *three a vies wits.*] "a vie," says Bailey, "is a wager, challenge, or invitation." Gifford, in a note to Every Man in his Humour, Act iv. sc. 1, says, "To *vie* was to hazard, to put down a certain sum upon a hand of cards; to *revie* was to cover it with a larger sum, by which the-challenged became the challenger, and was to be *revied* in his turn with a proportionate increase of stake. This vying and revying upon each other continued till one of the party lost courage and gave up the whole, or obtained, for a stipulated sum, a discovery of his antagonist's cards: when the best hand swept the table."—Nares' Glossary, 542.

P. 15, l. 15. *an old stabber at passage.*] "Passage," from the French " passe-dix." " Passage is a game at dice to be played at but by two, and it is performed with three dice. The caster throws continually till he hath thrown dubblets under ten, and then he is out and loseth, or dubblets above ten, and then he *passeth* and wins."—Compleat Gamester, 1680, p. 119. From the same excellent authority we learn that " stabbing the dice " was one of the tricks practised by the cheats of old times, a full account of which will be found at p. 12.

P. 15, l. 25. *spurne.*] i. e. kick.

P. 15, l. 28. *wood-sere.*] This word I cannot trace to any authority. Is it the sap which exudes from the ends of green wood when put into the fire?

P. 16, l. 2. *as an Estrich a two penie naile.*] Of the digestive powers of the ostrich the most extraordinary fables are related. In Skelton's Works by Dyce, i. 65, we have
" The *estryge* that wyll eate
An horshowe so great."
" Let them but remember that the *estridge* digesteth hard yron to preserve his health."—Lyly's Euphues, N 4. 6. See also Scot's Philomythie, 1616.

P. 16, l. 14. *biggin.*] A sort of cap. " Upon his head he wore a filthy coarse *biggin*, and next it a garnish of night caps."—Nash's Pierce Pennilesse.

P. 17, l. 12. *there is a book coming out of a hundred merrie tales.*] A work with this title was printed by John Rastell, and reprinted a few years ago by Singer. To read aloud these collections of " Merrie Tales" appears to have been a frequent winter evenings amusement.

P. 18, l. 1. *bable.*] the same as bauble.

P. 18, l. 4. *lambacke.*] To beat or bastinado. " Happy may

they call that daie wherein they are not *lambeaked* before night."—Discovery of a New World, 115.

P. 18, l. 27. *cleaue to Christ his dabitur in illa hora.*] That is, relying on Christ for words to utter when he comes to preach.

P. 19, l. 4, *If they cannot leuell, they will roue at thee.*] To rove is to shoot an arrow at a mark at an elevation, and not point blank. See Nares, 435.

P. 19, l. 8. *as Bull in quartering a knaues bodie.*] It is probable, from the allusion here, at p. 25, l. 10, and p. 28, l. 13, that Bull was the name of the common hangman.

P. 19, l. 23. *Alls.*] i. e. all is.

P. 20, l. 16. *bodges.*] botches ?

P. 23, l. 5. *Mar-martin.*] This is the title of one of the pamphlets against Martin Mar-prelate.

P. 23, l. 25. *cogge.*] i. e. to cheat.

P. 26, l. 22. *rippier.*] According to Minsheu, a "rippier" is a person who brings fish from the coast to sell in the interior.

P. 27, l. 1. *kixes.*] A dried stalk of hemlock or parsley is called a kex; the form here is plural. The word occurs under various modes of spelling in our old dramatists.

P. 27. l. 13. *Primero.*] A game at cards, said to be the oldest known in England. The curious may consult Nares for a particular description. It was considered a gambling game according to Greene :—

" SPENDALL. If there be cards i' the house, let's go to *primero.*

RASH. Primero, why I thought thou hadst not been so much gamester as to play at it."—Tu Quoque, O. P. vii. 2.

P. 28. l. 1. *Take away this beard, and giue me a pickede vaunt.*] Pike-devant. The beard cut to a sharp point in the middle, below the chin. It is seen in most of the portraits of Charles I. See Nares, 377.

P. 28, l. 3. *old Iohn of Paris garden.*] Paris Garden was a public place for the exhibition of bear and bull-baiting. The allusion here seems to apply to a monkey. We find, from an account of Paris Garden written in 1544, inserted in Collier's Annals of the Stage, iii. 279, that " At the same place a poney is baited, with a monkey on its back, defending itself against the dogs by kicking them ; and the shrieks of the monkey, when he sees the dogs hanging from the ears and neck of the pony, render the scene very laughable."

P. 28, l. 10. *if they floute, we will bring quippes.*] To flout or flyte, is to scold or to rate.

" Po. But what's a *quip ?*

Ma. We great girders call it a short saying of a sharp wit, with a bitter sense in a sweet word."—Alex. & Camp. O. P. ii. 113.

P. 28, l. 29. *Tobacco.*] This is the earliest notice of tobacco, in the form of snuff, with which I am acquainted. The reader who is curious on the subject of the culture and use of this plant in England, will find much information in the proclamations of James I. and Charles I. in Rymer's Fœdera.

P. 29, l. 26. *poore Iohns.*] Poor John is a coarse kind of fish; it is used here, by metonymy, for poor fellows.

P. 30, l. 2. *like quicksiluer into the bones.*] The full force of this passage will be understood better by a knowledge of the medical practice of the time.

P. 30. l. 29. *Liripoope.*] That is, a humour put on, an assumed character. A writer in the Gentleman's Magazine for Sept. 1818, mentions it as a clerical vestment, and quotes the Latin edition of Sparrow's Canons, 4to, 1675, where the word *Tippets* is rendered *Liripipia.* It is used also in the Statutes of Brazenose College, Oxford, in the same sense. Peck, in his Desiderata Curiosa, p. 570, 4to, 1779, when detailing the dress used by the Commons in the reign of Edward III. 1327-77, says, "their *lerripippes* reach to their heels, all jagged." " It was therefore," continues Peck, " identical with what we now call scarves."

P. 31, l. 10. *realme.*] Ream, of course.

P. 32, l. 6. *Would those Comedies might be allowed to be plaid that are pend.*] These comedies against Martin appear to be totally lost to us. That Martin Mar-Prelate had been exhibited on the stage we are certain, and in Nash's " Returne of the renowned Cavaliero Pasquill of England," 1589, an account is given of the manner in which he was exhibited :—" Methought *Vetus Comædia* began to pricke him at London in the right vaine, when shee brought foorth *Divinitie* with a scratcht face, holding of her hart, as if she were sicke, because *Martin* would have forced her ; but myssing of his purpose, he left the print of his nayles upon her cheekes, and poysoned her with a vomit, which he ministred

unto her to make her cast uppe her dignities and promotions."
It was, therefore, in the manner of an old Moral, and not with
the improvements which had recently been introduced into
dramatic poetry, that he was exhibited on the stage.

Strype, in his edition of Stow's Survey, alludes to the silencing
of the players in 1589, " because one Mr. Tylney had utterly,
for some reasons, disliked them."   Edmund Tylney was the
Master of the Revels at this time, a part of whose duty it was
to watch over the conduct of the players.   The exhibiting of
Martin Mar-Prelate on the stage induced him to make some
representations to Lord Burghley against the conduct of the
actors in the city.   The Lord Treasurer accordingly wrote to
the Lord Mayor, requiring him to put a stop to all theatrical
exhibitions within his jurisdiction.   The answer addressed to
Lord Burghley is as follows :—

" My very ho: good lord.   Where by a lre of your Lordships,
directed to Mr. Yonge, it appered unto me, that it was your ho:
pleasure I sholde geve order for the staie of all playes within
the cittie, in that Mr. Tilney did utterly mislike the same.
According to which your Lordships good pleasure, I presentlye
sent for suche players as I coulde heare of, so as there appered
yesterday before me the Lord Admiralls, and the Lord Straunges
players ; to whome I speciallie gave in charge, and required
them in her Majesty's name, to forbere playinge untill further
order might be geven for their allowance in that respect:
Whereuppon the Lord Admiralls players very dutifullie obeyed ;
but the others, in very contemptuous manner departing from
me, wente to the Crosse Keys, and played that afternoone to the
greate offence of the better sorte, that knew they were prohibited by order from your Lordship.   Which as I might not
suffer, so I sent for the said contemptuous persons, who haveing
no reason to alleadge for their contempte, I could do no less but
this evening committ tow of them to one of the Compters, and
do meane, according to your Lordships direction, to prohibite
all playing until your Lordship's pleasure therein be further
knowen.   And thus resting further to trouble your Lordship,
I moste humblie take my leave.   At London the sixte of No-
vember 1589.   Yr Lordships most humble

                              " John Harte, maior."

, Lansdowne MSS. No. 60, quoted in Collier, i. 272-3.

Within six days after the date of this letter, the Privy Council had considered the subject, and, to remedy the abuses, addressed three letters, to the Archbishop of Canterbury, the Lord Mayor of London, and the Master of the Revels, requiring the first to name a person " well learned in divinity," the second " to appoint a sufficient person learned and of judgement," and the last to act in conjunction with them, in licensing all plays to be acted in and about the city of London. These letters are as follow :—

Nov. 12, 1589. A letter to the Lord Archbishop of Canterbury.—" That whereas there hathe growne some inconvenience by common playes and enterludes in & about the cyttie of London, in [that] the players take upon [them] to handle in their plaies certen matters of Divinytie and State, unfitt to be suffered : for redresse whereof their Lordships have thought good to appointe some persons of judgment and understanding to viewe and examine their playes before they be permitted to present them publickly. His Lordship is desired that some fytt person well learned in divinity be appointed by him, to joyne with the M^r. of the Revelles, and one other to be nominated by the L: Maior, and they joyntly with some spede to viewe and consider of such Comedyes and Tragedies as are and shall be publickly played by the companies of players in and about the Cittie of London, and they to geve allowance of such as they shall thinke meete to be played, and to forbyd the rest."

To the Lord Mayor of London.—" That whereas their Lordships have already signifyed unto him to appoint a sufficient person learned and of judgement for the Cittie of London, to joyne with the M^r. of the Revelles, and with a Divine to be nominated by the Lord Archb. of Cant: for the reforminge of the plaies daylie exercysed and presented publickly in & about the Cittie of London, wherein the players take upon them without judgment or decorum to handle matters of Divinitie and State. He is required, if he have not as yet made choice of such a person, that he will soe do forthwith and there of geve knowledge to the Lord Archb. and the M^r. of the Revelles, that they may meet accordingly."

To the Master of the Revels.—" Requiring him with two others, the one to be appointed by the Lord Archb. of Canterbury, and the other by the Lord Maior of London, to be men of learning and judgment, and to call before them the severall companies of players (whose servaunts soever they be), and to require them by authorytie hereof to deliver unto them their books, that they may consider of the matters of their Comedyes and Tragedyes, and thereuppon to stryke out or reforme such parte and matters, as they shall fynd unfytt and undecent to be handled in plaies both for Divinitie & State; commanding the said Companies of players in her Majesties name, that they forbear to present and play publickly any Comedy or Tragedy, other than such as they three shall have seene and allowed: which if they shall not observe, they shall lett them know from their Lordships, that they shalbe not onely sevearly punished, but made [in]capable of the exercise of their profession for ever hereafter."—COLLIER's Annals of the Stage, i. 271-7.

P. 32, marginal note.] "If it be shewed at Paules," that is, by the children at St. Paul's; "the Theater," a play-house so called, was in Shoreditch; "Sainct Thomas a Watrings" was a place of execution for the county of Surrey; and the unfortunate Penry, to whom the Mar-Prelate libels have been attributed, was there hanged. It was situated close to the second milestone on the Kent road, where was a brook, dedicated to St. Thomas à Becket.

> "And forth we riden a litel more than pas
>   Unto the *watering of Seint Thomas,*
>   And then our hoste began his hors arest."
>
>   CHAUCER, Prol. C. T.

P. 32, l. 24. *Mardocheus.*] i. e. Mordecai.

P 33, l. 7. *Aue Cæsar.*] So in Skelton,

" Parot can say, *Cæsar, ave,* also."—Works by Dyce, ii. 6.
See also the Note in the same work, ii. 341.

P. 34, l. 9. *Springalls.*] A growing lad, a youth.

" Joseph, when he was sold to Potiphar, that great man, was a faire young *springall.*"—LATIMER's Sermons, fol. 190.

" There came two *springals* of full tender yeares."

                                   SPENSER, F. Q. b. v. ver. 6.

P. 35, l. 22. *cuckingstoole.*] " We have," says Johnson, " different modes of restraining evil. Stocks for the man, a *Duckingstool* for women, and a pound for beasts." The Cucking-stool, or Ducking-stool, for it had these and other names, was an engine invented for the punishment of scolds and unquiet women, by ducking them in the water, after having placed them in a stool or chair, fixed at the end of a long pole, by which they were immerged. See Brand's Popular Antiq. by Ellis.

P. 35, last line. *mubble fubbles.*] A cant term for any causeless depression of spirits.

"Our Mary Guitierez, when she was in the *mubble fubbles*, do you think I was mad for it."—Gayton's Festivous Notes, p. 46.

"Melancholy is the creast of courtiers armes, and now every companion, being in his *mubble fubbles*, says he is melancholy."—Lyly's Midas, v. 2.

P. 36, l. 20. *carde.*] cared.

P. 38, l. 9, 10. *celarent—ferio.*] Terms in logic.

P. 38, l. 15. *Ora whine meg.*] Mr. Dyce, in his Notes to Skelton, quotes from Laneham's Letter concerning the entertainment to Queen Elizabeth at Kenilworth Castle, in 1575, the following :—" What shoold I rehearz heer, what a bunch of Ballets and songs all auncient : As Broom broom on hill, So wo is me begon, troly lo, *Over a whinny Meg,*" &c.—Skelton's Works, by Dyce, ii. 340.

P. 38, l. 16. *shaking of the sheetes.*] The name of an old dance, often mentioned with a double entendre by our early dramatists.

P. 39, l. 2. *souterlie.*] A " sowter " is a cobler, from the Latin *sutor.*

"Our *sowters* had Crispine" [for their patron].
Scot's Discoverie of Witchcraft.

P. 39, l. 3. *frize iestes vpon fustion earnest.*] " Frieze " was a coarse warm woollen cloth, used for outer garments.

"Am I ridden with a Welch goat too ?
Shall I have a coxcomb of *frize ?*"
Merry Wives of Windsor, v. 5.

We have also *frieze* jerkins mentioned in the play of King Edw. I.

P. 39, l. 16. *flim flams.*] i. e. lies.

P. 39, l. 26. *glicks and girds.*] i. e. jests and sarcasms.

P. 39, l. 28. *Scogen.*] Scogan, John or Henry, respecting whom Ritson and Malone held long controversy, is represented by Shakspeare as having had his head broken by Falstaff in his youth. See 2 Hen. V. iii. 2. *Scoggin's Jests* are mentioned with *The Hundred Merry Tales* in *Wily Beguiled*, 1606·

> " such as can make a large discourse
> Out of Scoggin's Jests, or the Hundred Merry Tales,
> Marry, if you go any further 'tis beyond their reading."
>
> COLLIER's Annals of the Stage, iii. 441.

P. 41, l. 1. *Moldwarpe.*] i. e. the mole.

P. 41, l. 28. *Elder house.*] Alluding to the elders or heads in the Puritan form of Church government.

P. 41, last line. *fleech of mirth.*] i. e. for this turn or bout. I cannot trace " fleech" in any glossary.

P. 42. l. 3. *Martin's Matachine.*] Of this dance, Mr. Douce thus writes :—" It was well known in France and Italy, by the name of the dance of fools or *matachins*, who were habited in short jackets, with gilt paper helmets, long streamers tied to their shoulders, and bells to their legs. They carried in their hands a sword and buckler, with which they made a clashing noise, and performed various quick and sprightly evolutions."—DOUCE, Illustrations of Shakspeare, ii. 435.

THE END.

LONDON:
HUGH WILLIAMS, Printer, Ashby-street, Northampton-square.

𝕻uritan 𝕯iscipline 𝕿racts.

PLAINE PERCEVALL,

THE

PEACE-MAKER OF ENGLAND;

BEING

A REPLY

TO

MARTIN MAR-PRELATE.

𝕽eprinted from the 𝕭lack 𝕷etter 𝕰dition,

WITH

AN INTROCUCTION AND NOTES.

LONDON:

JOHN RUSSELL SMITH, 36, SOHO SQUARE.

M.DCCC.LX.

INTRODUCTION.

The following Tract, with that singular fatality which so often perpetuates error, has been generally, and but with scarcely an exception, attributed to Thomas Nash, who, it is well known, was one of the chief writers against Martin Mar-Prelate. The Rev. Mr. Maskell, in his "History of the Mar-Prelate Controversy," justly calls in question this universal consent, and concludes, with some plausibility, that "it is in fact a last gasp of the Puritans: an expression in their extremity of some desire of peace: a wish that they might for a time, until themselves spoke again, be let alone."—H. M. C. 199.

From its style alone we might conclude that Nash did not write it. It is remarkable also that the following lines,

> "If any aske why thou art clad so garish
> Say thou are dubd the forehorse of the parish,"

which appear at the end of the Tract, are to be found,

with a slight variation, in Gabriel Harvey's "Four Letters and Certain Sonnets," 1592, as an epitaph on Robert Greene,

> " Heere Bedlam is : and heere a Poet garish
> Gaily bedecked like forehorse of the parish ;"

and which there is good reason to believe were written by Gabriel Harvey, or his brother Richard. In this place, therefore, the direct testimony of Nash will be of importance.

" Some what I am priuie to the cause of Greenes inueighing against the three brothers. Thy hot-spirited brother Richard (a notable ruffian with his pen) hauing first tooke vpon him in his *blundring Persiual* to play the Iacke of both sides twixt Martin and vs, and snarled priuily at Pap-hatchet, Pasquil, and others, that opposde themselues against the open slaunder of that mightie platformer of Atheisme, presently after dribbed forth another fooles bolt, a booke I should say, which be christened *The Lambe of God.*"—NASH's *Strange Newes*, 1592, sig. 2.

Now if we refer to Plaine Percevall, we shall find evidence of this " privily snarling." The Dedication of it is, " To all whip Iohns and whip Iackes ; not forgetting the Caualiero Pasquill [Thomas Nash], or the Cooke Ruffian that drest a dish for Martins diet [Pap with a Hatchet, by John Lyly], and the residue of light fingred younkers which make euery word a blow, and euery booke a bobbe." Whether Greene is included amongst the " whip Iohns," or " whip Iackes," or the " light fingred younkers," is doubtful ; but scarcely a doubt can remain, after considering the character of the present Tract, in which the writer throughout plays the " Iacke of both sides," that it must be the " blundring Persiual," which Nash has fathered upon Richard Harvey.

The remarkable quarrel between Nash and Harvey is given in a very graphic manner by D'Israeli, in the " Calamities of · Authors." Unfortunately, however, but few facts can be gleaned from it; and it would appear, too, as if the origin of the quarrel had been misunderstood by him. The sketch which I have here given may serve to illustrate a very interesting period of our literary history; though so much of the contemporary literature of this period has perished, that it is not only a work of labour to give in a connected form any series of remarks on a like subject, but it renders on many occasions our conclusions doubtful or erroneous.

Gabriel Harvey and his brothers Richard and John were of good family, though their father carried on at Saffron Walden the humble trade of a ropemaker. This disagreeable fact becoming known, appears to have caused a great share of the annoyance which the brothers (and especially the elder of them) were fated to meet with in life. The circumstances of the father were sufficiently prosperous (" four sons him cost a thousand pounds at least") to enable him to send his three sons (four it is stated in Harvey's " Four Letters") to Cambridge. The elder, born about 1545, was educated at Christ's college, and took both his degrees in arts. He obtained a fellowship in Trinity-hall, and served the office of proctor. Having studied civil law, he obtained his grace for a degree in that faculty ; in 1585 he was admitted doctor of laws at Oxford, and subsequently practised as an advocate in the Prerogative Court of Canterbury at London. Richard, the second, we find in 1583 about to profess divinity; he subsequently entered the Church, and was presented to the vicarage of Saffron Walden. John, the younger, after obtaining his degree in medicine, settled at Lynn as a Physician, and died in July, 1592.

As early as 1577, Gabriel Harvey had given to the world his " Rhetor," and " Ciceronianus ;" and in the following year his " Gratulatio Valdenensium," and " Smithus," a Latin Poem on the death of Sir Thomas Smith, to whom it would appear he stood in the relation of nephew. It is to this period, or shortly after, we must refer the following autobiographical facts, mentioned in the " Four Letters," 1592.

" I was supposed not unmeet for the Oratorship of the University, which in that spring of mine age, for my exercise and credit I much affected; but mine own modest petition, my friends' diligent labour, our High Chancellor's most honourable and extraordinary commendation, were all peltingly defeated by a sly practice of the old Fox, whose acts and monuments shall never die."—HARVEY's *Four Letters, &c.* 1592, Reprint.

Whether the allusion here is to Harvey's " old controller Dr. Perne," whom he accuses of " playing fast and loose," or to John Fox the martyrologist, is not clear; but if to the latter, the fact itself, and the possession of such influence as is here supposed, have nowhere, as I am aware of, been noticed by his biographers.

In 1580 appeared the celebrated Letters between Harvey and Spenser the poet, entitled " Three Proper, and wittie, familiar Letters; lately passed betvveene tvvo Vniuersitie men : touching the Earthquake in Aprill last, and our English refourmed Versifying. With the Preface of a well willer to them both." To these were added shortly after, " Two other, very commendable Letters, of the same mens vvriting : both touching the foresaid Artificiall Versifying and certain other Particulars."

These letters would appear to have originated from his failure to obtain the Oratorship of the University. Shortly before this he had " curiously laboured some exact and exquisite points of study and practice, and greatly misliked the preposterous and untoward courses of divers good wits ill directed : there wanted not some sharp undeserved discourtesies to exasperate my mind." —HARVEY'S *Four Letters*, Reprint, 147.

Urged forward by various causes, (dislike, young and hot blood, and an invective vein,) these letters, written and circulated probably in manuscript amongst the friends of both, at last were surreptitiously printed.

" Letters may be privately written, that would not be-publicly divulged. . . . Many communications and writings may secretly pass between friends, even for an exercise of speech and style that are not otherwise convenient to be disclosed; it was the sinister hap of those unfortunate letters to fall into the hands of malicious enemies, or undiscreet friends, who ventured to imprint in earnest that was scribbled in jest (for the moody fit was soon over), and requited their private pleasure with my public displeasure : oh ! my inestimable and infinite displeasure.

" When there was no remedy but melancholy patience, and the sharpest part of those unlucky letters had been over-read at the Council Table, I was advised, by certain honourable and divers worshipful persons, to interpret my intention in more express terms ; and thereupon discoursed every particularity by way of articles or positions, in a large APOLOGY of my dutiful and entire affection to that flourishing University, my dear Mother ; which *Apology*, with not so few as forty such academical exer-cises, and sundry other politic discourses, I have hitherto sup-pressed, as unworthy the view of the busy world, or the enter-tainment of precious time : but peradventure these extraordinary provocations may work extraordinarily in me ; and though not in a passion, yet in conceit stir me up, to publish many tracts and discourses, that in certain considerations I meant ever to conceal, and to dedicate unto none but unto obscure darkness, or famous Vulcan.—G. HARVEY's *Four Letters*, Reprint, p. 15.

This " Apology" of Harvey does not appear to have been printed, and is probably for ever lost to us.

It must have been in the " Discourse touching the Earthquake in Aprill last," that the libellous matter was found, which led to the interference of the Privy Coun-cil ; and to this Lyly evidently alludes in the following sentence in Pap with a Hatchet :

" And one will we coniure vp, that writing a familiar Epistle about the naturall causes of an Earthquake, fell into the bowells of libelling, which made his eares quake for feare of clipping, he shall tickle you with taunts ; all his works bound close, are at least six sheetes in quarto, and he calls them the first tome of his familiar Epistle . . . . If he ioyne with us *perijsti* Martin, thy wit wil be massacred : if the toy take him to close with thee, then haue I my wish, *for this tenne yeres haue I lookt to lambacke him.*" [Reprint, 17, 18.]

Amongst the Letters between Harvey and Spenser, is a Poem by the former, entitled " Speculum Tuscanismi," which, by Harvey's enemies was construed into a libel on Edward Vere, Earl of Oxford, the story of whose exile and residence at Florence has been told by D'Israeli. Harvey says that it was Lyly who betrayed him.

" And that was all the fleeting that ever I felt, saving that another company of special good fellows (whereof he was none of the meanest that bravely threatened to conjure up one which should massacre Martin's wit, or should be lambacked himself with ten years' provision) would needs forsooth very courtly persuade the Earl of Oxford, that something in those letters, and namely, the *Mirror of Tuscanismo* was palpably intended against him." [*Four Letters*, p. 17.]

Though Harvey goes on to disclaim all reference to the Earl of Oxford, Nash tells us that he was " compelled to secrete himself for eight weeks in that noble mans house, for whom he had thus bladed," and that he afterwards was imprisoned in the Fleet, quoting the evidence of Thomas Watson in confirmation :

" But O what news of that good Gabriel Harvey
    Knowne to the world for a foole, and clapt in the.
        Fleet for a rimer."

In one of his Sonnets, Harvey replies :

" Whose eye but his that sits on slander's stool
    Did ever him in Fleet or prison see."

He also alludes to this charge of Nash in " Pierce's Supererogation :"

" As for his lewd supposals, and imputations of counterfeit

praises they are, like my imprisonment in the Fleet, of his strong phantasy, and do but imitate his own skill in falsifying of evidence, and suborning of witnesses to his purpose." [Reprint, p. 57.]

Harvey and Lyly were in early life friends. The former, in the second book of Pierce's Supererogation, thus commences :

" PAP-HATCHET (for the name of thy good nature is pitifully grown out of request) thy old acquaintance in the Savoy when young *Euphues* hatched the eggs that his elder friends laid, (surely *Euphues* was someway a pretty fellow : would God, *Lilly* had always been *Euphues* and never *Pap-hatchet*) that old ac- quaintance, now somewhat strangely saluted with a new remembrance, is neither lullabied with thy sweet *Pap*, or scare-crowed with thy sour *Hatchet*." [Reprint, p. 81.]

Lyly's Euphues came out in 1579 : and from the prefatory matter we learn that its author had previously been rusticated at Oxford, for glancing at some abuses. One of his first patrons was the Earl of Oxford ; but in 1582 he appears to have lost the favour of that nobleman ; this circumstance is stated in a letter which Lyly wrote upon the occasion to Lord Burghley, in which he protests his innocence. In what capacity he served Lord Oxford is not mentioned, but it may be gathered from the terms of the letter, that he occupied a place of pecuniary trust, which he was supposed to have abused. [COLLIER's *Hist. E. D. P.* iii. 175.]

The quarrel between Lyly and Gabriel Harvey would appear to have begun about 1580, and it is not unreasonable to suppose that it had reference to the

discharge of Lyly from his office in the family of the
Earl of Oxford.

In 1583, Richard Harvey, being as he says, "shortly
to profess Divinity," published " An Astrological Discourse vpon the great and notable Coniunction of the
tvvo superiour Planets, SATVRNE & Iupiter, which
shall happen the 28. day of April, 1583," which, having
been submitted to the censorship of Doctor Squire, son-
in-law to Abp. Whitgift, came out under his Lordship's
express sanction and encouragement. The prediction
in this absurd and foolish book did not take place, but
the author, according to Nash, had pawned his credit
upon it in these express terms: "If these things fall not
out in euerie poynt as I haue wrote, let mee for euer
hereafter loose the credit of my astronomie." [NASH's
Pierce Penniless, 8vo, p. 44, Reprint.] These express terms, however, do not appear in the book,
although the substance of what is quoted is the same.
[See R. HARVEY's *Astrol. Discourse*, p. 17, 1583.]

"Wel, so it happend, that he happend not to be a man of his
word: his astronomie broke his day with his creditors, and
Saturne and Jupiter proued honester men than all the worlde
tooke them for. Wherevpon the poore prognosticator was
readie to runne himselfe through with his Jacob's staffe, and cast
himselfe headlong from the top of a globe, (as a mountaine)
and breake his necke. The whole vniuersitie hyst at him,
Tarlton at the Theater made Iests of him, and Elderton consumed his ale-crammed nose to nothing in bear-bayting him
with whole bundells of ballets." [NASH's *Pierce Penniless*, 1592,
p. 44, Reprint.]

Here, then, we see one of the Harveys, and presently

shall find the three brothers, at variance with that gregarious herd of town wits, who, as actors or writers, were connected with the stage at this eventful period.

In 1589* Nash gave to the world the " firstlings of his folly " in authorship, being a preface to his friend Greene's " Arcadia," or " Menaphon." This was addressed " To the Gentlemen Students of both Universities," and in it he takes occasion to bestow just praise on Harvey's Latin versification; hence we may conclude with certainty, that the strife waged so many years between them had not then begun.

Whether any circumstances to us unknown occasioned the production of Lyly's Pap with a Hatchet, or merely his desire of attacking Gabriel Harvey under the mask of Martin Mar-prelate, is uncertain. Harvey tells us that he had been suspected by these mad copesmates [Greene, Lyly, and Nash] of being Martin; and Lyly, in the extract we have given above from Pap with a Hatchet, charges him with being the author of Martin's Epitome. It is most probable, however, that it was more for the purpose of attacking their common enemy that these writers engaged in a controversy so totally at variance in its object and end to their usual occupation, and not, as has been supposed, that they were patronized and encouraged by the dignitaries of the Church.

J. P.

---

* See Preface to the Reprint of " An Almond for a Parrot," 1845, where the reasons for this conclusion are given.

PLAINE PERCEVALL THE
Peace-Maker of England.

SWEETLY INDEVORING WITH HIS
blunt persuasions to botch vp a Reconciliation between MAR-TON
and Mar-tother.

*ompiled by lawfull art, that is to say, without witch craft, or sorcery
and referred specially to the Meridian and pole Artichocke of
Nomans Land: but may serue generally without
any great error, for more Countries
then Ile speake of.*

Quis furor aut hos,
Aut hos, arma sequi, ferrúmque lacessere iussit.

———————

Printed in Broad-streete at the signe
of the Pack-staffe.

TO THE NEW VPSTART MARTIN,

AND THE MISBEGOTTEN HEIRES
OF HIS BODY: his ouerthwart neighbor, Mar-
Martin, Mar-Mar-Martin, and so foorth following
the Traulila-lilismus, as farre as Will Solnes stut-
tring pronunciation may stumble ouer at a breath:
To all Whip Iohns, and Whip Iackes: not forget-
ting the Caualiero Pasquill, or the Cooke Ruffian,
that drest a dish for Martins diet, Marforms and
all Cutting Hufsnufs, Roisters, and the residew of
light fingred younkers, which make euery word a
blow, and euery booke a bobbe: Perceuall *the Peace-*
Maker of England, wisheth grace to the one party, of
the other Parish: and peace stichd vp in a Gaber-
dine without pleat or wrinckle, to the other party of
this Parish.

I WOULD it had bin PERCEVALS hap, to haue com to
the beginning of a friendly feast, or to the latter ending
of so dangerous a fraye. And I thought I had bin
faire for it at the first: for plodding through Aldersgate,
all armed as I was, with a quarter Ashe staffe on my
shoulder, and an emptie belly vnder my northern belt,
I spied me, a large **P.** with a wide mouth like a por-
radge pott, and being quicksented thrust forward on
the trale, and found it was Papp. But I cannot tell,
what the goodere came into my minde, but somewhat

it was, that persuaded me to trie before I tasted, and
looke before I licked: And though my sharpset-
stomach would haue straight fell into acquaintance, by
reason of some auncient familiaritie betweene a western
fellow, and a whitpot: yet bearing a braine as well
as a belly, I stood sauntring ouer it, like a whelp that
had scalded his mouth with lapping vp hotte water
Grewell: till I found that it was no meat indeed for
PERCEVALL, but rather a bone for MARTIN to digest,
if his stomach wold serue him: for though the first
ladlefull had a smacke as soft as pap, the next morsell,
a taste as sweet as a fig, and so forth: yet I see he that
was Cooke and Cater, thought to feed MARTIN with
these nunchiōs, as men feed Apes: with a bit and a
boxe on the eare. Why but soft maisters, faire plaie
and no snatching: is your feasting turned to a fray?
put vp, put vp your weapons, and be some wiser then
some. They were neuer tall fellows of their hands
that were such hacksters in the street: nor euer prooued
old wringers indeed, that fell out at their belly mettall.
Go to MARTIN, go to: I know a man is a man, though
he haue but a hose on his head (and thou hast a close
house on thine) but the greatest quarrellers meet often
with their ouer-match. Putcase thou hadst a good
cause (as alas I am a plaine fellow and not giuen to

swearing) yet a couple of these late Roysters would marre ten MARTINS, at the cracking of a stage Iest. They haue plaguy Clubfists, the one with his Counter-Cuffe, the other with his Country Cuffe, would quickly make a blew MARTIN. And you on the other side: what neede all this stir? this banding of kilcowes to fight with a shadow? If I were at home, within the precinctes of mine owne domination, I would charge you in Gods name and the Queens, to put vp your whinyards, you are men inough, able to deale one to one at handigripes, come cut and long taile: why should you offer to take the aduātage of the higher ground? Truly, truly, I will present you at the law day for a ryot, though I be neither side man for this Meridian, nor Warden, but to ward my selfe as I walke. There is more danger in breaking the Queenes Maiesties peace, then you are aware of. That mad companion MARTIN, you know, plaies least in sight, and serues you, as Æneas serued Turnus, ˚to make him fight with a mist in steed of a man: he doth but send his picture, to make triall of your affection towards him, as (my boy at home saies) Heliogabalus did, to search the humors of the Roman Senate. If you had vsed his Image somwhat more gentlie, within this space, hee would haue appeared in his likenes, incarnated or incased in some knaues skin or other I warrant you: beare with one grosse terme, so as I make no custome of it. Come on therfore MARTIN and the rest, house your selues in the next Tauerne, I will set my selfe (not a knaue betweene two honest men) but as a good fellow, betwixt the shadow of MARTIN, and the naturall shape of your selues, to trie whether I can stint this, Hold my dagger from your throat, or no.

Yours if you like mee :
mine owne if you strike me.
P.P.P.

Plaine Perceball.

HE was a tender harted fellow, though his luck were but hard, which hasting to take vp a quarrell, by the high way side, between a brace of Saint Nicholas Clargie men: was so curteously imbraced on both parties, that he tendered his purse for their truce, and swapt away his siluer for Copper retaile. Such copsmates would be examined, if it were but for Alcumists: and such a kind hart Chronicled, if it were but for a foole.

All this wind shakes none of my Corne, quoth *Perceuall*, whereupon Gossip Reason the chiefe actor in the pageant of my braine, and high speaker in the Parlament of my deuise, began this motherly, and well powdered tale. The medling Ape, that like a tall wood cleauer, assaying to rend a twopenny billet in two peeces, did wedge in his pettitoes, so fast, between the two clefts, that he stucke by the feete for a saie: and remained foorth comming at the discretion of those, whose occupation he enchrochd vpon before he was free: Short though were his prentiship, did he not pay for his learning? Tush *Perceuall*, hath no felicitie in these captious Intergatories. And therefore good

sweete Tenant Reason, speake plainely, and say Land-
lord mine (giue euery man his right) he that thrusts his
finger between the barke and the tree, is like to be
pinched: Counterfet *Martin*, or Counter *Martin*, let
them fight or be frinds, with a knaues name: encounter
not with them, they be like Gunnes, they carry fier in
their harts, and death in their mouths. If they get
thee within their reach: thou must come to knokham
faire, and what betweene the block and the beetle, be
thumpd like a stockfish, now gandmer are not these
your examples moralized? Pithy stuffe to keepe a
man from crossing the bowling Alley, for feare of a
broken shin. Or it moues me as much as the fatherly
Two an- rebuke of an old stander, moude that vniuer-
cient stan- sity post, which seemed to take the wall of a
ders, that
Senior and Senior. I cannot though you should bind
the post. me to such a stubborn post, as that graue
student met with in the darke, but carry one bucket of
water, when I heare the bels ring backward, and the
fire runne forward. They were in a fault, where the
fire first began: but first and last, helpe, quench all;
or else these high flying sparks will light on the heads
of vs all, and kindle in our bedstraw, if other folkes
lodging be no better then mine. Well fare London
yet, for a policie besides water (which they put in
practise too lately, the more was the pitty:) pull downe
the houses burning, lest they catch hold on their
neighbors. I, but you talke of cost, and commission.
That tricke would aske a long pole and a hoke, and
my quarter stafe is too short, except a man stood on

tiptoe. But now I remember my selfe, neuer will I ouerstraine my strength, nor play at hand ouer head so high, but where I may feele sure footing.

Giue me my spectacles, that I may see whether I dreame, or whether these sights be all in good sadnes, which I behold, sometime these madcaps be at a fray: sometimes at a feast: it makes no matter whether it be plaine dealing or iugling, take them at the best, and sit downe to their banket. And sith *Martin* and his brood hath furnished the first course, with sundry dishes, and saweed them throughly: and againe his beauie frinds *Pasquill, Marforius,* and the fresh Cater of late, haue counter coursd him, with messes somewhat hoat of the spice: (for the Pap had corns of long Pepper as big as a hatchet:) I follow like a plaine dunstable Groome, with salt and spoones on a trencher. Indeede you say true, *Sal sapit omnia:* and seruice without salt, by the rite of England, is a Cuckholds fee, if he claime it. Go to then, and take salt to your soppes, least sorrow attaint them. Make brine for your bull biefe, that it may sucke out those swelling corrupt affections that remaine somewhat rancke in the flesh. As for my spoons, those I brought, that I and my companions might haue one slap at the Spoone meat, wherein *Martin* boasted his Cookery: and the other set out their skill. They had neede be large long Spoons (say you) if I come to feed with such whipsters.

Martin cald his arguments spoon meat in his protest.

Let me alone, for my actiuity, at the dish meat, and a long arme, though my scoope be the shorter. *Perceuall,*

you are somewhat a mery man, as well as the rest,
according to your homely Countrey fashion.   Mary sir,
there is somewhat in it beside true working, and a
Gods name, quoth the good man, that checkt his wife,
for hopping about the house, and telling what the
schollers of Oxford paid for their good cheare: when
he no sooner stept ouer the threshold, but fell into the
same tune and taking; *and about they went.*   My
Masters be ware of *Martins* circle, for if his frinds or
his foes chop into it vnawares, they are like to daunce
after his pipe, and set themselues vpon a miry pinne,
(for so doth he) till his vnderpinning will faile him, I
doubt.

Come on *Martin*, put out (as the passenger said to
the Miller) not a knaues head, no keepe in, thou art
wiser then so, yet if wind doe not faile thee, thy late
Customers, which play more sacks to the mill, haue
brought greists or iests at least wise to be ground.   If
thy mill stones be not worne too blunt, for want of
pecking, there is picking meat for thee: make meale of
it, and take large tole to the enriching of the *Tolbot*
thou talkest off.

Martin me thinks the clacke of thy mill, is somewhat noisome to the whole countrey, thou liuest in;
either thou art well set on worke, or else, thou hast
wind at will to thy sailes.

I pray thee make once an *auricular confession,* tell
me in mine eare: is the desire of *Reformation* so deeply
imprinted in thine hart, as the terme is often printed in
thy papers?   Is it conscience or lucre, that spurgals

thy hackney pen, to force it take so high a hedge, as thou leapest at? I haue seene as mad a trick as this, when a Rancke rider hath put his horse to a hedge, and lay in the ditch for his labor. Thy foming mealy mouth betokeneth stomacke, and yoong vnbridled fits, for all that fatherly countenance, and graue vizard which sometimes thou vsest to plead the cause of thy *Reformation* vnder. No no, you vse the nostrils too much, and to many vnseasoned frumps, to come of that raze, that sincerely in time of superstition required *Reformation.* Whow? I go about to disgrace thee? No no I come but by the way of intreaty, as it were with a becke to admonish thee, that thou putst the wrong foote before, and therefore pull backe. Yet beare with me, if I doubt whether all be gold that glistereth, sith *Saint Martins* rings be but Copper within, though they be gilt without, sayes the Goldsmith. Idle termes came neuer from *Saint Paul,* nor reprochfull taunts from *Michaell:* yet *S. Paul,* no doubt, was mery in his daies: and the *Archangell,* you know, was at controuersie with the *Diuell.* Here againe whow? nay if I trot so heauily, I am neither for *Martins* riding, nor these three new mery mens reading. Gape *Martin* that I may see thy age, but take heed, thou bite me not: I thought so: the marke is not out of thy mouth, for thou hast a Colts tooth in thine head still: if thou wilt haue it drawne by fowle means, these *Roisters* haue beetles to knocke it out: if gently, let me be thy tooth drawer, I haue a kind hart of mine owne, and that name hath been good at such a practise heretofore.

Take heede *Martin*, a horse may ouer reach in a true pace, and thou play the foole though thou shouldst haue a good matter in hand. As for my part, I come not to take any part, I am none of those, which loue fending and proouing, if I can part you but for the time present, I am at my Iourneies end. Let the higher officers examine the cause, and find the fault (if al be true thou talkest of) where it is: yet (as a wel bearded Poet taught a Queene to speake in a Latine Enterlude) *Etsi causa repetentis bona, Mala sic petentis est.* Out vpon thee *Perceuall*, what gibberish is that? what, what, latine in the mouth of a plaine fellow? Nay I wot neere, but it hath left behind it a wale in my throate like a strange bodylouse in an vnknowne pasture. Wel *Martin*, *Sustine pro nunc*, stand by a trice, but looke you depart not the court, in paine of mine Indignation. Thou shalt perceiue that like a good sempster, I can cut euen by a threed, and part this quarrell without partiality. If I vse indifferency, call me not *Iohn Indifferent* now, for my good will: or if I lay my helping hand, to the cure of such a broile, without breach of peace, or danger of riot; say not thou as an olde *Pasquill* said being in a traunce of that famous and modest *Clarke Erasmus*, that I hang houering in the mid way betwixt heauen and hell: He no doubt, misused, for fancie sake the memory of a good man deceased: and thou in so saying shouldst mistake the good meaning of one wel *Disposed*. Stand by I say, till thy turne comes aboute againe.

Now, my Countrey men on the other part, make

your appearance, thinke not skorne that *Perceuall*, is somewhat in your tops, my sirnome is *Peace-Maker*, one that is but poorely regarded in *England*, bicause Peace hath been long plentifull: but yet one that may speake with some authority, as long as our most roiall *Peace-Mistres* holds the sterne (which God grant long she may.)   That faire, and fairest flower, in our garland, if she should faile: then were it high time for *Perceuall* and all *Peace-Makers*, to put vp their pipes, or else in steed of the soft violine, learne to sound a shrill trumpet. Well then, let a poore mans tale be hard amongst you. *Martin* is the man and the marke you shoot your forked arrowes at: if you strike his face you can raise no skin, for his forhead is brasse: nor fetch vp his blood, bicause he is giuen to blush no more thē my black dog at home: welfare a faire face vpon an ill paire of shoulders yet: if you pearce his hart, you can doo him little harme, for he is liude like a Cat: strike his toong, the biternes of the same, will trace out the Author of the wound, like the fish *Torpedo*, which being towchd, sends her venime alongst line and angle rod, till it cease on the finger, and so mar a fisher for euer.   Fie, fie, will you vpon a spleen, run vpon a Christen body, with full cry and open mouth?   Though indeed I cannot blame you, sith his proceedings were so vnchristianlike, if you tooke him for a Monster, or a Maddog: and so went about to worme him: but I am afraide such a carelesse curre, is cureles: wormeseede and reasons will doo him no good: and for other remedies that might come by incision, his wormeaten

B

Cōscience refuseth, (as *Dionysius* did the hands of his Barbar, for feare lest mistaking his beard, he would haue cut his throat) and therefore keeps him out of your Clutches.   Yt were good to keepe such a Cur in awe, but alas hurt him not, for a dogs mouth is medicineable, (they say:) *Verum est,* if he bite not where he should licke, I am answered.   But here is such likening Christianfolks to dogs; that I cannot away with it.   Shall we haue neighbors children, lie skufling in the kennel together by the eares like bride well birds? it is as good as a beare bayting for them, which loue neither, to see either touze other so bedlemlike. Neuer a beadle sturring? nor bear-heard at hand to put his staffe in the mouth of the beare, or pull off these dogs?   This will proue foule play: whosoeuer get the victorie, " Seu vincas, seu vincêris, maculêre necesse est si:" the rest was at my finger's end: but fare well it, since it is gone : Beare with my shittle remembrance.   I doe not thinke, though *Martin* and you be of diuerse Parishes, but you be all of one Church, saile all in one ship, and dwell all in one Commonwealth.   Nay you are all good subiects, or else I would the woorst were curbd with a checkthong, as bigge as a towpenny halter, for halting with a *Queene* so good and gratious.   All this hart burning betweene you, is but about the bounds of the. Parish, and the limits of the Church lands.   Let the yoouth be content to be infourmed of the Mearstones, by the Auncientry of the Parish: and not continew such bustling, back-biting, with facing and defacing one another to the vttermost: this is *Spight,* and not *Spirit,* or if it be, it is some *spightfull Spirit.* It were enough to entitle those *Browne sectaries* of the *Blacke Prince,* with the name of traytors, and not to cast them like squibs and wild fire within your owne hatches, and the body of your owne Common-wealth. Mary who began (say you:) *Martin* cald traytor first, he spake lauishly, and must heare as knauishly. Now the blood is vp; he that hath most gall in his garbage, thinks to win the goale. And he that hath most toong powder hopes to driue the other out of the field first. I could tell these eager younsters, how they might be euen with their Aduersary : giue faire words for foule : " Doe good against euill : and heape hoat burning coales vpon his head." That is a sentence sooner belieud bicause it is scripture, then put in practise, for all it is true.

Such a *Deane,* such a *Doctor,* slips within the compasse of treason cries *Martin.* Another, takes him by the nose with a paire of left-handed pincers, and puls him ouer the pumpes into the same puddle. Wot you what the little wagges saide, when they had beene telling many precious miracles of Robin-goodfellow and the diuell? We shall O P. P. there I plaid vpon thee to thy paine. speake so long of the diuell in iest, that he shall come amongst vs in good earnest: God warrant vs, and there withall, crost themselues, for it was in the old time: I would we could blesse vs from him, this newe time. But I am afraid, there will be so much talke of traitor, and so long vse of such bugs words, that some of our Male-contented **Hufsnuffs,** and Marprelats will prooue

their words master, yet I will nicke-name no bodie: I
am none of these tuft mockadoo mak-a-dooes: for
" Qui mochat, moccabitur" quoth the seruingman of
Abington.

And, as who shoulde say, they that named Rebels
oftenest with a breath, were the soundest winded
subiects: who can tell that? Not I: but sure I am,
that the boy which greeted his father with a letter clapt
full of commendations, commendations, and nothing but
commendations, prooude as vntoward a sonne, as he
that directed his superscription to his most obedient
parents.

If *Menippus*, or the *Man in the Moone*, be so quick-
sighted, that he beholds, these bitter sweete Iests, these
railing outcries: this shouing at *Prelats* to cast them
downe, and heauing at *Martin* to hang him vp for
Martilmas biefe: what would he imagine otherwise,
then as that stranger, which seeing a *Quintessence*
(beside the foole and the Maid Marian) of all the
picked yoouth, straind out of an whole Endship, footing
the Morris about a *May pole*. And he, not hearing
the crie of the hounds, for the barking of dogs, (that is
to say) the minstrelsie for the fidling, the tune for the
sound, nor the pipe for the noise of the tabor, bluntly
demaunded, if they were not all beside them selues, that
they so lipd and skipd whithout an occasion.

Backe with that leg *Perceuall:* Nouice as thou art,
dost thou thinke that we are some, all mad? Alas I
am a stranger, and cannot tel what your horse play
meanes. Learne, learne to vnderstand the occasion of

those actions: Their words are common? for euery
cut-purse vseth them at the Old Bayly, that Occasions
hath had any skill in his miniken Handsaw.   and ac-
                                              tions com-
I can tell who was acquainted with an olde mon.
sooker, that caries such *Potticall* verses of the *State of
Flanders,* in a linnen bag (though they be no baggage
neither) as would make a man thinke vpon driuing out
sides, and taking of parts as long as he liues.   My selfe
drinking hand to hand with the founder of them: for
lacke of a nutmeg, he gaue me a great and a lesse, to
grate in a spice bole, and this was the powder.

> " Orgia turbantem natum dum mactat Agaue,
>   Insana, insanum Penthea, credit aprum."

Had not he a long wind that sowpd vp these two at
a draught? and a good head that carried them away
without staggering, togither with their Appurtenances?
"Mad was the mother and kild hir wood sonne, &c."
That liquid Poet, had askt himselfe the question, who
was in the fault, that two factions were at daggers
drawing, till they were like to draw all to an vprore,
he answers like a slie slaue; *Ambo.* for that was his
meaning, though he wheeld about, seeking to declare
his mind, with a *Far Fetched Simile.*

But (say you) there is no reason in it, that we should
stand bound to the good a-bearing, except *Martin* were
bound to the peace.   Yf he snarle like a cur at vs, why
should not we prouide a Bastinado for him? and he
making an assault, to mount ouer our parke pales: why
may not we haue one cast in his Orchard, and a fling

at his Medlar tree? Mary sirs, for feare the Cudgell
fall downe againe upon a mans owne Costard. If a
swift running streame haue free passage along the
kennell, fare well it, you shall neuer heare worse of it:
but stop it, and *Hercules* like where it finds no way, it
wil make one: and so set the next neighbors medowes
all on a floate. When he began to skold first, you
should haue betooke him to an Ostler, to walke, while
you had cald an officer to chamber his toong.

So if you had done, his owne poison would haue
festered in his owne flesh. Prid and venime, if they
had so ranckly possessed his hart, they would haue set
his owne skin a strute, and burst his hide before this
time. I see the vaine is vp in the forhead, and *Martin*
shall haue as good as he brings, or else a free schoole of
skolds shal be set vp for the nonce. O that *M. Th.*
Cicero might rise againe, a little before his turne, and
see railing made a profession, *Slaunder* set in a *Shrine*,
and honored with the slaughter of many ripe wits, in
steed of a sacrifice: how would he blame England now,
(as he blamed *Athens* when he liude) for erecting
Chappels in honor of that dishonorable cowple: *Reproch*
Virtutes
enim non
vitia conse-
crare decet
Cic.de lc.2. and *Impudency:* or as he checkd his Countrey men the *Romans,* which had builded an
altar to the *Agewe,* and a monument to the
remembrance of *Cursed Fortune.* I cannot
tell what Spirituall Chappels, and Inuisible altars our
men set vp now a daies, but I am sure, one of the
Largest Churches in England is like to fall on his
maribons, and so mar the fashion of his bones, that it

may be cald *Allstones* here after.   Had *Martin* walkd
that way he might haue espide a great hole and a miserable maime in the body of that Church.   It is an ill
wind that blowes no man to good they say: yea but the
Prophet *Aggeus* would haue giuen counsaile to repaire
such a place of praier: if *Martin* himselfe crie Hauocke
at it, beleeue him not, *Aggeus* was a great deale the
honester man, although while he liude he was no saint.
Where was I? my iourney lies not that way: I was
about to say that the Printers had hard luck if they lost
by these matches that are made of late against *Martin*.
Whose states when I looke vpon, I am ready to crie at
as a Countrey man of mine did, when trauersing London
streets, he spide a Iacke an apes, in a gaie cote, sit
mooing on a Marchants bulke: Good Lord what knacks
are made for money, now adaies?

　　Speake a blooddy word in a Barbors shop, you make
a forfet: and good reason too, Cap him sirrra, if he pay
it not.   Speake a broad word or vse a grosse tearme
amongst huntsmen in chaze, you shall be leasht for your
labor: as one that disgraceth a gentlemans pastime and
game, with the termes of a heardsman.   And is there
no penaltie to represse such lauish ouer reachers as
offer legends of lies to the presse? *Martin*, he put those
lies into print vnlawfully, which he coind in hugger
mugger: and others opposite to his humor will haue
their lies lie open manifestly, if it be but to shew that
they dare put in for the whetstone, and make as lowd
lies as *Martin* the forman.   But who is the father of
such fruit, or the sower of such seede?   False witnes,

and lying was forbode by *Moses Law*, but is taken vp
now for a custome, of one lewd Customer, and hath got
Chapmen that will neuer lay it downe, except they
make their end as tedious to the indifferent Reader, as
his beginning was odious to the peaceable hearer.   He
that catcheth euery flying tale by the end, may chance
to take a frog for a fish, and doo as the boy, that bit a
snake by the head insteed of an eele.   Heresay is too
slender an euidence to spit a mans credit vpon, or to
broach a mans Conscience with kitchin termes or any
thing, nothing comes amisse to *Perceuall.*

I see neighbors how you croud backward, thinking
belike to ride vpon my Crupshoulders: I am no Ape
Carrier, I pray you defile not my sheeps russet Coate,
with your dirtie shoes yet: this home made Karsey,
and my plain speeches may haue as much wooll (I dare
not say so much wit) as is in your double pild veluet.
Blessed are the Peace-makers (I say:) and so are neither
the breeders nor fauourites of discord.   *Cursed are the
malitious inuentors of slanders;* and so are neither the
renewers nor continuers of Concord.   O so some of
those companions ply the boxe, to boxe a shadowe, and
beate their knuckels against a bare wall, and to get a
sure card on their side, either calles for Justice, and
seekes to incense our noble *Queene* against the other.
Indeed I confesse some of them haue great cause so to
doo, but what then?   Let hir imperiall Maiestie alone,
by hir gratious leasure, and wisedome, she will prepare
a boisterous snuffle, for such boisterous head-strong
Iaddes, as will be wincing.   Slow to wrath, and slower

to punishment, and alwaies like *Elizabeth*, she peaseth the sword of Iustice, with an vpright hand: when season serues, she will strike, and yet deuide so equally, that she hurts not one heire of an naturall subiect. No doubt she is the naturall mother of this Iland (if *Salomon* himselfe were Iudge) that is so tender ouer hir Sonnes and subiects. And they on the other side, stepdames, and most vnnaturall parents, that would haue their children dismembred and cut off in middle. Againe, those children be chaunglings, that in steede of sucking the milke, would sucke the blood of their nourses. Dost thou beleeue there be any *Fairies* then *Perceuall?* I cannot tell whether there be *Fairies*, but I am sure there is a foule *Diuell* that brings foorth changeable coloured vrchins, which can glister like a glose worme neare gold, looke pale and wan vpon Lead, and browne vpon Iron: tell me now, whether is such a one a *Chaungling*, a *Horselech*, or a *Chamelæon?* their Law: set downe your staffe, and pause a while, this beauie fardell hath bred a stitch in my short ribs. But well remembred, Crier, make an, o yes, for *Martin* to come into the Court. O Sir, do you stand vnder my sleeue, and I see you not? I pray God I haue not a foole at mine elbow, the *Diuell* you haue, quoth his beauy frinds. I thinke the mad slaue, hath tasted on a ferne-stalke, that he walkes so invisible.

I haue had conference *Martin*, with these ruffe *Roisters* that challendge thee at all weapons, from the forrest bill, to the bodkin. They seeme to blame a certaine *Pipe of Pistling*, that hath tooke the tip of thy

toong and a vaine of lauish iangling, that hath made
thy palate rise out of socket.   Their teeth water at
reuenge, and are sharpe set on edge: thy selfe was the
grindstone of their wits, and now if they cannot come at
the faire, to hold thy nose to the grindstone, they sweare
to chop thy Relickes and hacke thine hackle as small as
fewell to the fire.   I perceiue, and they would faine be
on thy Iacke for thy sawcines, that thou art principall
picker of the quarrell.

O *Martin*, honor gray heares, during thy nonage: or
else looke for dishonor and dotage if thou canst get
any competent yeers on thy backe, before thou pro-
curest a hempen chaine aboue thy shoulders.   Be thou
a yoong boy, or a stale Batchelar, (vnmaried thou art
by thine own *Protestation*) learne to reuerence those
two ornaments of a common-wealth, *Age* and *Authority*.
Barre this pert bearding of men reputed honest for their
behauiour, and honorable both for their calling and
counsaile: Leaue thrumming thy *Pibauld Iestes* with
Scripture, Iron and Clay will not be tempered togither.
Thy pamphlets which thou sendest into the broad world,
may well be *Pistles*, but certainely they be no *Gospels*.
The word of God is sufficient to worke the will of God,
and neede not thy friuolous medleis, thy humane traditions, or additions, either to qualifie the vertue, or
disgrace the enemies thereof, which thou pretend-
est, being thy selfe, I doubt, an archenemie to the
same.

Aske the Printer if he haue not a merier booke: this
fellow is falne so low into his dumps, that there is no

sport in reading him. Let me gape and stretch my selfe a little, and then hay we ye.

I find that in euery trade and occupation, there is a better and a worse, as there is in euery warpe of fish, a great and a lesse. There is a Shomaker, there is a Cobler: a Tailor, and a Botcher: a Marchant, and a Broker: a Haberdasher and a Pedlar: a Mason and a Dawber: a Minstrell and a Fidler: a Parson and a Uicar: a Minister and a Curat: there steps me in a third tricksie, neat, nimble, spruse Artificer into euery one of these occupations: and like a prickeard Mule will be of another distinct kind from either dame or sire. One standing all vpon his pumps and pantables, will be aboue a Shomaker. Another mounts vpon a loftier Shop bourd then a Tailor, and wil be none otherwise termde then a shaper of garments forsooth. Stand thy ground *Perceual*, neuer run through such a rablemēt of Craftsmen forward, and backeward, I am windles to follow thee so fast ouer and ouer so many trads. I haue thy meaning at one word, as well as at an hundred. Then sir if you be of such a sodaine conceipt, follow me step by step, from these handicrafts to matters of Religion. Some of conscience study to reforme their owne liues, and looke first into their own bosome : others to the intent that all the world might suppose, that nothing were amisse at home, like bad huswifes flie abroad, and search out publike imperfections, to busie their heads about. Some againe endeuor to practise, without a multiplying of words openly: others beare a ready toong in their heads, but bray them in a morter, they

will neuer be mortified in deeds: Some earnest protestants are precise in correcting their owne corrupt
affections, and in aduertising their brother kindly of his
faults as they fall: he goes for my money. Comes me
in an Hipocriticall younster, and he will be a Puritane,
and an ase before any that euer bare the name, or else
you abuse him. I haue heard of words that haue dege-
nerated into a worse signification from a better, but few
termes that were betterd by any that vsed them. I
hard say a good old Doctor (he shall haue my good
word though he be laid in his graue) found out *Puri-
tanisme* in *Papistry* (for so he termed their fained hipocrisie) when he dealt against *Iesuits:* then though we
cannot be too forward in a good matter, yet the diuel
can inuent sins in excesse, aswell as in defect. Men
haue great desire to be compted high fliers and deepe
swimmers, yet be the both daungerous exercises, considering that a man hath neither winges to beate the aire,
nor finnes to breake the water. *Adam* would haue
beene a *God*, but that his foote slipt, and he fel into a
state mortall. I do not thinke, *Martin*, but the olde
Serpent can tempt the perfectest *Eue* that euer was,
and then let *Eue* alone to perswade hir husband. But
thou hast no *Eue* to trouble thee: no but thou hast flesh
and blood to interrupt thee.

Nay *Perceuall*, now you wade into such particulars,
you are wide: stand not vpon the priuate censuring of
persons, lest thou seemest as senseles, as they which
determine vpon an Ale bench whether the passenger
that passeth by the lettise, be a *Saint* or a *Diuell*. Nay

ho there neighbor: chaue hard them say, that if a man
point with his finger in the Court of a Prince, he may
chaunce to forfet his whole fist for his sawcines: he
points faire, that disapoints his mouth of such a nourse,
as either of his hands be.

But there is one thing vsed amongst these *Marrers*
and *Markers* of folkes which maske with vizards of
Reformation, that stickes in my stomacke, and wil not
be digested. The greatest coursers, and professed hunters of dumbe dogs: such as wery themselues in hol-
lowing after that *Vermine*, and make their voices hoarse,
in crying out against them, are the very foster fathers,
that pester our Church with that Cattell. I wish that
we had none of these toong-tide Curs, that cannot
barkè, nor say buffe to a woulfes shadow: if it were
possible. But you that most cry out against them, why
haue you brought them vp no better? Why haue you
not taught some of those Puppes their lerrie? I will
take it vpon the credit of my selfe, an vpstantiall yeoman, that they most part of these mute shepheards are
hatchd vp vnder the wing of those which beate most
vpon the remoouing of dumbe dogs. I could giue you
some examples in Bedfordshire: a whole rablement at
least. A Preacher, if his conceipt be any thing swift,
that he can rolle it in the pulpit, must haue his reader
at his elbow, to fauor his voice. A Minister that hath
any thing a fat benefice, and a full belly, will haue his
Co-brother to assist him. And what must he be but
either an halfe-peny boy, or an idle craftsman, that shall
serue for meate, drinke and cloth, a little tutoring in

Diuinitie, and the reuersion of a benefice, when it fauls,
where his godfathers commendatorie letters may preuaile.   I could well like that men of some desert and
imploiment should haue their assistants, so they were
Preachers, but you shall not take them in that fault.
Where is the conscience of these criers out on blinde
guides become? not resident at home now: but abroad,
busie in inueighing against Bishops for their tolerations
graunted, to such as themselues haue preferred, commended, presented.   And by this *Leger-demaine* hath
the Common-wealth been robd of Tailors, Shoomakers,
and good Artificers, and the Church ouercharged with
bad Ministers: which thanke God, I dare saie in their
hearts (with that firehot Preacher) that they are so farre
from the Romish Religion, as they cannot vnderstand a
word of the Latine toong.   I tell you, this is a miserie
to heare, and a miserie to see: that such eager Callers
for *Reformation*, should plant slips of their owne gathering: supplant Magistrates for wincking at it, and make
the people beleeue, that they would haue it otherwise,
with all their hearts.   How dare these fellowes aspire
to further authoritie in Minister-making, when they
suffer their houses to be the Nourceries of such impo-
tent and impudent encrochers vpon Church-Offices?
What saie the people to this geare? tush, let the master
alone to speake for the man: he will commend him, for
his great profiting in knowledge vnder him: preferre
him for a peece of plaine doctrine; praise him, that he
is not infected with *Philosophie*, or such like *Vniuersitie
learning*: but especially that he is an honest man,

zealous, forward in Religion, and one that seekes for *Reformation.* This fellow cannot be misliked I warrant you: I, I that one word of *Reformation, Martin,* which hath been so much in thy mouth, and so greatly in thy request, hath made thy Customers swarme like Bees to the ringing of a Bason: but take heed, thine owne Cattaile sting thee not, when they shall taste what *Hemlockes* thou hast mingled, wherewith thine hiue was annointed.

But tush thy gossips will stand vpon it, that *Martins* clocke goes true, though the *Diuell* were in the *Horologe :* their rellish is altered so far with the sirope of selfe-loue, that Choller is called Zeale, and Melancholy, Mortification: whereupon followes swift iudgement that cuts all other from saluation: and some bad sullen conceipt peeuishly taken from their owne humorous imagination, that they would haue all stampt vpon, that be not of their stampe, or will not be strainde to their starke staring madnes. You had best saie now I speake against good men: *quatenus* they are good, *Martin,* I am their Orator, in the state demonstratiue to extoll them: but a wart is a wart if it were in the face of *Alexander:* frowardnes is frowardnes, if it were in my Father: sinne is sinne in holie *Dauid* himselfe. And *Socrates* had a wanton looke of his owne, though his schollers should beat the Phisiognomer for so saying. I would they were so good as I could wish them: we should haue better fruit, and more good deeds, which are now both thin sowne god wot, and thinner growne. Yet be they, as be may, I may be

thus bold with their masterships.   Beware of a heat,
for so long as a man is warme, he cannot feele his owne
imperfections, but thinketh that euerie man which
sweats not is keycold, such *firie Agues* fall soonest
into a surfeit, and founder themselues with their intem-
perate behauiour.   You shal haue a lame Iade, bridle,
and brag it vp and downe Smithfield, when he is a little
chafde, as though hee could stand on no ground for
lustines : set him vp in a stable, till he wax a litle cold,
and his limbes be so stiffe, he can stand on no ground
for lamenes.   Some of thy mates *Martin*, I am afraid,
be alwaies stirring so busily, least standing long still in
the open faire, they fall to downeright halting, and so
be disclosed for arrant heldings.   Such Iadish trickes
make a sound horse to be suspected, and some bipo-
crites, make earnest professors doubted of, yet neither
condemned so vnmercifullie as though there were no
way but one :- God forbid.   But leaue leaue, all the sort
of you, to boulster vp the faults of your own parishioners, and boult out the skapes of such as are none
of your sectaries.   One spakey Apple will make the
whole hourd smel, picke him out: One Hipocriticall
dissembler, will bring reproch vpon the whole brotherhood, cull him out: and although he defie the Surplice,
(which is a point of great valiancie) yet let him be put
to the choice of a whip or a white sheete : if he haue
offered in secrecie to defend this position.   *That a*
woman waking may lawfully graft Dianaes armes, vpon
the Temples of her husband sleeping.   You meane
vnhappily *Perceuall* whatsoeuer your wordes be: I

know a newst what *Circuit* you are in.   But is it not
a Religious deed to conceale the blemish of a brother,
least the *Gospell* be ill spoken of for his misdeeds?
As who should say the punishment of malefactors were
not the fruit of the Gospell? which heauenly and
blameles *Oracle* none but *Atheists* and *Miscreants*
will condemne for the shameles action, of such a one as
speakes of gospels in the day: but vseth I know not
what *nightspels* in the darke.   Neuer be afraid that
any which hath his fiue senses, will impute the fall of a
brother to the ouergreat knowledge he had in the scriptures: but to the slender practise and profite he made
in the same: for all his great boast.   Take heed, haue
an eye to the doore, least that, that Frierly *Si non castè*
Caueat creepe in amongst Protestants, where- *tamen cautè.*
by their ghostly Fathers wished a man to liue *Charily,*
though not chastly.

Whether will *Perceuall* and this weather holde? nay
no further *Martin,* thou maist spet in that hole, for ile
come no more there: here I pitch my staffe, and stand
to vrge thee, with these premises aboue named: thou
begannest first, and therefore giue not ouer last.   Thy
beginning was worst, let thine ending be best.   Controuersies be meate and drinke to the people: but doo not
cramme them with such gobbets, as may sticke in their
throats, least they hang the head on the shoulder, like
him that was slaine with an arrow at Tiburn prickes.
That is a new kinde of diet, with all my hart.   Yet sir,
when the steele and the flint be knockde togither, a
man may light his match by the sparkle: surely, but I

c 3

thinke tinder be verie danke now adaies, and though it take fire quickly, yet it takes light by leisure: for there hath been striking and iarring euer since, and a great while before, that a learned man somewhat on thy side, *Martin,* seemed to persuade that contention for good matters was good: you should haue his words: but

Car.　　that *Græcum est, non potest legi:* and yet I see no more Candles tinded thē wont to be, but a great many Beacons more fired then ought to be. You shall neuer make me belieue, that many Arguments turne soonest to Agreements. I haue seene them, which haue seene such hurly burlies about a couple, (that were no Fathers of the Church neither) *Aristotle* and *Ramus,* or els aske the Vniuersities, such a quoile with *pro* and *con,* such vrging of *Ergoes,* til they haue gone frō Art togither by the eares, and made their conclusions end with a Clunchfist, right like the old description of Logicke. My yoong maisters could not be content to whet their wits with such a cōtentiō: but fel to whetting their Tuskes at one another: like those children which sitting in the Chimney corner, some at one side, some at another, with the fire in the middle; fell to it with firebrands, when they should haue but warmde themselues and away. One litle sparke of dissention, is able to set a whole house, a Towne, an Vniuersitie, a Citie, a whole Realme on fire, the affections of young men be so readie to nourish it. Well then *Martin,* and you professed *Mar-Martins,* in presence of me *Perceuall* shake hands and be friendes, meet halfe way, and I standing iump in the middle will

crie aime to you both: so as you come not running with
force and maine, and crush me betwixt you for my good
will.   As for thine offence *Martin*, of higher Powers, I
dare vndertake, the Bishops seeke no blood, so as thy
rash attempt might be qualified with submission.   And
so did *Paul*, (els I am deceiued) either plead ignorance
for an excuse, or seem to recant and correct his ruffe
speech, he had made to a man in authority: belike he
was afraid least his example should haue animated any
pert Controulers of Magistracy, and therefore cut them
downe, which *should speake ill of the Ruler of the
people*.   How strangely looke these marchants on
both sides?   I would we had an Ostler to giue them a
turne or two till their sweating were done.   What mettall be they made of? their noise nothing like bels, and
yet a man may stop his eares to hear their dinne, with
honestie: it goes through my head, and makes a great
many moe deafe and displeased besides me.   They
agree like two drums, which are headed, the one with a
sheeps skin, the other with a wolfes hide.   It can neuer
be good musicke, that stands all vpon sharpes, and neuer
a flat: all diuisions framde with such long discords, and
not so much as a concord to end withall, argues a bad
eare, and a bungling *Artist*.   *Martin* and counter
Martin, be you not all Countrey men? make you no
account of that name? vnnaturall children, will you
distract your naturall mother? will you send Foxes
with fire brands at their tailes, to burne so forward a
crop of toward youth, so well eared, that they put vs in
hope alreadie of a timely haruest, and a plentifull

Gardiner for seuen yeeres after? send not a whirle-
winde amongst them, least beating one against another,
they dash out the Curnell, or be ledgde on the ground.

Go too I say, neuer straine curtesie, who shall begin:
beshrow him that comes lagge in so good a course as is
renewing of frindship. Downe with those great harts,
and bridle those angry fits, stand not in that clamorous
accusation of one another, the best of both may be
amended. Let the wisest be the forwardest, and the
most foole the frowardest. What ouerthwart companions be these, the more I perswade, the more they
looke askaunce ouer their shoulders: you turne the
wrong way and be too wayward. Remēber your
selues, walke about, and coole this flushing in the face,
lest it fume vp, and make you braine sicke. I would
faine doo some good vpon you: but when I lead a
horse to the water, if he will not drinke, what can I
doo, but whistle him. If my presens perswade nothing,
yet in mine absence, thinke of *Perceual,* and let him not
haue his name *Peace-Maker* for naught. I am sorry,
if I haue put my finger in the fire, and cannot quench
it: yet the best is, I can pull it out againe harmles, for a
wet finger burns not. I wil keepe me far enough from
the flame, though perhaps I may smell in the smoke, by
touching the brands.

O *Perceuall!* so some of these wil be-daube thee
with Inke, and plague thee with blacke and white: for
I see how they gird thee in their sleeues already. Tush
I can paint as fast as they, though perhaps not altogither
so faire. But a Iewes letter scrible scrable ouer the

Copurtenaunce of a mans countenance, will dash a body
wickedly. You see my quarter staffe, is it not a blesse
begger, thinke you? A washing blow of this is as good
as a Laundresse, it will wash for the names sake: it
can wipe a fellow ouer the thumbs, wring a man in
the withers, and must needs dry beate a skoundrell,
if it be artificially managed. Will you fight then
Perceuall? no truly, I had rather see my quarter ashe
staffe conuerted into ashes, then I would vse it against
any person: and then I am sure I shall not be pinchd
on the parsons side: for they would haue peace as
well as I. But let a Trauailor walke with his imple-
ments about him: A Dag case may be as good now
and then as a case of Dags. The sight of a *Hanger*
rusted in the sheath hanging by ones side, may safe
conduct a bodies purse, and saue a picking faint harted
theefe from hanging beside. But what if these Roisters
draw their Pen and Inkehornes, and so set vpon thee?
They may quickly set me vp, for I will be no *Peace-
Breaker*: yet if they howse me, I may chaunce to
thrust a wispe out of the window and so make them
waspish. O that is an excellent Auditor for a skold,
a cucking stoole will coole somewhat too much this
wether: but a wispe wil heate to the hart like Mal-
mesie. But you my Masters that striue, for this
supernaturall art of wrangling: let all matters be husht
and quiet a Godsname: if my toong ware currant
at the later end of my tale, and incur any suspition
that I am currish naturde, bicause I talke of my fence,
write my termes in the wind, or let them passe for

wind: and carrouse vp your owne quarrels in the
cup, and let the licour and they, like good fellowes,
march arme in arme, downe your throats. And so
hauing skinkde mine *Vltimum Vale* in a parting pot, I
put you both in a draught: And drinke to the funerals
of your Enimitie. Stay good neighbors, now I am for
your company.

Medio Tutissimus ibis.

This worke being finished, and red ouer and ouer by
the head of the parish, they called a vestry, wherin
they concluded, to write euery man some verses in the
commendation of the Author, bicause it was a custome
greatly taken vp in the Vniuersitie of late. And thus
they florish in their mother tong, as here followeth.

> *The gay bay Larell bow, that prancks my Cole,*
> *As speciall forehorse of my beanefed Teeme,*
> *Take* Perceuall, *and clap it on thy pole,*
> *Whose fortops such a branch doth well beseeme:*
>   *If any aske why thou art clad so garish:*
>   *Say thou art dubd the forehorse of the parish.*
>   *Quoth A. N. Carter.*

Hold hether, thou bell wether, of my fold,
Although thou hast dischargde thy duty well :
Surrender vp thy watch though it were gold :
For learned Perceuall *must beare the bell.*
     If (quoth my wether) it be Perceuall :
     Let him for me, take bell and hornes and all.
             Not so quoth G. A. Sheepheard.

Thy praises Perceuall *shall florish in my dary,*
My Paper, Curds, my Pen shall be a spoone,
Where I for aie will make thy praises tarry :
And if my Paper doe not sincke too soone,
     Else will I write them all vpon a cheese,
     That as the same increaseth, so may these.
             Quoth Goodman Bl. farmar.

The Coblers prophecy vpon the Author.

This patch here placd, the which I bast :
And sow so fast, shall sooner wast
            Then *Perceuals* renowne.

My shoe shall rend, my nall blade bend,
My lingels end, first shall I spend,
            Before his works goe downe.

At these assaies, thou gettest such praise,
As neer decaies, then goe thy waies,
            For I stand to the same.

If any such, by chaunce I tuch,
As seemes to grutch, for I speake so much,
            George Cobler is my name.

FINIS.

My frinds all fauor I beseech,
To yeeld our Perceuall *good speech :*
Husht Momus or my needell in thy breech.
                  Cast me the bottome of browne
                      threed hither.

All folkes of fauour I beseech,
To yeeld our Perceuall *good speech :*
Or else my needell in their breech.
                     Cast me hither the bottome
                       of browne threed.

So I will chalke thy praises vp,
And preach thy fame vpon a cup :
Remembring Perce, at euery sup.
                   But that I haue such hast of my
                     worke against Christide

                       Quoth N. G. Botcher.

Feceris Hufsnuffos scribendo relinquere Cuffos,
Necnon Martinos (appositiuè dico) malè natos cùm patre binos,
Et quoque Clubfistos omnes pacaueris istos,
Perceuall, ac idem (si possis) scindere pridem
Inceptas lites, vis, tanquam runcina, vites.
Es melior, (quid est Latinè propter.)   An Ale-house
To stablish friendship, or botch vp Peace in an Endship.

Twenty pound for a Dictionary.

Giuen in the Church loft.   By me H. D. Schollard
maker for fault of a better.

F I N I S.

Puritan Discipline Tracts.

AN ALMOND FOR A PARROT;

BEING

A REPLY

TO

MARTIN MAR-PRELATE.

Re-printed from the Black Letter Edition,

WITH

AN INTRODUCTION AND NOTES.

LONDON:
JOHN PETHERAM, 71, CHANCERY LANE.

1846.

INTRODUCTION.

ALTHOUGH I cannot at this time bring together positive and undoubted evidence of the authorship of the following tract, (because the materials are at present inaccessible to me,) at some future period, in the Introduction to one of his accredited productions, I hope to place the fact beyond the reach of cavil or question, that Thomas Nash, to whom public fame has given it, was the author.

Nash was of St. John's College, Cambridge, and took his degree of B.A. in 1585. He is supposed to have quitted the university in some disgrace about 1586, but of the cause we are entirely ignorant. The anonymous author of a tract called " Polymanteia," printed in 1595, thus alludes to it: "Cambridge, make thy two children friends; thou hast been unkind to one [Nash], to wean him before his time, and too fond

upon the other [Gabriel Harvey], to keep him so long
without preferment; the one is ancient and of small
reading; the other is young and full of wit." Nash
himself speaks of his beardless years, in Pierce Penniless; and Gabriel Harvey, in his Pierce's Supererogation,
1592, calls him " a gosling of the printing house;" and
in another place "a proper young man;" and elsewhere,
"a young man of the greenest spring, as beardless in
judgment as in face:" so that he must have taken his
degree of B.A. early in life, and we know that he never
proceeded Master of Arts.

It would appear from the Introduction to the following tract that Nash had visited Italy. Mr. Collier, in
his Introduction to Nash's Pierce Penniless [Shakspeare
Soc. 1842], says, "We find him [Nash] in London in
1587, in which year he wrote a very amusing and clever
introductory epistle to a tract by the celebrated Robert
Greene, called 'Menaphon,' afterwards better known
by the name of 'Greene's Arcadia,' the title it bore
in the later impressions. This seems to have been
Nash's earliest appearance in the character of an author"
[p. x. xi.], then adding in a note, "We take the date of
'Greene's Menaphon,' 1587, from the edition of that
author's 'Dramatic Works,' by the Rev. A. Dyce."
Mr. Collier apparently had forgotten that he had

himself stated some years before the fact of the Arcadia having been printed in 1587, "because in Greene's *Euphues*, his *Censure to Philautus*, of the same date, it is mentioned as already in print." [Hist. English Dramatic Poetry, vol. iii. p. 150.]

Whatever may be the date of the first edition of Greene's Menaphon, we have here only to do with Nash's Preface to that work, and, though Sir E. Brydges, in his reprint of it in 1814, mentions 1587, in which he is followed by the Rev. A. Dyce in 1831, [Greene's Works, ii. c. iii], by Mr. Collier above, in the same year, and again in 1842, all agreeing to fix the date of Nash's Preface in 1587; yet there is, if I mistake not, internal evidence that it could not have been written before the date of the first known edition, which is in 1589.

Of the accuracy of the extraordinary facts which Nash relates in the Introduction to the Almond for a Parrot [pp. 5, 6], I had expected to find confirmation in some book of travels of the time, but in this have not succeeded.

Nash, in his Preface to Menaphon, addressed "To the Gentlemen Students of both Universities," evidently

referring to the Puritans, mentions, "the most poi-
sonous Pasquils any dirty-mouthed *Martin* or Momus
ever composed;" of their "spitting *ergo* in the mouth
of every one they meet;" and, unless I am mistaken,
the following refers to Penry: " But when the irre-
gular idiot, that was up to the ears in divinity before
ever he met with *probabile* in the university, shall leave
pro et contra before he can scarcely pronounce it, and
come to correct commonweals that never heard of the
name of magistrate before he came to Cambridge, it
is no marvel if every alehouse vaunt the table of the
world turned upside down, since the child beateth his
father, and the ass whippeth his master." [Reprint of
Menaphon, in Archaica, Pref. xiii., 4to, 1814.] The
allusions in the whole sentence can only be explained
by referring them to Martin Mar-Prelate's " Epistle," .
"Epitome," &c., which were printed in 1588.

Secondly, Nash says, " It may be my *Anatomy of
Absurdities* may acquaint you *ere long* with my skill in
surgery." Now, the Anatomy of Absurdities came out
in 1589, and the expression " ere long " would scarcely
apply had this been written in 1587.

Thirdly, he says, " If I please, I will think my ignorance indebted unto you that applaud it, if not, what

rests but that I be excluded from your courtesy, like Apocrypha from your Bibles?"

This passage appears to refer to a fact which Martin Mar-Prelate states in his Epistle to the Terrible Priests. [Reprint, p. 4.] "The last lent [he is writing in 1588] there came a commaundement from his grace into Paules Church Yard, that no Byble should be bounde without the Apocripha." Strype, in his Life of Archbishop Whitgift, admits the order, and takes some pains to justify the Archbishop in issuing it. [See Strype's Whitgift, i. 590.—Cooper's Admonition, 1589.]

The foregoing inferences, however, are confirmed by the fact that there is an allusion in this Preface to a work which did not appear until 1589. Nash, in giving the roll of English Worthies, introduces the following passage: "I will not say but we had a HADDON, whose pen would have challenged the laurel from Homer; together with CAR, that came as near him as Virgil to Theocritus. But THOMAS NEWTON, with his *Leiland,* and GABRIEL HARVEY, with two or three other, is almost all the store that is left us at this hour." [Pref. to Menaphon, xviii.]

As Newton's *Leiland* is a work of unfrequent occur-rence, I subjoin the title at length: "Principum, ac illustrium aliquot & eruditorum in Anglia virorum, Encomia, Trophæa, Genethliaca & Epithalamia. A Joanne Lelando Antiquario conscripta, nunc primùm in lucem edita. Quibus etiam adiuncta sunt, Illustrissimorum aliquot Herôum, hodiè · viventium, aliorúmq; hinc indè Anglorum, ENCOMIA et EVLOGIA: à Thoma Newtono Cestreshyrio, succisiuis horulis exarata. Londini, apud Thomam Orwinum, Typographum. 1589," in 4to. This work may also contain internal evidence, in addition to the statement in the title-page, that it was first published in 1589. There is a poem at p. 122, "Ad Chr. Oclandum de Elizabetheide sua," which may refer to the first part of Ocland's Elizabetheis, which came out in 1582, but most probably refers to the second part, printed by Thomas Orwin, in 1589.

I should not have taken the trouble to investigate the contents of this Preface of Nash, "the firstlings of my folly," as he calls it himself [p. xxi], with such minuteness, but that it establishes beyond question the fact that Nash commenced his literary career in 1589, and not, as is generally supposed, in 1587.

In the following Introduction, Nash says, "For comming from Venice the last summer, and taking

Bergamo in my waye homeward to England." Now as
he afterwards alludes to the appearance of Martin
Mar-prelate in England, and also to the defeat of the
Spanish Armada, "neither Philip by his power," this
most probably was the latter part of the summer of
1588, and if he arrived in England towards the end
of 1588, there would be both time and opportunity
for him to write the various works, which, published in
1589, are attributed to him. There is every probability, therefore, that Nash. did visit Italy, that he was
there in 1588, and that, returning to England with his
mind enlarged by travel, he commenced his short, but
remarkable career in literature, which, after he had
undergone the painful vicissitudes to which authors by
profession have so often been subjected,

"Since none takes pitie of a scholler's neéde,"

was terminated by his death in 1601.

I shall not here enumerate the various works which
Nash wrote, because an opportunity will offer, in the
Introduction to one of his publications, to notice the
whole of them.

Whatever was the origin of the long and bitter
quarrel between Nash and Gabriel Harvey, from this

passage in the Preface to Menaphon, 1589, "and Gabriel Harvey, with two or three other, is almost all the store that is left us at this hour," we may reasonably infer that it was not in existence then. The origin, progress, and effect of this quarrel, which included Lyly, Greene, Nash, and the three Harveys, and the right understanding of which is necessary to elucidate the progress of the Martin Mar-Prelate Controversy, I hope to give in the Introduction to "Plaine Percevall the Peace-Maker of England," a tract uniformly attributed to Nash; but which he, in one of his publications, not only utterly disclaims, but charges it upon one of his most hated antagonists.

The internal evidence in favour of Nash, as the author of the Almond for a Parrot, is very strong; and cannot but appear to any one who is conversant with his "Christ's Tears over Jerusalem," a work containing more remarkable passages than any publication of the time that has ever fallen in my way. The description of Penry, at p. 39, beginning, "Where, what his estimation was," &c.; but more especially the paragraph at p. 21, beginning, "Talke as long as you will of the Ioyes of heaven," &c., may be compared with several passages in "Christ's Tears" wherein Nash describes the horrors endured by its inhabitants during the siege of Jerusalem.

With respect to the title "An Almond for a Parrat," the meaning appears obvious; it is evidently a cant term, and like "A Sop to Cerberus," means a stopper for the mouth. Mr. Halliwell, in his Dictionary of Archaic and Provincial Words, calls it "a kind of proverbial expression," but does not attempt to trace its origin. It is used by Skelton [Works by Dyce, ii. 4], by Webster [Works, iii. 122], and by Middleton [Works, iii. 112].

The original, from which the present tract is reprinted, is a small 4to, printed in black letter, consisting altogether of 28 pages. The "Protestation" is referred to at p. 11, "Pap with a Hatchet," at p. 12, and "Hay any worke for a Cooper," at p. 15, by which it is certain that its publication was subsequent to them, and may perhaps be referred to the latter end of the year 1589.

J. P.

London,
Nov. 28th, 1845.

An Almond for a Parrat,

Or

Cutbert Curry-knaues

Almes.

Fit for the knaue Martin, and the
rest of those impudent Beggers, that
can not be content to stay their stomakes
with a Benefice, but they will needes
breake their fastes with
our Bishops.

Rimarum sum plenus.

Therefore beware (gentle Reader) you
catch not the hicket with laughing.

Imprinted at a Place, not farre from a
Place, by the Assignes of Signior Some-body, and
are to be sold at his shoppe in Trouble-knaue
Street, at the signe of the
Standish.

TO THAT MOST
Comicall and conceited Caualeire
Monsieur du Kempe, Iestmonger and
Vice-gerent generall to the Ghost of Dicke Tarlton.

His louing brother Cutbert Curry-knaue sendeth Greeting.

BROTHER KEMPE, as many alhailes to thy person as there be haicocks in Iuly at Pancredge : So it is, that what for old acquaintance, and some other respectes of my pleasure, I haue thought good to offer here certaine spare stuffe to your protection, which if your sublimitie accept in good part, or vouchsafe to shadow with the curtaine of your countenance, I am yours till fatall destiny two yeares after doomes day. Many write bookes to knights and men of great place, and haue thankes, with promise of a further reward for their paines : others come of with a long Epistle to some rufling Courtier, that sweares swoundes and bloud as soone as euer their backe is turnd, a man can not goe in the streetes for these impudent beggers. To auoide therefore as well the worthlesse attendance on the one,

as the vsuall scorne of the other, I haue made choise of
thy amorous selfe to be the pleasant patron of my
papers. If thou wilt not accept of it in regard of the
enuy of some Citizens, that can not away with argument, Ile preferre it to the soule of Dick Tarlton, who
I know will entertaine it with thankes, imitating herein
that merry man Rablays, who dedicated most of his
workes to the soule of the old Queene of Nauarre
many yeares after her death, for that she was a maintainer of mirth in her life. Marry God send vs more
of her making, and then some of vs should not liue so
discontēted as we do: for now a dayes, a man can not
haue a bout with a Balletter, or write *Midas habet aures
asininas* in great Romaine letters, but hee shall bee in
daunger of a further displeasure. Well, come on it
what will, Martin and I will allow of no such doinges,
wee can cracke halfe a score blades in a backe-lane
though a Constable come not to part vs. Neither
must you thinke his worship is to pure to be such a
swasher, for as Scipio was called Africanus, not for
relieuing and restoring, but for subuerting and destroying
of Africa: so he and his companions are called Puritans, not for aduancing or supporting of puritie, by
their vnspotted integritie, but of their vndermining and
supplanting it by their manifold heresies. And in deed
therein he doth but apply himselfe to that hope which
his holinesse the Pope and other confederate forriners,

haue conceiued of his towardnesse. For comming from
Venice the last Summer, and taking Bergamo in my
waye homeward to England, it was my happe soiourning
there some foure or fiue dayes, to light in felowship
with that famous Francattip' Harlicken, who perceiuing
me to bee an English man by my habit and speech,
asked me many particulars, of the order and maner of
our playes, which he termed by the name of representations : amongst other talke he enquired of me if I
knew any such Parabolano here in London, as Signior
Chiarlatano Kempino. Very well (quoth I,) and haue
beene oft in his company. He hearing me say so,
began to embrace me a new, and offered me all the
courtesie he colde for his sake, saying, although he
knew him not, yet for the report he, had hard of his
pleasance, hee colde not but bee in loue with his perfections being absent. As we were thus discoursing,
I hard such ringing of belles, such singing, such
shouting, as though Rhodes had beene recouered, or the
Turke quite driuen out of Christendome, therewithal
I might behold an hundreth bonefiers together, tables
spred in the open streetes, and banquets brought in of
all handes. Demaunding the reason of him that was
next me, he told the newes was there (thankes be to
God,) that there was a famous Schismatike one Martin
newe sprung vp in England, who by his bookes, libels,
and writings, had brought that to passe, which neither

the Pope by his Seminaries, Philip by his power, nor all the holy League by their vnderhand practises and policies could at any time effect: for wheras they liued at vnitie before, and might by no meanes be drawne vnto discord, hee hath inuented such quiddities to set them together by the eares, that now the temporaltie is readie to plucke out the throtes of the Cleargie, and subiects to withdraw their allegeance from their Souerayne: so that in short time, it is hoped they will bee vp in armes one against another, whiles we aduantaged by this domesticall enuy, may inuade them vnawares, when they shall not be able to resist. I, sory to heare of these triumphes, coulde not rest till I had related these tidinges to my countrimen. If thou hast them at the second hand, (fellow Kempe) impute it to the intercepting of my papers, that haue stayed for a good winde, euer since the beginning of winter. Now they are arriued, make much of them, and with the credit of thy clownery, protect thy Cutbert from Carpers.

Thine in the way of brotherhood,
Cutbert Curry-knaue,

An Almond for a Parrat.

WELCOME Mayster *Martin* from the dead, and much good ioy may you haue of your stage-like resurrection. It was told me by the vndanted purseuants of your sonnes, and credibly beleeued in regard of your sinnes, that your grout-headed holinesse had turnd vppe your heeles like a tired iade in a medow, and snorted out your scornefull soule, like a mesled hogge on a mucke-hill, which had it not beene false as the deuill woulde haue it, that long tongd doctresse Dame *Law*. muste haue beene faint (in spite of insperation) to haue giuen ouer speaking in the congregation, and employ her Parrats tong in stead of a winde-clapper to scarre the crowes from thy carrion. But profound *Cliffe* the ecclesiasticall cobler, interrupted from his morning exercise with this false alarum, broke vp his brotherly loue-meeting abruptly, when the spirite had but newly moued him, and betooke him to his solitary shoppe, abutting on the backe side of a bulke. Nor was his souterly sorrow so hippocritically ingratefull, but he determined in the aboundance of his teares, that made a ful tide in his blacking tubbe, to haue stitcht vp your traytourshippe a tumbe of vntand leather, wherein *tan-quam culeolo insutus*, hee mought haue sought his for-tune in the seas.   But I know not how this parracides exequies were prorogd, in so much as a brother in Christ of his at Northampton, fetcht a more thriftier president of funeralls piping hot from the primitiue church, which including but a few words and those passing well expounded, kept his wainscot from waste, and his linnen from wearing, sufficeth he tombled his wife naked into the earth at high noone, without sheete or shroude to couer her shame, breathing ouer her in an audible voice : Naked came I out of my mothers wombe, and naked shall I returne againe.   Tut, tut, a thousand of these pranks make no discord in my young maisters discipline, whose reformed fraternity, quoat Scripture so confidently, as if they had lately purchast a commission of *cum priuilegio ad interpretandum solum*, from Christ and his twelue Apostls.   And in deede who knowes whether Maister *Martin* being inspired, as earst one of his faction, who hearing the waites play vnder his window very early, insulted most impudently, that in the midst of his morning praiers, he was presented with the melody of Angels, so hee in like manner shoulde vaunt of some reuelation, wherein the full sinode of *Lucifers* ministers angells assembled, did par-lament all their enuy to the subuersion of our esta-blished ministry, and then comes forth some more subtile spirite of hipocrisie, which offers himself to be a false prophet in the mouths of our *Martinists*, to whom the whole sedition house of hel condiscending,

break vp their sessions, and send this seducer into the
world, where finding no such mutinous seate, as the
heart of our seconde *Pilate Marprelate*, he chose it in
steade of a worser, to bee vnto England as *Zidkiah* son
of *Chenaanah* was vnto *Ahab*. Beare with me good
Maister Pistle-monger, if in comparing thy knauery,
my full points seeme as tedious to thy puritane perusers,
as the Northren mans mile, and a waybitte to the
weary passenger, for I tell thee troth, till I see what
market commission thou hast to assiste any mans sentences, I will neuer subscribe to thy periode prescisme.
And hearest thou old *Martin*, did all thy libells iointly
shroude so much substance of diuinity in their out-
landish letters, as that one periode of vniformity in
T. C. directing to obedience, I would thinke God had
bin mercifull to thee in inspiring thy soule with some
one separate motion, from reprobation, but when whole
reames of paper are blotted with thy huperbolical blasphemies and religious matters of controversy more then
massacred by thy prophane scurrility, I cā but suppose
thy hart y^t house swept and garnished, into the which
the foule spirit returned with other 7. spirits worse
then himself. Malicious hipocryt, didst thou so much
malign the successeful thriuings of the Gospell, that
thou shouldst filch thy selfe, as a new disease into our
gouernement? wert thou the last instrument of Sathans
enuy, that as the abhortiue childe of a *Chaos* of heresies,
thou sholdst adorne thy false dealing with the induments
of discipline? Me thinks I see thee smile from vnder
thy double-fact hood, to thinke howe craftily thou hast

crept into mens cōsciences : but wouldst thou obserue,
how if thy alarums haue prosperd in our peaceable
ears, that make no more breach into our state, then
the iron hornes of those hony .tōgd prophets into the
arraies of the *Aramites*, Chro. 2. and tenth Chap. thou
wouldest with *Achitophell* return to thy house (at least
if thou hast any) and hang thy selfe in a melancholie,
for that thy counsaile was turned to follye.   When I
first saw thy books, I ascribed thy impudence to the
Calabrian wonders of 88. but when 89. beheld thee in
a new sute, I imagined the excesse of our sins, sent thee
forth to geue railing sentence against vs, as *Simei* against
Dauid in the 2. of Kings. Yet seely sophister wouldest
thou return the sobrietie of thy morning wittes to this
ouerworne Simile, that the rodde which was made to
correct *post destinatum finem*, is cast into the fire, thy
despaire would deeme euery darke hole, the entraunce
into hell, thy soule being the cittie, whereof the deuill
is made free by endenture.   And be it true which pit-
tying report hath auouched, *Herostratus* desire to be
famous, made thee to seale him a conueiance of it many
yeares since, so that now thy notorious pamphlets hauing
passed the Presse, it is to be feared he will come ouer
thee for couenantes ere many yeares to an end.   It
may bee thou hast redde *Foxes* Monuments more idlely,
where lighting on the example of Luther, that by his
praiers importunitie, made the deuil to deliuer vp the
obligation of his dānation, that sold the ioies of Heauē,
for the inheritance of earth, thou hopest in like manner
in the age of thine iniquities to bee restored to eternity,

by the vncessant inuocation of the Church which thou
termest Antichristian. Deceiue not thy selfe thou man
of security, for the enemy of *Adam* is no poeticall
Argus, that his eies should be put out by thy arguments.
I tell thee troth, he wil be-pistle thee so peuishly, with
allegations of vnuenidall sinnes, as though hee were
borne within two houses of Battle bridge. It is not thy
despairing protestations, can make thy peace with God,
whose church thou hast sought to deuide, as did *Herods*
souldiers his garmentes : wele geue thee leaue to tell vs
a smooth tale of the intercepting of thy treasons, and
curry fauour like a crafty foxe, with the ciuill magistrate in politique termes of feare and reuerence, but thy
heart is no more disguised in this hypocriticall apparel,
then a trenchour *Aristippus* in the coate of a Parasite.
Why discourse I so soberly, with the mortal enemy of
modesty, when as the filth of the stewes, distild into
ribauldry termes, cannot confectionate a more intempe-
rate stile then his Pamphlets. Thou calst our Bishops
wicked by comparison, whereas (wert thou strooken as
thou protests with the vntoward euents of thy villanies)
thou shouldst find the defilings of the 7. deadly sins, to
haue broght thee by a pleasant pollution, within the
possitiue degree of damnation. What talk I to him, of
hel or damnation, whom *Lucifer* hath furnisht to infection, with the painted poison of snout-holy deuotion,
and all the powers of darknesse, haue adorned as an
intelligencer to their kingdome, of the infirmities in our
flourishing Church of England. To this purpose haue
they inspired him with a most scurrile spirite of lying,

that when his eagle-sighted enuy can truely atract no
argument of infamy, his *poetica licentia*, may haue a
fresh supply of possibilities, that encrease by cōtinuance
to a compleat libell of leasings.   All you that be schollers, read but his last challenge, wherein he laies about
him so lamely, as though of his limping brother *Pag.*
hee had lately learned to play at cudgels.   But how
euer his crazed cause goes on crutches, that was earst
so brauely encountered by *Pasquin* and *Marphoreus,*
and not many moneths since most wittily scofte at by
the extemporall endeuour of the pleasant author of
Pap with a hatchet: yet is not the good olde creeple
vtterly discouraged, or driuen cleane from his dounghill,
but he meanes to make the persecuted Coblers once
more merrie.   Yet by your leaue his other dayes daunger is not so fully disgested, that he shuld forget the
sanctified martyrs his brethren, those runagate Printers,
to whose reuenge he bequeatheth a large Pistle of
rayling Epithites, and mistearmeth our Bishoppes
authoritie, with a whole *Textor* of tyrannie.   A few of
whose milder tearms are of this making, wicked Priests,
presumptuous Priests, proude Prelates, arrogant Bishops, horseleeches, butchers, persecutors of the truth,
Lamhethical whelps, Spanish Inquisitours.   Thinke
you this myrie mouthed mate, a partaker of heauenly
inspiration, that thus aboundes in his vncharitable railings : yet are these nothing in comparison of his auncient burlibond adiunctes, that so pester his former
edition with their vnweldie phrase, as no true syllogisme can haue elbowe roome where they are.   In

which Alphabet these that followe may bee placed: bounsing Priests, terrible Priests, venerable Maisters, proud and pontificall Patripolitians. Gentle reader, I giue you but a tast of them by the waie, that you may knowe them the next time you meete them in your dish, and learne to discerne a poysonous scorpion from wholesome fish. *Martin* you must thinke, was moude, when his gun-pouder papers were fired aboute his eares, and the spendthriftes his Printers, haled to the prison their patrimonies. Wherefore I cannot blame him though he sends abroade his Letters of supplication, in behalfe of his seruants that did but his bidding. The Church, the Church is persecuted amongst you my maisters, and *Martin* gettes nere a superintendentship by the shift, but let not *Meg Law.* crie once more to the Churchwardens for her foode, least shee bring with her a campe royall of scoldes, to scratch out your eyes. Oh she will declaime brauely ouer a Cuckstoole, and plaie the gyant in a narrowe lane with her distaffe. Maister *Cooper* shall haue his stipend still at Paules chaine, or else shee will sweat for it. I lyke such a wench that will stande to her tackling, why Bishoppes are but men, and she will carrie a *Martin* in her plackarde in despite of the proudest of them all. Learne of her you London Matrones, to make hodie-peeles of your husbandes, and leade them like good soules up and downe the streetes by the hornes, let it be seene by your courages in scolding, that women haue soules, which a balde eloquent brother of yours, denide not long since in his Sermon at Lichfielde. I, I, my maisters, you

may mocke, on as you see cause, but I warrant you the
good olde true-pennie *Marprelate* is not so merrie, hee
sits ruminating under an oake, or in the bottome of a
haystacke, whose bloud shall be first spilte in the
reformation of the Church.   And not without cause,
for hee that hath so lately felte the paine of worming
and launcing, cannot but stande in awe of *Buls* slicing
tooles one two moneths after.   O it is a hairebrande
whooresonne, and well seene in Phlebotomie, if a but
once take knife in hande, cha will as soone let out the
seditious humours forth a Martinistes bodie, as the best
he in England, that hath bin twentie yeeres practioners
in Surgerie, Good munckie face Machiuell, shew but
thy head once, and trie him at my request, and if he
doe it not more handsomely, then those whom thou
callest Butchers and Horseleeches, then neuer trust an
olde ladde whilest thou liuest.   How euer it · happens,
thou bearest thy resolution in thy mouth at highe
midnight, and hast Scripture enough to carrie thee to
heauen, though thou wert hangde to morrowe.   We
feare not men that can kill the bodie, quoth *Martin*,
because we feare God, who can cast both bodie and
soule into vnquenchable fire.   Doest thou feare God in
deede, I praie thee good hedge-creeper how shall we
knowe that? What, by the smoothing of thy face, the
simpering of thy mouth, or staring of thy eies? Why if
that be to feare God, Ile haue a spare fellowe shall
make mee a whole quest of faces for three farthinges,
But thou wilt peraduenture saie, by thy obedience vnto
him.   Then will I catechise thee more kindly with a

fewe more Christian questions: the first whereof shall
be this, wherein thou placest obedience, which if thou
aunswerest, by doing that which God hath commaunded
in his worde: then would I knowe of thee, whether
that of Paul be Canonicall or Apocripha, He that
resisteth the magistrate, resisteth the ordinaunce of God.
And here I am sure to be had by the eares with a
Geneua note of the distinction of magistrates, but all
that shall not serue your turnes, for Ile driue you from
your *Dic Ecclesiæ* ere I have done, ware the vnmasking
of *Martin*, when it comes tis lyke to bee a shrewde
Pistle, I can tell you. Prepare your argumentes as
you will, for *Mar-Martin Iunior*, meanes to make such
hauocke of you in that his next peece of seruice, as all
your borrowed weapons of simple T. C. shall not bee
able to withstande. For your olde soaking Demonstrationer, that hath scrapte vp such a deale of Scripture
to so lyttle purpose, Ile leaue his confusion to the
vacaunt leasure of our grauer Diuines, who I knowe,
did they but once sette penne to paper, woulde grinde
his discipline to powder. Thou art the man, olde
Martin of Englande, that I am to deale withall, that
striues to outstrip all our writers in witte, and iustle
our gouernement forth of doores with a iest. What, wee
must not let you passe with such fauourable tearmes,
as our graue Fathers haue done, your Bookes must bee
lookt ouer, and you beaten lyke a dogge for your lying.
I thinke, I thinke I shall haue occasion to close with you
sweetlie in your Hay anie worke for a Cooper, and
cutte off the traynes of your tedious syllogismes, that

c 2

nowe haue no lesse then seauen or eight Termini wait-
ing on them.   Fortifie your ruinous buildinges betimes,
and saie hee was your friende that badde you: for I
can tell you thus much, a whole hoast of *Pasquils* are
comming vppon you, who will so beleaguer your paper
walles, as that not one idle worde shall escape the edge
of their wit.   I giue thee but a brauado now, to let thee
knowe I am thine enemie, but the next time you see *Mar-
Martine* in armes, bidde your sonnes and your familie
prouide them to God-warde, for I am eagerly bent to
revenge, and not one of them shall escape, no not T. C.
himselfe as full as he is of his myracles.   But to pur-
sue maister Protestationer in his common place of persecution.   I remember we talkt euen now of a dudgen
destinction from which my Bedlam brother *Wig.* and
poltfoote *Pag.* with the rest of those patches, striue to
deriue theyr discipline disobedience.   Our Ecclesiasticall gouernment and gouernours say they, are wicked
and vnlawfull.   Why? because Sir *Peter* nor Sir *Paul*
were neuer Archbishoppes of Canterbury, London, or
Yorke.   They were Fisher-men, and were not able.
When *Cæsars* Officers demaunded their tribute to make
fiue groates amongst them, then what reason is it our
Bishoppes should inioy their five hundreds, nay, that
which is more, their thousand and two thousands?
They were none of these Cartercaps, Graduates nor
Doctors, therfore why should we tie our Ministrie
to the prophane studies of the Vniuersitie.   What is
Logicke but the highe waie to wrangling, contayning
in it a world of bibble babble.   Neede we anie of your

Greeke, Latine, Hebrue, or anie such gibbrige, when wee haue the word of God in English? Go to, go to, you are a great company of vaine men, that stand vpon your degrees and tongues, with tittle tattle, I cannot tell what, when as (if you looke into the matter as you ought) the Apostles knew neare a Letter of the booke. I wis it were not two pins hurt, if your Colledges wer fired ouer your heades, and you turnde a begging forth your fellowshippes, like Fryers and Monkes vp and downe the Countrie. I marie sir, this is somewhat like, now *Martin* speakes like himselfe, I dare saie for him good man, he could be contented there were nere a maister of Art, Bachelour of Diuinitie, Doctor or Bishop in England, on that condition he prest Fishermen, scullers, Coopers, Stitchers, Weauers and Coblers into theyr places. You talke of a Harmonie of the Churches, but heere would be a consort of knauerie worth the publishing to all posteritie. Would you not laugh to see *Cli.* the Cobler, and *New.* the souter, ierking out theyr elbowes in euerie Pulpit. Why, I am sure Ladie *Law.* would fast mans flesh a whole moneth together, but shee woulde giue either of them a gowne cloth on that condition. My self doe knowe a zealous Preacher in Ipswich, that beeing but a while a goe a stage player, will now take vpon him to brandish a Text agaynst *Bishoppes, as well as the best Martinist in all Suffolke. Why, I praie you goe no farther then Batter. haue wee not there a reuerent Pastour of *Martines* owne making, that vnderstands not a bit of Latine, nor neuer dyd so much as looke towards the Vniuersitie in

his life, yet you see for a neede he can helpe discipline
out of the durt, and come ouer our Cleargie verie handsomely with an heere is to bee noted.   Oh he is olde
dogge at expounding, and deade sure at a Catechisme,
always prouided, that it bee but halfe a sheete long,
and he be two yeeres about it.   And well too my
maisters, for such a one that vauntes himselfe to bee as
hee is, as good a Gentleman euerie inch of him, as anie
is in all Stafford sheere.   Bee what he will, one thing
I wote, hee is seldome without a good Cheese in his
studie, besides apples and nuttes, although his wife can
neuer come at them.   I hearde not long since of a
stoute conference hee had with a yong scholer, who
taking my Deske-man somewhat tardie in his disputations, told him hee was inspired with too much Logique.
Where vnto hee replyed with this solempne protestatiō,
I thank God, al the world cannot accuse me of that
arte.   I hope anon maister *Martin*, I shall bee meetelie
euen with you for your knauerie, if I goe but two mile
further in your Ministrie.   It is not the Primitiue
Church shall beare out the Vicar of little *Down.* in
Norfolke, in groaping his owne hennes, like a Cot-
queane, I am to come ouer him when I have more
leasure, for his tenne shillings Sermons at Thetforde:
wherein if he raue as hee was wont to doe, Ile make
him wishe that hee had been still Vsher of Westminister.
Well, to the purpose.   You saie Bishoppes are no
Magistrates, because they are no lawfull Magistrates.
Is it euen so brother *Timothie*, will it neuer be better,
must I euer leade you vp and downe antiquitie by the

nose lyke an Asse. May neither Scriptures nor Fathers
goe for paiment with you, but still you will bee reducing
vs to the president of the persecuted Church, and so
confounde the discipline of warre and peace? If you
will needes make vs the apes of all their extremities,
why doe not you vrge the vse of that communitie
wherein *Ananias* and *Saphira* were vnfaythfull. Perswade Noble men and Gentlemen to sell theyr landes,
and laie the money at your feete, take awaie the title
of mine and thine from amongst vs, and let the worlde
knowe you heereafter by the name of Anabaptistes.
Admit that the authoritie of Bishoppes were as vnlawfull as you woulde make it, yet since it is imposed vnto
them by the Princes owne mouth, and ratified by the
approbation of so many Kings and Emperours, as well
in their particular Parliamentes as generall counsayles,
you are bounde in conscience to reuerence it, and in all
humilitie to regarde it, insomuch as Christ denide not
tribute to *Cæsar* an vsurper, nor appealde from *Pilate*
a Pagan, who occupied that place by the intrusion of
tyrannie. Were the Israelites in captiuitie, anie whit
exempted from the obedience of subiectes, in that they
liued vnder the scepter of *Nabuchodonesor* an Idolater,
who had blasphemed their God, defaced their Temple,
and defiled their holie vesselles. Nay, are they not
expresslie commaunded by the Lordes owne mouth, to
honour him as their King: Howe can they then escape
the dampnation of contempte, that beeing priuate subiectes to such a vertuous Soueraigne, as is zealous of
Gods glorie will controll her, disposing of honours, and

oppose vnto publique derision, those the especiall pillers and ornamentes of her state, whome shee hath graced from their infancie, with so many sundrie ascentes of dignities. But were this all, then shoulde not treason bee such a braunche of your religion as it is. Haue not you and your followers vndermined her Graces Throane, as much as traytours might: call to minde the badde practise of your brother the Booke-binder and his accomplishes at Burie, who beeing as hotte spirited as your worshippes, in the schismaticall subiect of reformation, and seeing it woulde not come of halfe kindlie to theyr contentment, made no more a doe, but added this newe Posie to her Maiesties armes. Those that bee neither hotte nor colde, Ile spue them out of my mouth, sayth the Lorde. Denie this, and Ile bring a whole Assizes, as *Obsignatos testes* of your trecherie. To come neerer to thee Brother *Martin*. Hast not thou in thy firste booke agaynst Doctour *Bridges*, as also in Hay anie worke for Cooper, excluded her Highnesse from all Ecclesiasticall gouernement, saying she hath neyther skill nor commission, as shee is a Magistrate, to substitute anie member or minister in the Church. And in an other place, that there is neither vse nor place in the Church for members, ministers or officers of the magistrates making. If this wyll not come in compasse of treason, then farewell the title of Supremacie, and welcome agayne vnto Poperie. By this time I thinke, good-man Puritan, that thou art perswaded, that I knowe as well as thy owne conscience thee, namely *Martin Makebate* of Englande, to bee a moste scuruie and beggerlie benefactor to obedience, and *per consequens*, to feare neyther men, nor that God who can cast both bodie and soule into vnquenchable fire. In which respect I neyther account you of the Churche, nor esteeme of your bloude, otherwise then the bloud of Infidelles. Talke as long as you will of the ioyes of heauen, or paines of hell, and turne from your selues the terrour of that iudgement howe you will, which shall bereaue blushing iniquitie of the figge leaues of hypocrisie, yet will the eie of immortalitie discerne of your painted pollutions, as the euer-liuing foode of perdition. The humours of my eies are the habitations of fountaines, and the circumference of my heart the enclosure of fearefull contrition, when I thinke howe many soules at that moment, shall carrie the name of *Martine* on their foreheads to the vale of confusion, in whose innocent bloude thou swimming to hell, shalt haue the tormentes of tenne thousande thousande sinners at once, inflicted vppon thee. There will enuie, mallice and dissimulation bee euer calling for vengeance agaynst thee, and incite whole legions of deuilles to thy deathlesse lamentation. Mercie will saie vnto thee, I knowe thee not, and Repentaunce, what have I to doe with thee. All hopes shall shake the head at thee, and saie, there goes the poyson of puritie, the perfection of impietie, the serpentine seducer of simplicitie. Zeale her selfe will crie out vppon thee, and curse the time that euer shee was maskte by thy mallice, who lyke a blinde leader of the blinde, sufferedst her to stumble at euerie steppe in Religion, and madest her seeke in the dimnesse of her sight, to murther her mother the Churche, from whose pappes thou lyke an enuious dogge but yesterdaie pluckest her. Howe euer proude scorner, thy whoorishe impudencie, may happen heereafter to insiste in the derision of these fearfull denuntiations, and sporte thy iesters penne at the speach of my soule, yet take heede least despayre bee predominant in the daie of thy death, and thou in steade of calling for mercie to thy Iesus, repeate more oftner to thy selfe, *Sic morior damnatus vt Iudas!* And thus much *Martin*, in the way of compassion, haue I spoke for thy edification, moued therto by a brotherly commiseration, which if thou bee not too desperate in thy deuilish attempts, may reform thy heart to remorse, and thy pamphletes to some more profitable theame of repentance. But now haue at thee for the goodnesse of the cause, of which thou saist: We must not reason from the successe.

Trust me therein thou hast spoke wiser then thou art aware of, for if a man should imagine of fruite by the rottennesse, of garmentes by the moath frets, of wine by the sowrnesse, I warrant him for euer being good costerd-monger, broker, or vintner whiles he liues. Therefore we must not measure of *Martin* as he is allied to *Elderton*, or tongd like *Will Tong*, as he was attired like an Ape on yᵉ stage, or sits writing of Pāphlets, in some spare out-house, but as is *Mar-Prelat* of England as he surpasseth King and collier, in crying, So ho ho, brother *Bridges*. Wo ho ho, *Iohn* a London. Ha ha he, Doctor *Copecotes*. Doe this and I warrant you, for sauoring of the fleshe, though you take the

oportunity of the spirite, with euery sister in Christ.
Beholde the state of the low Countryes, since your
Plaintife Pistler, will needs make the comparison, suppose *Martin* to be the map of *Belgia dilacerata*, whose
chiefe prouinces as they are wholye possessed with
Spaniards, so thinke his hart and soule enhabited with
spiet, they Romists in the matter of Religion, and he a
Papist in supremacies contradiction, her inward partes
possessed with Anabaptists, and Lutherans, and his
more priuate opinions polluted with the dregs of them
both, her farthest borders of Holland and Zeland,
peopled God wot with a small number of vnperfite
Protestants, and the furthest and fewest of his thoughts,
taken vppe with some odde true points of Religion,
How now Father *Martin*, haue not I hit your meaning
patte in this comparison. Say, wil you haue any more
such interpretations, if you say *Amen* to it. Ile also
reconcile your allegoricall induction of France, to the
present constitutiō of your frowardnes: but that shal
not neede, since the misery of the one is the mirrour of
the other, and the Reader must suppose that *Martin*
would neare haue compared himselfe to Flaunders nor
France, but as they reflect by allusion the distraction
of his factions faith. Howe euer you take him at the
worst, yet is his welchnes perswaded, that the Lord
hath some speciell purpose, by preuentinge of his presse,
to try who they be that are hipocrites, and what they
be yᵗ are innocent: And not vnlike too, for hauing interrupted the trafique of honestye, so long as thou hast
with thy coūterfet knauery, tis more the hie time thy

vnder-hād treachery, were broght to the touchstone of
authority.   You think we know not how pretily your
Printers were shrouded vnder the name of salt-peter-
men, so that who but *Hodgkins, Tomlins* and *Sims,* at
the vndermining of a house, and vndoing of poore men,
by diggyng vp their floars, and breaking down their
wals.   No, no, we neuer heard how orderly they
pretended the printing of Accidences, when my L. of
Darbies men came to see what they were a doing, what
though they damned themselues about the deniall of
the deede, is periury such a matter amongst puritans.
Tush they account it no sin as long as it is in the way
of protestation, being in the mind of a good old fellow
in Cambridge, who sitting in S. *Iohns* as Senior at
the fellowes election, was reprehended by some of his
betters, for that hee gaue his voice with a dunce like
himself, contrary to oath, statute and conscience: why
quoth hee, I neither respect oath, statute, nor conscience,
but only the glory of God.   Men are but men and may
erre, yea goodman *Spe.* himselfe in Paules church-yard,
although he saith he hath no sinne, what maruaile is it
then, though some corruption cleaue vnto our aged
Gentleman by his owne confession.   Learne of me to
iudge charitably, and thinke that nature tooke a
scouring purgation, when she voided all her imperfections
in the birth of one *Martin:* which if it be so, hee is
not to be blamed, since as *Arist.* sayes, *vitia naturæ
nō sunt reprehendenda.*   Gibe on, gibe on, and see if
your father *Mar-martin* will beare you out in it or no,
you thinke the good sweet-faced prelate, *Masse Martin,*

hath neuer broke sword in ruffians hal, yes that he hath
more then one or two, if the truth were known, and
fought for his wench as brauely as the best of them all,
therefore take heede how you come in his way, least
hee belabour you with his crabtree stile for your lustines, and teache you howe to looke into a *Martins*
neaste againe while you live. Alas you are but young,
and neuer knewe what his Bumfeging ment, for if you
did, you woulde thinke fiue hundreth fistes about your
eares, were more then Phisicke in a frosty morning.
Write or fight which you will, our champion is for you
at all weapones, whether you choose the worde or the
sworde, neither comes amisse to him, he neuer took his
domesticall dissention in hand to leaue it soone. All
England must bee vp together by the eares, before his
penne rest in peace, nor shall his rebellious mutinies,
which he shrouds vnder the age of *Martinisme,* haue
any *intermedium,* till religions prosperity and our
Christian libertye, mis-termed of him by the last yeare
of Lambethisme, doe perishe from amongst vs, and
depart to our enemies: then shall you see, what seditious
buildinges will arise on the vnfortunate foundations of
his folly, and what contentious increase will come from
the schoole of contempt.

> *If they will needes ouerthrowe mee*
> *let them goe in hand with the*
> *exploite &c.*

HOLLA, holla brother *Martin,* you are to hasty, what,
Winter is no time to make warres in, you were best

D

stay til summer, and then both our brains wilbe in a
better temperature, but I think ere that time your
witte wilbe welny worn thredbare, and your banquerout
inuention, cleane out at the elbowes, then are we well
holpen vp with a witnesse, if the aged champion of
Warwicke, doe not lay to his shoulders, and support
discipline ready to lie in the dust, with some or other
demonstration.   I can tell you *Phil. Stu.* is a tall man
also for that purpose.   What his Anatomy of Abuses
for all that, will serue very fitly for an Antipast, before
one of *Egertons* Sermons, I would see the best of your
Trauerses write such a treatise as he hath done, against
short heeld pantoffles.   But one thing it is great pitty
of him, that being such a good fellow as hee is, hee
shoulde speake against dice, so as he doth : neuerthelesse ther is some hope of him, for as I heard not lōg
since, a brother of his, meting him by chance (as
theeues meete at the gallowes) after many christian
questions of the well fare of his persecuted brethren,
and sistern, askt him when they should haue a game at
tables together, by the grace of God the next Sabaoth,
quoth *Phil.* and then if it shal so seeme good to his
prouidence, haue at you for ames ase and the dise.
I forgette to tel you what a stirre he keepes against
dumbe ministers, and neuer writes nor talkes of them,
but hee calleth them minstrels, when his mastershippe
in his minority, plaide the Reader in Chesshire, for fiue
marke a yeare and a canuas dublet, couenanted besides,
that in consideration of that stipend, he make cleane the
patrones bootes euerye time hee came to towne.   What

need more words to proue him a protestāt, did not he
behaue himselfe like a true Christian, when hee went a
wooing for his friend *Clarke*, I warrant you hee saide
not God saue you, or God speed you, with good euen
or good morrow, as our prophane woers are wont, but
stept close to her, with peace bee with you, very de-
murely, and then told her a long tale, that in so much
as widowhoode, was an vncleane lyfe, and subiect to
many temptations, shee might doe well to reconcile her
selfe to the Church of God, in the holy ordinance of
matrimony. Manye wordes past to this purpose, but I
wotte well the conclusion was this, that since she had
hitherto conuerst with none but vnregenerate persons,
and was vtterly carelesse of the communion of Saints,
she would let him that was a man of God, put a new
spirite into her, by carnall population, and so engraft
her into the fellowshippe of the faithfull, to which that
shee might more willingly agree, hee offered her a
spicke and spanne new Geneua Bible, that his attendant
Italian had brought with him to make vp the bargaine.
But for all the Scripture he could alledge, it should not
bee, *Phil. Stu.* was no meate for her tooth, God wote
he could not get a penyworth of leachery on such a
pawne as his Bible was, the man behinde the painted
· · cloth mard all, and so O griefe, a good Sabaoths day
work was lost. Stand to it *Mar-martin Iunior* and
thou art good inough for ten thousand of them, tickle me
my *Phil.* a litle more in the flanke, and make him
winche like a resty iade, whereto a dreaming deuine of
Cambridge, in a certain priuate Sermon of his, com-

pared the wicked. Saist thou me so good heart, then
haue at you Maister Compositor, with the constructiō
of *Sunt oculos clari qui cernis sydera tanquam.* If you
be remembred you were once put to your trumpes
about it in *Wolfes* Printing-house, when as you would
ncedes haue *clari* the infinitiue moode of a verbe
passiue, which determined you went forwards after this
order. *Sunt* there are, *oculos* eies, *qui* the which, *cernis*
thou doest see, *clari* to be cleare, *tanquam sydera* as the
Stars. Excellent well done of an old Maister of Arte,
yet why may not hee by authority challenge to himselfe
for this one peece of worke the degrees hee neuer tooke.
Learning is a iewel my maisters, make much of it, and
Phil. Stu. a Gentleman euery haire of his head, whom
although you doe not regard according as he deserues,
yet I warrant you *Martin* makes more accoúnt of him
then so, who hath substituted him long since (if the
truth were well boulted out) amongst the number of
those priuy *Martinists,* which he threatens to place in
euery parish. I am more then halfe weary of tracing too
and fro in this cursed common wealth, where sinfull
simplicitye pufte vppe with the pride of singularity,
seekes to peruerte the name and methode of magistracy.
But as the most of their arguments, are drawn from our
graue fathers infirmities, so al their outrageous endeuors
haue their ofspring from affected vainglory.   Agreeing
Hug. lib. with the saying of *Hug.* "Innobedientiæ mor-
de duob.
abusio.   bus ex superbiæ tumore procedit, sicut sanies
ex vlcere." The disease of disobedience proceeds from
the swelling of pride, as madnesse from some vntollera-

ble vlcer. The cause whereof *Gregory* thus expresseth. "Dum plus exquirunt" saith he, "contemplando quam capiunt, vsque ad peruersa dogmata erumpunt, Greg. lib. 8. et dum veritatis discipuli esse negligunt, humiliter magistri erroris fiunt." Whiles by study they search out more then they vnderstand, they breake forth into peruerse opinions, and whiles they neglect to be the schollers of truth, they most basely become the schoolemaisters of error. For such is the boldnesse of our boyish deuines, that they will leape into the pulpet, before they haue learned *Stans puer ad mensam,* and talke very desperately of dicipline, before they can construe, *Qui mihi discipulus.* "Qui venit institui" saith *Cassiodorus,* "antequam instituatur, alios instituere cupit," &c. The nouice that comes to be informed, desireth to enforme others, before he bee enformed himselfe, and to teach before hee bee taught, to prescribe lawes before he hath redde *Litleton,* and play the subtile Philosopher, before he knowes the order of his sillables: he wil needes haue subiects, before he can subiugate his affections, and couets the office of a commander, before he hath learned to stoupe to the admonitions of his elders, and beginneth to instruct and perswade, before he bee instructed and perswaded in any kind of art, which their folly once fuelled with ye frowardnesse of blind zeal, makes thē cōfound cōtempt with gods true worship, and open their mouths against his ordinance, as did the Prophets against *Ieroboams* hil altars. T. C. in Cambridge first inuented this violent innouation, when as his mounting ambition, went through euery kinde of *Ambitus,* to

compasse the office of the Vicechauncelour-ship. But
after he saw himselfe disfauourd in his first insolence,
and that the suffrages of the vniuersity, would not
discend to his dissentious indignityes, his seditious
discontent deuised the meanes to discredite that gouernement, which he through his il behauiour might not
aspire to.   Thē began his inueterat malice, to vnder-
mine the foundations of our societies, and reduce our
Colledges to the schooles of the Prophets, to discard all
degrees of art as antichristian, to condemne all decency
in the ministery as diabolicall, and exclude all ecclesiasticall superiority forth the Church as *Apocripha*.   No
sooner had these new fangled positions entred the tables
of young students, but Singularity the eldest childe of
heresy, consulted with male-conted melācholy, how to
bring this misbegottē scisme to a monarchy.   To which
purpose hipocriticall zeale, was addrest as a pursuiuant
into all places of Suff. Norff. Essex and Midlesex,
with expresse commandement from the sinod of Saints,
to proclaime T. C. supreme head of the Church.   This
past on thus, whiles the sworde of iustice, slept in his
scaberd, whose vnprouident eie neglecting the beginning
of such burnings, hath added a more confirmed fury to
the flame, which hath now taken hold on yᵉ buildings
of our bishopricks.   How it hath raged in those quar-
ters before mentioned to yᵉ vtter impouerishing of the
allegeance of the communalty, and lamentable vndoing
of the estimation of diuers other knights and gentlemen,
the whole course of the high commission may testify.
Nether was this plague of apostacy vndeserued of their

inconstancy, who forsook yᵉ true service of God, to
worship the idoll of Warwicke.   Put case his reading be
gret and his malice more, that he hath plodded through
ten cart loade of paper, and bin the death of ten thousand
pound of candels, yet as *Gregory* saith, " perit omne
quod agitur, si non humilitate custodiatur." Greg. lib. mor.
Whatsoeuer is done doth vanish to infamy, if it be not
vpholden by humility: What childe doth not see into
the pride of his heart, that first entertained the impudency of controlling antiquity, and preferd the poison of
his owne peruerse opinions, before the experience of so
many Churches, counsails and fathers. "Quæ Ber. 2. ser.
maior superioria," saith *Bernarde*, "quam vt resur.
vnus homo toti congregationi iudicium suum preferat tan-
quā ipse solus habeat spiritū Dei." What greater pride
then that one man should aduance his iudgement, aboue
the sentence of a whole congregation, as if he alone had
the spirit of God.   Pride ouerthrew the towr of *Babell*,
prostrated *Golias*, hūg vp *Haman*, kild *Nichanor*,
consumed *Herod*, destroied *Antiochus*, drowned *Pharao*,
subuerted *Senacherib*, and I hope will also confound
arrogant T. C. and all his accomplishes in the Lords
good time.   And now that I haue vnburdened my
shoulders of the weight of his learning, Ile ribroste my
brother *Martin* a litle, for obiecting to my Lord Archbishop, the not answering of his bookes.   Therefore
first would I know of sweete M. sauce malapert whether
he would haue the care of the common-wealth, and
forseing consultation of domestical and forreine affaires,
resigned to the retorting of T. C. his vnreuerent railings.

Next what such equall proportion his mastership finds
in their places, that the grauity and mildnes of the one,
should stoupe his attention so low, as the iangling leuity
of the other.   Were there no other thing to refrayn his
grace, from combating with a common barretour then
this, that in *discordia nemo benedicit Dominum*, it were
sufficient to pleade his absence from this inferiour fight.
But when he considers that saiyng of *Augustine*, "Nullus
est modus inimicitiis, nisi ob tempus obtēperemus iratis,"
ther is no meane of mallice, vnles for a time we giue
place to the furious, and that which another sais, "Sicut
nihil est deformius quam respondere furiosis ita, nihil
vtilius quam tacere prouocatis."   As there is nothing
more vnseemely then to aunswere the froward, so there
is nothing more profitable then scilence to such as are
prouokt.   Let him vse the libertye of his speache as
hee please, and detracte from his learninge in what
tearmes hee see cause, yet will all Christendome admire
his perfection, when T. C. his singularitie shall go a
begging vp and downe the low Countries.   I will not
gainsaie but your reuerend Pastor may haue as knauish
a vaine in writing as your selfe, and fasten a slander on
the Saintes of heauen, as soone as anie of your sect, for
Ierome su-   "nil tam facile est," as Ierom sayth, "quam
per Oseam.   ociosum et dormientem de aliorum labore et
vigiliis disputare."   There is nothing so easie for a man
that is sluggish and idle, as to call in question others
mens watchings and labours.   "Mens praua," sayth *Gre-*
Greg. 15.   *gorie*, "semper in laboribus est, quia aut moli-
tur mala quæ inferat, vel metuit nè sibi ab aliis infeānt,

et quicquid contra proximos cogitat, hoc contra se, a proximus cogitari formidat." A wicked mind liues in continuall toile, because it eyther meditates the iniuries which he is about to inferre, or feares some reproch to be inferred by others, and whatsoeuer bee pretendes agaynst his neighbor, the same he mistrusts to be pretended against himselfe. If T. C. hath made thee his atturney, to vrge the not answering of his bookes, then I praie thee bee my Mercurie this once, and tell him thus much from *Mar-Martine*, that he hath vndone more Printers with his py-bald pamphlets, then his dish-clout dicipline will sette vp agayne this seauen yeeres. Much inkehorne stuffe hath hee vttered in a iarring stile, and intruded a greate deale of trashe to our cares by a daintie figure of *idem peridem*, but for anie new peece of arte he hath shewed in those idle editions, other then that his famous aduersary hath before time confuted, he may wel enough bequeth it to Dunce or Dorbel, whēce his blundering capacity is lineally descended. What maister T. C. you think that no man dare touch you, because you haue plaid the scuruie scolde anie time these twentie yeeres, but Ile so hamper your holynes for all the offences of your youth, as all geering puritans shall haue small cause to insult and reioyce at my silence. Then see whether I dare stand to the defence of your defame or no. Take heede good-man Howlyglasse, that I make not such a hole in your coate the nexte Tearme, as *Martine* and his sonnes shall not sowe vp in hast, I tel you I am a shreud fellow at the vncasing of a fox, and haue cats

eyes to looke into euerie corner of a Puritans house.   I
warrant you my brother *Pag.* will saie so, by that time
I haue talkte with him a little, who although hee bee
none of the straightest men that euer God made, yet
hath he as good skill in milche bullocks, as anie huswife
within fortie miles of his head.   Let him alone, and if
he doe not know by a cowes water, how many pintes of
milke she will give in a yeere, then wyll he neuer help
his wife to make cheese agayn whiles hee liues: and
without offence to his Pastorshippe bee it spoken, hee
will saie pretyly well to a henne, if shee bee not too
olde, always prouided, shee haue a neaste of cleane
strawe in his studie, and hee groape her with his owne
bandes euening and morning.   Then see if hee doe not
make three pounds a yeere of her ouer and aboue all
costes and charges.   I marie sir, is not this a husbande
in deede, that besides the multiplying of the Church of
God, in his householde ministerie, will keepe his wife
and familie by crosse bargaines a whole twelue moneth.
What woulde he doe my maisters, if he had two good
legges, that wil thus bestirre him in his vocation with
one and a stump.   The world may saie he is lame,
and so forth, but hee that had seene him runne from
Houns. the other daie, for getting his maide with childe,
woulde neuer thinke so.   I meruaile with what face
our Bishoppes could depriue such a man of God, that
beeing knowen to bee a most heauenly whooremaister,
a passing zealous worldling, and a most mortified
schismatique, was fitter iwis to teache men then boyes.
Bee ruled by *Martine,* and send him home into Deuon-

sheere, or else hee will wrappe all your Cleargie once
agayne in Lazarus winding sheete. Which fauour if
hee obtayne contrarie to desert, I woulde wishe him as
a friend, neare more to vrge Fathers to sweare at the
Funt, that the children that are brought thether to be
christned, are of none but their owne begetting, lest
olde *Ragdale* plie him as he did in times past, about
the shoulders with his plowe staffe. Haue with you
Giles Wig. to Sidborough, and let us haue you make
another Sermon of *Sedgwickes* pack-prickes: or such
another Prayer as you did of three hours long, when
as a friend of yours (that best knew your armes) cast
in the Rammes hornes at your windowe. If you be
remembred, it was the same time, when you cride,
Come wife, come seruants, let vs fall on our knees, and
praie to the Lorde God to deliuer vs from all euill
temptation, for the deuill is euen new gone by, and looke
where he hath throwne in his hornes at the windowe.
Giles, Giles, I haue to talke with you for your sau-
cinesse with the right Honorable the Earle of Huntington, in whose presence you (though of all other vnworthie) then beeing, when conuersant with other Gentlemen, hee calde for a boule of Beere, which brought,
and set downe by him, and he yet busie in talke, you
tooke verie orderlie from before him, and trilled it off
without anie more bones, bidding his man if he would,
goe fill him another. And what of all this I praie you,
was that such a wonderous matter, doth *Giles* care for
anie of your Lordes, Earles, Barons or Bishops. No,
no, no barrell better herring with him: we are all made

of one and the selfe same molde, and *Adam* signifieth
but red earth.   I could tell you a tale worth the hearing, that would counteruaile *Glib.* of Haustead, were it
not that it woulde make M. *Wig.* as cholerike, as when
he burst in the Church maugre excōmunication, and
knockt the keies about yᵉ Sextens head, for not opening
vnto him.   Come on it what wil, in spite of midsūmer
moone, you shal haue it as it is, therefore attend good
people to the vnfortunate sequele. G. W. of Wig. house,
in the land of little Wittam, chosen to the place and
function of a pastor, by those reuerend elders of the
Church, Hicke, Hob and John, Cutbert C. the Cobler,
and New. the broomseller *cum multis aliis que nunc*
prescribere longum est, at length seased (after many
yeeres stragling on the superintendentship of Sidborough,
wher hauing worn out three or four pulpits with the
vnreasonable bounsing of his fistes, it was his chance on
a time to haue one quarrell more to another of them:
so that no sooner mounted on her backe, but he began
to spurre her with his heeles, to boxe her about the
eares with his elbowes, and so pittiously misuse her in
euerie part, as would haue greeued anie heathen Ioyner
to the heart, to beholde.   Nor coulde his Text containe
him in this choler, or pleade anie pardon or pittie for
this poore pulpit, but he wold needes ride her to death
from one Diocesse to another, from Yorke to London,
from London to Canterbury, from Canterburie to Winchester, and all without a baite, insomuch, that tyred in
his waie homeward to his Text, he had stucke in the
myre for anie more matter hee had, had not Iohn a

Borhead come into the church as he did. Whom he
espying in good time, crost the midwaie of a sentence to
let flie at him in this manner. As for the discipline
which those wretches doe hinder, looke, looke good
people where that vile whooremaster Iohn a Borhead comes in piping hot from Clayphams wife.
Whose verie sight put him so cleane besides himselfe,
that he could neyther goe forward nor backward, but
stil repeated, Iohn a Borhead, Iohn a Borhead, that
vild whooremaister Iohn a Borhead: to whom with the
Father, the Sonne, and the holy Ghost, be al honor and
praise both now and for euer. Ah hah maister *Martine*,
what get you nowe by your red cap? Whether was
Clayphams wife or Iohn a Borhead more in fault, for
marring this good sermon. If I. a Borhead, then is it
not best for him to come in my brother *Wig*. waie,
least he stabbe him, as hee did the Drumme once for
playing after seruice. How euer it was, may it please
you Lordes of the spiritualtie, in consideration of these
laudible premises, to sende him home to his charge,
that hee may once more preache in the yewe tree. My
brother *Vd*. of Kingston thinkes Ile spare him for his
wiues sake, that is reported to be as good a wench as
euer playde her prises at Pancredge, although she is
not altogether such a gyantesse, as my brother *Wig*.
female, but *forma fragulis*, and Ale is not worth a
button, if it be too stale. Wherefore prepare you good
neighbour *V*. to vnder-goe the crosse of persecution.
Martine hath vaunted you to be a venterous knight, and
I doe meane to breake a launce with you, ere you and

E

I part. Wherfore what saie you nowe to the matter,
is Christ descended of bastardisme or no, as you gaue
out in the pulpyt? Would you not haue your tongue
cut out for your blasphemie if you wer wel serued?
Are you a notable preacher of the word of God, and a
vehement reprouer of sin, that thus seeke to discredit
the fleshly descent of our Sauiour, I thought you such
another, when I first sawe you emblazoned in *Martins*
bookes. Tis you that are so holy, that you wil not
forsooth be seene to handle anie monie, nor take golde
though it shoulde filch it selfe into your purse, but if
God moued the heartes of anie of your brethren or
sistren in the Lord, to bring in pots, beds or houshold
stuffe into your house, you would go out of doores of
purpose whiles it was brought in, and then if anie man
aske you, how you come so well storde, your answere
is that you know not how, but only by the prouidence
of God. I must belabour you when all is done, for
your backbiting and slandering of your honest neighbours, and open inueighing against the established
gouernment in your sermons. Helpe him *Martin,* or
else his vpbraided absurdities will make thee repent
that euer thou belyedst or disgracedst *Hone, Cottington*
or *Chatfield* in his cause. May it please you therefore
that are in authoritie, considering how reuerently hee
hath abused Christs birthright, to restore him to preach
that the blockes and stones of Kingstone, do not crie
out against you. I followe the riuers of folly, whiles
the fountaines of infection do propagate their poison.
Martin all this while thinkes himself in league with

obscuritie, whiles Phebus the discouerer of Mars and
Venus adultery, hath streamed his bright day light into
the net where he daunceth. Blush squint-eied caitife,
since thy couert no more wil contain thee. *Cælum te
contegit non habes vrnam.* Therfore let al posteritie
that shall heare of his knauerie, attend the discouery
which now I will make of his villanie. *Pen. I. Pen.*
welch *Pen. Pen.* the Protestationer, Demonstrationer,
Supplicationer, Appellationer, *Pen.* the father, *Pen.* the
sonne, *Pen. Martin Iunior, Martin Martinus, Pen.* the
scholler of Oxford to his friend in Cambridge, *Pen.*
totum in toto, et totum in qualibet parte, was somtimes
(if I be not deceiued) a scholler of that house in Cambridge whereof D. *Per.* was maister. Where, what his
estimation was, the scorn wherin he liued can best relate.
For the constitution of his bodie, it was so cleane contrarie to all phisiognomie of fame, that a man wold haue
iudged by his face, God and nature deuising our disgrace, had enclosde a close stoole in skinne, and set a
serpentine soule, like a counterfet diamond, more deepe
in dong. Neither was this monster of Cracouia
vnmarkt from his bastardisme to mischiefe: but as he
was begotten in adultery and conceiued in the heate of
lust, so was he brought into the world on a tempestuous
daie, and borne in that houre when all planets wer
opposite. Predestination y^t foresaw how crooked he
should proue in his waies, enioyned incest to spawne
him splay-footed. Eternitie, that knew how aukward
he shoulde looke to all honesty, consulted with Con-
ception to make him squint-eied, and the deuill that

discouered by the heauens disposition on his birth-day,
how great a lim of his kingdom was comming into the
world, prouided a rustie superficies wherinto wrapt him,
as soone as euer he was separated from his mothers
wombe: in euerie part whereof these words of blessing
were most artificially engrauen, *Crine ruber, niger ore,
breuis pede, lumine lustus.*   To leaue his natiuitie to
the Church porch, where the parish found him, and
come to his riper yeres, that now had learnd *Puerilis,*
of the poore mans boy, and nere as pretily entred in
Aue Marie English, as any parish clarke in those parts.
I am to tel you how laudibly he behaued himselfe in
Peterhouse, during the time of his subsistership.   First
therfore he began with his religion at his first comming
thether, *Hoc scitote viri,* that he was as arrant a papist
as euer came out of Wales.   I tell you *I. a P.* in those
daies, would haue run a false gallop ouer his beades
with anie man in England, and helpt the Priest for a
shift to saie Massse at high midnight, which if need
were, I doubt not but he would do at this houre.   It
was not for nothing my masters, that he so be-baited his
betters, for shewing the people the relique of our Ladies
smock in his sermon, and open detecting of all their
other blind superstition.   Say what you will, he is a
close lad, and can carrie a ring in his mouth, though all
the world see it not: what though hee now dissemble
with the time, and disguise his Spanish heart in a Pre-
cisians habit.   May not he hereafter proue a necessarie
mēber in conspiracies common wealth, and aduantage
the holy league as much in this meanes of sedition, as

all *Philips* power by inuasion. Simple English men, that cannot see into pollicie before it supprise your peace, nor interrupt the ambition of trechery, before it hath besieged your prosperitie. Doe you beholde whiles innouations bud, and do not you feare lest your children and family be poisoned with the fruit. The Scythians are barbarous, yet more fore-seeing then you, who so detested al forren innouations, tēding to the derogation of theyr ancient customes, that they kild Anacharsis for no other cause, but for y^t he performed the rights of Sibil after the manner of the Grecians. What should I vpbraide your simplicitie with the Epidaurians prouident subtiltie, who fearing least their Countrie men shoulde attract innouations from other nations, and especially from their riotous neighbors the Illirians, interdicted theyr merchants from al trafick with them, or trauaile vnto them, but least they should be vtterly destitute of their commodities, they chose a graue man amongst them, knowen to be of good gouern-ment and reputation, who dealt continually for the whole Countrie in the waie of exchange, and meruail-ously augmented their wealth by the reuerence of his wisedome. But you fond men, as in garments so in gouernment continually affecting new fashions, thinke no man can be saued y^t hath not bin at Geneua. Your beleefe forsooth must be of that Scottish kinde, and your Bibles of the primitiue print, else your consciences God wot, are not of the cannonical cut, nor your opinions of the Apostles stamp. *Pen.* with Pan, hath contended with Appollo, and you lyke Midasses, haue

ouerprised his musick. Good God, y^t a Welch harpe
should inchant so many English harts to their confusiõ,
especially hauing nere a string belonging to it, but a
treble. Had a syren sung, and I drownd in attending
her descante. I would haue bequeathed my bane to
her beautie, but when Cerberus shall barke and I turne
back to listen, thē let me perish without pittie, in the
delight of my liuing destruction. Deceit hath tooke vp
his seat in a dunce, and you thinke him a saint, because
he comes not in the shape of a deuil. We know M.
Pen. intus et in cute, first for a papist, then for a
Brownist, next for an Anabaptist, and last for ye blasphemous *Martin,* whose spirite is the concrete compound of all these vnpardonable heresies. But had not
the frantike practise of his youth throughly founded his
confirmed age in this furie, I woulde haue imagined his
vpstart spite, a wõder aboue usual speech, whereas now
the coniectures drawen from his cradles, detract frõ his
mallice all maruels. For whiles hee was yet a fresh
man in Peterhouse, and had scarce tasted, as we say,
of *Setons modalibus,* he began to affect factions in
art, and shew himselfe openly a studious disgracer of
antiquitie. Who then such an vnnatural enemie to
Aristotle, or such a new-fãgled friend vnto *Ramus.*
This one thing I am sure of, hee neuer went for other
then an asse, amongst his companions and equalles, yet
such a mutinous block-head was he alwaies accounted,
that through town and Colledge he was cõmonly called
the seditious dunce. For one while he would be
libelling against *Arist.* and all his followers he knew,

another while hee would all to be-rime Doctour *Perne*,
for his new statutes, and make a by-word of his bald
pate, yea had the Dean, President, or any other officer
neuer so litle angerd him, they were sure ere the
weeke went about to haue hard of it, in some libell or
other. This humour helde him at that time, when, by
conuersing with French men neare Christes Colledge, of
a Papist hee became a Brownist, how afterwards from
a Brownist hee fell to bee an Anabaptist, I referre it to
those that knewe his after behauiour in Oxford. But
for his last discent, *a malo in peius* from an Anabaptist
to be that infamous *Martin*, impute it to the age of
his heresies, that are now in there Harvest. Neither
would I haue you thinke there was no more heades in
it then his owne, For I can assure you to the contrary,
that moste of the Puritane preachers in Northampton
shire, Warwick shire, Sufolke and Northffolke, haue
eyther brought stone, strawe or morter to the building
of this *Martin*. Only *Pen.* found nothing but *ry*, which
the last part of his name, affordeth sufficiently, you may
see what it is for a nest of hornets to hiue together, oh
they wil make braue combes to choake bees withal, if
they be let alone but one quarter, not so much as T. C.
himselfe, but will haue the helpe of his fellow Brethren,
if he hath any thing to write against Bishops, were not
al the elected in Cambridge, assembled about the shaping
of the confutation of the Remish Testament, O so
deuoutly they met euery Friday at Saint *Laurence* his
Monastery, wher the counsails and fathers, were distributed amongst seueral companies, and euery one of the

reformed society sent there combined quotations weeke
by weeke in a Capcase, to my brother *Thomas*, yet
wandring beyond sea, such a Chaos of common places,
no apothegmatical *Lycosthenes* euer conceited. Bishops
were the smallest bugs, that were aimed at in this
extraordinary beneuolence, God shield, the court haue
escapt their collectiōs. Some thing it would proue in
the end if it wer published, that is pouldred with the
brains of so many Puritan springols, and polluted with
the pains of such an infinite number of Asses. Much
good do it you M. *Martin*, how like you my stile, am
not I old *Ille ego qui quondam* at ye besleeuing of a
sichophant. Alas poore. idiot, thou thinkest no man
can write but thy selfe, or frame his pen to delight,
except he straine curtesie with one of thy Northren
figures, but if authority do not moderate, the fiery
feruence of my enflamed zeale, ile assaile thee from
terme to terme with *Archilochus*, in such a compleat
armour of Iambicks, as the very reflexcye of my fury,
shall make thee driue thy father before thee to the
gallows, for begetting thee in such a bloody houre. O
God that we two might bee permitted but one quarter,
to try it out by the teeth for the best benefice in
England, then would I distill my wit into incke, and
my soule into argumentes, but I would driue this
Danus from his dunghill, and make him faune like a
dog for fauour at the magistrates feete. But it is our
English policy to aduantage our enemies by delaies,
and resist a multitude with a fewe, which makes
sediton seede before the haruesters of our souls

suppose it in the blade: it is not the spirite of
mildenesse y^t must moderat the hart of folly, dogs must
be beaten with staues, and stuborn slaues cōtrolled
with stripes. Authority best knows how to diet these
bedlamites, although *Segnior Penry* in his last waste
paper hath subscribed our magistrats infants. Repent,
repent thou runnagate lozill, and play not the Seminary
any longer in corners, least thy chiefest benefactors
forsake thee, and recouer the pouerty of their fines,
by bringing the pursiuants to thy forme. I heare some
vnderhande whisperers, and greeneheaded nouices
exclaime against our Bishops, for not granting thee
disputation. Alas alas brother *Martin* it may not be:
for thou art known to be such a stale hackster, with
thy welch hooke, that no honest man wil debase
himselfe in buckling with such a braggar. But suppose we should send some Crepundio forth our schools
to beat thee about the eares with *ergo*. Where should
this *sillogistica concertatio* be solemnized: what in our
Vniuersity schooles at Oxford, or in *puluere Philo-
sophico* at Cambridge. No they were erected in time
of Popery, and must be new built againe before they
can giue any accesse to his arguments. Truly I am
afraide y^t this Generall counsaile, must be holden at
Geneua, when al is done, for I know no place in
En[g]land holy inough for their turne, except it be some
barne or out-house about Bury, or some odde blind
cottage in the hart of Warwicke shire, and thither
peraduenture, these good honest opponents would
repaire without grudging. Prouided alwaies that they

haue ther horse-hire and other charges allowed them
out of the poor mans box, or els it is no bargain. All
this fadges wel yet, if we had once determined who
shold be father of the act. Why what a question
is that, when we haue so many persecuted elders
abroad. The blinde, the halt, or the lame, or any
serues the turn with them, so he hath not on a cloak
with sleues, or a cap of the vniuersity cut. Imagin
that place to be furnished, where shall we finde
moderators, that may deale indifferently twixt both
parts. *Machiuell* is dead many a yeare agoe, or els he
had bene a fit man for this may-game, therefore whom
shal we haue now, since it must be neither yours
nor ours. Some vpstart countrey Gentleman, that
hath vndone all his tenants by oppression, euen such
a one as *Scar.* of Warwicke shire, that being a noted
Martinist, be frinded his poor coppi-holder *Criar,*
and turnd him out of all that ere he had very orderly.
How thinke you my lay brethren? is not here a trim
conuocation towards. But mark the end of it, and
then you may haps see odde buffeting with the
buttond bookes, and battring down of bishopricks.
Giles of Sidborough wil off his gown at least, and
make demonstrations of Logique with his fists like
Zeno, what though he be low and cannot reach so
hie as an Archbishop, may not he stād like a
iackanapes on his wiues shoulders, and scold for the
best game with all that come. He is sauing a
reuerence a spritish dispu[t]er, and a pestilent felow at
an vnperfect sillogisme. Nay mark me well, and

take me at my words, he shal speake false Latine, forge a text, abuse a Bishop, or make a lie of reuelation for more then I speak off with any man in Englād. Neither do I flatter him herin for he hears me not, if I did, it were no matter, considering that *virtus laudata crescit.*

From iest to ernest, I appeale to you Gentlemen, how ridiculous in pollicy this disputation would proue if it were granted. First for there Bibles, the touchstone of all controuersies, they must bee of their fouorites translation, or els they will deny there authority as friuolous. Admit they go to the original (which but few of them vnderstand) they wil haue euery man his sundry interpretation. Let our deuines alledge any text, they will expound it as they list, say the fathers or other auncient writers what they will. For such is the growth of their arrogancy, that they are not ashamed to compare themselus with *Ierome* or *Austen,* and in their tedious sermons preach against them as prophane. If this thē bee any betraying of the wretchednesse of our cause (as they call it) not to dispute with them that deny all principles, not to contend with thē that wilbe tride by none but themselus, I refer it to all considerate iudgementes, that haue no more experiēce in the actions of peace then a reasonable soule may afford. The more pacified sort of our Puritans, would needs perswade the world, that it is nought but a learned ministry which their chāpion *Martin* endeuors : were it no otherwise his pardon were easely sealed, but

those that know the treasō of his books, can report
of his mallice against Bishops.   One thing I am
perswaded, that he neither respects the propagation
of the Gospel, nor the prosperity of the Church, but
only the benefite that may fall to him and his
boulsterers,   by   the   distribution   of   Bishoprickes.
Beshrewe mee but those Church-liuings would come
well to decayed courtiers.   O howe meerilye the
Dice would runne, if our lustye laddes might goe
to hazard for halfe a dozen of these Dioses[es].   Not
a page but woulde haue a flinge at some or other
impropriation or personage: and in conclusion, those
liuings which now maintaine so many schollers and
students, would in two or three yeares be all spent
in a Tauerne amongst a consort of queanes and fidlers,
that might carouse on their wine-bench to the confusion
of religion.   Well, to proceede in this text of
reformation: is not this thy meaning *Martin*, that
thou wouldest haue two and fiftie thousand Pastors,
for two and fiftie thousand Parish churches in England
and Wales.   If thou saiest the word, we will haue a
place in both Vniuersities, begin in Oxford first with
the fresh-men, and so go vp to the heades of the
Vniuersitie, and then count how many thou canst
make.   Our Beadles that know the number best,
would needes perswade vs, that of all sortes, there
is not full three thousand: in Cambridge they say
there is not so many by a thousand, then call thy
wits together, and imagin with thy selfe, out of these
three thousand, and two thousand of all gatherings,

how many good preachers may be mustered, some
foure hundreth as I gesse, peraduenture thou maist
rebate them to some fiftie or threescore, because there
is no more open-mouthes of thy profession in both
Vniuersities: How farre this fiftie is from fiftie
thousand, a farthing worth of Arithmetike will teach
you: where wilt thou haue then a competent number
to fill vp those defects of dum ministers: inspiration
I perceiue must helpe to patch vp your knauerie,
and then welfare the cobler of Norwitch, that being
one morning somthing earelie at Saint Androwes,
and the Preacher not come before the Psalme was
ended, stept vp into the pulpet verie deuoutly, and
made me a good thriftie exhortation in the praise
of plaine dealing. If this bee not true, aske the
Maior that committed him to prison for his labour.
Such another Doctour would he proue, that standing
in election for a liuing that was then in her Maiesties
bestowing, came to be examined by men of grauitie
in the circumstance of his sufficiencie, who discending
eft soones into his vnschooled simplicitie, gaue him
this litle English to be made in Latin. There be
three Creedes, the Nycen Creede, Athanatius Creede,
and the Apostles Creede, all which ought to be
belieued vpon paine of damnation. The good simple
superintendant, that saw himselfe so hardly beset,
craued respite to compasse this vulgar, which graunted,
after some deliberation he began thus to go forward,
" Tria sunt Creda, vnum Niceni, alterum Athanasii,
tertium Apostolorum, quæ omnes debent esse creditum,

F

sub pœna condemnationis." I marrie Sir, here is
apeece of scholershippe of the new cut, which for
the goodnesse of the Latin might haue borne a part
in the Pewteres paggeant. I keepe a register of ten
thousand such knacks. Why, there is not a Presician
in England that hath abused arte, or mistoken a
metaphor but I haue his name in blacke and white,
what say you to that zealous sheepebyter of your
owne edition in Cambridge, that saide the wicked
had a scabbe, a braune, and a crust on their conscience,
being so full of their wilie gilies, that we that are
the true children of God can not tell how to concerne
them: or was not hee a sound carde, that talking
of the maiestie and authoritie of the scriptures, said
they were the sweete meates of Saintes, the houshold
stuffe of heauen, and the home spunne cloth of the
Lords own loombes, being deliuered from the stonebow
of his mouth, when he appeared in glory on mount
Sinay: But this is nothing to the good sport of that
is behinde. What, I must tell you of a fellow that
trolles in his rethorike like *Martin* in his riddles.
This hors-holy father preaching on a time in Saint
Maries at Oxford, came off with this mannerly
comparison: There is an vglie and monstrous beast
in our tongue called a hogge, and this vgly and
monstrous beast in boistrous and tempesteous weather
lifts vp his snoute into the ayre, and cryes wrough,
wrough: euen so (deare people) the children of God
in the troublesome time of temptations, cry, Our helpe
is in the name of the Lord. Such another woodcocke

was he of Yarmouth, that said openly in the pulpet, whosoeuer weares a vayle, is an whore without exception, and on an other time, two women comming to be churched, whereof the one wore a vaile, the other went without. He began his thankesgiuing in this forme: Let vs giue God thankes for the safe deliuery of one of our sisters, for the other let vs not giue God thankes, for she is a straunger, and we haue nothing to doe with her, I take her to be *Dinah* the harlot, that sat by the high way side, for she hath a vayle ouer her face. In the next place to him, shall he be put that railing on the Papists in his Sermon, alledged this argument to confute their religion, Nay (saith he) you may gather what a wicked and spotted religion this papistrie is, for Campion himselfe that was accounted their chiefest piller, was reported to haue had the poxe. I haue another in my tables, that handling that place of *Iosua* where *Rahab* entertained his spies, would needes conclude all Inkeepers to be harlots, because *Rahab* the harlot was an Inkeeper. I shall run my penne out of breath, if I articulate all the examples of their absurdeties that I could. Haue not Trinitie Hall men in Cambridge a preaching brother in Bury yet in sute, for saying all ciuillians were papists. To let him passe for a patch, that being maister of none of the meanest Colledges in Cambridge, and by the oth of his admission, bound to take no money for preferments, made answere to one that offered him fortie markes to make his sonne fellow:

God forbid I should take any money for it is against
my oth, but if you will giue me it in plate, Ile
pleasure him in what I may. This is the dreamer
if you be aduised, that is indebted aboue two
thousand houres to the Vn[iu]ersitie, which he hath
borrowed by three and foure at a time vpon seuerall
sundayes preaching as it came to his course: it is a
shame for him, that he doth not pay them, professing
such puritie as he doth. *Martin,* thou seest I
come not abruptly to thee like a rednosde ieaster,
that in the pride of his pottle-pots curries ouer a
reuelling riffe raffe of Tapsterly tauntes, and course
hempen quippes, such as our brokerly wits doe filsh
out of Bull the Hangmans budget, but I speake
plaine English, and call thee a knaue in thine owne
language. All the generation of you are Hipocrites
and belli-gods, that deuoure as much good meat
in one of your brotherly loue meetings, as would
wel-nye victuall the Queenes ships a whole moneth.
It is a shame for you to exclame so against Cardes,
and play thus vnreasonably at Maw as you do.
Gaffe *Martin,* doe you remember whom you vpbraided
by Primero? well let not me take you at Noddy
anie more, least I present you to the parish for a
gamster, this the ninth set that you haue lost, and
yet you will not leaue off. Beware *Anthony Munday*
be not euen with you for calling him Iudas, and lay
open your false carding to the stage of all mens
scorne. I maruell *Pasquill* comes not away with his
legends, considering that the date of his promise is

more then expired. It seemes he stayes for some Saintes that are yet to suffer, and wants none but *Martin* to make vp his legend of Martyres, if it be so I woulde thou wouldest come aloft quickly, that we might haue this good sport altogether, and not liue euer in expectation of that which is not. O I could furnish him to the proofe with such a packet of male and female professors, as the world might not patterne. A good old dunstable doctor here in London, should be the formost of them, that saide his wife was as good as our Ladie: and another time quarrelling with one of his neighbours that was a sadler, about setting vp of the Organs, in a good zeale he lift vp his fist, and stroke out two of his fore teeth, like a right man of peace: where haue you lived my brethren, that you haue not heard of that learned Presbiter, that talking how *Adam* fell by eating of the Apple, discourst thus: *Adam* eate the Apple and gaue it to his wife, whereby is to be noted that the man cate and the woman eate, the man eate, but how, a snap and away: the woman eat, but how, she laide her thumbe on the stalke, and her finger on the coare and bitte it ouerthwart, in which byting it ouerthwart, she broke all the commaundements, insomuch as vnder ten greene spots the ten cōmandments in euery Apple are comprised: and besides that corrupted her fiue senses. From whence wee may gather this obseruation, that a woman alwaies eates an Apple ouerthwart. Why, this is sound diuinitie, and apt for to edify, *Sed*

abeundum est mihi, and from the Cleargie must I
leape to the Laytie. Wherefore God euen good
man *Dauy* of Canterbury, and better lucke betide
thee and thy limbes, then when thou dauncedst a
whole sunday at a wedding, and afterwardes repenting they selfe of thy prophane agilitie, thou entredst
into a more serious meditation against what table
thou hadst sinned, or what part was the principall
in this antike iniquitie. The eyes they were the
formost in this enditement, but the legs, (O those
leude legs,) they brought him thither, they kept
him there, they leapt, they daunced, and I leualted
to the Vials of vanitie: wherefore, what didst thou
but like a true christian chastised them accordingly.
The scripture saith, if thine eye offend thee, plucke
it out, *Dauy* saith, my hose and shoes haue
offended mee, therefore will I plucke them off.
This text thus applyed, off went the wollen stockings
with a trice, and they with the good neates leather
shoes were cast both into the bottom of a well.
The sinners thus punished, and all parties pleased,
home went the pilgrim *Dauy* barefoote and barelegge.
And now since wind and tide serues, now I care
not if I cut ouer to Ipswitch: there is a Cowdresser
there that I am sure. will entertaine me if she be
not dead, great *Iane* of Ipswitch they call her, one
that hath beene a tender mother to many a Martinist
in her time, and hath a very good insight in a
canne of strong wine. A good vertuous Matrone
is she and a wise, hauing no fault but this, that

she will be drunke once a day, and then she lyes
her downe on her bedde, and cryes, O my God,
my God, thou knowest I am drunke, and why I
should offend thee my God by spuing thus, as I
do. I haue not beene in Essex yet, but Ile set
in my staffe there as I go home, for I haue a petition
for my brother that made the Sermon of Repentance
to deliuer vp for me to the Councell: but it must
not be such a one as he deliuered for him selfe
to my Lord Treasurer, beginning with O sweet
Margery, could thy eyes see so fare, thy hands
feele so farre, or thy eares heare so farre &c. for
then euerie seruing man will mocke vs, but it must
be of another tune, with most pitifully complaining,
that a man can not call an Asse, asse, but he shall
be had *coram nobis*. In this vaine enough, because
actions of the case are chargeable, and Guilde
men vncharitable. If the dogge *Martin* barke againe,
Ile hold him tugge for two or three courses, and
then beware my blacke booke you were best,
for I haue not halfe emboweld my register. Amend,
amend, and glorie no more in your hipocrisie, least
your pride and vaine glory betray our prosperitie
to our enimies, and procure the Lords vengeance to
dwell in the gates of our citie. The simple are
abused, the ignorant deluded, and Gods truth most
pitifully peruerted, and thou art that most wretched
seducer, that vnder wolues raiment deuourest widowes
houses. Visions are ceast, and all extraordinarie
reuelation ended, although a good fellow in Cambridge,

hearing all thinges might be obtained by prayer, prayed two dayes and two nightes for visions: wherefore broach no more heresies vnder colour of inspiration: if thou doest, thou art like to heare of me by the next Carrier.   And so bon nute to your Noddishippe.

Yours to command as your owne
for two or three cudgellings at all times.

Cutbert Curriknaue
the yonger.

NOTES.

PAGE 9, line 28. *induments*] from *induo*, Latin, to put on; cover over. The word, as a noun, does not occur in Todd's Johnson nor in Nares.

"Diana's shape and habit them *indued.*"—*Sandys' Ovid*, b. ii.
> "One first matter all
> *Indu'd* with various forms."—*Milton, Par. Lost.*

P. 11, l. 6. *unuenidall sinnes*] Unvenial? it seems used in contradistinction to venial.

P. 11, l. 8. *despairing protestations*] This is an allusion to "The Protestatyon of Martin Mar-Prelat, wherein notwithstanding the surprizing of the printer, he maketh it known vnto the world that he feareth, neither proud priest, Antichristian pope, tiranous prellate, nor godlesse catercap."

P. 12, l. 28. *burlibond*] Todd, in his edition of Johnson, has adduced one illustration of the word *burly*, which approximates to the meaning here, that of loud, boisterous; derived, as he supposes from *borlen*, Teut., to make a noise. Though neither in Nares nor Todd, it will be found in Nash's Pierce Penniless [Reprint, Shaksp. Soc., p. 25]: "The most grosse and senseless proud dolts are the Danes, who stand so much vpon their vnweldie *burlibound* souldiery, that they account of no man that

G

hath not a battle-axe at his girdle to hough dogs with, or weares
not a cock's fether in a thrumb hat like a caualier: briefly, he is
the *best foole bragart* under heaven."

P. 13, l. 25. *hodie-peeles*] Nash, in his *Anatomie of Absurdities*,
uses the word *hoddy-peke*, there implying cuckold, which is the
meaning it bears in this place.

"Who under her husband's that *hoddy-peke's* nose must have
all the distilling dew of his delicate rose."

P. 14, l. 2. *true-pennie*] See the Notes to the Reprint of
"Hay any Worke for Cooper," p. 79.

P. 14, l. 7. *Buls slicing.*] Bull was the name of the common
hangman; he is quoted some two or three times in "Pap with a
Hatchet," and in many of the Dramas of the time.

P. 15, l. 21. *Old Martin of England.*] An allusion to the "Iust
censure and reproofe of Martin Iunior, by his reuerend and elder
brother Martin Senior."

P. 16, l. 14. *dudgen distinction.*] I am unable to explain this.

P. 16, last line. *bibble-babble.*] Idle talk.

"Malvolio, Malvolio, thy wits the heaven restore! endeavour
thyself to sleep, leave thy vain *bibble babble.*"

Shakspeare, Twelfth Night.

P. 17, l. 1. *gibbrige*] Gibberish.

P. 17, l. 19. *Cli. the Cobler, &c.*] Cliffe, Newman, Lawson.

P. 22, l. 25. *Will Tong,*] I cannot give any account of this
worthy, unless Will. Kempe, who succeeded the celebrated
Tarlton, is meant. Elderton's name is well known, his rimes
and ballets are the subject of frequent allusion in the dramas and
pamphlets of the time. See "Pap with a Hatchet," [Reprint,
p. 14]. Harvey's "Pierce's Supererogation." [Reprint, p. 181.]

P. 23, l. 25. *his Welchnes.*] An allusion to Penry.

P. 24, l. 4. *Hodgkins, Tomlins and Sims.*] Hodgkins, and his two men, Tomlyn and Symms, who were employed to print the Mar-Prelate Tracts after Waldegrave's press had been broken up, were seized at Manchester in printing "More work for the Cooper." Their examination will be found in Strype's Annals, vii. 602-5.—See also much information in Sutcliffe's Answer to Job Throckmorton, p. 72, 4to, 1595.

P. 25, l. 8. *Bumfeging.*] *i. e.* belabouring. The word does not occur in Nares. In "Hay any Worke for Cooper," Martin says, "For ise so bumfeg the Cooper," &c. [Reprint, p. 24.]

P. 26, l. 5. *the aged champion of Warwicke.*] *i. e.* Thomas Cartwright.

P. 26, l. 8. *Phi. Stu.*] Philip Stubbes, the brother-in-law of Cartwright. His "Anatomy of Abuses," was printed in 1589.

P. 31, l. 24. *ribrost.*] To belabour, to beat soundly.
"I have been pinched in flesh, and well *ribroasted* under my former masters; but I'm in now for skin and all."—*L'Estrange.*

P. 35, l. 26. *anie more bones.*] *i. e.* without scruple.
"Perjury will easily donne with him that hath made *no bones* of murther."—*Bp. Hall, Cases of Conscience.*

P. 39, l. 6. *Pen. &c.*] Nash is evidently mistaken in attributing all the Mar-Prelate Tracts to him. The description which follows powerfully reminds us of Nash's characteristic portrait of Gabriel Harvey.

P. 44, l. 2. *Capcase.*] A small travelling case, according to Nares, 72.

P. 50, l. 8. *sheepe byter.*] A petty thief.
"There are political *sheepbiters* as well as pastoral, betrayers of publick trusts as of private."—*L'Estrange.*
"May it please Gentle Pierce in the divine fury of his ravished spirit, to be graciously good unto his poor friends, who would be somewhat loth to be silly sheep for the wolf, or other *sheepbiter.*"—*G. Harvey's Pierce's Supererogation.*

P. 51, L. 26. *patch.*]   *i. e.* a fool.

P. 51, l. 21. *Maw.*]   An old game at cards; the pun is not a bad one.

P. 52, l. 26. *Beware Anthony Munday.*]   A well known writer and translator of various works.   I have not met with the passage alluded to.

THE END.

LONDON:
HUGH WILLIAMS, PRINTER, ASHBY-STREET.

Puritan Discipline Tracts.

AN EPISTLE

TO

THE TERRIBLE PRIESTS

OF THE

CONVOCATION HOUSE:

BY

MARTIN MAR-PRELATE, Gentleman.

Re-printed from the Black Letter Edition,

WITH

AN INTRODUCTION AND NOTES.

Second Edition.

LONDON:

JOHN PETHERAM, 71, CHANCERY LANE.

1843.

Prospectus.

THE following Tracts relating to the controversy between the Puritans and the Church of England, during the reign of Elizabeth, on Discipline, &c. are suggested for publication, on the same plan as the first, which is already published. Those who are desirous of subscribing for the whole, or for any one of them separately, should give early and specific directions to this effect. A limited number only will be printed beyond the subscription.

1. Oh read ouer D. Iohn Bridges, for it is a worthy worke, or an Epistle to the terrible Priests of the Confocation House : with Introduction and Notes. 8vo, [pp. 82,] cloth, lettered. Price, to subscribers, 2s. ; to non-subscribers, 3s. *Already published.*

2. Oh read ouer D. Iohn Bridges, or an Epitome of the fyrst Booke of that right worshipfull volume written against the Puritanes. Printed on the other hand of some of the priests. *Preparing for publication, and will be from 72 to 84 pages.* Subscription, 2s.

3. A Brieff discours off the troubles begonne at Franckford in Germany, Anno Domini 1554. Abowte the booke off common prayer and Ceremonies, and continued by the Englishe men theyre, to thende off Q. Marys Raigne. 1575. *Reprinted in 1642, and subsequently in the Phœnix,* 1707.

4. A Brief discourse against the outward Apparell and Ministering Garments of the Popish Church, 1566 ; *and other tracts on the Habits, printed about the same time.*

5. An Admonition to the Parliament. A Second Admonition to the Parliament. *Without place or date.* [1572.]

6. Certain Articles, collected and taken, (as it is thought) by the Byshops out of a little Boke, entituled an Admonition to the Parliament, with an Answere to the same, containing a Confirmation of the sayde Booke in shorte Notes.
Imprinted we know where and whan,
Judge you the place and you can. · [1572.]

7. Counter-Poyson : or, the Certaine Forme of Ecclesiasticall Government. London, *without date.* [1584.]

8. A Defence of the Reasons of the Counterpoyson. 1586.

9. A lamentable Complaint of the Commonalty by way of Supplication to the High Court of Parliament for a learned Ministery. *Without place.* 1585.

10. A briefe discovery of the untruths and Slanders contained in a Sermon by D. Bancroft, Feb. 8, 1588, and set forth in print by John Penry. 1588.

11. The State of the Church of Englande laide open, in a conference betweene Diotrephes a Byshoppe, Tertullus a Papiste, Demetrius a Usurer, Pandochus an Innkeeper, and Paul a Preacher of the Word of God. R. Waldegrave. *Without date.*

12. A Countercuffe given to Martin Junior, by the venturous, hardie, and renouned Pasquill of England, Caualiero. 1589.

13. The First parte of Pasquils Apologie. Wherein he renders a reason to his friendes for his long silence, and gallops the fielde with the Treatise of Reformation. 1590.

14. A Myrror for Martinists and all other Schismatiques, which in these dangerous daies doe breake the Godlie Unity and disturbe the Christian Peace of the Church, by T. T. J. Wolfe. 1590.

15. A Whip for an Ape ; or Martin displaied ; Marre Mar-Martin, or Marre Martins medling in a manner misliked. 1589. With a collection of other pieces in verse relating to the same subject.

16. Ha'ye any work for a Cooper ? penned and compiled by Martin Marprelate. 1590.

17. The Protestation of Martin Marprelat. 1589.

18. The unlawfull Practises of Prelates against Godly Ministers, the Maintainers of the Discipline of God. *No date.* [1590.]

19. Pappe with a hatchet, alias a figge for my God sonne, or Cracke me this nut, or a Countrie Cuffe, that is a sound boxe of the eare for the idiot Martin to hold his peace, written by one who dares call a dog a dog. [1590.]

20. Pasquill's returne to England from the other side of the Seas, and his meeting with Marforious at London upon the Royal Exchange. If my breath be so hote that I burn my mouth, suppose I was printed in Pepper Allie, A.D. 1589.

21. Martin's Months Minde, that is a Certaine Report, and True Description of the Death and Funeral, of Olde Martin Marre-Prelate, the great Make-bate of England, and Father of the Factious. 1589.

22. Plaine Percevall, the Peace-Maker of England, sweetly indevoring with his blunt Persuasions to botch up a Reconciliation between Mar-ton and Mar-tother.

23. A Selection from the very scarce collection printed at Edinburgh in 1593, by R. Waldegrave, entitled " A Part of a Register, contayning sundrie Memorable Matters, written by divers godly and learned in our time, which stande for, and desire the Reformation of our Church, in Discipline and Ceremonies, accordinge to the pure Worde of God, and the Lawe of our Lande."

24. A Collection of certaine Sclaunderous Articles, given out by the Bishoppes against such faithful Christians as they now vniustly deteyne in their prisons, together with the answeare of the prisoners thereto : Also the some [sum] of certaine conferences had in the Fleete. 1590.

25. The Examination of Henry Barrow, John Greenwood, and John Penry, before the High Commissioners and Lords of the Council, with their Answer to the many Questions, why they would not take an oath, and why they refused to hear or have communion in the Church of England, also Mr. Penry's Declaration of his Faith and Allegiance to her Majesty, &c. faithfully penned by the Prisoners themselves.

26. D. Bancroft's rashness in rayling against the Church of Scotland, and some reasons rendred why the Answer thereunto hath not hitherto come forth, by J. D. a brother of the said Church of Scotland. Edinburgh, by R. Waldegrave. 1590.

INTRODUCTION.

THE original, from which the following tract is re-printed, is a small quarto volume, in black letter, of 52 pages. There are several tracts which bear the general title of Martin Mar-Prelate, Martin Senior, Martin Junior, &c., but this, which is the "Epistle," and another, called the "Epitome," are frequently con-founded together, arising probably from the similarity of appearance in the titles, the first paragraph in each being exactly alike, and the second very similar, though in other respects they differ; and, whereas the "Epis-tle" was printed "oversea," the "Epitome" (which is a continuation of the Epistle) was "Printed on the other hand of some of the Priests," both without date, though it must have been towards the end of 1588, which may be collected from several circumstances mentioned in the tracts themselves; and, from the appearance of the type, they were most probably printed by Richard Schilders, at Middleburgh, in Zea-land. Another reason, perhaps, why these two tracts are so frequently confounded together, may arise from both having been written against the same work, namely, "Dr. John Bridges' Defence of the Government of the Church of England for Ecclesiastical Matters against a Treatise of Ecclesiastical Government," &c., a quarto of 1500 pages, the bulk of which, in more than one instance, appears to have excited Martin's spleen.

The authors of Martin Mar-Prelate were never discovered; it is, however, probable that John Penry, "the hot-headed Welshman," as his enemies called him, was the author. He confessedly wrote several works on behalf of the Puritan cause, and in 1593 suffered death for them.

In the following tract the reader will have an opportunity of judging of the manner in which the other works, announced in the Prospectus, (should sufficient encouragement be given to continue them,) will be published. In the text I have faithfully adhered to the original copy, both in orthography and punctuation; in the notes to the giving some few particulars for illustrating the allusions in the text. Although some of the words to be met with are now obsolete, the readers, into whose hands it will come, will hardly require a glossary of them. The same care in the text, and, I trust, even more attention in the notes, will be given to the subsequent publications.

In conclusion, I must disclaim any personal or politico-religious feelings in bringing once more before the world these curious productions of by-gone times. Personality and scurrility were used freely by the Martinists and their opponents; and however much it is to be wished that they had written with a gravity and decorum more suited to the object they had in view, I could only give that which I found, faithfully and unreservedly, and this I have done.

J. P.

London, Sept. 20th, 1842.

Oh read ouer D. Iohn Bridges, for it is a worthy worke:

Or an epitome of the
fyrste Booke of that right worshipfull vo-
lume, written against the Puritanes, in the defence
of the noble cleargie, by as worshipfull a prieste, Iohn
Bridges, Presbyter, Priest or elder, doctor of Diuillitie,
and Deane of Sarum.   Wherein the arguments
of the puritans are wisely prevented, that
when they come to answere M. Doctor,
they must needes say something
that hath bene spoken.

Compiled for the behoofe and overthrow
of the Parsons, Fyckers, and Currats, thàt have lernt
their Catechismes, and are past grace: By the
reverend and worthie Martin Marprelate
gentleman, and dedicated to the
Confocationhouse.

The Epitome is not yet published, but it shall
be when the Bishops are at conuenient leysure to
view the same. In the meane time, let them
be content with this learned Epistle.

Printed oversea, in Europe, within two fur-
longs of a Bounsing Priest, at the cost and
charges of M. Marprelate, gentleman.

RIGHT PUISANTE, AND TERRIBLE PRIESTS,

MY CLEARGIE MASTERS OF THE CONFOCATION-HOUSE,
WHETHER FICKERS GENERALL, WORSHIPFULL PALTRIPOLITANE,
OR ANY OTHER OF THE HOLY LEAGUE OF SUBSCRIPTION :
THIS WORKE I RECOMMEND VNTO THEM WITH ALL MY HEART, WITH
A DESIRE TO SEE THEM ALL SO PROUIDED FOR ONE DAY,
AS I WOULD WISH, WHICH I PROMISE THEM
SHALL NOT BE AT ALL TO THEIR HURT.

RIGHT poysond, persecuting and terrible priests, the theame of mine Epistle, vnto your venerable master-domes, is of two parts (and the Epitome of our brother Bridges his booke, shall come out speedily). First, most pitifully complayning, Martin Marprelate, &c. Secondly, may it please your good worships, &c.

Most pitifully complayning therefore, you are to vnderstand, that D. Bridges hath written in your defence, a most senceles book, and I cannot very often at one breath come to a full point, when I read the same.

Againe, may it please you to giue me leaue to play the Duns for the nonce as well as he, otherwise dealing with master doctors booke, I cannot keepe *decorum personæ*. And may it please you, if I be too absurd in any place (either in this Epistle, or that Epitome) to ride to Sarum, and thanke his Deanship for it. Because I could not deal with his booke commendablie according to order, vnles I should be sometimes tediously dunstical and absurd. For I haue heard som· cleargie men

B

say, that M. Bridges was a verie patch and a duns, when he was in Cambridg. And some say, sauing your reuerence that are Bb. that he is as very a knaue, and enemy vnto the sinceritie of religion, as any popish prelate in Rome. But the patche can doe the cause of sinceritie no hurt. Naye, he hath in this booke wonderfully graced the same by writing against it. For I haue hard some say, that whosoeuer will read his booke, shall as euidently see the goodnes of the cause of reformation, and the poore poore, poore nakednes of your gouernment, as almost in reading all master Cartwright's workes. This was a very great ouersight in his grace of Cant. to suffer such a booke to come· out. For besides that an Archb. is very weakely defended by masse Deane, he hath also by this meanes prouoked many to write against his gracious fatherhood, who perhaps neuer ment to take pen in hand. And brother Bridges, mark what Martin tels you, you will shortly I hope haue twenty fistes about your eares more thē your own. Take heed of writing against Puritanes while you liue, yet they say that his grace woulde not haue the booke to be published, and if you marke, you you shall not finde seene and allowed in the title of the booke. Well fare old mother experience yet, the burnt childe dreads the fire: his grace will cary to his graue I warrant you, the blowes which M. Cartwright gaue him in this cause: and therefore no maruell though he was loth to haue any other so banged as he himselfe was to his woe. Others say that Iohn Cant. ouersawe euery proofe. If he did, then he ouersaw many a

foule salecisme, many a senceles period, and far more
slanders. Slanders my friends? I thinke so. For what
will you say, if our brother Bridges, and our cosen
Cosins, with manye others, haue had their grace of the
Bb. *ad practicandum* in Flanders? Howe could their
gouernment stand, vnles they should slander their brethren, and make her Maiestie beleeue, that the Church
gouernment prescribed in the worde, would ouerthrow
her regiment, if it were receiued in our Church, and
that the seekers of reformation, are a sort of Malcontents, and enemies vnto the state.

Item may it please your worthy worshipps, to receive
this curteously to favour at my hand, without choller or
laughing. For my L. of Winchester is very chollericke
and peeuish, so are his betters at Lambeth, and D.
Cosins hath a very good grace in iesting, and I woulde
he had a little more grace, and a handful or two more
of learning, against he answer the Abstract next. Nay
beleeue me, it is inough for him to answere the Counterpoyson. And I am none of the malicious sectaries,
wherof Iohn of London spake the last Lent, 1588. in
his letters written to the Archdeacon of Essex, to forbid
publike fastes. Ha, ha, D. Copcot are ye there, why
do not you answere the confutation of your sermõ
at Pauls crosse? ¶It is a shame for your grace Iohn of
Cant. that Cartwrights bookes haue bene now a dozen
yeares almost vnanswered: you first prouoked him to
write, and you first haue receiued the foyle. If you
can answer those books, why do you suffer the Puritans
to insult and reioyce at your silence. If you cannot,

why are you an Archb. He hath prooued the calling to be vnlawfull and Antichristian. You dare not stand to the defence of it. Now most pitifully complayneth, M. Marprelate, desireth you either to aunswere what bathe beene written against the gracelesnes of your Archbishoprick, or to giue ouer the same, and to be a meanes that no byshop in the land, be a Lord any more. I hope one day her Maiestie will either see that the L. Bb. prooue their calling lawfull by the word, or as Iohn of London prophesied saying, come downe you bishopps from your thousands, and content you with your hundreds, let your diet be pristlike and not prince-lik, &c. quoth Iohn Elmar in his Harborow of faithful subiects. But I pray you B. Iohn dissolue this one question to your brother Martin: if this prophesie of yours come to passe in your dayes, who shal be B. of London? And will you not sweare as commonly you do, like a lewd swag, and say, by my faith, by my faith my masters, this geare goeth hard with us. Nowe may it please your grace with ye rest of your worships, to procure that the Puritans may one day haue a free dispu-tatiõ with you, about ye cõtrouersies of the Church, and if you be not set at a flat *non plus*, and quite ouer-throwen, ile be a Lord B. my selfe: looke to your selues, I thinke you haue not long to raigne. Amen. And take heed brethren of your reuerend and learned brother, Martin Marprelate. For he meaneth in these reasons following I can tell you, to proue that you ought not to be maintained by the authoritie of the Magistrate, in any Christian commonwealth : Martin is a shrewd fellow, and reasoneth thus. Those that are pettie popes and pettie Antichrists, ought not to be maintained in anie Christian commonwealth. But euerie Lord B. in England, as for ilsample, Iohn of Cant. Iohn of London, Iohn Excetor, Iohn Rochester, Thomas of Winchester. The B. of Lincolne, of Worcester, of Peterborow, and to be briefe, all the Bb. in England, Wales, and Ireland, are pettie popes, and pettie Antichristes. Therefore no Lord B. (nowe I pray thee good Martin speake out, if euer thou diddest speake out, that hir Maiestie and the counsell may heare thee) is to be tollerated in any christian common welth: and therefore neither Iohn of Cant. Iohn of London, &c. are to be tollerated in any christian commonwelth. *What malapert knaues are these that cannot be content to stand by and here, but they must teach a gentleman how to speake.*

What say you now brother Bridges is it good writing against Puritanes. Can you denie any part of your learned brother Martin his syllogisme. We denie your minor M. Marprelat say the Bb. and their assóciats. Yea my learned masters, are you good at that? what do you brethren? say me that againe? do you denie my minor? And *Looke the doctors booke, pag. 107. lyme 20. and Pag. 113. line 13.* that be all you can say, to denie L. Bb. to be pettie popes, turne me loose to the priests in y‍ᵗ point, for I am olde suersvie at the proofe of such matters, ile presently marre the fashion of their Lorships.

They are pettie popes, and pettie Antichrists, whosoeuer vsurpe the authority of pastors ouer them, who by the ordinance of God, are to bee vnder no pastors. For none but Antichristian popes and popelings euer claimed this authoritie vnto themselues, especiallie when it was gainsaid, and accounted Antichristian, generally by the most Churches in the world.   But our L. bishops vsurpe authoritie ouer those, who by the ordinance of God, are to be vnder no pastors, and that in such an age, as wherein this authoritie is gainsaid, and accounted Antichristian, generally by all the Churches in the world for ye most part.   Therefore our L. Bb. what sayest thou man, our L. bishopps, (I say) as Iohn of Canterburie, Thomas of Winchester (I will spare Iohn of London for this time, for it may be he is at boules, and it is pitie to trouble my good brother, lest he should sweare too bad) my reuerend prelate of Litchfielde, with the rest of that swinishe rable, are pettie Antichrists, pettie popes, proud prelates, intollerable withstanders of reformation, enemies of the gospell, and most couetous wretched priests.   This is a pretie

M. Marprelate you put more than the question in the conclusion of your syllogisme.

matter, y^t standers by, must be so busie in other mens games : why sawceboxes must you be pratling ? you are as mannerly as bishops, in medling with that you haue nothing to doe, as they do in taking vpon them ciuill offices.   I thinke for any maners either they or you haue, that you were brought up in Bridewell.   But it is well that since you last interrupted me (for now this is the second time) you seeme to haue lernt your *Cato de moribus* in that you keepe your selues on the margent.   Woulde you be answered ?   Then you must know, that I haue set downe nothing but the trueth in the conclusion, and the syllogismes are mine owne,

I may do what I will with them, and thus holde you
content. But what say you my horned masters of the
Confocation house? you denie my minor againe I know.
And thus I prooue it. First

That our Prelates vsurpe their authoritie.

They vsurpe their authoritie, who violently and vnlawfully, retaine those vnder their gouernment, that
both woulde and ought (if they might) to shake of that
yoke wherewith they are kept vnder. But our Lord
bishops retaine such (namely other pastors) and vnlawfully vnder their yoke, who both woulde and ought to
reiect the same. For all the pastors in the land, that
deserue the names of pastors, are against their wil
vnder the bishops iurisdictions. And they are vnlawfully detained by them, because no pastor can be lawfully kept vnder the pastoral (I meane not the ciuill)
authoritie of any one man. Therfore our Bb. and
proud popish, presumptuous, profane, paultrie, pestilent
and pernicious prelates, bishop of Hereforde and
all : are first vsurpers to beginne the matter withall.
Secondly

Our Prelates claime this authoritie ouer those, who by
the ordinance of God, are to be vnder no Pastors.

That is, they claime pastorall authoritie ouer other
ministers and pastors, who by the ordinaunce of God,
are appointed to be pastors and shepheards to feede
others, and not sheep, or such as are to haue shepheards, by whõ they are to be fedd and ouerseene :
whiche authoritie the bishops claime vnto themselues.
For they say that they are pastors of al the pastors

B 4

within their dioces. And take this of M. Marprelates
worde, that there is no pastor of pastors, but he is a
pope. For who but a pope will claime this authoritie..
Thirdly,

This authoritie of our L. Bb. in England, is accounted
Antichristian of the most Churches in the worlde.

As of the Heluetian, the Scottish, French, Bohemian,
and the Churches of the low countries, the Churches of
Polonia, Denmarke, within the dominions of the Count˜
Palatine, of the Churches in Saxonie, and Sweuia, &c.
which you shall see euidently proued in the Harmonie
of the Confessions of all those Churches, Section the
eleuenth. Which Harmonie, was translated and printed,.
by that puritan Cambridg printer, Thomas Thomas.
And although the booke came out by publike authoritie,
yet by your leaue the Bishops haue called them in, as
things against their state. And trust me, his grace will
owe that puritane printer as good a turne, as hee paide
vnto Robert Walde-graue for his sawciness in printing
my frend and deare brother Diotrephes his Dialogue.
Well frend Thomas I warne you before hand, looke to
your selfe.

And now brethren byshops, if you wil not beleeue
me, I wil set down the very words of the French confession, contayned page 359. of the Harmonie. We
beleeue (saith the confession, art 30.) that all true pastors, in what place soeuer they be placed, haue the same,
and equall authority among theselues, giuen vnto them
vnder Iesus Christ the only head, and the chiefe
alone vniuersal bishop: and that therefore it is not

lawfull for anye Churche to challenge vnto it selfe, dominion or soueraignty ouer any other. What an horrible heresie is this, wil some say, why? gentle Martin, is it possible y* these words of the French confession should be true? is it possible that there ought to be an equallity betweene his Grace and the Deane of Sarum, or som other hedge priest: Martin saith it ought be so, why then Martin if it shoulde be so, howe will the byshops satisfie the reader in this poynt? Alas simple fellow whatsoeuer thou art, I perceiue thou dost not mark the words of the confession: My good brethren haue long since taken order for this geare: For the Confession doth not say that all Pastors, but that all true Pastors, and all Pastors that are vnder Iesus Christ, are of equall authority. So that all men see that my brethren, which are neyther true Pastors, nor I feare me vnder Jesus Christ, ar not to be of equall authority. And because this doth not touch them, I will end this whole learned discourse with the words of Pope Gregorie, vnto Iohn bishop of Constantinople (for I haue red somthing in my dayes) which words you shall finde in our owne Englishe Confession, written by a bish. page 361. of the Harmony. The Popes words be these, "He is also the king of pride, he is Lucifer, which preferreth himself before his brethren, he hath forsaken the fayth, and is the forerunner of Antichriste." And haue not I quited my selfe like a man, and dealt very valiantly, in prouing that my lerned brethren the L. bishops ought not to be in any christian

[marginal note:] At a dead lift well fare a good glose.

[marginal note:] Put the case that my Lord of Canterbury is such a one.

common wealth, because they are pettie Popes, and
pettie Antichristes.   But what doe you say, if by this
lustie syllogisme of mine owne making, I proue thē
Popes once more for recreations sake.

Whosoeuer therefore clayme vnto themselues pastorall

Why Mar-
tin, what
meanest
thou? Cer-
tainely an
thou takest
that course
but a while,
thou wilt set
thy good
brethren at
their wits
end.
authoritie ouer those Christians, with whome
they cannot possiblie at any time altogether
in the same congregation sanctifie the Sabboth : they are vsurping prelats, Popes and
pettie Antichrists : For did you euer here of
anye but of Popes and dumb ministers, that
woulde challenge the authority of Pastors
ouer those Christians, vnto whom they could
not possiblie on the Sabboths discharge the dutie of
pastors : But our L. Bb. challenge vnto themselues
pastorall authoritie ouer them, vnto whom they cannot
possiblie on the Sabboth, discharge the duty of Pastors,
vz. ouer people inhabiting diuers shires distant asunder,
with whom, gathered together on the Sabboth, they
cannot by order of nature, performe any dutie of Pastors : Therefore all the L. Bishops in England, Ireland
and Wales (and for the good wil I beare to the reuerende brethren, I will speake as loud as euer I can) All
our L. Bb. I saye, are pettie Popes, and pettie vsurping
Antichristes, and I thinke if they will still continue to
be so, that they will breed yong Popes and Antichristes: *per consequens*, neyther they nor theyr broode,
are to be tollerated in any Christian common wealth,
quoth Martin Marprelate.   There is my judgment of
you brethren, make yᵉ most of it, I hope it will neuer

be worth a byshopricke vnto you : reply when you dare, you shall haue as good as you bring. And if you durst but dispute with my worship in these poynts, I doubt not but you should be sent home by weeping crosse. I wold wish you my venerable masters for all that, to answere my resons, or out of doubt you will prooue pettie Antichristes, Your corner caps and tippets will do nothing in this poynt.

Most pitifully complayneth, Martin Marprelate, vnto your honorable masterships, that certayn theeues, hauing stolne from dyars in Thames streat, as much cloth as came to 30. pound, did hide the sayd cloth in Fulham, which is a place within the territories of the Lord dumbe Iohn, who by occupation is Lord Bish. of London : The theeues were apprehended, the cloth came within your clouches Don Iohn of London, and al is fish that comes to the net with your good honor. The theeues being taken, the dyars came to challenge their cloth : Iohn London the bishop, said it was his owne, because it was taken within his owne Lordship. But sayth he, if the cloth be yours, let the law go vpon the theeues, and then ile talke farther with you : wel, one or two of the theeues were executed, and at their deathes con- fessed that to be the cloth which the bishop had, but the dyars coulde not get their cloth, nor cannot vnto this day, no though one of their honors wrote vnto him to restore the cloth vuto the poore men. What reason were it he should giue thē their own, as though he could not tell how to put it vuto good vses as well as the right owners. It is very good blew, and so would

serue well for the liueries of his men, and it was good
greene, fit to make quishions and couerings for tables.
Brother London, you were best to make restitution, it
is playne theft and horrible oppression: Boner would
haue blusht, to haue bene taken with the like fact.
The popish sort your brethren, will commend this vnto
posteritie by writing assure your selfe.   The dyars
names are Baughin, Swan and Price: They dwell at

My booke the old swan in Thames streat, I warrant you
shall come
with a wit- Martin will be found no lyar, he bringeth in
ness before
the high nothing without testimonie.   And therefore
commission. I haue set downe the mens names and the
places of their aboade, y* you of this conspiration house
may finde out this slaunder of trueth, against the L. of
good London.   It was not therefore for nothing (Iohn
of London I perceiue) that Mistris Lawson the shrew at
Pauls gate, and enemie to all dumb dogs and tyrannicall
Prelates in the land : bad you throw downe your selfe
at hir Maiesties feet, acknowledging your selfe to be
vnsauory salt, and to craue pardon of her highnes, because you had so long deceiued her and her people :
You might well ynough craue pardon for your theft, for
Martin wil stand to it, that the detayning of the mens
cloth is plain theft.

Riddle me a riddle what is that, his grace threatened ·
to send Mistris Lawson to Bridewell, because she shewed
the good father D. Perne, a way how to get his name
out of the booke of Martyrs, where the turnecoat is
canonized for burning Bucers bones : Dame Lawson
aunswered, that she was an honest Citizens wife, a man

well knowen, and therefore bad his Grace an he would, send his uncle Shorie thither. Ha ha ha: Now good your grace you shall haue small gaynes in medling with Margrete Lawson I can tell you. For if she be cited before *Tarquinius Superbus* D. Stanop, she will desire him to deal as fauorablie with her in that cause, as he would with Mistris Blackwell, tse tse tse, wil it neuer be better with you mistris Lawson.

Sohow, brother Bridges, when wil you answere the booke intituled, an answere to Bridges his slanders: nay I thinke you had more need to gather a beneuolence among the Cleargie, to pay Cbarde toward the printing of your booke, or els labour to his grace to get him another protection, for men wil giue no mony for your book, vnles it be to stop mustard pots, as your brother Cosins answer to the Abstract did. You haue bin a worthy writer as they say of a long time, your first book was a proper Enterlude, called Gammar Gurtons needle. But I thinke that this trifle, which sheweth the author to haue had some witte and inuention in him, was none of your doing: Because your bookes seeme to proceede from the braynes of a woodcocke, as hauing neyther wit nor learning. Secondly, you haue to your mediocritie written against the Papists: And since that time, you haue written a sheete in rime, of all the names attributed vnto the Lorde in the Bible, a worthy monument: what hath the hedge priest my brother written anye more? O is, I crye him mercy, he hath written this great volume which now I haue in hand against his brethren. The qualities of this booke are many, M. D.

sheweth himselfe to be very skilfull in the learning of
ob and *Sol*, if euer you red olde Fa-Briccot upon
Aristotle: M. Deanes manner of writing and his, are
not much vnlike, Doctor Terence of Oxforde and this
Doctor, may be neere of kindred for their learning.
There bee periods in this learned booke of great reason,
though altogether without sence.   I will giue you a
proof or two, page 441.   "And although" (sayth the
Doctor) "Paul afterward, 1 Cor. 1. 14. mentioning this
Sosthenes, Crispus, term him not there, the archgouer-
and not
Crispus was nour of the Iewes Synagogue, yet as it farther
one of the
72. Disci- appeareth, Acts 18. 17. by Sosthenes, who
ples. was long before a faythfull Christian, and as
some alledge out of Eusebius lib. 1. cap. 13. he was
also one of the 72. Disciples chosen by Christ."

Fleering, ieering, leering : there is at all no sence in
this period.   For the words (yet afterward) vuto the
ende, M. D. minde was so set vpon a byshopricke, that
he brought nothing concerning Crispus to aunswere the
word (yet) Therefore I will helpe my reuerende brother
to make the sentence in this sort.   And although, &c.
yet afterwarde my learned brother, D. Yong, Bish. of
Rochester, hauing the presentation of a benefice in his
hand, presented himselfe thereunto, euen of meere good-
wil.   I Iohn of Rochester, present Iohn Young quoth
the bishop.   Nowe iudge you good readers, whether
Martin sayth not true, that there is too much cousenage
now a dayes among the cleargie men.

This sentence following of M. Deanes, hath as good
sence as the former, page 655.   The D. citeth these

wordes out of the learned Discourse. " God graunt that in steede of ordinarye formes of prayers, wee may haue preaching in all places." And in steede of Amen, God forbidd saye I, quoth the Doctor, with another prayer to the contrarye, (nowe marke my masters, whether you can finde anye sence in this contrarye prayer, for I assure you reuerende Martin can find none) " if it be his good will not so much (good lord) to pun- These be the nish vs, that this our brethrens prayer should D. owne be graunted." If this be a senceles kind of words. writing, I would there were neuer a Lord bishop in England.

And lerned brother Bridges, a man might almost run himselfe out of breath before he could come to a full point in many places in your booke, page 69. line 3. speaking of the extraordinarye giftes in the Apostles time, you haue this sweete learning. " Yea some of them haue for a great part of the time, continued euen till our times, and yet continue, as the operation of great workes, or if they meane miracles, which were not ordinary no not in that extraordinary time, and as the hipocrites had them, so might and had diuers of the papists, and yet their cause neuer the better, and the like may we say of the gift of speking with tongs, who who! which haue not bin with studie before learned, Dean take breath and as Anthonie, &c. and diuers also among the then to it ancient fathers, and some among the papists, againe. and some among vs, haue not bene destitute of the giftes of prophesying, and much more may I saye this of the gift of healing, for none of those giftes or graces

giuen then or since, or yet to men infer the grace of
Gods election to be of necessitie to saluation."

Here is a good matter deliuered in as good Grama-
ticall words : But what say you if M. Do. can prooue
that Peter was prince of the Apostles ?   That is popery
Both these
poynts are
set down
page 448.
line 3.(quoth Martin) to begin withal.   Nay but
what say you if he proueth that one priest
among the residue, may haue a lawfull superiour authoritie ouer the vniuersall bodye of
the Church, is not this plaine treason?   Is forsooth, if a
puritane had written it : But Mas Deane of Sarum that
wrote these things, is a man that fauoreth bishops, a
nonresident, one that will not sticke to play a game at
Cards, and sweare by his trothe : and therefore he may
write against the puritans what he will, his grace of
Canterbury will giue a verye Catholike exposition thereof.   This geare maynteineth the crowne of Canterbury,
and what matter is it though hee write for the mainte-
naunce thereof, all the treason in the world.   It wil
neuer come vuto hir Maiesties care, as my friend Tertullus in the poore Dialogue that the bishops lately
burned hath set downe.   His grace is able to salue the
matter well inough: yea my brother Bridges himselfe
can aunswere this poynt.   For hee hath written otherwise, page 288. line 26. in these wordes : " Neither is
all gouernment taken away from all, though a moderate
superior gouernment be giuen of all to some, and not
yet of all in all the Churche to one, but to one ouer
some in seuerall and particular Churches."   The Deane
wil say, that concerning the superioritie of bishops this

is the meaning. As concerning the treason, written page 448. it may be the foxe D. Perne, who helped him as they say, to make this worthy volume, was the author of it.

Now brethren, if any of you that are of the Confocation house, would knowe howe I can prooue M. Deane to haue written flatt treason, page 448. as I haue before set downe : draw neere, and with your patience I will proue it so, that M. Deane will stand to his owne words, which I care not if they be sett downe: page 448. line 3. Thus you shall read, " Doth S. Peter then forbid that any one Elder should haue and exercise any superior gouernment ouer the cleargie," vnderstanding the cleargie in this sence, " if he doth not but alloweth it, and his selfe practized it: thē howsoeuer both the *I commend thee yet good D. for thy good English tongue.* name, both of gouerning and cleargy may be abused, the matter is cleare, that one priest or elder among the residue, may haue a superior authority ouer the cleargie, that is, ouer all the vniuersall bodie of the church, in euery parti- *Cleare quoth he, yea who will make any question thereof.* cular or seuerall congregation, and so not only ouer the people, but also ouer the whol order of ministers."

Would your worships knowe howe I can shew and conuince my brother Bridges, to haue set downe flat treason in the former words, Then haue at you Deane. ·
1. It is treason to affirme her Maiestie to be *Looke Stat. 13. Elizabeth.* an infidell or not to be contayned in the bodie of the Church. 2. It is treason to saye that one priest or elder, may haue a lawfull superiour

authoritie ouer hir Maiestie. Take your spectacles then, and spell your owne words, and you shall finde that you haue affirmed eyther of these 2. poynts. For you affirme that a priest may haue a lawfull superior authoritie ouer the vniuersall bodie of the Churche. And you dare not denie her Maiestie to bee contayned within the vniversall bodie of the Church. Therefore to helpe you to spell your conclusion, you haue written treason, if you will be as good as your writing : your learned frend Martin (for no brother M. Deane if you be a traytor) would not mistake you, and therefore say what you can for your selfe : you meane not that this priest shalbe ouer all the church : do you? but howe shall we knowe that? forsooth because you saye that this superioritie must be in euery particular or seuerall congregation. Is this your aunswere brother Iohn? why what sence is there in these words? One priest may haue a superior authoritie ouer the vniuersall body of the Church, in euery particular or seuerall congregation? The vniuersal bodie of the Church, is now become a particular or seuerall congregation with you? And in good earnest Deane Iohn, tell me howe many orders of ministers be there in a particular cōgregation? For there must bee orders of ministers in the congregation, where you meane this bounsing priest should haue his superioritie, and because this cannot be in seuerall and particular congregations : therefore you cannot meane by these words, ouer the vniuersall bodye of the Church, any other thing, then the whole Church militant : But you would mende your answere? And say that this superior priest must be an Englishe priest and no forrainer : As for ilsample, his grace of Canterbury is an English priest. Do you

A good il-sample.

meane then, that his grace should be this superior priest, who by Sir Peters allowaunce may haue a lawfull superior authoritie ouer the vniuersall bodie of the Churche ? Truely I doe not

Sir Peter neuer alow-ed this.

meane so. And good now, do not abuse his graces worship in this sort, by making him a Pope. Be it you meane this hie priest should be no stranger, yet your treason is as great or greater. For you will haue her Maiesty tò be subiect vnto her owne subiect and seruant. And if it be treason to say that the Pope, who hath princes and Cardinalls for his seruants, being far better than were Iohn with his Canterburinesse, may haue a lawfull superior authoritie ouer her Maiesty, as one being contained with in the vniuersall bodie of the Church : is it not much more trayterous to say, that an Englishe vassall may haue this authoritie ouer his Soueraigne. And brother Iohn, did Sir Peter his selfe in deede practize this authoritie ? whie what a priest was he? Did he alow others to haue this authority. Truly this is more then euer I knew til now. Yet notwithstanding, I thinke he neuer wore corner cap and tippet in all his

Here be those that can be bar-barous as well as masse Deane.

life, nor yet euer subscribed to my Lord of Canterbury his articles : Now the question is, whom Sir Peter his selfe nowe alloweth to be this bouncing priest? the Pope of Rome yea or no ? No in no càse, for that is against the statute. For will my brother Bridges saye that the

Pope may haue a lawfull superior authoritie ouer his Grace of Canterbury? Ile neuer beleeue him though he saye so. Neyther will I saye that his Grace is an Infidell, (nor yet sweare that he is much bet-ter) and therefore M. Deane meaneth not that the Pope shoulde bee this highe Priest. No brother Martin (quoth M. Deane) you saye true, I meane not that the Pope is this priest of Sir Peter. And I haue many reasons why I shoulde denie him this authoritie. First he is a massemonger, that is, a professed idolater. 2. He weareth a triple crowne, so doth not my Lorde of Canterbury. 3. He hath his seat in Romish Babylon in Rome within Italie : you know ye nomber 666. in the Reuelation signifieth *La-tenios*, that is, the man of Rome, or *Ecclesia Italike*, the Italian church. Lastly, he must haue men to kisse his toes, and must be carried vpon mens shulders, and must haue princes and kings to attend vpon him, which shew-eth his horrible pride. Sir Peters vniuersall priest and mine, shalbe no such priest I trow, ka Mas Doctor. No shall not Doctor Iohn, I con thee thank. Then thy vniuersall priest, 1. must be no idolator, 2. must be no proude priest, and haue neuer a triple crowne (and yet I hope he may weare as braue a sattin gowne as my Lord of Winchester weareth, and be as cholericke as he) 3. he must haue his seat out of Italie, as for fashion sake, at *Lambehith Hippo*, &c. but at Rome in no case. If I should examine these properties, I thinke some of them, if not all, haue bene accidents vnto English priests. For how many Bb. are there in England, which haue

His grace shall neuer get me to sweare against my conscience.

not either said masse, or helped the priest to say masse
or bene present at it? As for the triple crowne, Pope
Ioan the English harlot hath woon it: So did Vrbane
the 5. an English man. And concerning pride, I hope
that our Bb. howe liuing, haue to their mediocritie taken
order, that some Popes may be inferior vnto them, as
for ilsample, his Canterburinesse, &c. And I cannot
see how the planting of the chaire in Rome anye more
then Canterbury, can make a Pope. Seeing that Cle-
ment the 5. Iohn 22. Benedict 12. and all other Popes,
from the yeare 1306. vuto 1375. sate not in Rome, but
for the most part at Avinion in Fraunce. But notwithstanding all this, out of your meaning masse D. such a
simple ingram man as I am, in these poynts, of vniuersall superior priests, I finde three differences betweene my L. of Peterborough, or any other our high
priests in England, and the Popes holines: and 3. impe-
diments to hinder the Pope from being Sir Peters high
priest and yours, vz. his idolatrie, 2. his triple crowne,
3. his seat at Rome. But if Hildebrande Pope of
Rome, had beene a professor of the trueth (as his grace
Doctor turnecoats (Perne I shoulde saye) scholler is)
had worne no triple crowne, had bene Archbishop of
Canterbury (and I think we haue had Hildebrands there
ere nowe) then he might by the iudgement of the learned
Bridges, and the allowance of that Peter, which his
selfe practized that authoritie, haue a lawful superior
authority ouer the vniuersal bodie of the Church. And
what a worthy Canterbury Pope had this bin, to be
called my Lords grease? Thus you see Brother Bridges,

M. Marprelate an please him, is able to make a yonger
brother of you : he hath before proued, that if euer you
be Archb. of Canterbury (for you wrote this foule
heape against the holy Discipline of Christ, (as Whitgift
did the like) in hope to bee the next Pope of Lambeth)
that then you shalbe a pettie Pope, and a pettie Antichrist : Nay he hath prooued you to haue deserued a
cawdell of Hempseed, and a playster of neckweed, as
weel as some of your brethren the papists.   And now
brother Bridges once again, is it good writing against
the Puritans.   Take me at my word, vnlesse you answere the former poynt of Antichristianisme, and this of
treason, I will neuer write again to my bre[thren] the
Bb. but as to vsurpers and Antichristes, and I shall
take you for no better then an enemie to her Maiesties
Supremacie.   And because you haue taken vppon you
to defend L. Bb. though you be as very a sot as euer
liued, (outcept dumb Iohn of London againe) yet you
shall answere my reasons, or else I will so course you,
as you were neuer coursed since you were a Symonical
Deane, you shall not deale with my worshipp, as Iohn
with his Canterburinesse did with Thomas Cartwright,
whiche Iohn, left the cause you defend in the plaine
field, and for shame threw downe his weapons with a
desperate purpose to runne away, and leaue the cause,
as he like a coward hath done : For this dozen yeares
we neuer saw any thing of his in printe for the defence
of his cause, and poore M. Cartwright doth content himselfe with the victorie, which the other will not (though
in deed he hath by his silence) seeme to grant.   But

I will not be this vsed at your hands, for vnlesse you
answere me, or confesse (and that in print) Ha, prieste
that all L. Bb. in England, Wales, Ireland, ile bang you,
or else neuer
yea and Scotlande to, are pettie popes, and trust me.
plaine vsurpers, and pettie Antichristes : Ile kindle such
a fire in the holes of these foxes, as shall neuer be
quenched as long as there is a L. B. in England. And
who but the worthie Martin can doe so valiantly. Page
560. master Deane bringeth in Aretius, to proue that
kneeling at the communion is not offensiue. And how
is the argument concluded think you? for sooth euen
thus. Aretius saith, that in Berne they receiue the com-
muniō sitting or standing : therefore saith my brother
Bridges, kneeling at the communion is not vnlawfull.
I maruell whether he was not hatched in a goose nest,
that would thus conclude.

In another place, page 226. or thereabouts, he prooueth
that one man may haue two spirituall liuings, My brother
because the puritans themselues saye, that one Bridges
nowe rea-
charge may haue two ministers, to wit, a soneth in
good earnest
Pastor and a Doctor. And these be some of for nonresi-
the good profes whereby our established go- dents.
uernment is vphelde.

It would make a man laugh, to see how many trickes
the Doctor hath to coosen the sielie puritans in his book,
he can now and then without any noyse, What a craf-
alleadge an author clean against himselfe, tie knaue is
masse
and I warrant you, wipe his mouth cleanly, Deane.
and looke another way, as though it had not bene he.
I haue laught as though I had bene tickled, to see with

what sleight he can throw in a popish reason, and who
sawe him? And with what art, he can conuaye himselfe from the question, and goe to another matter? it is
wonderfull to thinke. But what would not a Deane do
to get a bishoppricke? In this one poynt, for sparing
labour he is to bee admired, that he hath set downe
vnder his owne name, those things which (to speak as I
think) he neuer wrote himselfe. So let the puritans
aunswere when they will, he hath so much of other
mens helpes, and such contrarieties in this book, that
when they bring one thing against him out of his owne
writings, he wil bring another place out of the sayd
booke, flat contrary to that, and say that the latter is
his, and not the former. For the former, it may bee,
was some other friends, not so fullie seen in the cause,
as presbyter Iohn Bridges was. The reason of these
contrarieties was uery expedient: because many had a
hand in the worke, euery man wrote his own minde,
and masse doctor ioyned the whole together.

Nowe forasmuch as he hath playd the worthy workeman, I will bestow an Epitaph vpon his graue when he
dyeth, which is thus :

" Here lies Iohn Bridges, a worthie Presbyter he
was."

But what if he be a B. before he die? what brethren? doe you not thinke that I haue two strings to
my bow, is vs haue I, and thus I sing, if he chance to
be a bishop.

" Here lies Iohn Bridges late Bishop, friend to the
Papa."

I care not an I now leaue masse Deanes worship, and be eloquent once in my dayes : yet brother Bridges, a worde or two more with you, ere we depart, I praye you where may a mā buie such another gelding, and borow such another hundred poundes, as you bestowed vpon your good patron Sir Edward Horsey, for his good worde in helping you to your Deanry : go to, go to, I perceiue you will prooue a goose. Deale closeliar for shame the next time : must I needs come to the knoledge of these things ? What if I should report abroad, that cleargie men come vnto their promotions by Simonie ? haue not you giuen me iuste cause ? I thinke Simonie be the bishops lacky. Tarleton tooke him not long since in Don Iohn of Londons cellor.

Well nowe to mine eloquence, for I can doe it I tell you. Who made the porter of his gate a dumb minister ? Dumbe Iohn of London. Who abuseth her Maiesties subiects, in vrging them to subscribe contrary to lawe ? Iohn of London. Who abuseth the high commission, as much as any ? Iohn London, (and D. Stanop to) Whoe bound an Essex minister, in 200.1. to weare the surplice on Easter day last? Iohn London. Who hath cut downe the Elmes at Fulham ? Iohn London. Who is a carnall defender of the breache of the Sabboth in all the places of his abode ? Iohn London. *Ile make you weary of it dumbe John, except you leaue persecuting.* Who forbiddeth men to humble themselues in fasting and prayer before the Lorde, and then can say vnto the preachers, now you were best to tell the people, that we forbidd fastes? Iohn London. Who goeth to bowles

vpon the Sabboth ?   Dumbe dunsticall Iohn of good
London, hath done all this.   I will for this time leaue
this figure, and tell your venerable masterdomes a tale
worth the hearing : I had it at the second hand : if he
that tolde it me, added any thing, I do not commende
him, but I forgiue him : The matter is this.   A man
dying in Fulham, made one of the bishopp of Londons
men his executor.   The man had bequeathed certaine
Legacies vnto a poore shephearde in the towne.   The
shepheard could get nothing of the bishops man, and
therefore made his mone vuto a gentleman of Fulham,
that belongeth to the court of requests.   The gentlemans
name is M. Madox.   The poore mans case came to bee
tryed in the court of Requestes.   The B. man desired
his masters helpe : Dumb Iohn wrote to the Masters
of requests to this effect, and I think these were his
wordes.

"My masters of the requests, the bearer hereof being
my man, hath a cause before you : in as much as I
vnderstande howe the matter standeth, I praye you let
my man be discharged the court, and I will see an
agreement made.   Fare you well."   The letter came to
M. D. Dale, he answered it in this sort.

"My Lorde of London, this man deliuered your letter, I pray you giue him his dinner on Christmas day
for his labour, and fare you well."

Dumbe Iohn not speeding this way, sent for the sayd
M. Madox : he came, some rough words passed on both
sides, Presbyter Iohn sayde, master Madox was verye
sawcie, especially seeing he knew before whom he spake :

namely, the Lord of Fulham. Wherevnto the gentleman answered, that he had bene a pore freeholder in
Fulham, before Don Iohn came to be L. there, hoping
also to be so, when he and all his brood (my Ladle his
daughter and all) shoulde be gone. At the hearing of
this speeche, the waspe got my brother by the nose,
which mad him in his rage to affirme, that he woulde
be L. of Fulham as long as he liued, in despight of all
England. Naye softe there, quoth M. Madox, except
her Maiestie I pray you, that is my meaning, ka dumb
Iohn, and I tell thee Madox, that thou art but a Iacke
to vse me so : master Madoxe replying, sayd that in
deed his name was Iohn, and if euery Iohn were a Iacke,
he was content to bee a Iacke (there he hit my L. ouer
the thumbs)   The B. growing in choller, sayd y^t master
Madox his name did shewe what he was, for sayth he,
thy name is mad Oxe, which declareth thee to be an
vnruly and mad beast.   M. Madox answered againe,
that the B. name, if it were descanted vpon, did most
significantly shew his qualities.   For said he, you are
called Elmar, but you may be better called marelme,
for you haue marred all the Elmes in Fulham : hauing
cut them all downe.   This farre is my worthy story, as
worthye to bee printed, as any part of Deane Iohns
booke, I am sure.

Item, may it please you that are L. Bb. to shewe
your brother Martin, how you can escape the danger of
a premunire, seeinge you vrge her Maiesties subiects to
subscribe, cleane contrary to the Statute 13. Elizabeth.
What haue you to shew for your selues, for I tell you,

I heard some say, that for vrging subscription, you were all within the premunire, insomuch that you haue bene driuen closely to buie your pardons, you haue forfayted all that you haue vnto her Maiestie, and your persons are voyde of her Maiesties protection : you knowe the danger of a premunire, I trowe ? Well but tell me what you haue to shewe for your selues ? her Maiesties pre-rogatiue ? haue you ? Then I hope you haue it vnder seale. No I warrant you, her Maiesty is too wise for that. For it shall neuer be sayde, that she euer author-ized such vngodly proceedings, to the dishonor of God, and the wounding of the consciences of her best subiects. Seeing you haue nothing to shew that it is her Maiesties will, why should any man subscribe contrary to statute ? Forsooth mē must beleue such honest creatures as you are on your words ? must they ? As though you would not lye : yes, yes, bishops will lye' like dogs. They were neuer yet well beaten for their lying.

May it please your honorable worships, to let worthy Martin vnderstand, why your Canterburinesse and the rest of the L. Bb. fauor papists and recusants, rather thē puritans. For if a puritane preacher, hauing a recusant in his parrish, and shall go about to deale with the recu-sant for not comming to Church. Sir will the recusant say, you and I will answere the matter before his grace, (or other the high commissioners, as L. Bb. Seeuillaines (I meane) popish doctors of the bawdie courts.) And assoone as the matter is made knowne vnto my Lorde, the preacher is sure to go by the worst, and the recusant to carie all the honestie : Yea the preacher shalbe a busie enuious fellow, one that doth not obserue the booke, and conforme himself according vnto order, and perhaps go home by beggers bush, for any benefice he hath to liue vpon. For it may be the Bb. will be so good vnto him, as to depriue him for not subscribing. As for the recusant, he is known to be a man that must haue the libertie of his conscience. Is this good dealing brethren. And is it good dealing, that poore men should be so troubled to the chaunccellors courte, that they are euen wearie of their liues, for such horrible oppression as there raignes. I tell you D. Stannop (for all you are so proude) a premunire will take you by the backe one day, for oppressing and tyrannizing ouer her Maiesties subiects as you doe.

Doth your grace remember, what the Iesuit at New-gate sayde of you, namely, that my Lorde of Canterbury should surely be a Cardinall, if euer poperie did come againe into England: (yea and that a braue Cardinall to) what a knaue was this Iesuit? beleeue me I would not say thus much of my Lord of Canterburie, for a thou-sand pound, lest a *Scandalum magnatum* should be had against me: But well fare him that sayd thought is free.

Pitifully complayning, is there any reason, (my Lords grace) why knaue Thackwell the printer, which printed popishe and trayterous welshe bookes in Wales, shoulde haue more fauour at your gracelesse handes, then poore Walde-graue, who neuer printed book against you, that contayneth eyther treason or impietie. Thackwell is at libertie to walke where he will, and permitted to make

the most he could of his presse and letters: whereas
Robert Walde-graue dares not shew his face for the
blood-thirstie desire you haue for his life, onely for
printing of bookes which toucheth the bishops Myters.
You know that Walde-graues printing presse and Letters were takken away: his presse being timber, was
sawen and hewed in pieces, the yron work battered and
made vnseruiceable, his Letters melted, with cases and
other tooles defaced (by Iohn Woolfe, alias Machiuill,
Beadle of the Stacioners, and most tormenting execu-
tioner of Walde-graues goods) and he himselfe vtterly
depriued for euer printing againe, hauing a wife and sixe
small children.   Will this monstrous crueltie neuer be
reuenged thinke you?   When Walde-graues goods was
to be spoiled and defaced, there were some printers,
that rather then all the goods should be spoyled, offered
money for it, towardes the reliefe of the mans wife and
children, but this coulde not be obtayned, and yet
popishe Thackwell, though hee printed popish and trayterous bookes, may haue the fauor to make money of
his presse and letters. And reason to. For Walde-
graues profession ouerthroweth the popedome of Lambehith, but Thackwels popery maintayneth the same.
And now that Walde-graue hath neither presse nor letters, his grace may dine and sup the quieter.   But
looke to it brother Canterburie, certainly without your
A fyrebrand repentance, I feare me, you shalbe * Hilde-
in deede.   brand in deed.   Walde-graue hath left house
and home, by reason of your vnnaturall tyrannie: hauing
left behinde him a poore wife and sixe Orphanes, with-

out any thing to relieue them. (For the husband, you haue bereaued both of his trade and goods) Be you assured that the crie of these will one day preuaile against you, vnlesse you desist from persecuting. And good your grace, I do now remember my selfe More knau-
of another printer, that had presse and letter ery.
in a place called Charterhouse in London (in Anno 1587: neere about the time of the Scottish Queenes death) inteligence was giuen vnto your good grace of the same, by some of the Stacioners of London, it was made knowen vnto you what worke was in hand, what letter the booke was on, what volume, vz. in 8o. in halfe sheetes, what workemen wrohgt on the same : namely, I. C. the Earle of Arundels man and three of his seruants, with their seuerall names, what liberallitie was bestowed on those workemen, and by whom, &c. Your grace gaue the Stacioners the hearing of this matter, but to this daye the parties were neuer calde in Coram for it : but yet by your leaue my Lord, vpon this inform- ation vnto your honorable worship, the sta- Is not he a
cioners had newes, that it was made knowne very Pope in deed that
vuto the printers, what was done vnto your thus hideth poperie and
good grace, and presently in steed of the work knauery.
which was in hand, there was other appointed, as they saye, authorized by your Lordship. I will not saye it was your owne doing, but by your sleeue, It may be
thought is free. And my good L. (nay you you hindred her Maiestie
shalbe none of my L. but M. Whitgift and of many thou'sands of
you will) are you partiall or no in all your pounds.
actions tell me ? yes you are ? I wil stand to it ? did

c 4

you get a decree in the high court of Starchamber onely
for Walde-graue? if it bee in generall (and you not
partiall) why fet you not that printing presse and letters
out of Charterhouse, and destroye them as you did
Walde-graues? Why did you not apprehend the parties,
why? Because it was poperie at the least, that was
printed in Charterhouse : and that maintayneth the
crowne of Canterburye? And what is more tollerable
than popery? Did not your grace of late erecte a new
printer contrary to the foresayd decree? One Thomas
Orwine (who sometimes wrought popish bookes in corners : namely Iesus Psalter, our Ladies Psalter, &c.)
with condition he should print no such seditious bookes
as Walde-graue hath done? Why my Lord?
Walde-graue neuer printed any thing against

This is no
knauery my
Lord.

the state, but onely against the vsurped state
of your Paultripolitanship, and your pope holy brethren,
the Lorde B. and your Antichristian swinish rable, being
intollerable withstanders of reformation, enemies of the
Gospell, and most couetous wretched, and popish
priests.

Nowe most pitifully complayning, Martin Marprelate :
That the papistes will needs make vs beleeue, that our
good Iohn of Canterbury and they, are at no great iarre
in religion. For Reignolds the papist at Rheimes, in
his booke against M. Whitakers, cōmendeth the works
written by his grace, for the defence of the corruption
in our Churche, against T. Cartwright. And sayth that
the said Iohn Cant. hath many things in him, which
euidently shew a catholike perswasion. Alas my mas-

ters shall we loose our metropolitan in this sort. Yet
the note is a good note, that we may take heed the
Spaniards steale him not away, it were not amisse if
her Maiestie knew of it. Wee need not fear (if we can
keep him) the Spaniards and our other popish enemies,
because our metropolitans religion and theirs differ not
much. In the article of Christes descending into hell,
they iumpe in one right pat: and in the mayntenaunce of
the hierarchie of Bb. and ascribing the name of priest,
vnto them that are ministers of the gospel. I know not
whether my next tale will be acceptable vnto his grace or
not. But haue it among you my masters : M. Wiggington the pastor of Sidborough, is a man not altogether
unknowen vuto you. And I think his worshipfull grace
got little or nothing by medling with him, although he
hath depriued him. My tale is of his depriuation, which
was after this sort. The good quiet people of Syd-
borough, being troubled for certaine yeares with the
sayde Wiggington, and many of them being infected by
him with the true knowledge of the gospell, by the
worde preached (which is an heresie, that his grace
doth mortally abhorre and persecute) at length grew in
disliking with their pastor, because the seuere man did
vrge nothing but obedience vuto the gospell. Well,
they came to his grace to finde a remedie hereof:
desiring him that Wiggington might be depriued. His
grace could find no law to depriue him, no although the
pastor defied the Archb. to his face, and would giue
him no better title then Iohn Whitgift, such buggs
words, being in these daies accounted no lesse then high

treason against a Paltripolitan: Though since that time,
I think his grace hath bin well enured to beare the
name of Pope of Lambeth, Iohn Cant. the prelate of
Lambeth, with diuers other titles agreeable to his function.   Well Sidborogh men proceeded against their
pastor, his grace woulde not depriue him, because he
coulde finde no law to warrant him therein, and he will
do little contrary to law, for fear of a premunire, vnles
it be at a dead lift, to depriue a puritan preacher.
Then in deed he will do against lawe, against God, and
against his owne conscience, rather then that heresie of
preaching should preuail.   One man of Sidborough,
whose name is Atkinson, was very eger among the rest,
to haue his pastor depriued: and because his grace
woulde not heare them but departed away, this Atkinson desired his grace to resolue him and his neighbours
of one poynt which something troubled them : and that
was, whether his grace or Wiggington were of the deuill.
For quoth he, you are so contrary the one from the
other, that both of you cannot possibly be of God.   If
he be of God, it is certaine you are of the deuill, and so
cannot long stand: for he will be your ouerthrowe.
Amen.   If you are of God, then he is of the diuell as
wee thinke him to be, and so he being of the deuill,
will not you depriue him? why shoulde you suffer such
a one to trouble the Church.   Now if he be of God,
why is your course so contrary to his? and rather, why
do not you follow him, that we may do so to?   Truely,
if you do not depriue him, we will thinke him to be of
God, and go home with him, with gentler good will

towardes him, then we came hyther with hatred, and
looke you for a fall. His grace hearing this northen
logicke, was mooued on the sodaine you must thinke,
promised to depriue Wiggington, and so he did. This
Atkinson this winter 1587. came vp to London, being
as it seemed afflicted in conscience for this fact, desired
Wiggington to pardone him and offred to kneele before
her Maiestie, that Wiggington might bee restored againe
to his place, and to stande to the trueth hereof, to his
graces teeth. The man is yet aliue, he may be sent
for, if you thinke that M. Martin hath reported an vntrueth. No I warrant you, you shall not take mee to
haue fraught my booke with lyes and slaunders, as Iohn
Whitgift, and the Deane of Sarum did theirs. I speak
not of things by heresay as of reports, but I bring my
witnesses to prooue my matters.

May it please you to yeeld vnto a suite that I haue
to your worships. I pray you send Wiggington home
vnto his charge againe, I can tell you it was a foule
ouersight in his grace, to send for him out of the North
to London, that he might outface him at his owne doore.
He woulde do his Canterburines lesse hurt if he were at
his charge, then now he doth. Let the Templars haue
M. Trauers their preacher restored againe vuto them,
hee is nowe at leysure to worke your priesthood a woe
I hope. If suche another booke as the Ecclesiast. Discipline was, drop out of his budget, it were as good for
the Bb. to lie a day and a night in little ease in the
Counter. He is an od fellowe in folowing an argument,
and you know he hath a smooth tong, either in Latine

or English.   And if my L. of Winchester vnderstood,
eyther Greeke or Hebrew, as they say he hath no great
skill in neyther : I woulde pray your priesdomes to tell
me which is the better scholler, Walter Trauers, · or
Thomas Cooper.   Will you not send M. Wyborne to
Northampton, that he may see some fruits of the seed
he sowed there 16. or 18. yeares ago.   That old man
Wiborne, hath more good learning in him, and more fit
gifts for the ministery in his little toe, then many braces
of our Lord Bb.   Restore him to preaching againe for
Except per-
secuting
Greene-
fielde. shame.   M. Paget shalbe welcome to Deuon-
shire, he is more fit to teach men then boyes.
I marueile with what face a man that had
done so much good in the Churche as he did among a
rude people, could be depriued.

Briefely, may it please you to let the Gospell haue a
free course, and restore vnto their former libertie in
preaching, all the preachers that you haue put to silence :
and this far is my first suit.

My 2. suit is a most earnest request vnto you, that
are the hinderers of the publishing of the confutation of
the Rhemish Testament by M. Cartwright, may be
published.   A resonable request, the granting whereof,
I dare assure you, would be most acceptable vnto all
that feare God, and newes of wofull sequell vnto the
papists.   For shall I tell you what I heard once, from
the mouth of a man of great learning and deepe iudgement, who sawe some part of Master Cartwrights answere to the sayde Rhemish and trayterous Raffodie ?
His iudgment was this.   That M. Cartwright had dealt

so soundly against the papists, that for the answering and confuting of the aduersary, that one worke woulde be sufficient alone. He farther added, that y⁰ aduersary was confuted by strange and vnknown reasons, that would set them at their wits end, when they see them-selues assayled with such weapons, whereof they neuer once drempt, that they should be stroken at. And wil your grace or any els, that are the hinderers of the publishing of this worke, still bereaue the Church of so worthy a Iewell: nay, so strong an armour against the enemie. If you deny me this request, I will not threaten you, but my brother Bridges, and Iohn Whitgiftes bookes shall smoke for this geare, ile haue my peni-worths of them for it.

Now may it please you to examine my worthines your brother Martin, and see whether I saide not true in the storie of Gyles Wiggington, where I haue set downe, yᵗ the preaching of the word is an heresie, which his grace doth mortally abhorre and persecute, I can prooue it without doubt. And first that he persecuteth the preaching of the worde (whether it be an heresie or not) both in the preacher and the hearer : the articles of subscription, the silencing of so many learned and worthy preachers do euidently shew, and if you doubt hereof, let my worshipp vnderstand thereof, and in my next treatize, I shal prooue the matter to be cleare with a witnes, and I hope to your smal commendations, that will deny such a cleare point. On the other side, that he accounteth preaching to be an heresie, I am now to insist on the proofe of that poynt. But first you must know, that he did not account simple preaching to be an heresie, but to holde that preaching is the onely ordinary meanes to saluation, this he accounteth as an beresie, this he mortally condemned.   The case thus stoode, Iohn Penrie the welsheman (I thinke his grace and my brother Lon. don, would be better acquain[ted] with him and they could tell howe) about the beginning of Lent, 1587. offered a supplication and a booke to the Parliament, entreating that some order might be taken, for calling his countrie vnto the knowledge of God.   For his holde attempt, he was called before his grace with others of the high commission, as Thomas of Winchester, Iohn London, &c.   After that his grace had eased his sto- macke in calling him boy, knaue, varlet, slanderer, libeller, lewde boy, lewd slaunderer, &c. (this is true, for I haue seene the notes of their conference) at the length a poynt of his booke began to be examined, where nonresidents are thought intollerable.   Here the Lorde of good London asked M. Penrie, what he could say against that kinde of cattell, aunswere was made that they were odious in the sight of God and man, because as much as in them lie, they bereaue the people ouer whom they thrust themselues, of the ordinarie meanes of saluation, which was the word preached.   Iohn Lon- don demaunded whether preaching was the onely meanes to saluation ?   Penrie answered, that it was the onely ordinarie meanes, although the Lorde was not so tyed vnto it, but that hee could extraordinarily vse other meanes.   That preaching was the onely ordinary meanes, he confirmed it by those places of scripture, Rom. 10.

14. 1 Cor. 1. 21. Ephes. 1. 13. This point being a
long time canuassed, at the lēgth his worship of Winchester rose vp, and mildly after his manner, brast forth
into these words. I assure you my Lords, it is an exe-
crable heresie: An heresie (quoth Iohn Penry) I thanke
God that euer I knewe that heresie: It is such an
heresie, that I will by the grace of God, sooner leaue
my life then I will leaue it. What sir, (quoth the
Archb.) I tell thee it is an heresie, and thou shalt
recant it as an heresie? Naye (quoth Penrie) neuer so
long as I liue godwilling. I will leaue this storie for
shame, I am weary to hear your grace so absurd. What
say you to this geare my masters of the confocation
house? we shal haue shortly a good religion in England
among the bishops? if Paule be sayd of them to write
an heresie. I haue hard some say, that his grace will
speake against his own conscience? It is true. The
proofe whereof shalbe his dealing with another welshman, one M. Euans. An honorable personage, Ambrose
Dudley, nowe Earle of Warwicke (and long may he be
so, to the glorie of God, the good of his Church, and
the comfort of al his) in the singular loue he bare to the
town of Warwick, would haue placed M. Euans there.
To the ende that master Euans might be receiued with a
fauorable subscription, &c. he offered the subscription
which the Stat. requireth (wherevnto men may subscribe
with a good conscience): The earl sent him with his
letter, to his gracelesnes of Cant. thinking to obtaine so
smal a curtesy at his hands. And I am sure, if he be
Ambrose Dudley, the noble Earle of Warwicke (whose

famous exploytes, both in peace and war, this whole
land hath cause to remember with thankfulnes) y^t he is
able to requite your kindnes, M. Iohn Cant.   O said
his grace to M. Euans, I knowe you to be worthy a
better place then Warwicke is, and I would very gladly
gratifie my Lord, but surely, there is a Lord
in heuen whom I feare, and therefore I can‑
not admit you without subscription.   Thus

O Mon-
strous hypo-
crite.

the man with his poore patrone, the earle of Warwick,
were reiected by your grace, and the poore earle to
this day, knoweth not how to finde the fauour at your
hands, that the man may be placed there.   I tell you
true Iohn Canter.   If I were a noble man, and a Counsellor to, I should be sicke of the splene : nay I could
not beare this at your hands, to be vsed of a priest thus,
contrary to the law of God and this land.   It is no
maruell though his honor could not obtaine this small
suit at your graceles hands, for I haue hearde your owne
men say, that you will not be beholding to neuer a
noble man in this land, for you were the 2. person, &c.
Nay your own selfe spake proudly, yea and that like a
pope : when as a worthy knight was a suter vnto your
holines, for one of Gods deare children (whom you haue
kept and do keepe in prison) for his libertie.   You
answered him he should lie there stil, vnles he would
put in sureties vpon such bonds as neuer the like were
hard of : and said further, that you are the 2. person in
the land, and neuer a noble man, nor Counsellor in this
lande should release him : Onely her Maiestie may
release him, and that you were sure, shee would not.

Doe you thinke this to be he (I pray you) that was
sometime doctor Pernes boy, and carried his cloak-bagg
after him? Beleeue me he hath leapt lustily? And do
not you knowe that after it is full sea, there
followeth an eb? Remember your brother Is not this
Haman? Do you think there is neuer a ambitious
Mordecai to step to our Gracious Hester, for wretche at
the highest
thinke you.
preseruing the liues of her faithfullest and best subiects,
whō you so mortally hate, and bitterly persecute? I
hope you haue not long to raigne. Amen. And you
M. bishop of Worcester, how delt you with master
Evans in the same case? Do you thinke that I do not
know your knauerye? you could by law require no
other subscription of master Evans then he offered, and
yet forsoth, you would not receiue it at his handes,
vnlesse he woulde also enter into a bonde, to obserue
the booke of common prayer in euerie poynt, will law
permit you to play the tyrant in this sort bishop? I
shall see the premunire on the bones of you one day for
these pranks. And the masmonger your neighbor the
B. of Glocester, thinks to go free, because in his sermon
at Paules crosse, preached 1586. in the Parliament time,
he affirmed, that beefe and brewesse had made him a
papist. But this will not serue his turne: woulde you
know what he did? why he conuented an honest draper
of Glocester, one Singleton, and vrged him being a lay
mā to subscribe vnto the booke. The man affirming
that no such thing cold be required of him by law,
denied to subscribe: Vpon his deniall the B. sent him
to prison. Is it euen so, you old popish priest? dare

you imprison lay men for not subscribing? It were not good for your corner cap that her maiestie knew her subiects to be thus delt with. And if this be euer made knowen vnto her, I hope to see you in for a bird. But brother Winchester, you of all other men are most wretched, for you openly in the audience of many hundreds, at sir Marie Oueries church the last lent, 1587. pronounced that men might finde fault, if they were O blasphem- disposed to quarrell, as well with the Scrip-
ous wretche. ture, as with the booke of Common praier. Who coulde heare this comparison without trembling. But lest you should thinke, that he hath not as good a gift in speaking against his conscience, as my L. of Cant. is endued with: you are to vnderstand, that both in that sermon of his, and in another which he preached at the court the same Lent, he protested before God, A flattering and the congregation where he stood, y^t there
hypocrit. was not in the world at this day: nay there had not bin since the Apostles time, such a flourishing estate of a Church, as we haue now in England. Is it any maruaile that we haue so many swine, dumbe dogs, nonresidents, with their iourneimen the hedge priests, so many lewd liuers, as theeues, murtherers, adulterers, drunkards, cormorants, raschals, so many ignorant and atheistical dolts, so many couetous popish Bb. in our ministery: and so many and so monstrous corruptions in our Church, and yet likely to haue no redresse: Seeing our impudent, shamelesse, and wainscote faced bishops, like beasts, contrary to the knowledge of all men, and against their own consciences, dare in the eares of her

Maiestie, affirme all to be well, where there is nothing but sores and blisters, yea where the grief is euen deadly at the heart. Nay saies my L. of Winchester (like a monstrous hypocrite, for he is a very duns, not able to defende an argument, but till he come to the pinch, he will cog and face it out, for his face is made of seasoned wainscot, and wil lie as fast as a dog can trot) I haue said it, I doe say it, and I haue said it. And say I, you shall one day answere it (without repentance) for abusing the Church of God and her Maiestie in this sort. I would wish you to leaue this villanie, and the rest of your diuellishe practises against God his saintes, lest you answere it where your pieuish and chollerick simplicitie will not excuse you. I am ashamed to think that the Churche of England shoulde haue these wretches for the eyes thereof, that woulde haue the people content themselues with bare reading onely, and holde that they may be saued thereby ordinarily. But this is true of our Bb. and they are afraid that any thing should be published abrod, whereby the common people should learne, that the only way to saluation, is by the word preached. There was the last sommer a little catechisme, made by M. Dauison and printed by Waldegraue : but before he coulde print it, it must be authorized by the Bb. either Cante. or London, he went to Cant. to haue it licensed, his grace committed it to doctor Neuerbegood (Wood) he read it ouer in halfe a yeare, the booke is a great one of two sheets of paper. In one place of the booke, the meanes of saluation was attributed to the worde preached : and what did he

thinke you? he blotted out the word (preached) and
would not haue that word printed, so ascribing the way
to work mens saluation to the worde read.   Thus they
doe to suppresse the trueth, and to keep men in ignorance.
Iohn Cant. was the first father of this horrible error in
our Church, for he hath defended it in print, and now
as you haue hard, accounteth the contrary to be heresie.
And popish Goodman, Abbot of Westminster, preaching vpon 12. Rom. 1. said, that so much preaching as
in some places we haue is an vnreasonable seruice of
God.   Scribes, Pharises, and hypocrits, that will
neither enter in [y]our selues, nor suffer those that will,
to enter into heauen.

May it please your Priestdomes to vnderstand, that
doctor Cottington Archdeacon of Surrey, being belike
bankerout in his owne countrie, commeth to Kingstone
vpon Thames of meere good will that he beareth to the
towne (I should say, to vserer Haruies good chear and
money bags) being out at the heeles with all other
vserers, and knowing him to be a professed aduersary
to M. Vdall, (a notable preacher of the Gospell, and
vehement reprouer of sinne) taketh the aduantage of
their controuersie, and hoping to borow some of the
vserers money : setteth himself most vehemently against
M. Vdall, to do whatsoeuer Haruie the vserer will haue
him: and taketh the helpe of his iourniman doctor Hone,
the veriest coxcombe that euer wore veluet cap, and an
ancient foe to M. Vdall, because (in deed) he is popish
dolt, and (to make up a messe) Steuen Chatfield, the
vicker of Kingston, as very a bankerout and duns as

Doc. Cottington (although he haue consumed all the money he gathered to build a Colledge at Kingstone) must come and be resident there, that M. Vdall may haue his mouth stopped, and why? forsoth because your friend M. Haruie woulde haue it so: for sayth Haruie, he rayleth in his sermons, is that true? Doth he rail, when he reproueth thee (and such notorious varlets as thou art) for thy vsery, for thy oppressing of the poore, for buying the houses ouer their heads that loue the gospell, and the Lord his faythfull minister? (M. Vdall) And art not thou a monstrous atheist, a belly God, a carnall wicked wretch, and what not. M. Chatfield you thinke I see not your knauery? is vs do I, you cannot daunce so cunningly in a net but I can spie you out? shal I tel you why you sow pillows vnder Haruies elbowes? Why man, it is because you would borow an 100. pound of him? Go to you Asse, and take in M. Vdall againe (for Haruie I can tell, is as craftie a knaue as you, he will not lend his money to such bankerouts, as Duns Cottington and you are) and you do not restore M. Vdall againe to preach, I will so lay open your vilenes, y^t I will make the very stoones in Kingstone streets shall smell of your knaueries. Nowe if a man aske M. Cottington why M. Vdall is put to silence? forsoth saith he, for not fauoring the Churche gouernement present. Doc. Hone (Cottingtons iourniman, a popish D. of the baudy court) saith by his troth, for making such variance in the town. M. Chat-field seemeth to sorie for it, &c. But what cause was alleaged why M. Vdall must preach no longer? surely this onely? that he had not my L. of Winchesters licence vnder seale to shew : and because this was thought not to be sufficient to satisfie the people : Hone the baudie Doctor, charged him to be a sectarie, a schismatike, yea he affirmed plainly, that the gospell out of his mouth was blasphemie. Popish Hone, do you say so? do ye? you are a knaue I tel you? by ye same token your friend Chatfield spent thirteene score pounds in distributing briefes, for a gathering towards the erecting of a Colledge at Kingstone upon Thames.

Wohohow, brother London, do you remember Thomas Allen and Richard Alworth, marchants of London, being executors to George Allen somtimes your grocer, but now deceased: who came vnto you on easter wednesday last being at your masterdoms pallace in Londō, hauing bene often to speake with you before and could not, yet now they met with you: who tolde you they were executors vnto one George Allen (somtimes) your grocer, and among other his debts, we finde you indebted vnto him, in the some of 19. pound and vpward, desiring you to let them haue the money, for that they were to dispose of it according to that trust he reposed in them.

Can B. face, cog, lie and cos^n or n^? thinke you. You answered them sweetly (after you had pawsed a while) in this manner: You are raskals, you are villaines, you are arraunt knaues, I owe you nought, I haue a generall quittance to shew. Sir (sayd they) shew vs your discharge, and we are satisfied. No (quoth he) I will shew you none, go sue me, go sue me. Then sayd one of the merchants, doe you thus vse vs for asking our due? Wee

would you should know, we are no suche vile persons.
Done Iohn of London (hearing their answere) cried out,
saying: Hence away, Citizens? nay you are Dumbe
raskcals, you are worse then wicked mam- Iohn of
Londōs
mon (so lifting vp both his hands, and flinging blessing.
them downe againe, said) You are theeues, you are
Coseners: take that for a bishops blessing, and so get
you hence.   But when they would haue aunswered, his
men thrust them out of the dores.   But shortly after,
he perceiued they went about to bring the matter to
farther tryial: he sent a messenger vnto them confessing
the debt, but they cannot get their money to this day.
What reason is it they should haue their mony? hath he
not bestowed his liberallitie alreadie on them?   Can
they not be satisfied with the blessing of this braue
bounsing priest?   But brethren bishops, I pray you tell
me? hath not your brother Londō, a notable brazen
face to vse these men so for their owne?   I told you,
Martin will be proued no lyar, in that he saith that
Bb. are cogging and cosening knaues.   This priest went
to buffets with his sonne in law, for a bloodie nose,
well fare all good tokens.   The last lent there came a
commaundement from his grace into Paules Churchyard,
that no Byble should be bounde without the Apocripha.
Monstrous and vngodly wretches, that to maintaine their
owne outragious proceedings, thus mingle heauen and
earth together, and woulde make the spirite of God, to
be the author of prophane bookes.   I am hardly drawn
to a merie vaine from such waightie matters.

But you see my worshipfull priestes of this crue to

whom I write, what a perilous fellow M. Marprelate is :
he vnderstands of all your knauerie, and it may be he
keepes a register of them : vnlesse you amend, they
shall al come into the light one day.   And you brethren
bishops, take this warning from me.   If you doe not
leaue your persecuting of godly christians and good
subiectes, that seeke to liue vprightly in the feare of
God, and the obedience of her Maiestie, all your dealing shalbe made knowen vnto the world.   And ise be
sure to make you an example to all posterities.   You
see I haue taken some paynes with you alreadie, and
I will owe you a better turne, and pay it you with
aduauntage, at the least thirteene to the dozen, vnles
you obserue these conditions of peace which I drawe
betweene me and you.   For I assure you, I make not
your doings known for anie malliee that I beare vnto
you, but the hurt that you doe unto Gods Churche,
leaue you your wickednesse, and ile leaue the reuealing
of your knaueries.

☞ *Conditions of Peace to be inuiolablie kept for euer,*
betweene the reuerend and worthy master Martin Mar-
prelate gentleman on the one partie, and the reuerend
fathers his brethren, the Lord bishops of this lande.

1. *In primis*, the said Lord Bb. must promise and
obserue, without fraud or collusion, and that as much as
in them lyeth, they labor to promote the preaching of
the worde in euery part of this land.

2. That hereafter they admitt none vnto the minis-

terie, but such as shalbe knowen, both for their godlinesse and learning, to be fit for the ministerie, and not
these neyther without cure, vnlesse they be Colledge
ministers of eyther of the Vniuersities, and in no case
they suffer any to be nonresidents : and that they suffer
M. Cartwrightes answere to the Rhemish Testament to
be published.

3. That neyther they nor their seruants, vz. their
Archdèacons, Chancellors, nor any other of the high
commission, which serue their vile affections, vrge any
to subscribe contrary to the statute 13. Eliza. and that
they suspend or silence none, but such, as either for
their false doctrine, or euill life, shall shew themselues,
to be vnworthy the places of ministers : so that none be
suspended or silenced, eyther for speaking (when their
text giueth them occasion) against the corruptions of the
Church, for refusing to weare the surplice, cap, tippet,
&c. or omitting the corruptions of the booke of common
prayers, as churching of women, the crosse in baptisme,
the ring in marriage, &c.

4. That none be molested by them or any their aforesaid seruants, for this my booke, for not kneeling at the
communion, or for resorting on the Saboth (if they
haue not preachers of their owne) to heare the word
preached, and to receiue the Sacraments.

5. Lastly, that neuer hereafter they profane excommunication as they haue done, by excommunicating
alone in their chambers, and that for trifles : yea before
mens causes be heard. That they neuer forbid publike
fasts, molest either preacher, or hearer, for being present

D

at such assemblies. Briefly, that they neuer slander the
cause of reformation, or the furtherers thereof, in terming the cause by the name of Anabaptisterie, schisme,
&c. and the men puritans, and enemies to the state.

These be the conditions, which you brethren bishops,
shalbe bound to keepe inuiolably on your behalfe. And
I your brother Martin on the other side, do faithfully
promise vpon the performaunce of the premisses by you,
neuer to make any more of your knauery knowne vnto
the worlde. And howbeit that I haue before threatened
my brother Bridges, in the cause of his superior priest,
and your Antichristian callings : notwithstanding, I will
write no more of your dealings, vnles you violate the
former conditions. The conditions you see, are so reasonable, I might binde you to giue ouer your places
which are Antichristian: but I doe not, lest men shoulde
thinke me to quarrell, and seeke occasions for the nonce
to fall out with my brethrē. Therefore I require no
more but such things as all the worlde will thinke you
vnworthy to liue, if you grant them not. And this I
doe the rather, because you should not, according to
your olde fashion, say yᵗ my worship doth for mallice
lay opē your infirmities : nay I haue published not one
of your secret falts, what you haue not blushed to commit in the face of the sun, and in the iustfiing whereof
you yet stand, these things onely haue I published.
The best seruants of God I know, haue their infirmities.
But none of thē will stand in the maintenance of their
corruptions as you do, and that to the dishonour of God
and the ruine of his Church. You must either amend,

or shortly you will bring our church to ruine: therfore it is time that your dealings were better looked vnto.

You will go about I know, to proue my booke to be a libell, but I haue preuented you of y^t aduantage in lawe, both in bringing in nothing but matters of fact, whiche may easily be prooued, if you dare denie them: and also in setting my name to my booke. Well I offer you peace vpon the former conditions, if you will keepe them, but if you violate thē either in whole or in part (for why should you breake anye one of them) then your learned brother Martin doth proclaime open war against you, and entendeth to worke your woe 2. maner of wayes as followeth. First I will watch you at euery halfe turne, and whatsoeuer you do amisse, I will presently publish it: you shall not call one honest man before you, but I will get his examination (and you thinke I shall knowe nothing of the oppression of your tenants by your briberie, &c.) and publish it, if you deal not according to the former conditions. To this purpose I wil place a yong Martin in euerie diocesse, which may take notice of you practizes. Do you think that you shalbe suffred any longer, to break the law of God, and to tyrannize ouer his people her Maiesties subiectes, and no man tell you of it? No I warrant you. And rather then I will be disappointed of my purpose, I will place a Martin in euerie parish. In part of Suffolk and Essex, I thinke I were best to haue 2. in a parishe. I hope in time they shalbe as worthie Martins as their father is, euery one of them able to mar a prelate. Marke what wil be the issue of these things, if you still

keep your olde byas. I knowe you would not haue
your dealings so knowne vnto the worlde, as I and my
sonnes will blase them. Secondly, al the books that I
haue in store already of your doings, shalbe published
vpon the breache of the former couenants or any of
them. Here I know some will demand what these
bookes are, because saith one, I warrant you, there will
be old sport, I hope olde father Palinod D. Perne, shall
be in there by the weekes. Why my masters of the
cleargie, did you neuer heare of my books in deed?
Foe, then you neuer heard of good sport in your life.
The catalogue of their names, and the arguments of
some are as followeth. As for my booke
named "Epistomastix," I make no mention
thereof at this time. First my "Paradoxes,"
2. my "Dialogues," 3. my "Miscelanea," 4. my "Va-
riæ leiciones," 5. "Martins dreame," 6. "Of the liues
and doings of English popes," 7. my "Itinerarium, or
visitations," 8. my "Lambathismes." In my "Paradoxes" shalbe handled som points, which the cōmon
sort haue not greatly considered of: as 1 That our prelates, if they professed popery, could not do so much
hurt vnto Gods Church as now they do. 2 That the
Diuell is not better practized in bowling and swering
then Iohn of London is, with other like points. What
shalbe handled in my 2. 3. 4. 5. and 6. bookes, you
shall know when you read them.

Mine "Iterarium" shalbe a booke of no great profit,
eyther to the Church or commonwealth: and yet had
nede to be in follio, or else iudge you by this that fol_

*Mine Epi-
tome is
readie.*

loweth. I meane to make a suruey into all the diocesse
in this land, that I may keepe a visitation among my
cleargie men. I would wish them to keepe good rule,
and to amend their manners against I come. For I
shall paint them in their coulers, if I finde any thing
amisse: In this booke I wil note all their memorable
pranckes. As for example, if I finde anye priest to
haue done as Sir Gefferie Iones of Warwicke shire did,
that must be set downe in my visitations, and I thinke
I had need to haue many Scribes, and many reames of
paper for this purpose. The said sir Iefferie Iones,
committed a part verie well beseeming his priesthood,
which was after this maner. Sir Ieffry once in an alehouse (I doe desire the reader to beare with me, though
according to M. Bridges his fashion, I write false Englishe in this sentence) whereunto he resorted for his
morning draught, either because his hostesse woulde
haue him pay the olde score before he should run any
further, or the new, or els because the gamesters his
companions wan all his monie at trey trip: tooke such
vnkindenes at the alehouse, that he sware he would
neuer goe againe into it. Although this rash vow of
the good priest, was made to the great losse of the ale-
wife, who by means of sir Iefferie was woont to haue
good vtterance for her ale: yet I think the tap had
great quietnes and ease therby, which coulde not be
quiet so much as an houre in the day, as long as Sir
Iefferie resorted vnto the house, how sweete it was,
poore sir Iones felt the discommoditie of his rashe vowe.
Then alas, he was in a woe case, as you know: for his

stomacke could not be at all strengthened with the drink
he got abroad.   But better were a man not to feele his
discommoditie, then not to be able to redresse the same.
Therefore at length sir Iefferie bethought him of a feat
whereby he might both visit the alestond, and also keepe
his othe.   And so he hired a man to carie him vpon his
backe to the alehouse, by this meanes he did not goe,
but was caried thither, wherevnto he made a vow neuer
to go.   I doubt not in my visitation, but to get a hundreth of these stratagemes, especially if I trauell neere
where any of the vickers of hell are.   As in Surrie,
Northampton, and Oxforde shires.   And I would wish
the Purcivants and the Stacioners, with the Woolfe
their beadle, not to be so redy to molest honest men.
And Stacioners, I would wish you not to be so francke
with your bribes, as you were to Thomas Draper, I can
tell you his grace had need to prouide a bag ful of
Items for you, if you be so liberal.   Were you so foolish
(or so malicious against Walde-graue) to giue that knaue
Draper fiue pounds to betray him into your wretched
hands : he brought you to Kingstone vpon Thames, with
Purcivants to take him, where he should be a printing
books in a Tinkars house : (your selues being disguised
so, that Walde-graue might not know you, for of Citizens you were becom ruffians).   There you were to
seek that could not be found, and many such iournies
may you make.   But when you came to London, you
laid Thomas Draper in the Counter for cosenage.   O
well bowlde, when Iohn of London throwes his bowle,
he will runne after it, and crie rub, rub, rub, and say the

diuill go with thee. But what thinke you shalbe handled
in my "Lambathismes?" Truely this, I will there
make a comparison of Iohn Whitgifts Canterburines,
with Iohn Bridges his Lambathismes. To speake in
plaine English, I will there set downe the flowers of
errors, popishe and others, wherewith those two'worthie
men haue stuffed the bookes which they haue written
against the cause of reformation, in the defence of the
gouernment of Bb. I haue in this book as you shal see,
gathered some flowers out of Iohn of Londons booke,
but my "Lambathismes" shalbe done otherwise I trow.

And now if it may please you of the Confocationhouse,
to here of any of the former books, then break the
league which I offer to make with you, but if you
woulde haue my friendship, as I seeke yours, then let
me see that you persecute no more, and especially, that
you trouble none for this booke of mine. For this must
be an especiall article of our agreement, as you know.
And Deane Iohn, for your part, you must plaie the fool
no more in the pulpit : we will end this matter with a
prettie storie of a certaine mischance that befell a B.
corner cap, as followeth. Olde doctor Turner (I meane
not D. Perne the old turner) had a dog full of good
quallities. D. Turner hauing inuited a B. to his table,
in dinner while called his dog, and told him that the B.
did sweat (you must think he labored hard ouer his
trencher) The dogg flies at the B. and tooke of his
corner capp (he thought belike it had bene a cheese
cake) and so away goes the dog with it to his master.
Truely my masters of the cleargie, I woulde neuer weare

D 4

corner cap againe, seeing dogs runne away with them :
and here endeth the storie.

May it please you that are of this house, to tell me
the cause, when you haue leysure, why so many opinions
and errors are risen in our Church, concerning the ministery, and the ioyning with preaching and vnpreaching
ministers. To tell you my opinion in your eare, I
thinke it to be want of preaching, and I thinke your
worships to haue bene the cause of all this stir. Some
puritans holde readers for no ministers, som hold you
our worthy Bb. for little better then faire parchment
readers, and say that you haue no learning. Now whether readers be ministers or no, and whether our bishops
be learned or no, I woulde wish you brethren bishops,
and you brethren puritans, to make no great controuersie, but rather labor that all euil ministers may be
turned out of the Church, and so I hope there shoulde
be a speedie ende of all those questions betweene you.
For then I doubt not, but that Lord bishops whereat the
puritans so repine, shoulde be in a faire reckoning within short space, euen the next to the dore saue the
dog : and I see that you bishopps are well towardes this
promotion alreadie. And truely, though the puritans
should neuer so much repine at the matter, yet I tell
you true, I am glad that you are so esteemed among mē.
And for mine owne part, I think my masters, that manie
of you our Lord Bb. and cleargie men, are men verie
notorious for their learning and preaching. And hereof
vnder Benedicite betweene you and me, (the puritanes
may stand aside nowe) I will bring you some instances.

First his grace and my L. of Winchester haue bene verie notable clarkes, euer since M. doctor Sparke set them at a *non plus* (some of their honors being present) in the conference betweene him and M. Trauers on the puritans side, and the two Archbishops and the B. of Winchester on the other side.   D. Sparks argument was drawn from the corruption of the translation of the 28. verse of the 105. Psalme, in the booke of Common prayer, and the contrarietie of the translations allowed by the Bb. themselues.   For in the book of Common prayer you shal read thus : And they were not obedient vnto his word (which is a plain corruptiō of the text) in other priuiledged English translations it is, And they were not disobedient vnto his word, which is according to the veritie of the originall.   By the way ere I go any fur-ther, I would know with what conscience, either my brother Cant. or any els of our Bb. can vrge men to allow such palpable corruptions by subscribing vnto thinges meere contrarie to the word.   Here also I would shew by the way, and I woulde haue al my sonnes to note, that their vncle Canterburies drift in vrging sub-scription, is not the vnity of the church (as he would pretende) but the maintenance of his owne pride and corruption, which should soon come to yᵉ ground, if the worde had free passage : and therefore he prooueth the same, by stopping the mouthes of yᵉ sincere preachers thereof.   For if the vnitie of the Church had bene his end, why hath not he amended this fault in all the books that haue bene printed since that time, which now is not so little as 3 yeares, in which time, many thousand of

books of Common praier haue bin printed. If he had
other busines in hand then the amending of the booke of
Common prayer? why had he not, nay why doth he not
leaue vrging of subscription vntill that be amended?
Can he and his hirelings haue time to imprison and
depriue men, because they will not sinne, by approuing
lyes vpon the holy ghost (which thinges they cannot,
nor could not chuse but commit, whosoeuer will or haue
subscribed vnto the booke and Articles) And can he
haue no time in 3. or 4. yeares to correct most grose
and vngodly faultes in the print, whereof the putting
out of one syllable, euen three letters (dis) would haue
amended this place. But it lieth not in his grace to
amende the corruptions of the booke. Belike it lieth in
him to doe nothing but sinne, and to compell men
against their consciences to sinne, or else to bring
extreme miserie vpon them. If it laye not in him, yet
he might haue acquainted the Parliament (for there was
a Parliament since the time he knew this fault) with the
corruptions of the booke. And I will come neerer home
to him then so, in the Article concerning the gouernment
whereunto men are vrged to subscribe. You must (say
the Articles) protest that there is nothing in the minis-
terý of the Church of England, that is not according
to yᵉ word, or to such like effect they speake. I say
that I cannot subscribe vnto this article, becáuse contrary to the expresse commandement of our sauiour
Christ, and the examples of his Apostles, there be Lords
in yᵉ ministeriė, or such as wold be accoūted ministers,
will also be called and accoūted Lords, and bear ciuill

offices, the words of Christ are those. The kinges of
the Gentils raigne ouer them, and they that beare rule
ouer them, are called gracious Lords, but you shall not
be so, Luk. 22. 25. 26. I saye that out of this place,
it is manifest, that it is vtterly vnlawfull for a minister
to be a Lord: that is, for any L. B. to be in the ministerie : and therefore I cannot subscribe vnto that Article
which would haue me iustifie this to be lawfull. Nowe
I will cease this point, because I doubt not but the
Articles of subscription, wilbe shortly so made out of
fashion, that the Bb. will be ashamed of them themselues : and if no other will take them in hande, ile
turne one of mine owne breede vnto them, eyther Martin senior, or some of his brethren.

To go forward, his Lordship of Winchester is a great
Clarke, for he hath translated his Dictionarie, called
Copers Dictionarie, verbatim out of Robert Stephanus
his Thesaurus, and ilfauored to they say. But what
do I speake of our bishops learning, as long as bishop
Ouerton, bishopp Bickley, bishop Middleton, the Deane
of Westminster, doctor Cole, D. Bell, with many others,
are liuing, I doubt me whether all the famous dunses be
dead. And if you woulde haue an ilsample of an excellent pulpit man in deede, go no further then the B. of
Glocester nowe liuing: And in him you shall finde a
plaine instance of such a one as I meane. On a time
he preaching at Worcester before he was B. vpon Sir
Iohns day: as he trauersed his matter, and discoursed
vpon many points, he came at the length vnto the very
pithe of his whol sermon, contained in the distinction of

the name of Iohn, which he then shewing all his learning at once, full learnedly handled after this manner.
Iohn, Iohn, the grace of God, the grace of God, the
grace of God: gracious Iohn, not graceles Iohn, but
gracious Iohn. Iohn, holy Iohn, holy Iohn, not Iohn
ful of holes, but holy Iohn. If he shewed not himselfe
learned in this sermond, then hath he bene a duns all
his life. In the same sermon, two seuerall Iohns, the
father and the sonne, that had beene both recusants,
being brought publikely to confesse their faults, this
worthy doctor, by reason that the yong man hauing bene
poysoned beyond the seas with popery, was more
obstinate then his father, and by all likelihood, he was
ye cause of his fathers peruersenesse: with a vehement
exclamatiō, able to pearce a cobweb, called on the father
aloud in this patheticall and perswading sort. Old
Iohn, olde Iohn, be not led away by the Syren sounds,
and inticements of yong Iohn, if yong Iohn will go to the
diuell, the diuell go with him. The puritans it may be,
will here obiect, that this worthy man was endued with
these famous gifts before he was B. whereas since that
time, say they, he is not able to say bo to a goose.
You wey this man belike my masters, according to the
rest of our Bb. But I assure you it is not so with him.
For the last Lent in a sermon he made in Glocester
towne, he shewed him selfe to be the man that he was
before. For he did in open pulpit confirme the trueth
of his text to be authenticall, being the prophesie of
Isaiah, out of the book of Cōmon prayer, whiche otherwise would (it is to be feared) haue proued Apocrypha.

His text was, a childe is borne vuto vs, which after he sweetly repeated very often as before, to the great destruction and admiration of the hearers, saying: A child is borne, a child is borne, a child is borne vnto vs this (sayth he) is proued you know, where in that worthy verse of the booke of Common prayer. Thy honorable true and onely sonne. Afterward, repeating the same words againe: A childe is borne vuto vs, a childe is borne vnto vs: here sayth hee, I might take occasion to commende that worthy verse in our Latenie, where this is made very manifest, that y* prophet here speaketh. By thy Natiuitie and circumcision. What should I prosecute the condemnation of this man, as though other our Bb. and pulpit men haue not as commendable gifts as he.

And once againe to you brother Bridges, you haue set downe a flanting reason, in the 75. page of your book, against the continuance of the gouernment which the Puritans labor for, and I finde the same syllogisme concluded in no mood: therefore what if I was ashamed to put it downe? But seeing it is your will, to laye on the puritans with it as it is, put your corner cap a litle nere a toe side, that we may see your partie coullered beard, and with what a manly countenance, you giue your brethren this scouring. And I hope this will please you, my cleargie masters, as well as if I tolde you how our brother Bridges plaid my L. of Winchesters foole, in sir Maries pulpit in Cambridg, but no word of that: now to my reason.

Some kinde of ministerie ordained by the Lorde, was

temporarie (saith he) as for example, the Mosaicall priesthood, and the ministerie of Apostles, prophets, &c. But the ministerie of pastors, doctors, elders and deacons, was ordayned by the Lord: Therefore it was temporarie.

Alacke, alacke deane Iohn, what haue you done now? The puritanes will be O the bones of you too badd, for this kinde of arguing, and they wil reason after this sort.

1 Some man in the land (say they) weareth a wooden dagger and a coxcombe, as for example, his grace of Canterburies foole, doctor Pernes cosen and yours: you presbyter Iohn Catercap, are some man in the land: Therefore by this reason, you wear a woodden dagger and a coxcombe.   2 Some presbyter prieste or elder in the English ministerie, is called the vicker of hell.   As for example one about Oxford, another neere Northampton, and the parson of Micklaim in Surrie: But the dean of Sarum Iohn Catercap, is some priest in the Englishe ministerie: Ergo he is the vicker of hell. 3 Some presbyter priest or elder, preaching at Pauls crosse 1587. tould a tale of a leadden shoinghorne, and spake of Catekissing: and preaching at the Court on another time, thrust his hand into his pocket, and drew out a piece of sarsnet, saying, behold a relique of Maries smocke: and thrusting his hand into the other pocket, drew out either a linnen or a wollen rag, saying, behold a relique of Iosephs breeches.   But quoth he, there is no reason why Maries smocke shoulde be of sarsnet, seeing Iosephs breeches were not of silke.   This prist

being lately demanded whether he should be bishop of Eli, answered that he had now no great hope to B. of Eli: and therefore quoth he, I may say well inough, Eli, Eli, Lammasabacthani. Eli, Eli, why hast thou forsaken me. Alluding very blasphemously vnto the words which our Sauiour Christe spake, in his greatest agonie vpon the crosse. The same priest calling before him one M. Benison a preacher, and would haue vrged him to take his othe, to answere to such articles as he would propounde against him, who answered saying, brother bishop, I wil not sweare, except I know to what? with that the priest fell sicke of the splene, and began to sweare by his fayth: quoth Benison, a Bishop should preache fayth, and not sweare by it. This priest being in his malancholicke mood, sent him to the Clincke, where he lay till her Maiestie was made priuie of his tyrannie, and then released to the priests wo. As for example, the B. of Londoo did al those things and more to: For lying at his house at Haddam in Essex, vpon the Sabboth day (wanting his bowling mates) tooke his seruantes and went a heymaking, the godly ministers round about being exercised (though against his commandement) in fasting and prayer: But you Iohn Catercap, are some presbyter priest or Elder: Therefore you prophaned the word and ministerie in this sort. 4 Some presbyter priest or elder in the land, is accused (and euen now the matter is in triall before his grace and his brethren) to haue two wiues, and to marie his brother vnto a woman vpon her death bedd, shee being past recouerie. As for example, the B. of sir Dauies in

Wales, is this priest as they saye: But you presbyter
Iohn, are some priest: Therefore you haue committed
all these vnnaturall parts.   5 Some priest preaching at
the funeralls of one who died, not onely being condemned
by the lawe of God and of the land, for attempting
matters against her Maiesties person and the state, but
also dyed an obstinate and professed papist, and without
anye repentance for her enterprises against her Maiestie
and the state : prayed that his soule, and the soules of
all the rest there present, might be with the soule of the
vnrepentant papist departed.   As for example, the B.
of Lincolne did this at Peterborough, August. 2. 1587.
But you are som priest : Ergo you made such a prayer.
6 Some priest in yᵉ land lately made, or verie shortly
meaneth to make, as they say, an olde acquaintance of
his owne, Richard Patrick, clothier of Worcester, of the
reading ministery.   As for example, his grace of Canter.
is this priest : But you brother Sarum are som priest as
wel as he : Ergo you haue thrust a bankerout clothier
in the ministerie.   7 Some priest hauing giuen a man
(whose wife had plaid the harlot) leaue to marie another,
desiring the man long after he had bene maried to
another woman, to shewe him his letters of diuorcement,
with promise to deliuer them againe : But hauing receiued them, they are retained of him most iniuriously
vnto this day, and he troubleth the man for hauing two
wiues : as for example, the B. of sir Asse is this priest :
But you dean Catercap are som priest : Ergo you do
men such open iniurie.   8 Some men that breake the
lawe of God are traytors to her Maiestie, as for example,

the Iesuites. But all our bishops are some men that breake the law of God, because they continue in vnlawful callings: Ergo by your reason they are traitors to her maiestie, but I deny your argument, for there may be manie breaches of the law of God, whereof they may be guiltie, and yet no traytors. 9 Some men that will not haue their Lordships, and their callings examined by the worde, are limbs of Antichrist, as for example, the Pope and his Cardinals : But our L. bishops are some men which will not haue their lordships and their callings tried by the word : Therefore they are limbs of Antichrist. 10 Some men would play the turncoats, with the B. of Glocester, D. Renold, D. Perne (I wil let D. Goodman Abbot of West. alone now) But all the L. bishops, and you brother catercap are some men : Ergo you would becom papists againe. 11 Some men dare not dispute with their aduersaries, lest their vngodly callings shoulde be ouerthrowen, and they compelled to walke more orderly : But our Bb. are some men : Ergo they dare not dispute lest their vngodly callings and places shoulde be ouerthrowen. 12 Som men are theeues and foul murtherers before God, as for example, all nonresidents : Euerie L. bishop is a nonresident : Ergo he is a thiefe and a foule murtherer before God. 13 Some men are become Apostataes frō their ministerie, sinners against their owne consciences, persecuters of their brethren, sacriligious Church robbers, withstanders of the known trueth, for their owne filthie lukers sake, and are afraid lest the gospel and the holy discipline thereof should be receiued in euerie

place : But our Bb. are some men : Therfore (by your
reson M. doctor) they are become Apostaes from their
ministerie,. sinners against their owne consciences, persecutors of their brethren, sacriligious Church robbers,
and withstanders of the knowen truth, &c.   14 Som
priest is a pope, as for example, that priest which is
bishop of Rome is a Pope : But his grace of Cant. is
some prieśt : Therefore M. Bridges, by your maner of
reasoning, he is a Pope.   You may see what harme you
haue done by dealing so loosely.   I knowe not what I
shall say to these puritans reasons ?   They must needs
be good, if yours be sound.   Admit their syllogisms
offended in form as yours doth : yet the common people, and especially dame Lawson, and the gentlewoman,
whose man demanded of her, whē she sat at the B. of
Londons fire : why mistris wil you sit by Caiphas his
fire ? will finde an vnhappy trueth in many of these
conclusions, when as yours is most false.   And many of
their propositions are tried truths, hauing many eye and
eare witnesses liuing.

Men when commonly they dedicate bookes vuto any,
enter into commendations of those vuto whom they
write.   But I care not an I owe you my cleargie masters a commendations, and pay you when you better
deserue it.   In stead thereof, I will giue you some good
counsel and aduice, which if you followe, I assure you
it will be the better for you.

First I would aduise you as before I haue said, to set
at libertie all the preachers that you haue restrained
frō preaching : otherwise it shalbe the worse for you,

my reason is this. The people are altogether discontented for want of teachers. Some of them alreadie
runne into corners, and more are like, because you
keepe the meanes of knowledge from them. Running
into corners will breed Anabaptistrie, Anabaptistrie will
allienate the heartes of the subiects from their lawfull
gouernour. And you are the cause hereof. And wil
not her Maiestie then think you, require the hearts of
her subiectes at your handes, whē she shal vnderstand
that they are alienated (as God forbid they should) from
her by your means? yes I warrant you. And if they
should put vp a supplication vuto her highnesse, that
their preachers might be restored vnto them, I doubt
not but they should be heard. I can tell you she tend-
reth the estate of her people, and will not discourage
their hearts, in casting of their suits, to maynetaine your
pride and couetousnesse: you were then better to set
the preachers at libertie, then to suffer your cruelty and
euill dealing to be made known vnto her. For so they
shall be sure I doubt not to preuaile in their suit, and
you to go by the worse. And try if her Maiestie be
not shortly mooued in this suit. To it my masters
roundly, you that meane to deale herein, and on my life
you set the prelats in such a quandare, as they shal not
know wher to stand. Now M. Prelates I will giue you
some more counsell, follow it. Repent cleargie men,
and especially bishopps, preach fayth Bb. and sweare
no more by it, giue ouer your Lordly callings: reform
your families and your children: They are the patterne
of loosenesse, withstand not the knowen truth no longer:

you haue seduced her Maiestie and her people.   Praye
her Maiestie to forgiue you, and the Lord first to put
away your sinnes.   Your gouerment is Antichristian,
deceiue the Lord no longer thereby : You wil grow
from cuil to worse vnlesse betimes you return.   You
are now worse then you were 29. yeeres ago : write no
more against the cause of reformation : Your vngodlinesse is made more manifest by your writings : And because you cannot answer what hath bene written against
you, yeeld vnto the trueth.   If you should write, deal
syllogistically : For you shame your selues, when you
vse any continued speach, because your stile is so rude
and barbarous.   Raile no more in the pulpitt against
good men, you do more hurt to your selues, and your
owne desperat cause, in one of your rayling sermons,
then you could in speaking for reformation.   For euerie
man that hath any light of religion in him will examine
your groundes, which being found ridiculous (as they
are) will be decided, and your cause made odious.
Abuse not the high cōmission as you do, against the best
subiects.   The commission it selfe was ordained for
very good purposes, but it is most horriblie abused by
you, and turned cleane contrarie to the ende wherefore
it was ordayned.   Helpe the poore people to the meanes
of their saluation, that perish in their ignorance : make
restitution vnto your tenants, and such as from whome
you haue wrongfully extorted any thing : Vsurpe no
longer, the authoritie of making of ministers and excommunication: Let poore men be no more molested in your
vngodly courts : Studie more then you doe, and preache

oftener : Fauor nonresidents and papists no longer : labor to clense ye ministery of the swarms of ignorant
guides, wherewith it hath bin defiled : Make conscience
of breaking the Sabboth, by bowling and tabling : Be
ringleaders of prophanenes no longer vnto the people :
Take no more bribes : Leaue your Symonie : Fauor
learning more then you doe, and especially godly learning : Stretch your credit if you haue any to the furtherance of the gospell : You haue ioyned the prophanation
of the magistracie, to the corruption of the ministerie :
Leaue this sinne. All in a word, become good christians,
and so you shall become good subiects, and leaue your
tyrannie. And I would aduise you, let me here no
more of your euill dealing.

Giuen at my Castle between two Wales, neither foure
dayes from penilesse benche, nor yet at the West ende
of Shrofftide : but the foureteenth yeare at the least, of
the age of Charing crosse, within a yeare of Midsommer,
betweene twelue and twelue of the clocke. *Anno ponti-
ficatus vestri Quinto*, and I hope *vltimo* of all Englishe
Popes.

By your learned and worthie brother,

MARTIN MARPRELATE.

NOTES.

Page 3, line 16. *D. Cosins hath a very good grace in iesting*] The allusion is to the "Abstract of certain Acts of Parliament of cer. tain Injunctions," &c., published in 1584, and which Dr. Cosins replied to by authority of Archbishop Whitgift, in the same year. The Counterpoyson was printed in 1584, which Dr. Copcot an. swered in a Latin sermon, preached at Paul's Cross, in 1585. The sermon does not appear to have been printed, for the author of "A Defense of the Reasons of the Counterpoyson," 1586, tells us, "the author of the Counterpoyson never could get the answeres *in writing, as nowe I haue got them.* Since that I myself have fallen upon the *whole sermon in writing,* so that it seemeth it goeth from hand to hande amongst those who delight in it."

P. 3, l. 26. *Cartwrights bookes*] The controversy between Whit. gift and Cartwright began in 1572 with the publication of the "Admonition to the Parliament." According to Neal [Hist. Puritans, i. 231. ed. 1822] it was drawn up by Field, a minister, assisted by Wilcox, and revised by others. The authors pre- sented it to the House, for which they were committed to New- gate Oct. 8, 1572. The Admonition was, however, suffered to be printed, and in the course of two years passed through three or four editions. [Strype's Parker, 347.] The imprisonment of Field and Wilcox occasioned the publication of a "Second Admo- nition," written by Cartwright, and two other tracts, entitled "An Exhortation to the Bishops to deal brotherly with their brethren," and another "Exhortation to the Bishops to answer the Admonition." The bishops, thinking it necessary to reply, appointed Whitgift to the work, and, before it came out, it under- went the revision and correction of Archbishop Parker, Dr. Pern, Bishop of Ely, and Dr. Cooper, Bishop of Lincoln. It was enti- tled "An Answeare to a certain Libel, entitled *An Admonition to the Parliament,* 1572." Cartwright to this replied in 1573, in "A Replye to an Answere made of Dr. VVhitgifte againste the Admonition to the Parliament." Whitgift then published "The Defence of the Aunswere to the Admonition against the Replie of T. C. 1574." The following year came out, "The Second Replie," and, in 1577, "The Rest of the Second Replie of Thomas Cart-vuright agaynst Master Doctor Vuhitgifts Second Ansvuer touch-ing the Church Discipline." To this "Second Replie" no answer was returned, and hence Martin, writing towards the end of 1588, says, "You first prouoked him to write, and you first haue receiued the foyle;" and, in allusion to the same sub-ject at p. 22, "For this dozen yeares we neuer saw any thing of his [Whitgift's] in printe for the defence of this cause, and poore M. Cartwright doth content himselfe with the victorie, which the other will not (though in deed he hath by his silence) seeme to grant."

P. 4, l. 13. *quoth John Elmar in his Harborow of faithful sub-iects.*] Written in reply to John Knox's "first Blast of the Trum-pet against the Monstrous Regiment of Women," it is entitled "An Harborowe for Faithful and Trewe Subiects against the late blowne Blast, concerning the Government of Wemen, anno MDlix. Strasborowe the 26 of April."

P. 8, l. 13. *Which Harmonie, was* translated *and printed by that puritan Cambridg printer, Thomas Thomas.*] A new edition of the "Harmony of the Confessions" has recently issued from the press, edited by the Rev. Peter Hall. Its value is much enhanced by the addition of the Articles of the Church of England, 1562, and of Ireland, 1615, the Judgment of the Synod of Dort, and the Westminster Confession, with an Index to the Doctrines in the Harmony. The editor, in a Note appended to the Intro-duction, has thrown some discredit on the statement that Thomas Thomas was the translator of the Harmony, but in the two direct references which Martin has made to it, I find he is accurate; and a fair inference may be drawn that in other respects his testimony to a matter of fact may be received. Thomas was a Fellow, and Master of Arts, of King's College, Cambridge, and the author of the Dictionary which bears the name of Thomas Tho-masius, first published in 1588. He was licensed printer to the University 3 May, 1582, but nothing of his is known before 1584. This was occasioned by the Stationers' Company having, on some plea or other, seized his press. Another license was granted to him Feb. 11, 1584. Strype [Annals 3. 442] has given the following account: "A new press had been set up at Cambridge, and in 1586 the Harmony, translated out of the Latin, was printing there, which for some reasons was not allowed to be printed in London. Whitgift sent his Letter to the Vice-chancellor and

Heads to cause the said book to be stayed from printing ;" it
was, however, published the same year, and it might be, as
Strype says, "after some review or correction of it," for it has
" alowed by publique authoritie " in the title-page, and that the
" bishops called them in " may be collected from the following
entry in the Stationers' Register A, quoted by Herbert, p. 1417,
under the year 1589-90, " Whereas all the seiz'd books were sold
to Mr. Byshop, be it remembered that 40 of them being Har.
monies of the Churches rated at ijs le peece, were had from him
by warrant of my Ld. of Cant. and remain at Lambeth, with Mr.
Doctor Cosens."

P. 8, l. 20. *Diotrephes his Dialogue*] See another allusion to the
same work at p. 16 : " as my friend Tertullus says in the poor
Dialogue that the Bishops burned hath lately set down." The
title is, " The State of the Church of England laide open in a
Conference betweene Diotrephes a Byshoppe, Tertullus a Papiste,
Demetrius a Usurer, Pandochus an Innekeeper, and Paul a
preacher of the Word of God," printed by Waldegrave, without
date, in 1588. *See Note to p. 30, l. 28.*

P. 13, l. 18. *Gammer Gurton's Needle*] Martin here is correct
when he tells the doctor this is none of his doing. The author
was John Still, Bishop of Bath and Wells, and though acted
before, " in Christes Colledge Cambridge," is not known to have
been printed until 1575. It is reprinted in Collier's Old Plays.

P. 25, l. 14. *Tarleton*] Allusion to this celebrated actor and
buffoon is frequent in the old dramatists. In 1583 he was chosen
one of the Queen's twelve players. He died Sept. 3, 1588. In
" A Whip for an Ape, or Martin displaied," 1589, he is thus
noticed,—

" Now Tarleton's dead the Consort lacks a vice,
    For knave and fool thou must bear pricke and price :"

and again, in some Rhymes against Martin,—

" These tinkers terms and barbers jests first Tarleton on the stage,
    Then Martin in his bookes of lies, hath put in every page."

P. 29, l. 15. *the Iesuit at Newgate*] probably Edmund Campion,
who was executed in 1581, although Whitgift was not " Lord of
Canterbury" until 1583.

P. 30, l. 9. *John Wolfe*] Was chosen beadle of the Stationers'
Company in 1587. According to Herbert [1170] he was in
special favour with the court of assistants, and chosen from his

diligence in hunting out and giving intelligence of books disorderly printed. Herbert has given a catalogue of the numerous books printed by and licensed to him.

P. 30, l. 28. *Waldegraue hath left house and home*] An entry in the Register of the Stationers' Company explains the cause of proceeding against him. "May 13, 1588. Whereas Mr. Caldock, warden, Thomas Woodcock, Oliver Wilkes, and John Wolf, on the 16 April last, upon search of Rob. Walgraues house, did seise of his and bring to Stationershall according to the late decrees of the Starre-chamber, and by vertue thereof, a presse with twoo paire of cases with certain Pica Romane, and Pica Italian letters, with diuers books entituled ' The state of the Church of Englande laid open,' &c. For that Walgraue without aucthority and contrary to the said Decrees had printed the said book. Yt is now in full Court, ordered and agreed by force of the said decrees and according to the same, That the said books shall be burnte and the said presse, letters and printing stuffe defaced and made unserviceable." [Herbert, 1145, who gives the Star-Chamber Decrees.] Waldegrave, after this, by the assistance of friends, collected money, and commenced printing at Edinburgh in 1590, being printer to James VI. In that year he brought out the Confession of the Church of Scotland, and on the reverse of the title is the king's patent. [Given by Herbert, 1507.] Until James's accession to the crown of England, in 1603, he remained in Scotland, and then removed to London. The last book which Herbert quotes as being printed by him in Edinburgh is dated in 1600, but in 1602 I find his name to " Cartwright's Answer to the Preface of the Rhemish Testament," printed there in that year.

P. 32, l. 10. *one Thomas Orwin*] " Mar. 4, 1587-8. At a court holden this day yt is ordeyned and decreed that T. Orwyn shall from henceforth leave off from further dealinge with printinge whatsoever till such time as the Master, Wardens, and four of the Court of Assistants shall present his name to the High Commissioners," &c.; which it appears they did, for on the 7th March the Archbishop of Canterbury, the Bishop of London, Dr. Cosin, and Dr. Walker addressed a letter to the Court of Stationers, on which he was elected a printer, and presented 14th May to the Archbishop and others, and admitted the 20th May, 1588, to be a printer according to the said decree. [Stationers' Register, quoted in Herbert.]

E

P. 32, l. 25. *For Reignolds the papist at Rheimes in his booke against M. Whitakers*] The first Roman Catholic translation of the New Testament into English, was printed by John Fogny, at Rheims, in 1582, to which Whitaker replied in the same year, and was answered by W. Rainoldes in " A Refutation of sundry Reprehensions, Cavils and false Sleightes, by which M. Whitaker laboureth to deface the late English translation, and Catholike annotations of the New Testament, and the Booke of the Dis. covery of heretical Corruptions. Paris, 1583," in 12mo. To this Whitaker then rejoined in " An Answer to W. Rainolds' Refuta. tion of Sundry Reprehensions," &c., 1585, in 8vo.

P. 35, l. 26. *If suche another booke as the Ecclesiast. Discipline*] Strype [Annals, iii. 285] has given us the following account of this work. " The Brief and Plain Declaration was written in Latin in 1574, and reprinted in English 1584. It seemed to be printed beyond sea. [ed. 1584.] Travers, I think, was the author. The Epistle commendatory is T. Cartwright's," and the reason why it was written in Latin, he says, was that it might be read by the Queen, " who was delighted with things written in Latin." Bancroft, who lived at the time, has given us a more particular account in his " Survey of the Pretended Holy Discipline," and in his " Dangerous Positions," both printed in 1593. About the year 1583, where before the platforme of Geneva (for it was left at large in Cartwright's books) had been followed, now there was a particular draught made for England, with a new form of common prayer therein prescribed. It was published the following year, but there were found some imperfections in it, which were referred to Travers to be corrected by him; and being performed, it came out again in 1586, but it was then severed from the book of common prayer. About Sturbridge fair time, in 1589, another synod, or general meeting, was held in St. John's College, Cambridge, where some other corrections and additions were made, after which those present voluntarily agreed to subscribe it. [See Bancroft's Survey, 66, and Dangerous Positions, 68, 89.] Neal, under the year 1584, states, that " whilst printing at Cambridge, it was seized at the press; the Archbishop advised that all the copies should be burnt as factious and seditious, but one was found in Mr. Cartwright's study after his death, and reprinted in 1644." [Neal, i. 358.]

. P. 36, l. 22. *the Confutation of the Rhemish Testament may be published*] Clark, in his Life of Cartwright, tells us, that on the publication of the New Testament at Rheims, Queen Elizabeth sent to Beza, requesting him to answer it. Beza replied, that she had one in her own kingdom far abler than he was to perform such a work, mentioning Cartwright. In the preface to the Confutation, first printed in 1618, we have the following account: "The first remarkable motive it seemeth came from Sir F. Walsingham, who herein as in other affaires, was accounted the mouth and hand of the late Queen and State, by whom M. Cartwright was not onely incited to begin this busines, but assured also of such aid as should be necessarie for the finishing thereof, to which purpose he sent him an hundred pounds towards the charges, which buying of books and procuring of writers was like to bring upon him. This was about the year 1583, as appeareth by the date of M. Cartwright's letters in answer of the aforesaid motive, which testifie also of the receipt of that hundred pounds." Being also earnestly solicited by several eminent divines of Cambridge, as well as the ministers of London and Suffolk, Cartwright begun the work, and had made considerable progress, when "thorough the envious opposition of some potent adversaries, he met with so great discouragement and hinderances, that he was moved oftimes to lay pen aside, as appears by the letter of 1586 to a noble Earle and Privie Councellor of great note in answer of a letter to encourage him in the work and to understand the forwardness thereof, and by another of 1590, wherein he certifieth the said Earle that about four years before he had received commandment from the archbishop that then was [Whitgift] to deal no further in it, and yet upon special solicitation and encouragements both by him and some other honorable personages he had at last taken pen in hand againe;" but, receiving new discouragements from his great adversaries, together with his continual employment in the ministry, he was prevented from finishing it. The copy remained for 30 years in MS., and had become somewhat eaten by mice, so that, as published in 1618, the missing parts, and all after Revelations xv., are completed from Fulke's work on the same subject. Pierce, in his Vindication, hints that Queen Elizabeth furnished the money that Walsingham sent to him; but if she had done so, the Archbishop would hardly have interfered in opposition to her will.

P. 43, l. 22. *There was the last sommer a little catechisme, made by M. Dawison*] Herbert, in quoting the title, [p. 1588,] refers to Maunsell's Catalogue, p. 29; but a copy was in Heber's collection,

[Bib. Heber. ii. p. 25,] the title of which is, " A short Christian Institution made first for the use of a private family, and now communicated by the Author to other Flocks and Families, by J. D.," printed by R. Waldegrave, without date, in 1588.

P. 47, l. 24. *that no Byble should be bounde without the Apocri-pha*] Fuller [Ch. Hist. bk. ix.] states, that amongst other things discussed at the assemblies of the Puritans was the question, "Whether the books called Apocryphal were warrantable to be read publicly in the church as the canonical Scripture?" but it must be evident to those who are acquainted with their history, that they rejected the whole as uncanonical. In 1588 Martin denounces it as an attempt to mingle heaven and earth together. In 1592 we find the following language in a Petition to her Majesty : "Sundrie of the Prelates do preach and take their texts out of the Apocrypha, wherein they go beyond their commission, unless the Apocrypha be a part of Scripture, as one of the Bishops doth entitle it." [Petition, &c., 66.] In 1604 we find, from the Apology of the Lincolnshire Ministers, that one of their objections to the Book of Common Prayer was because "It does too much honour to the Apocryphal writings, commanding many of them to be read for first lessons under the name of Holy Scripture."

P. 54, l. 29. *O well bowlde, when Iohn of London throwes his bowle*] An allusion to the favourite amusement of Bishop Aylmer. For further particulars the reader is referred to Strype's Life of Aylmer.

P. 55, l. 22. *olde Doctor Turner*] Probably Dr. William Turner, author of the English Herbal, a New Book of Spiritual Physik, and other works.

THE END.

LONDON :

GILBERT AND RIVINGTON, PRINTERS, ST. JOHN'S SQUARE.